MACMILLAN
TEACHER'S EDITION · GRADE 8

Senior Authors: Barbara Staton, Merrill Staton **Authors:** Vincent Lawrence, Michael Jothen, Jeanne Knorr (Contributing Author)

MUSIC and YOU

Innovative, sequenced instruction for you, the teacher

Macmillan Publishing Company
866 Third Avenue, New York, NY 10022
Collier Macmillan Canada, Inc.
Collier Macmillan Publishers, London

Printed in the United States of America

ISBN: 0-02-295016-8
9 8 7 6 5 4 3 2 1

TABLE OF CONTENTS

COMPONENTS

Grade	7	8
Pupil's Editions	✓	✓
Teacher's Editions	✓	✓
Teacher's Resource Package	✓	✓
Piano Accompaniment Books	✓	✓
Records/ Compact Discs	✓	✓

BARBARA STATON

Barbara Staton has taught music at all levels, kindergarten through college, and for eight years was music television teacher for the State of Georgia. She is author of a four-volume series of books and records designed to teach music concepts through movement. She holds a B.S. degree in Music Education and an M.A. in Dance and Related Arts. Mrs. Staton has written numerous songs for television and recordings and is a composer member of ASCAP.

DR. MERRILL STATON

Dr. Merrill Staton earned his M.A. and Ed.D. degrees from Teachers College, Columbia University, and is nationally known as a music educator, choral conductor, singer, ASCAP composer, and record producer. He has been music director of and has conducted the Merrill Staton Voices on many network TV series and recordings. Dr. Staton has been a leader in the field of music education for over thirty years, and pioneered the use of children's voices on recordings for education.

DR. VINCENT LAWRENCE

Dr. Vincent Lawrence received his Ph.D. from Case Western Reserve University. He is currently Professor of Music at Towson State University in Maryland, where he is Chairperson of the Division of Music Education and directs the University Chorale. Dr. Lawrence has taught general music in the Baltimore County public schools. He has also served as adjudicator and clinician on national, state, and local levels.

DR. MICHAEL JOTHEN

Dr. Michael Jothen earned his degrees at St. Olaf College, Case Western Reserve University, and Ohio State University. He is widely published as a choral composer and has served as a guest conductor, clinician, adjudicator, and curriculum consultant throughout the United States. His teaching experience includes positions at the University of Northern Colorado, Ohio State University, and in public schools in Michigan and Ohio. Dr. Jothen is Supervisor of Vocal and General Music for the Baltimore County public schools in Towson, Maryland.

JEANNE KNORR (Contributing Author)

Jeanne Knorr teaches music education and theory at Towson State University in Maryland, and is pursuing her Ph.D. She has taught vocal and instrumental music at all levels. Ms. Knorr holds a Dalcroze-Orff-Kodály Certificate from the Manhattan School of Music and a Dalcroze Certificate from the Longy School of Music.

SPECIAL CONTRIBUTORS

Dr. Betty Atterbury – *Special Education*
University of Southern Maine, Gorham, Maine
Alex Campbell – *Choral Music*
Jefferson County Schools, Golden, Colorado
Mary Frances Early – *African-American Music*
Atlanta Public Schools, Atlanta, Georgia
Dr. JaFran Jones – *Ethnomusicology*
Bowling Green State University, Bowling Green, Ohio

RECORDINGS

Dr. Merrill Staton – *Conductor and Executive Producer of Recordings*

CONSULTANTS

Teri Burdette – *Signing*
Barnsley Elementary, Rockville, Maryland
Gregory Clouspy – *Choral Music & Show Swing Choir*
Franklin Senior High, Resistertown, Maryland
Marilyn Copeland Davidson – *Curriculum*
Pequannock Schools, Pequannock, New Jersey
Ruth Landis Drucker – *Women in Music*
Towson State University, Towson, Maryland
Dr. Robert A. Duke – *Educational Testing*
University of Texas, Austin, Texas
Nancy Ferguson – *Orff*
University of Arizona, Tucson, Arizona
Donna Brink Fox – *Choral Music*
Eastman School of Music, Rochester, New York
Dr. Judith A. Jellison – *Educational Testing*
University of Texas, Austin, Texas
Jeanne Knorr – *Dalcroze*
Towson State University, Towson, Maryland
Tom Kosmala – *General Music*
Pittsburgh Public Schools, Pittsburgh, Pennsylvania
Carl J. Nygard, Jr. – *Choral Music*
Fleetwood, Pennsylvania
Jane Pippart – *Kodály*
West Chester University, West Chester, Pennsylvania
Dr. Susan Snyder – *Cooperative Learning*
Greenwich Public Schools, Greenwich, Connecticut
Cynthia Stephens – *Choral Music & Movement*
Patapsco Middle School, Ellicott City, Maryland
Mollie Tower – *General Music*
Austin Independent School District, Austin, Texas
José A. Villarrubia – *Spanish-American Music*
Towson State University, Towson, Maryland

CONTRIBUTING WRITERS

Clifford D. Alper – *Musicology*
Dr. James Muse Anthony – *Musicology*
David Bauguess – *Choral Sight Reading*
Glen Cashman – *Jazz*
Larry Harms – *Keyboard*
Bernard Hynson – *Guitar, Grade 7*
Gilbert Meerder – *Listening Maps*
Michael Yockel – *American Popular Music*

TEACHER ADVISORY BOARD

Russ Abraham – *Music Specialist*
Dewey Fundamental Elementary, Fairoaks, California
Robert Coffman – *Music Specialist*
Deep Creek Middle School, Essex, Maryland
Nancy Cox – *Choral Director*
Northeast Junior High, Altus, Oklahoma
Clayton Miller – *Music Specialist*
Albert Leonard Junior High, New Rochelle, New York
Carolyn Roberts – *Music Specialist*
Los Angeles, California
Cynthia Terry – *Music Specialist*
Thomasville Heights Elementary, Atlanta, Georgia
Mollie Tower – *Music Supervisor*
Austin Independent Schools, Austin, Texas
Kathy Zellner
Wellwood Elementary, Pikesville, Maryland

MUSIC AND YOU —THE CREATIVE DIFFERENCE

Active involvement in composition, creative movement, critical listening, and sophisticated singing and playing activities gives students confidence and pride in their abilities.

PHILOSOPHY
related specifically to the needs and interests of middle/junior high school students

Step-by-step sequencing of concepts and skills helps students understand the different elements of music and why they enjoy their favorite music styles.

Integration of current music practices of Orff, Kodály, and Dalcroze with traditional instruction engages an adolescent's mind, body, and spirit in the making of music.

PROGRAM PHILOSOPHY

The diversity of course offerings in music, student enrollments, varying scheduling patterns, and instruments and equipment available in middle and junior high schools demands a music program with a flexible organization and varied contents. Further, the particular interests, needs, and skill abilities of this age group dictate the importance of content that is musically meaningful and relevant to a teenager's world.

To answer these needs, MUSIC AND YOU offers a flexible organization of general music core units, choral singing, instrumental skill development, and special study sections of high interest that can be taught independently or integrated with one another for a 6-week, 9-week or full semester course. Students are involved in lessons, and challenged to build skills in listening, playing, improvising, or singing. Music examples of rock, synth-pop, reggae, bluegrass, jazz, and movie themes are used in addition to traditional music in order to focus on more contemporary sounds of the students' world.

MUSIC AND YOU represents a fusion of the best current practices in the teaching of music. Important trends in music education over the past two decades have tended to split the ranks of music educators, resulting in a concentration of energies in one mode of teaching. The authors of MUSIC AND YOU feel it is time to integrate, not isolate these approaches using their proven practices in reaching and teaching music students today. The MUSIC AND YOU series synthesizes the wealth of research derived from the Comprehensive Musicianship Project, Manhattanville Project, Kodály Institute, Dalcroze Society, Orff-Schulwerk, aesthetic education movements, and current learning theory for this age level, and presents these materials in an easy to use sequential format.

The value of sequencing in the learning process has been an established practice in most other subject areas. Music educators have not had a structured and truly sequential course of study available in a basic music series. Working from a master Scope and Sequence for Grades K through 8, the authors have identified

measurable objectives for each of the units and sections. The presence of a measurable sequence for learning frees the teacher, and in turn the student, to be more creative.

The design of each lesson includes clearly stated objectives, motivators to capture the students' interest and focus them on the learning to take place, step-by-step teaching procedures, reinforcement of concepts, and appraisals that match the lesson objectives. Unit and section reviews offer an informal checking for understanding. Formal written evaluations are in the TEACHER'S RESOURCE PACKAGES. These materials are designed to make assessment of growth quick and easy and yet result in a high level of confidence and satisfaction for both students and teachers.

MUSIC AND YOU for middle/junior high school offers the flexibility and appealing music with related activities that enables teachers to meet the variety of needs and interests of their students.

ORCHESTRATE YOUR OWN CREATIVE APPROACH TO TEACHING

ORGANIZATION
Each Pupil Book presents 8 Units of General Music Instruction and 3 Supplementary Sections

GENERAL MUSIC
Units 1–8 – listening lessons, songs, music topics, concepts, music reading and Play-Along Accompaniments
Unit Reviews and Evaluations

VOCAL/CHORAL
Grades 7 and 8
Vocal and Ensemble Development
Choral Singing Section
Sight Reading Preparations

SPECIAL STUDY SECTIONS
Grade 7
American Popular Music
Musical – "Those Who Have Gone Before"
Grade 8
Western Musical Styles
Music of the World's Cultures

INSTRUMENTAL
Grade 7
Keyboard and Guitar Section
Accompaniments and Lyrics to Songs in the American Popular Music Section
Integrated Recorder
Grade 8
Keyboards of Today
Playing the Guitar
Integrated Recorder

GENERAL MUSIC

The first eight units of each book may be used for a 6-week, 9-week, or semester course in general music. Concepts and music reading are taught through listening lessons, songs, and different topics of study. The material in Unit 1 forms the basic structure for all the units that follow and should be taught first as the "core" unit.

A new feature called "Play Along" Accompaniments is an integral part of the teaching process in each unit. "Play Along" Accompaniments are simple rhythmic, melodic, and harmonic scores, written in the pupil books for students to perform on Orff and percussion instruments, recorder, guitar, and keyboard as they listen to recorded music.

VOCAL/CHORAL

The Choral Singing sections in Grades 7 and 8 can be used as additional repertoire for choruses, ensembles, and glee clubs, or integrated into general music classes. Songs have been carefully chosen with respect to the interests and singing abilities of adolescents and the particular needs of the cambiata voice. Concepts and music reading are sequenced throughout this section so students can build

vocal and reading skills gradually. To help students follow their parts in songs, difficult melodic, rhythmic, and harmonic patterns in the song are isolated in a "Preparation" page that precedes the song. By allowing students to focus visually on these patterns before sight reading them in the music, they will be able to sing with accuracy and learn the music more quickly.

SPECIAL SECTIONS

There are four special sections of study in MUSIC AND YOU that can either be integrated into lessons from the general music units or taught separately. The American Popular Music section in Grade 7 explores the development of different types of American popular music from 1900 to the present. It includes background information on famous composers and performers, and offers students an opportunity to learn to play some of the songs in the section.

The Grade 7 musical, "Those Who Have Gone Before" by Hank Beebe, is a complete work for the stage and includes songs, a script, and staging instructions.

Western Musical Styles and Music of the World's Cultures in Grade 8 are sections that lead students to develop a familiarity

with and knowledge about different musical styles.

INSTRUMENTAL

Students are given the opportunity to develop instrumental skills through the "Play Along" Accompaniments. Special keyboard and guitar sections contain additional instrumental instruction that develop playing and note-reading skills.

Grade 7
Keyboard and Guitar
Accompaniments and Lyrics to Songs in the American Popular Music Section

Grade 8
Keyboards of Today
Playing the Guitar

In a guitar or keyboard class, these separate sections could be used as a source to supplement any keyboard or guitar method book.

MUSIC and YOU

SEQUENCED LESSON PLANS FREE YOU TO BE CREATIVE

MUSIC AND YOU features an innovative Teaching Plan that *integrates* current music practices such as Orff, Kodály and Dalcroze, rather than *isolating* them.

Each lesson outlines specific objectives, step-by-step teaching procedures and appraisals that save you time and energy for reaching and teaching your students.

Teaching Suggestions are easily organized for all teachers by color coding and placement on the teacher's page.

☐ Lesson preparation information
☐ Basic teaching plan
☐ Extended activities for in-depth study

Additional background materials are provided in the *Extension* section at the bottom of most pages.

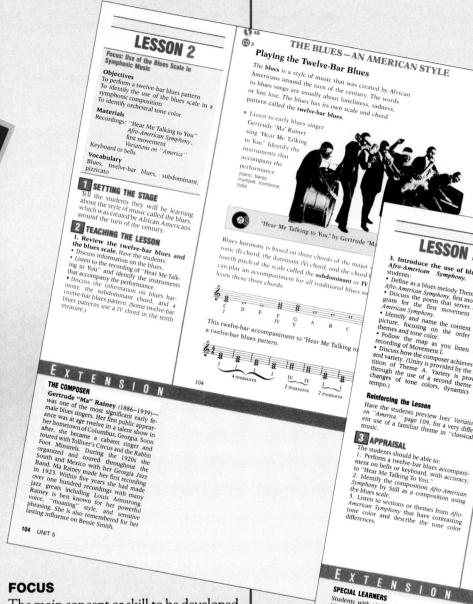

FOCUS
The main concept or skill to be developed in the lesson

Objectives
Specific goals to be accomplished

Materials
Materials and equipment needed

Vocabulary
Important terms introduced or used in the lesson

1 SETTING THE STAGE
A creative "lesson starter" related to the Focus

2 TEACHING THE LESSON
A basic instructional statement (in bold print), followed by step-by-step student behaviors

EXTENSION
This section may include More Music Teaching Ideas as well as Biographies, Curriculum Connections, alternate Songbook selections, Cooperative Learning, Vocal Development, and Suggestions for Special Learners.

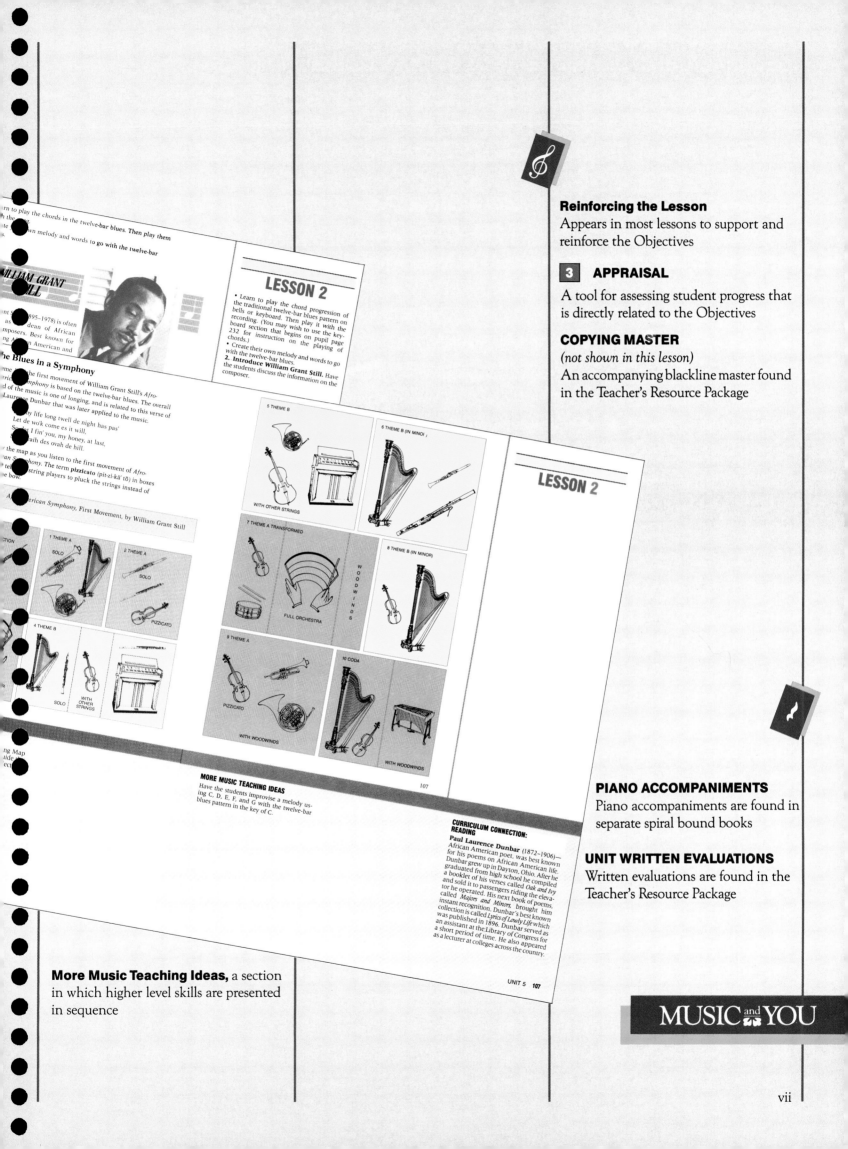

Reinforcing the Lesson

Appears in most lessons to support and reinforce the Objectives

3 APPRAISAL

A tool for assessing student progress that is directly related to the Objectives

COPYING MASTER

(not shown in this lesson)
An accompanying blackline master found in the Teacher's Resource Package

PIANO ACCOMPANIMENTS

Piano accompaniments are found in separate spiral bound books

UNIT WRITTEN EVALUATIONS

Written evaluations are found in the Teacher's Resource Package

More Music Teaching Ideas, a section in which higher level skills are presented in sequence

MUSIC and YOU

Eight basic units are designed for a complete 6-week, 9-week, or semester course. Music concepts, sight reading and playing skills presented in each unit are consistently *sequenced* through listening lessons, songs, related study topics, play-along accompaniments, and unit review and evaluation.

• Study subjects that interest and motivate teenagers

• A rich resource of songs arranged for teenage voices

• Listening lessons feature music from today's world

Wham!

George Michael and Andrew Ridgeley of the British group Wham! first met in school in their hometown of Bushey, England. George and Andrew wanted to be pop stars, and in their first group, the Executives, they started writing songs together. Although they were making records as Wham! as early as 1980, they did not produce a top American hit until the release of "Wake Me Up Before You Go-Go" in 1984. Other Wham! hits were "Freedom," "I'm Your Man," and "Christmas."

Wham! achieved international status after the release of "Careless Whisper" in 1985. At the invitation of the Youth Federation of China, Wham! became the first major Western rock band to perform in the People's Republic. Following the release of their third album *Music From the Edge of Heaven*, in 1986, George and Andrew broke up as a duo to follow solo careers.

Wham! in performance.

George Michael and Andrew Ridgeley

(Grade 8, page 122)

Singing the Blues

"The Walkin' Blues" also is based on the blues scale.

Learn to sing "The Walkin' Blues."

The Walkin' Blues

Words and Music by Bob Summers

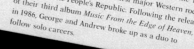

I've got the blues from my head down to my toes down in my shoes. I've got the
that feel ing it's time to
'cause when those blues come down, I've got to
the walk-in' blues.
doo wah doo wah doo, I The
wah doo wah doo. I got-ta
the blues, I the walk-in' blues.
Walk, walk, walk, yes, I'm a-walk-in'.
walk, walk, yes, I'm a-walk-in'.

(Grade 7, page 128)

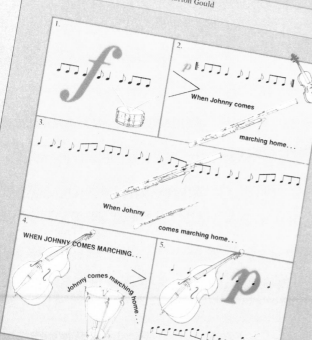

• Follow the map of *American Salute*. Listen to the theme and identify how each variation changes the melody, rhythm, texture, dynamics, tone color, and tempo.

American Salute by Morton Gould

1. *f*
2. *p* When Johnny comes
3. marching home...
   When Johnny
4. WHEN JOHNNY COMES MARCHING...
   comes marching home...
5. 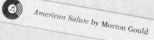 Johnny comes marching home... *p*

158

(Grade 7, page 158)

Over 20 additional songs for each grade level can be integrated into general music classes or repertoires for glee clubs, choruses and ensembles. Unison and 2-3-4-part songs accommodate the musical tastes and talents of 7th and 8th graders. Concepts and music reading skills are *sequenced* so that vocal and sight reading skills build gradually and *correctly*. Special focus in Grades 7 and 8 is on:

- Vocal Warm-up and Development
- Ensemble Singing Suggestions
- Reading Preparations

NEW **READING PREPARATION**

To help students follow their parts more accurately, difficult melodic, rhythmic and harmonic patterns are isolated on a *Preparations* page. Students can focus on these patterns visually before having to sight read them in the music.

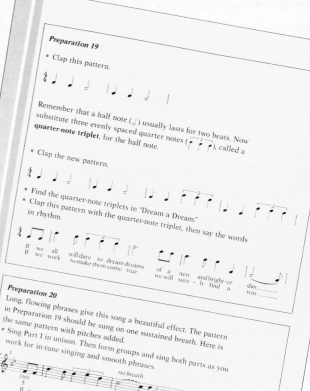

- *26 choral selections in Grade 7*
- *23 choral selections in Grade 8*

MUSIC and YOU

ACTIVE PARTICIPATION BRINGS A CLASS TO ITS FEET!

Instrumental lessons for guitar, keyboard, and recorder will help students develop playing skills.

NEW **PLAY-ALONG ACCOMPANIMENTS**

What better way for students to develop instrumental skills quickly and confidently than to play along with a record. Play-Along Accompaniments are simple rhythmic, melodic and harmonic scores that students can follow while learning basic note reading.

Play-Along Accompaniments for guitar, keyboard, percussion, recorder, and Orff instruments are used throughout General Music Units, supplementary sections, and are an integral part of the teaching process.

Grade 8 harmonic accompaniment

Grade 8 melodic accompaniment

Grade 7 Orff accompaniment

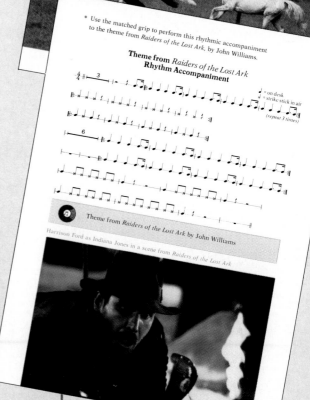

Grade 7 rhythmic accompaniment

VARIATIONS ON A STUDY THEME AROUSE STUDENTS' INTEREST

How have different types of music evolved to influence music of today? What makes American popular music different from music of other cultures? What can we learn about our ancestors' music to help us better understand their heritage, and our own?

Special Study Sections in MUSIC AND YOU help students develop a familiarity with the many forms music can take—and the many ways music remains part of our shared, living history.

AMERICAN POPULAR MUSIC
Grade 7

Explore the development of ragtime, blues, musical comedy and other popular styles from 1900 to the present. Background information on famous composers and performers is included along with songs students can learn to play.

MUSICAL
Grade 7

Humorous scenarios about our musical heritage come with songs, script, staging instructions, and recorded orchestrations for complete musical production. "Those Who Have Gone Before" is ideal for spring production.

MUSIC OF THE WORLD'S CULTURES
Grade 8

Reggae, calypso, oriental, and other styles from around the world help students appreciate the differences and similarities between cultures—and their influence on American pop music today.

WESTERN MUSICAL STYLES
Grade 8

Romantic, Baroque, and Renaissance are among the classical styles students learn to identify and analyze. Historical background and class activities put each musical style into perspective.

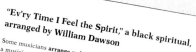

Michael Jackson

One popular musician who began his career early is Michael Jackson. Michael has been popular since he and his brothers formed the Jackson Five in their hometown of Gary, Indiana. In 1969, when Michael sang the lead on the Jackson Five's first hit, "I Want You Back," he was only ten years old. With the help of Diana Ross and Motown Records, the Jackson Five became one of the most successful groups in America and abroad. Michael Jackson has recorded more than a dozen hit records with his brothers and has had numerous successes on his own. His tremendous appeal was reflected in his 1983 hit "Beat It," from the album *Thriller.* You will find guitar and keyboard accompaniments to "Beat It" on pages 274–275.

Michael Jackson has had a strong influence on the popular culture of the 1980s. He helped create music videos of several songs from *Thriller,* one of the best-selling albums of all time. The videos show Michael's talent as a dancer as well as a singer.

Michael Jackson, 1987

The Jackson Five in performance. Michael is second from right.

"Ev'ry Time I Feel the Spirit," a black spiritual, arranged by William Dawson

Some musicians **arrange** rather than compose music. In arranging, a musician takes an existing composition and resets it for a different combination of musical resources. For example, a work for two voices may be rearranged for two clarinets.

One of the challenges an arranger faces is not to let the arrangement overpower the unique qualities of the original music. "Ev'ry Time I Feel the Spirit" illustrates William Dawson's sensitive feeling in preserving the characteristics of spirituals in his choral arrangements.

Tone Colors in the Music of India

The melody of *Madhu Kauns* is performed on a *sitar* (si' tär). The sitar is a twenty-six-stringed instrument somewhat like a lute. The performer uses six of these strings to play a melody. The rest of the strings vibrate when the melody is played, resulting in a continuous layer of sound.

Top, girls from northern India. Above, Ravi Shankar (center), a world-famous sitar player. The other performers in his ensemble play the tambura (right), a stringed instrument that produces the drone pitches, and the tabla (left), drums.

• Listen again to *Madhu Kauns* and focus on the sound of the sitar.

Madhu Kauns (excerpt)

The sitar melodies combine with the drone pitch and repeated rhythms played on hand drums to give Indian music its distinctive sound.

The traditional music of India is performed in concert settings. Members of an Indian audience are familiar with the repeated rhythms. As they listen they frequently move their hands silently in time to the rhythm. How is this different from the way an audience in the United States might respond?

214

MUSIC and YOU

Listen for the Macmillan excellence in recorded songs, poems, and listening selections.

BRAVO! FOR MERRILL STATON
Our Executive Record Producer and Conductor

Merrill Staton pioneered the recording of children's voices for song instruction and introduced the technique of divided tracks to demonstrate how different musical parts fit together. For MUSIC AND YOU he features adolescent voices as vocal models in the program's 120 recorded songs.

RECORDINGS OF THE HIGHEST TECHNICAL QUALITY

Songs, poems, accompaniments, and listening selections in MUSIC AND YOU were recorded with divided tracks, locked bands, and stereophonic sound for years of enjoyment and classroom use.

OUR NEW RECORDINGS FEATURE:

• The natural sound of teenagers' voices as vocal models.

• Divided parts highlight vocal parts on separate tracks so students can hear one part at a time while learning to harmonize.

• Divided tracks highlight instrumental accompaniments and vocal performances on separate tracks.

Our thanks to the students and adults around the country who recorded for MUSIC AND YOU.

There are simple measures of student growth and understanding in MUSIC AND YOU.

2. Review and Just Checking are informal evaluations at the end of each unit of the pupil's book that quickly assess understanding.

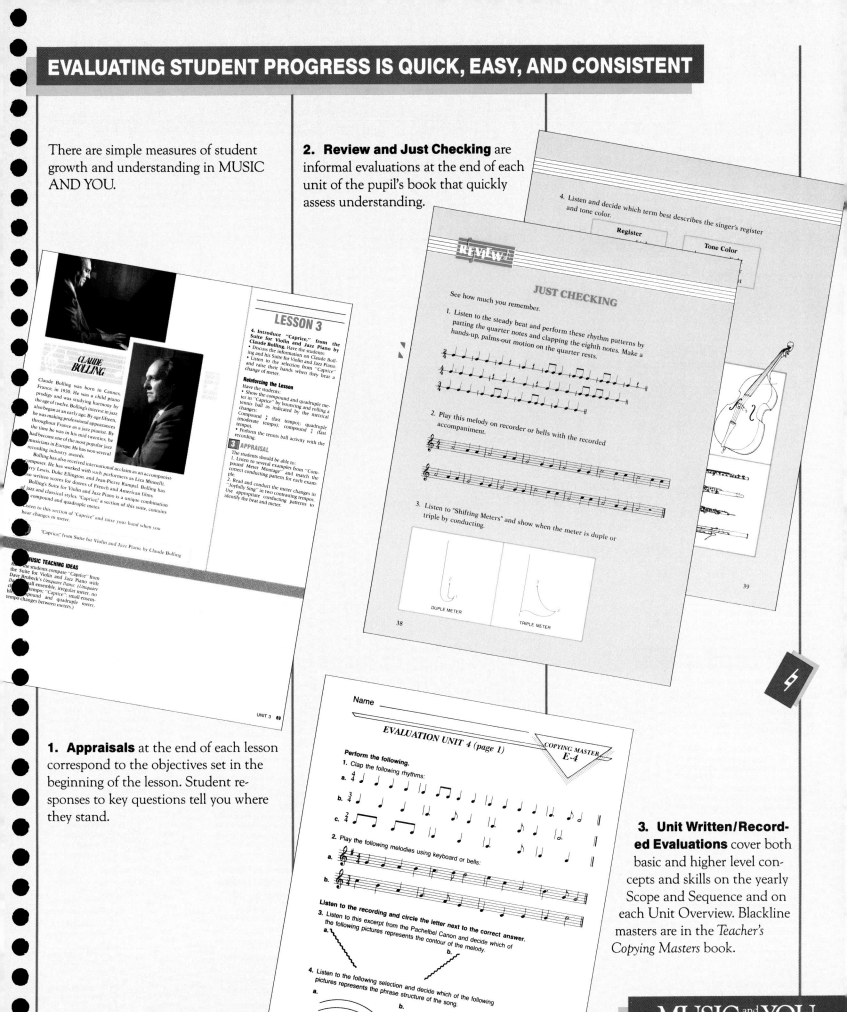

1. Appraisals at the end of each lesson correspond to the objectives set in the beginning of the lesson. Student responses to key questions tell you where they stand.

3. Unit Written/Recorded Evaluations cover both basic and higher level concepts and skills on the yearly Scope and Sequence and on each Unit Overview. Blackline masters are in the *Teacher's Copying Masters* book.

MUSIC and YOU

xiii

A consistent Teaching Plan focuses on concepts and skills that are first experienced, then identified and labeled, creatively reinforced, and finally evaluated.

Boldface type indicates a *basic concept or skill* is measured.

Concepts and skills are measured informally in the Pupil books at the end of each unit.

Written Unit Evaluations are provided in *Teacher's Copying Masters*.

ELEMENTS OF MUSIC	UNIT 1 EXPLORING MUSICAL STYLES Objectives	UNIT 2 RHYTHM PLAYS A ROLE Objectives	UNIT 3 RHYTHM SETS THE BEAT Objectives
Dynamics	Identify contrasting dynamics in different style periods **Define and identify $<$ and $>$** Identify *forte, piano*	Identify dynamic changes in a composition	
Tone Color	Identify and show understanding of tone color **Identify synthesizer** Identify instruments and their sounds	Identify tone color changes Perform melodic accompaniments on bells, recorder, or keyboard	Follow a tone color flow chart Identify tone colors
Tempo	Identify contrasting tempos (slow, moderate, fast)		Determine tempo relationships in the music Conduct patterns to fit the tempo
Duration/ Rhythm	**Perform rhythms to a steady beat** Identify meter contrasts **Experience and label syncopation**	**Identify duple, triple, and quadruple meter** **Identify meter changes** Perform, listen to, and identify irregular meter in $\frac{5}{4}$ and $\frac{7}{8}$	**Identify, define, perform, and conduct in compound meter** Identify meter changes **Identify polyrhythms**
Pitch	Identify major and minor in a composition **Read and perform a melody**	Hear, sing songs within a range of B-e'	Hear, sing songs within a range of G-e♭'
Texture	**Identify, define I and V chords** Experience musical textures	Perform a melodic accompaniment	Perform a rhythm accompaniment
Form	**Identify A and B sections, ternary (ABA) form** Identify verse and refrain	Conduct a musical composition having a strophic form	Follow a listening map of a composition having the form: Introduction, A, B, Bridge, Improvisation, Bridge, B, Coda
Style	**Identify compositions from different cultures and style periods** Create and perform music	Listen to and discuss the jazz style Discuss nationalism in the romantic style period **Classify musical examples according to style period**	Listen to a song from a musical and music that combines jazz and classical style Discuss salsa
Reading	Read percussion and melodic scores using ♪, ♩, ♪, ♩., ─, o, ─	Practice known notations Use $\overset{3}{\sqcap}$, ♩. ♩.	Read ♫, ♩ ♪, ♩. in $\frac{6}{8}$ Read ♫, ♪, ♫ ♪ ♪, ♩, ♩ in $\frac{4}{4}$

UNIT 4	UNIT 5	UNIT 6	UNIT 7	UNIT 8
MELODY Objectives	**HARMONY** Objectives	**FORM AND STYLE** Objectives	**ELEMENTS OF FORM** Objectives	**TONE COLOR IN DIFFERENT STYLES** Objectives
	Identify dynamic changes Determine how dynamics create a mood in the music	**Discuss ways in which dynamics affect mood in music** Listen to, identify, and perform contrasting dynamics	Follow dynamics from a listening map Listen to and identify contrasting dynamics	Listen to, identify, and perform contrasting dynamics
Perform retrograde on percussion instruments Perform a song on bells or keyboard and classroom instruments	Identify bright and dark tone colors Determine appropriate tone colors for a composition	Creatively explore tone colors **Perform melodic accompaniment on bells, guitar, keyboard, or recorder**	Listen to and identify the orchestra	**Discuss traditional and nontraditional tone colors** **Perform vocal tone colors** **Listen to prepared piano and steel band** **Identify new sounds from found objects** **Identify synthesizer**
	Determine appropriate tempo for the composition	**Discuss ways in which tempo affects mood in music** **Identify tempo of a composition**	Perform a free form composition keeping a steady tempo	Read and perform sounds at different tempos
Clap the rhythm of the melody as a canon Perform rhythms containing meter changes		**Perform a rhythmic motive** Perform steady beat Perform music with changing meters	**Identify rhythmic motives** **Define** *legato* **and** *staccato* **articulation**	**Read and perform a rhythm score**
Learn pitch organization **Define twelve-tone music** **Perform a tone row and its retrograde**	**Listen to and identify key changes** **Define register and modulation** **Identify bitonality**	**Discuss how mode can express the mood of music**	Follow a melodic listening map Create a melodic motive Identify pitch levels and major/minor tonality Read and perform spoken music	**Read and perform pitch sounds from a score**
Define harmony and consonance **Identify and define polyphonic, monophonic, and homophonic texture** **Perform melodic accompaniment**	Perform accompaniments in minor tonality **Identify, play tonic, subdominant, dominant chords in C**	Perform melodic accompaniments		
Analyze phrase length	**Perform the twelve-bar blues progression** Listen to, discuss, and create variations	**Listen to and identify phrases of different lengths** Identify, create, and perform rhythmic and melodic motives **Identify motive**	**Discuss and identify motives** **Discuss sonata allegro form** **Listen to and identify free form** Discuss, create, and perform a composition in free form	
Discuss a composer from the baroque period Discuss the music of Schoenberg **Identify atonal music**	Sing a song in Spanish Discuss the blues and music by an African American composer **Identify and discuss bitonal music** **Discuss and identify the art song**	Discuss the style of a popular group of the 1980s Discuss musical characteristics of the romantic period and 20th century	**Identify musical characteristics of the classical and neoclassical style period** **Identify program music**	**Discuss the pipe organ and synthesizer** Discuss composers **Discuss ways to produce new sounds from voices and traditional instruments** Discuss the electronic revolution **Identify composer Vangelis**
Follow listening map using ♪ ♪, ♫. ♩. ♪	Read and play ♩. on g, a, b♭, b♮, c	Read and play chord patterns Dm Gm B♭ Am throughout a song	Read *staccato* and *legato* patterns:	Read and play rhythm scores for contemporary music using

XV

ELEMENTS OF MUSIC	UNIT 1 OBJECTIVES	Lesson 1 CORE Focus: Style, Reggae	Lesson 2 Focus: Western and Non-Western Styles	Lesson 3 Focus: I and V Chords, Syncopation	Lesson 4 Focus: Instrumental Tone Color, Dynamics
Dynamics	Identify contrasting dynamics in different style periods **Define and identify** < **and** > Identify *piano/forte*				Identify contrasting dynamics Demonstrate understanding of dynamics Define and identify *piano (p), forte (f),* > and <
Tone Color	Identify and show understanding of tone color **Identify synthesizer** Identify instruments and their sounds	Identify vocal and instrumental tone colors Perform accompaniments on recorder or keyboard	Perform a rhythm accompaniment on percussion instruments	Play harmonic patterns with song on bells, keyboard, or guitar Select percussion instruments for performing rhythms	Identify sounds of Japanese instruments Demonstrate understanding of tone color
Tempo	Identify contrasting tempos (slow, moderate, fast)		Identify contrasting tempos (fast, slow)		Identify contrasting tempos (slow, moderate, fast)
Duration/ Rhythm	**Perform rhythms to a steady beat** Identify meter contrasts **Experience and label syncopation**	Read and perform a rhythm accompaniment Tap the steady beat	Tap steady beat and clap beat subdivision Perform a rhythm accompaniment Create rhythm patterns	Perform syncopated rhythm patterns	Tap a steady beat Create an improvised percussion part in the style of Japanese music
Pitch	Identify major and minor in a composition **Read and perform a melody Identify, define and perform I and V chords**	Perform a melody Read and perform a chord sequence Listen to and identify contrasting melody Create a melodic accompaniment		Create melodic patterns Sing a song with a range of e-d¹	Define methods of tone production in a Japanese instrument
Texture	Experience musical textures			Define, identify, perform tonic and dominant chords, roots	
Form	**Identify A and B sections, ternary (ABA) form** Identify verse and refrain	Identify A and B sections		Identify verse and refrain of a song	
Style	**Identify compositions from different cultures and style periods** Create and perform music	Identify, discuss, and listen to the reggae style	Discuss, identify, and compare musical styles	Identify, discuss, and listen to calypso music	Discuss and listen to Japanese song Create and perform a sound composition
Reading	Read percussion and melodic scores using ♪,ɤ,♩,ξ,♩·,♩,═,◦,─	Identify A and B sections	Read rhythm scores with ♪,ɤ,♩,ξ	Read melodic notation using ♩	Identify < (cres.), > (decres.), *p,f*

PURPOSE Unit 1: EXPLORING MUSICAL STYLES

In this unit the students will review and/or experience rhythm, pitch, tone color, meter, texture, and form. They will gain an understanding of musical styles through listening and performing.

SUGGESTED TIME FRAME

September				October			

FOCUS

- Style, Reggae
- Western and Non-Western Styles
- I and V Chords, Syncopation
- Instrumental Tone Color, Dynamics
- Historical Style Periods
- Baroque Style
- Major and Minor, Romantic Style
- Synth-Pop Style, Steady Beat

Lesson 5 Focus: Historical Style Periods	Lesson 6 Focus: Baroque Style	Lesson 7 Focus: Major and Minor, Romantic Style	Lesson 8 Focus: Synth-Pop Style, Steady Beat
Listen for different functions of dynamics in various style periods	Follow dynamic changes indicated on a musical map while listening to a composition (*p*, *f*, $<$)	Discuss the contrast of dynamics in a composition	
Perform a melody on recorder, bells, or keyboard Listen to and identify tone colors associated with various style periods	Identify contrasts in tone color Identify tone colors on a musical map while listening to a composition		Identify synthesized sound as a characteristic of synth-pop style Discuss the capabilities of a synthesizer
	Discuss tempo contrasts in a composition Identify a *ritardando*		
Listen to and identify the use of rhythm in various style periods	Identify meter contrasts Identify duple and triple meter Define meter, measure, and bar line Play steady beat		Read and perform a rhythmic accompaniment pattern using drumsticks Identify accent
Perform a melody with accuracy Listen for characteristics of melody in the various style periods		Identify major and minor chords Perform D major and D minor chords Determine how to change a chord from major to minor Analyze the tonality of a composition Sing a song with a range of B♭-e♭'	Perform a melodic accompaniment
Experience textures of various styles			
	Follow a musical map showing the form of a composition Define and identify ternary (ABA) form	Identify major and minor sections Analyze the form of a composition Identify the themes in a composition	
Listen to, discuss, and classify representative compositions from each historical time period Identify musical characteristics of the major historical time periods	Identify and discuss characteristics of baroque style Analyze a composition in baroque style Discuss the French composer Jean Baptiste Lully	Identify the musical characteristics of the romantic period Study a composition by the French composer Georges Bizet	Discuss, listen to, and perform synth-pop style
♩. ♪	Follow listening map Use duple meter, triple meter, measure, bar line, ritardando, $\frac{2}{2}$, $\frac{3}{4}$, 𝄽, ♩, 𝅝, 𝄐		Read percussion score with ♪. ♫, 𝄾, ♩, 𝄽, −, −, $\frac{2}{−}$

BULLETIN BOARD

Prepare strips of tagboard with the labels shown. Center the label STYLE MONTAGE at the top of the bulletin board, with "Reggae" in the middle of the board and the other labels around the edges of the board. Have the students collect pictures to illustrate the style, performer, culture, or period being discussed at the time, and surround the centered label with those illustrations. As you move through the unit, let the students select what they think is the best illustration of the style most recently covered. Continue the process until you have completed the unit and have one ideal illustration for each category.

LESSON 1

UNIT 1
EXPLORING
MUSICAL
STYLES

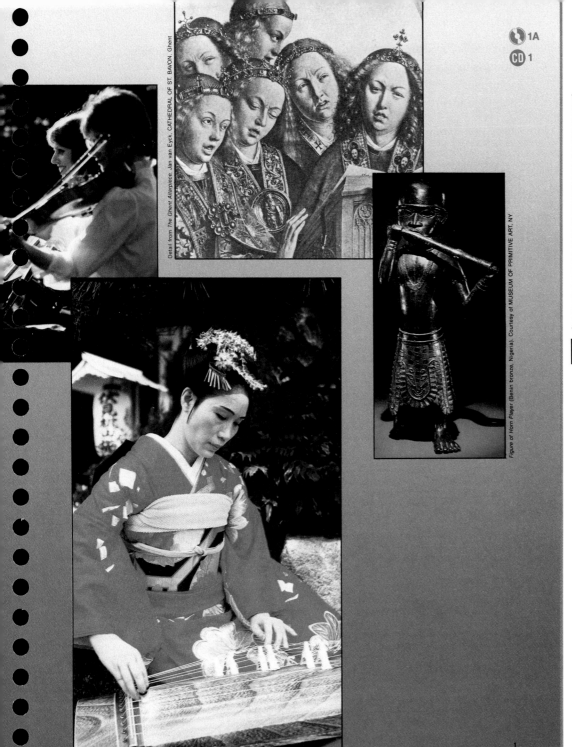

1

LESSON 1

Focus: Style, Reggae

Objectives
To identify and define style
To identify A and B sections
To perform a melodic accompaniment
To identify and define reggae style

Materials
Recordings: "Style Montage"
               "Elements"
Keyboard or recorder

Vocabulary
Quarter note, quarter rest, repeat signs, half note, whole note, chord, reggae, ska, dub

1 SETTING THE STAGE

Tell the students that they will be discussing contrasting musical styles and studying the Caribbean style called reggae.

THE ARTIST

Jan Van Eyck (yän van īk) (ca 1380–1441)—was one of the first artists to use oil painting. He is known for using natural lighting, vivid colors, and precise details of clothes and jewelry. Jan Van Eyck probably worked with his brother Hubert on *The Ghent Altarpiece*, a huge painting that is filled with many figures and consists of 26 panels in a frame. A detail of the altarpiece is shown here.

LESSON 1

2 TEACHING THE LESSON

1. Introduce style. Have the students discuss the information on style.

2. Introduce different musical styles. Have the students:

• Discuss the pictures representing music styles.

• Listen to "Style Montage" and follow the pictures that represent each musical selection.

• Listen to and describe "Elements," using the musical terms illustrated on pages 2 and 3.

Musical styles differ throughout the world. Every composer hopes that his or her style will be distinctive. Music from different countries has different sounds. Listening to a variety of music can help you identify the source.

• As you listen, follow the pictures on pages x and 1 that represent the musical selections in "Style Montage."

 "Style Montage"

A Caribbean Style

• Listen to "Elements" by Black Uhuru ($\overline{oo}$-h$\overline{oo}$' r$\overline{oo}$). Use illustrations on pages 2 and 3 to help you describe the musical characteristics of the selection.

 "Elements," by Black Uhuru

percussion instruments   voices in chorus

strong beat   weak beat

2

E X T E N S I O N

- Tap the steady **quarter note** (♩) beat with your foot and clap the rhythm pattern as you listen to "Elements" again. Make a silent palms-up motion on each **quarter rest** (𝄽). The **repeat signs** (‖: :‖) mean play the pattern again.

"Elements" has two different melodies. Call them A and B. Each time the A or B melody is played it is primarily vocal or instrumental.

- Follow the chart as you listen to the music one more time. Decide what should replace each question mark. How different is A' (A-prime) from A? A': instrumental solo

	1.	2.	3.	4.	5.	6.	7.	8.	9.	10.
	Introduction	A	B	? A	? B	? A	A'	? B	? A	Coda (Conclusion)
Mostly Vocal or Instrumental	I	V	V	? V	? V	? V	I	? V	? V	I

solo   voices with instruments   accent

3

3. Introduce steady beat and different melodies in "Elements." Have the students:
- Clap the rhythm pattern as they listen to "Elements" and identify the tempo. (tempo is slow)
- Listen to recording of "Elements" (with call numbers). Identify the sections of the composition by writing the letter A or B on a sheet of paper as each number is called.
- Identify vocal or instrumental tone colors used in each section.
- Analyze and discuss answers.

SPECIAL LEARNERS

Exceptional students who are visually impaired or who need a visual cue for coordinating motor and reading tasks will benefit from enlarged notation for the rhythm pattern accompaniment. Some mainstreamed students also may need a teacher cue to clap on the correct beats.

Exceptional students who need visual cues to coordinate visual and reading tasks will benefit from an overhead transparency of the chart on pupil page 3. As the selection is played, pause at the end of each section to allow the students to fill in the chart with the correct responses. Then mark the correct response on the transparency so students can confirm their answers.

LESSON 1

4. Prepare performing "Elements."
Have the students:
• Practice the melodic and harmonic accompaniments. (You may wish to use the keyboard section that begins on pupil page 232 for instruction on the playing of chords.)
• Perform the melodic and harmonic accompaniments with the recording as indicated.

• Play this melody on a keyboard instrument or recorder. Each **half note** (♩) sounds as long as two quarter notes. Each **whole note** (o) sounds as long as four quarter notes.

E D   D C   C   D

• Play these chords on a keyboard instrument. A **chord** consists of three or more pitches sounding together. To play **G♯ (G-sharp)** on the keyboard, find the black key to the right of G.

F		Em		Dm		1 C	2 E
C	C	B	B	A	A	G	B
A	A	G	G	F	F	E	G♯
F	F	E	E	D	D	C	E

• Listen to "Elements" again. Play the melody above during the A section and the chords during the B section.

These photos show some popular reggae artists. On this page are scenes of Black Uhuru in performance.

4

SPECIAL LEARNERS
Use an overhead transparency of pupil page 4 to assist students in following the notation for the melodic and harmonic accompaniments to "Elements." Point to the beginning of each phrase.

Reggae

"Elements" is an example of a style of music called **reggae** (re' gā) that developed during the 1960s on the island of Jamaica in the Caribbean. Reggae music is very popular throughout the Caribbean islands, and its popularity has gradually spread to the United States and other parts of the world.

Reggae grew out of *ska* music, a fast, lively musical style that featured the trumpet, trombone, and saxophone. Ska was popular in Jamaica during the early 1960s. However, musical tastes and performances gradually changed. Songs became slower, rhythms became catchier, and a rhythm section of guitar, bass guitar, and drums replaced the brass instruments. The first song to mention this unique style of music by name was "Do the Reggay," recorded by Toots and the Maytals in 1968.

Early reggae music featured scratchy rhythm guitars, booming bass guitars, and a slow beat. Trumpets, trombones, and saxophones could still be heard on some recordings, and piano and organ were often used to fill out the sound. Hundreds of songs were written and recorded at this time in Kingston, the capital of Jamaica.

Recently, *dub* poetry has flourished in Jamaica and has made an impact in the United States and England. Dub consists of rhythmically spoken political poems "dubbed" over a reggae background, in a style similar to rap music. Dub poetry has rapidly become a way of expressing national pride in Caribbean countries.

Left, the reggae group Aswad. Above, Bob Marley, perhaps the most famous reggae artist, in performance.

5

5. Introduce reggae style. Have the students discuss the background information on reggae.
You may wish to use the following item as a basis for further discussion.
Reggae is a musical style that was created on the Caribbean island of Jamaica. This style has characteristic sounds and rhythm patterns specific to a particular group or geographical area. Select several groups or countries and discuss the characteristics of their musical styles. (Fiddles and twangy guitars are often associated with country music; the sound of blues is tied to jazz.)

Reinforcing the Lesson

Discuss with the students why they chose certain pictures to represent a particular style on pages x-1; encourage them to use the terms on pages 2 and 3.

3 APPRAISAL

The students should be able to:
1. Listen to two stylistically contrasting compositions and discuss similarities or differences in the composers' use of such elements as tempo, form, tone color and accompaniment.
2. Identify A and B sections.
3. Read and perform the melodic accompaniment to "Elements" with accuracy.
4. Verbally identify reggae style to include at least three characteristic sounds and rhythm patterns specific to this style.

MORE MUSIC TEACHING IDEAS

Have the students:
1. Create their own melodic accompaniments to "Elements."
2. List other popular performers whose music reflects the reggae style. (Answers will vary.)

LESSON 2

Focus: Comparing Western and Non-Western Styles

Objectives
To identify and define contrasting styles
To perform a rhythmic accompaniment containing eighth notes and eighth rests

Materials
Recordings: *Bwala*
              Kyrie
              African Sanctus
Percussion instruments

Vocabulary
Style, eighth note, tempo, eighth rest

1 SETTING THE STAGE
Have the students review the musical terms on pages 2 and 3.

2 TEACHING THE LESSON

1. Introduce contrasting styles. Have the students:
• Listen to and contrast *Bwala* and Kyrie. Try to identify their origins.
• Examine the photos and determine which musical selection they would associate with each of the sculptures. (Kyrie—English sculpture; *Bwala*—African sculpture)

STYLE MAKES THE DIFFERENCE

CD 1. Listen to *Bwala*, a dance from Uganda, and the Kyrie (kir′ ē-ā) from the Mass in G Minor by Ralph Vaughan Williams. What characteristics of each composition might help you identify its origin? Answers may vary.

> 🎵 *Bwala* (dance from Uganda)
> Kyrie from Mass in G Minor, by Ralph Vaughan Williams

In different cultures many things vary. The people may speak different languages. The foods they eat and the clothes they wear also may be different. The art and architecture produced by different cultures also have their own unique characteristics.

Detail from *Sir Osbert Sitwell*, Frank Dobson, THE TATE GALLERY, London

Wooden Mask, Songe tribe, Zaire

The sculpture on the left is by a twentieth-century English artist. The sculpture on the right is by an artist of the Songe tribe in Zaire. Although they both have the same subject, their styles are quite different.

6

E X T E N S I O N

THE COMPOSER

Ralph Vaughan Williams (1872–1958) was born in Gloucestershire, England. His interest in music was sparked by his grandmother, who encouraged him to study piano and violin. He later went on to study composition and organ at Trinity College, Cambridge.

Vaughan Williams had great pride in his homeland. He loved his country's folk music—"the lilt of the chorus in a music hall . . . the children dancing to a barrel organ . . . the cries of street peddlers." His own music was greatly influenced by the many songs he collected and wrote down.

Besides composing, Vaughan Williams taught, wrote about music, conducted at choral festivals, and always encouraged young musicians.

Music from different times and cultures sounds different. The **style** of a culture is a unique mixture of its characteristics. The style of a musical composition is the unique mixture of its musical and cultural characteristics.

In *African Sanctus*, a new musical style results from combining the musical characteristics of different cultures. *Bwala* with its percussion, strong steady beat, and accents is combined with the choral singing tradition of Western cultures.

- Listen to *African Sanctus*. As each number is called, decide whether the music sounds more African or more Western. In which sections is it hard to make a choice? Western: 1, 3, 4, 6, 10, 11; African: 2, 5, 9; both: 7, 8

 African Sanctus, by David Fanshawe

The style of *African Sanctus* is unique. The musical characteristics of two cultures have been combined to create music in a new style.

- Tap the steady quarter-note beat played on the drum as you listen to the opening choral part of *African Sanctus*. Then tap the following patterns as you listen again. Make a palms-up, silent motion for each quarter rest.

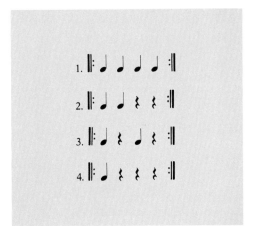

7

2. Introduce *African Sanctus*. Have the students:
- Discuss the information on style.
- Discuss the combination of musical styles in *African Sanctus*.
- Listen to *African Sanctus* (with call numbers).
- Determine which selections are in an African or a Western style, or both.

3. Prepare students to perform the percussion part to *African Sanctus*. Have the students:
- Listen to the recording of *African Sanctus* (call number 1) and tap the steady beat played by the drum. (Assign the note value of quarter note to the steady beat.)
- Tap the rhythm patterns as they listen again.

THE COMPOSER

David Fanshawe—English composer, was born in Paignton, Devonshire, in 1942. He was educated at St. George's Choir School and Stowe. He later won the Foundation Scholarship to the Royal College of Music, where he studied composition. His professional debut as a piano soloist–composer was at Queen Elizabeth Hall in 1970. Fanshawe has written scores for radio, film, and television programs. Journeys through Europe, the Far East, and Africa have resulted in compositions that merge local folk melodies and rhythms with Western musical traditions.

LESSON 2

- Listen to the recording of *African Sanctus* again (call number 1) and clap two sounds for each beat, counting aloud from 1 to 8. (Assign the note value of eighth notes to each subdivision.)
- Listen to the second and third sections of *African Sanctus* and clap and count the eighth-note subdivisions in the new tempo.
- Form six groups, with each group performing a line of the percussion score.
- Practice lines 1 and 2, 3 and 4, and 5 and 6 separately and then together.
- Perform with the recording of *African Sanctus* beginning with call number 3.
- Select percussion instruments and perform the patterns as an accompaniment to *African Sanctus*.
- Respond to the Challenge! by creating their own rhythm patterns to *African Sanctus*.

Reinforcing the Lesson
Discuss what distinguishes an African style from a Western one. (more complicated rhythms, different instruments)

3 APPRAISAL
The students should be able to:
1. Listen to a composition representative of Western style and one representative of non-Western style, and identify salient musical characteristics of each. Discuss at least two similarities and two differences in the cultures' music.
2. Read and perform with accuracy a percussion accompaniment to *African Sanctus* containing eighth notes and eighth rests.

Each quarter note can be divided into two **eighth notes** (♪♪).

- Listen again to the opening choral section of *African Sanctus*, and clap two eighth-note sounds for each beat. As you clap, count aloud from 1 to 8, giving each clap one count.
- Listen to the second and third sections of *African Sanctus*. Clap and count the eighth notes in these sections. Is the new **tempo,** or speed of the beat, faster or slower than that of the first section? faster
- Listen to the complete *African Sanctus*. Perform these patterns with the choral sections by clapping and counting each line. Make the silent, palms-up motion for the **eighth rest** (⁷).

- Select percussion instruments and play the patterns above as an accompaniment to *African Sanctus*.

> **CHALLENGE** Create your own patterns to accompany *African Sanctus*.

8

E X T E N S I O N

EXTRA HELP
The success of the *African Sanctus* activity will be enhanced if the groups are paired— 1 and 2, 3 and 4, and 5 and 6—to perform the rhythms.

SPECIAL LEARNERS
Divide the class into two groups, each having a mixture of mainstreamed and regular students. Use an overhead transparency of pupil page 8 with different color cues for each pair of lines. Have each group play the even- or odd-numbered lines as you point to each pair of lines on the color-coded overhead transparency.

MORE MUSIC TEACHING IDEAS
Have the students:
1. Create their own rhythmic accompaniments to *African Sanctus*.
2. Create their own musical style by combining two or more contrasting styles, for example, melodies from the classics set with a rock-style rhythmic accompaniment.

Left, drummers at a festival in Vuaben, Ghana. Above, celebration at a baby-naming ceremony in Accra, Ghana. Below, South African women perform a mine dance.

9

LESSON 3

Focus: Recognition of I and V Chords, Syncopation

Objectives
To identify calypso style
To become familiar with syncopation
To identify and perform the I and V chords (and their roots)

Materials
Recordings: "Run Joe"
"Elements"
"Two-Chord Strut" (optional)
Keyboard, bells, recorder, guitar

Vocabulary
Calypso, syncopation, tonic, key tone, dominant, root

1 SETTING THE STAGE
Tell the students that they will be learning about another Caribbean style.

2 TEACHING THE LESSON

1. Introduce calypso. Have the students:
• Discuss the information on calypso and syncopation.
• Listen to the recording and sing the refrain (changing voices can sing an octave lower).

2. Introduce "Run Joe." have the students:
• Perform the rhythm patterns on the verse and refrain with the recording. (The pattern to be performed during the verse can be introduced by rote.)
• Sing the verses and refrain with the recording.

1A, 5A

CD 1, 4

CALYPSO STYLE
Key: G major   **Starting Pitch:** G   **Scale Tones:** *la, ti, do re mi fa so*

"Run Joe" is a **calypso** song about two brothers who get into trouble. Calypso texts are usually witty, making fun of political and economic issues. The music is rhythmic, danceable, and cheerful. It achieves its unique lilt by stressing melodic notes just ahead of or just behind the steady beat. This type of off-the-beat rhythm is called **syncopation.** Calypso music evolved in Trinidad, in the West Indies, toward the end of the nineteenth century. It also exhibits a strong African influence.

Run Joe

Words and music by Dr. Walt Merrick, Joe Willoughby, and Louis Jordan

2. When you get home, you get to bed
   Call a doctor and tie your head.
   Can't tell Ma to invent a lie.
   Got to have a good alibi.

3. When the Judge ask me how I plea
   Not guilty, sir, most decidedly.
   You can see, judge, at a glance
   I'm the victim of circumstance.

4. If the judge believe what I say
   I'll be home by the break of day.
   If he don't, I'll be looking cute
   Behind the bars in my striped suit.

5. Mother told me not long ago
   Keep away from that worthless Joe.
   If I heard what my mama say
   Wouldn't be in this mess today.

10

E X T E N S I O N

CURRICULUM CONNECTION: SOCIAL STUDIES

Calypso—a type of folk music that comes from Trinidad. It originated in the work songs of the African slaves. The word *calypso* is thought to have come from the African word *kai-so,* which means bravo.

In calypso the words are more important than the music. They usually reflect local events, gossip, or personal philosophy. Cleverness in making up words and rhymes on the spot is the sign of a virtuoso calypso singer. Almost any instrument can be used to accompany the calypso singer. Commonly used instruments are bamboo pieces, rattles, drums, flutes, and guitars.

MORE MUSIC TEACHING IDEAS

Have the students select rhythm instruments to perform the rhythm patterns while singing "Run Joe."

- Perform this pattern during the verses of the song.

- Perform this pattern during the refrain. Pat your lap with your right and left hands.

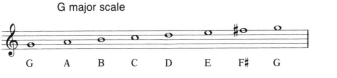

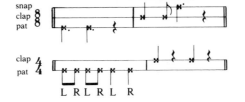

You can accompany the refrain of "Run Joe" on guitar or keyboard using two chords built on G, the first (I), and D, the fifth (V), pitches of the **G major scale.**

The G or I chord is called the **tonic** chord and is built on the most important pitch or tone of this scale, the **key tone** or home tone. The D or V chord is built on the fifth pitch of this scale and is called the **dominant** chord.

- Listen to the refrain of "Run Joe." Place your palms down on your desk when you hear the I chord. Turn your palms upward when you hear the V chord.

The lowest pitch of each of these chords is called the **root.**

- Give the letter names of the roots of the I and V chords. G and D
- Play the root of each chord on keyboard as you sing the refrain.
- Play the chords (I and V) as you sing the refrain.
- Play this pattern on bells or keyboard as you sing the refrain.

 CHALLENGE Create your own melodic pattern on keyboard, bells, or recorder to play on the word *Joe* as you sing the refrain. Use these five pitches. Play your accompaniment as you sing the song.

G A B D E

11

3. Introduce the accompaniment to the refrain of "Run Joe." Have the students:
- Discuss the information on the major scale and chords.
- Label the two I and V chords.
- Listen to the refrain of "Run Joe" and identify tonic and dominant chords as indicated.
- Identify and label the root of each chord and play the root of each chord to the refrain of "Run Joe."
- Form two groups. Each group will play one of the chords as it comes up on keyboard, bells, or guitar with the recording.

4. Introduce the melodic accompaniment to "Run Joe." Have the students:
- Play the melodic accompaniment to "Run Joe" on bells or keyboard as they sing the refrain.
- Respond to the Challenge! by creating their own four-beat melodic patterns. Use the five pitches of the G pentatonic scale.

Reinforcing the Lesson

Have the students review "Elements" on page 2 to distinguish between syncopated and nonsyncopated styles.

3 APPRAISAL

The students should be able to:
1. Listen to a composition in calypso style and then list in writing at least three musical characteristics that can be identified with calypso style.
2. Perform the I and V chords and roots in "Run Joe" on keyboard, guitar, or bells.
3. Listen to several musical examples of syncopated and nonsyncopated melodies and identify each example using pencil and paper procedures.

MORE MUSIC TEACHING IDEAS

Have the students:
1. Perform other selections that use the I and V chords, for example, "Tom Dooley."
2. Listen to "Two-Chord Strut" to identify tonic and dominant chord changes.

VOCAL DEVELOPMENT

Sing the refrain on a sustained *oo* vowel to contrast with the marcato articulation of the verse.

SPECIAL LEARNERS

Speech cues that reinforce the rhythms will help exceptional students perform the accompaniments. Have the class make up their own speech patterns from "Run Joe" such as, "Run, Joe, po-lice here" for the rhythm during the verse, or "Mo and Joe are run-ning fast-er" for the rhythm in the refrain. (Or you may wish to invent the speech patterns.)

LESSON 4

Focus: Instrumental Tone Color, Dynamics

Objectives
To identify instrumental tone color
To identify and label dynamic changes
To create an original composition

Materials
Recordings: *Satto*
          "Rainbow Writing"
          "Dreams"
          "Bravado"
          Bwala
          Kyrie
High and low drums
Pitched and unpitched classroom instruments

Vocabulary
Tone color, dynamics, piano, forte, crescendo, decrescendo

1 SETTING THE STAGE

Tell the students they will be identifying the sounds of instruments in Japanese music and creating their own sound compositions.

2 TEACHING THE LESSON

1. Introduce Japanese instruments and *Satto*. Have the students:
• Listen to *Satto* and determine how sound is produced on each instrument they hear.

A STYLE FROM THE FAR EAST

Satto (sä′ tō) or "Wind Dance" by Katsutoshi Nagasawa (kät′ sōō-tō-shē nä′ gä-sä-wä) was composed for the theater in 1975 to suggest the feeling of the ancient Japanese spirit of the wind.

• Listen to *Satto.* You will hear several Japanese instruments. Decide how sound is produced on each of the instruments. blowing; striking

Satto, by Katsutoshi Nagasawa

These photos show Japanese instruments, flutes (above) and drums (right).

12

A procession crossing a river at a Japanese festival

• Listen to *Satto* and softly tap the steady beat.
• Identify the tempo.
• Identify the contrasting tone colors used. (percussion and woodwind)
• Discuss the information on dynamics.
• Show the dynamic changes in *Satto* by clapping the steady beat lightly when the music is loud and tapping the back of the hand when the music is soft.

• Listen again and tap the steady beat. Is the tempo slow, moderate, or fast?   fast

Contrast in *Satto* is achieved by the use of different *tone colors* and *dynamic* changes.

Tone color refers to the sound of the different instruments used. **Dynamics** are the levels of loudness and softness in music. They are shown by the abbreviations of the Italian words *piano* (**p**) for soft and *forte* (**f**) for loud.

To show gradual changes from one dynamic level to another, symbols and words are used.

crescendo (cresc.)   get gradually louder

decrescendo (decresc.)   get gradually softer

• Listen to *Satto* once again to identify the dynamic changes. Clap the steady beat lightly when the music is loud. Tap the beat on the back of your hand when the music is soft.

13

MORE MUSIC TEACHING IDEAS
Have the students create an improvised percussion part on high and low drums in the style of *Satto* to demonstrate contrasts of tone color and dynamics.

LESSON 4

2. Prepare to create a sound composition. Have the students:
• Discuss the information about creating a sound composition.
• Read the poems aloud.
• Choose one poem and create a composition that will make a sound picture of the poem. (Help the students decide which tone colors, dynamics, and tempo they will use.)
• Practice and perform the composition. (Provide a limited time framework in which to complete the composition. You may wish to tape record each composition for appraisal. You may wish to use one of the poems to develop a composition as a model for the class.)

Create a Sound Composition

Composers often get ideas from other art forms such as theater or poetry. You, too, will have the opportunity to be a composer and create a sound composition based on one of these poems.

• Read the poems aloud. Select one of them and create an original composition that will make a sound picture of the poem. Decide what tone colors, dynamics, and tempo you will use.
• Practice and perform your composition. Have other students guess which poem inspired your composition.

Rainbow Writing

Nasturtiums with
their orange cries
flare like trumpets;
their music dies.

Golden harps
of butterflies;
the strings are mute
in autumn skies.

Vermilion chords,
then silent gray;
the last notes of
the song of day.

Rainbow colors
fade from sight,
come back to me
when I write.
—*Eve Merriam*

14

E X T E N S I O N

CURRICULUM CONNECTION: READING

Eve Merriam—born in 1916, is a writer of poetry, fiction, nonfiction, and plays for both adults and children. She has won several awards for her writing. Her poetry often contains humorous plays on words and expresses a joyful exploration of the world.

Langston Hughes (1902–1967)— was born in Joplin, Missouri, and grew up in other cities of the Midwest. Known mainly for his poetry, he also wrote fiction, non-fiction, and drama. His poetry portrays the urban African American experience in everyday language. It conveys the rhythms of colloquial speech and of popular music.

TEACHER INFORMATION

Music and You uses the term *African American* when referring to Americans of African descent.

COOPERATIVE LEARNING

Have the students work in cooperative groups of four to create a sound composition based on the poems on pages 14 and 15. Have the group decide on a poem for the project. For creating the sound picture of the poem, all four members of the group should decide on the tone colors, dynamics, and tempo that will be used. Possible roles to be assigned are recorder, to notate a graph score that includes one idea from each group member, and conductor, to research and lead the performance once the basic decisions have been made. Each cooperative group will perform its sound piece for the rest of the class. For another day, duplicate the graph score of each co-

Dreams

Hold fast to dreams
For if dreams die
Life is a broken-winged bird
That cannot fly.

Hold fast to dreams
For when dreams go
Life is a barren field
Frozen with snow.

—Langston Hughes

Bravado

Have I not walked without an upward look
Of caution under stars that very well
Might not have missed me when they shot and fell?
It was a risk I had to take—and took.

—Robert Frost

15

operative group and have other members of the class perform the sound pieces by reading the graph scores. Discuss the results.

Reinforcing the Lesson
Review *Bwala* and Kyrie on page 6. Discuss the contrasts in dynamics.

3 APPRAISAL

The students should be able to:
1. Identify the tone color of Japanese woodwind and percussion instruments and the method of tonal production for each.
2. Listen to several musical examples demonstrating clear examples of piano, forte, crescendo or decrescendo, and identify the correct dynamic symbol for each.
3. Create a composition to represent a sound picture of a poem and, within the composition, include contrasts in tone color, dynamics, and tempo.

CURRICULUM CONNECTION: READING

Robert Frost (1874–1963)— was one of the greatest of twentieth-century poets. His poetry is characterized by plain language, a graceful style, and powerful images. Born in the West, Frost moved to New England at age eleven and was influenced by the region's countryside, colloquial speech, and attitudes. He briefly attended Dartmouth College and Harvard University. Frost also worked for a short time as a schoolteacher, newspaper editor, mill worker, and farmer. His first books, published in England, brought him international recognition. He later won four Pulitzer Prizes for his poetry.

LESSON 5

Focus: Historical Style Periods

Objectives
To identify the major historical style periods and their musical characteristics
To perform a melody on keyboard, bells, or recorder

Materials
Recordings: "Historical Style Montage"
"Style Montage"
Keyboard, bells, or recorder

Vocabulary
Renaissance, baroque, classical, romantic, twentieth century

1 SETTING THE STAGE
Tell the students European musical styles can be organized into major historical style periods.

2 TEACHING THE LESSON

1. Introduce European-Western styles.
Have the students:
• Discuss the information on "Ode to Joy" and Beethoven's Symphony No. 9.
• Listen to the "Historical Style Montage."
• Prepare to perform "Ode to Joy" melody on keyboards, bells, or recorders.
• Identify phrases that are similar. (1, 2, and 4) (If students are having difficulty with the third phrase, have them play phrases 1, 2, and 4.)
• Perform "Ode to Joy" as they listen to the "Historical Style Montage." (The students should begin after the Beethoven excerpt.)
• Identify the number of times they played "Ode to Joy" as they listened to "Historical Style Montage." (five times)
• Describe the musical characteristics of each of the five settings. (Encourage the students to use general descriptions of tempo, rhythm, dynamics, and tone color.)

THE EUROPEAN-WESTERN STYLES

Symphony No. 9 by the German composer Ludwig van Beethoven (lood′ vig vän bā′ tō-ven) contains one of the most famous melodies ever written, the "Ode to Joy."

• Listen to the "Historical Style Montage." It first presents the "Ode to Joy" as Beethoven used it in his Symphony No. 9 and then as it might have sounded if used by composers who lived as much as four hundred years before Beethoven, or as much as one hundred fifty years after.

How is each performance different? Think about tone color, instruments, dynamics, and tempo to help you decide. Answers will vary.

 "Historical Style Montage"

• Perform the "Ode to Joy" on keyboard, bells, or recorder as you listen to the "Historical Style Montage." Begin after the Beethoven example.

"Ode to Joy" from Symphony No. 9, Fourth Movement

Ludwig van Beethoven

16

EXTENSION

SPECIAL LEARNERS

Prepare an overhead transparency of pupil page 16 if the class contains mainstreamed students who have visual impairments or difficulty reading notation. Write the names of the notes under phrases 1 and 3. It may also be necessary to point to the beginning of each phrase as the students are performing the theme. This will enable the mainstreamed students to coordinate the auditory with the visual activity.

Each time you performed the "Ode to Joy," it was in a different musical style. In European-Western music the terms *Renaissance, baroque, classical, romantic,* and *twentieth century* are used to describe each of the musical styles.

Renaissance   Both religious and secular music, predominantly vocal, instruments used in secular music

Baroque   Steady rhythm, organ used to accompany religious music, secular music written for small groups

Classical   Short, tuneful melodies, gradual dynamic changes, restrained expression of emotions

Romantic   Longer, often complex melodies, more open expression of emotions

Twentieth Century   Unusual rhythms, emphasis on unusual tone colors, great emphasis on experimentation

• Listen to the "Historical Style Montage" again. Identify the order in which the style periods are presented. Use the musical descriptions above to explain your choices.

17

2. Introduce the European-Western style: the differences. Have the students:
• Identify the major historical style periods and their major characteristics.
• Listen to the "Historical Style Montage." Identify the order in which the style periods are presented. (The five styles are: baroque, Renaissance, classical, twentieth century, romantic.)

Reinforcing the Lesson
Review "Style Montage" on page 2. Have the students follow the pictures that represent each musical section.

3 APPRAISAL
The students should be able to:
1. Match the names of the major historical style periods—Renaissance, baroque, classical, romantic, and twentieth century—to brief written descriptions of salient musical characteristics of those styles.
2. Perform "Ode to Joy" on keyboard, bells, or recorder with melodic and rhythmic accuracy.

MORE MUSIC TEACHING IDEAS
Have the students listen to, identify, and classify selected recordings representative of the major style periods if available.

LESSON 6

Focus: Baroque Style

Objectives
To identify duple and triple meter
To review and identify orchestral tone colors
To identify ternary (ABA) form of a composition
To identify the musical characteristics of a baroque composition

Materials
Recordings: ''Marche'' (excerpt)
''Marche''
''Historical Style Montage''
''Spring'' from *The Four Seasons* (optional)
Keyboard, recorder, percussion instruments

Vocabulary
Meter, duple meter, triple meter, measure, bar line, ritardando, coda, ternary

1 SETTING THE STAGE
Play Lully's ''Marche'' as the students enter the room. Tell them this music is typical of baroque style.

2 TEACHING THE LESSON

1. Introduce duple meter and triple meter conducting patterns. Have the students:
• Discuss the information on duple meter and triple meter.
• Perform the duple meter and triple meter rhythms.
• Listen to the excerpt from Lully's ''Marche.''
• Identify which conducting pattern shows the meter for each section.
• Describe the contrast in tempo between the two sections.
• Listen to the entire ''Marche'' and conduct showing duple and triple meter.

Conducting a Baroque Composition

''Marche'' by Jean Baptiste Lully (zhän' bäp-tēst' lyōō-lē') has sections in different **meters,** or groupings of beats. Beats grouped in twos are **duple meter.** Beats grouped in threes are in **triple meter.** Groups of beats are shown in **measures** that are separated by **bar lines.**

These are the conducting patterns for duple and triple meter. The photographs show the patterns when the conductor faces you.

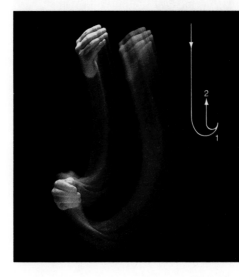 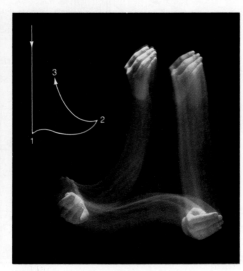

• Listen to the excerpt from Lully's ''Marche.'' It has A and B sections. Tell which conducting pattern to use for each section. Describe the contrast in tempo between the two sections. duple, triple; B is faster than A

   ''Marche'' (excerpt) by Jean Baptiste Lully

• Listen to the entire ''Marche'' and conduct showing duple and triple meter.

   ''Marche'' by Jean Baptiste Lully

18

LESSON 6

2. Introduce the composer. Have the students discuss the information on Lully. You may wish to use some of the following items as a basis for further discussion.

1. Discuss the use of the words *important* and *influential.* Name people in the twentieth century who have been "important and influential" in political and social affairs. (Martin Luther King, Jr.—social justice, Eleanor Roosevelt—social reform; Mahatma Gandhi—social and political reform; Winston Churchill—political leadership)

2. Lully died a rich and famous man. Discuss the concept of fame. Name some famous contemporary musicians. (Philip Glass, Bruce Springsteen, Andrew Lloyd Webber, Leonard Bernstein, and so on)

JEAN BAPTISTE LULLY

Jean Baptiste Lully

Jean Baptiste Lully (1632–1697) became King Louis XIV's most important and influential composer, producing operas and ballets to entertain the French court. For fifteen years Lully controlled much of the music performed in Paris. He was so popular that he was able to persuade King Louis XIV to force other composers to move away from Paris. Thus Lully managed to eliminate most of his competition. He earned enormous sums of money, but no amount ever seemed enough.

An unusual accident caused Lully's death. Instead of using a baton, conductors in those days often kept the steady beat by tapping a large stick on the floor. While conducting this way, Lully struck his own foot. An infection developed, which resulted in his death a month later.

During his career Lully wrote a great deal of dance music. His interest in orchestral tone color can be seen in the wide range of instruments he used in his works.

19

LESSON 6

3. Introduce the listening map of "Marche." Have the students:
• Become familiar with the format of the map. As each number is called:
Section A
1. Follow each measure of the notation in rhythm.
2. Touch the picture of the instrument family that is heard. (strings, then woodwinds)
3. Follow each measure of notation in rhythm.
4. Follow the bridge section followed by the ritardando.

Analyzing a Baroque Composition

• Listen to Lully's "Marche" again and follow the map by pointing to each measure when the music is provided. When no music is shown, point to the pictures that represent the meter, tone color, dynamics, and form. At call number 4, **ritardando** (ri-tär-dän' dō) means a gradual slowing down of the tempo. At call number 9, the **coda** is the concluding section.

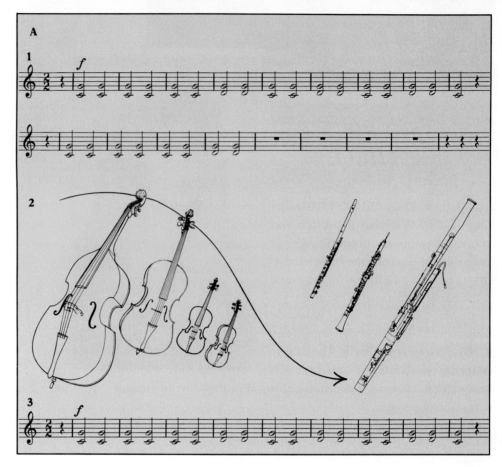

20

E X T E N S I O N

SPECIAL LEARNERS

Prepare an overhead transparency of pupil pages 20 and 21 if your class contains exceptional students who will have difficulty following notation. Point to each measure of the notation. It may help these students first to listen to the A section and tap the beat before following the listening map.

LISTENING

You may wish to use the Listening Map overhead transparency to help guide the students through the listening selection.

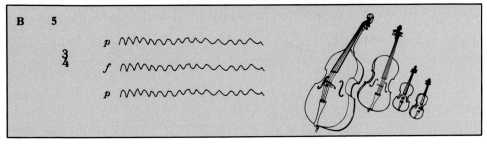

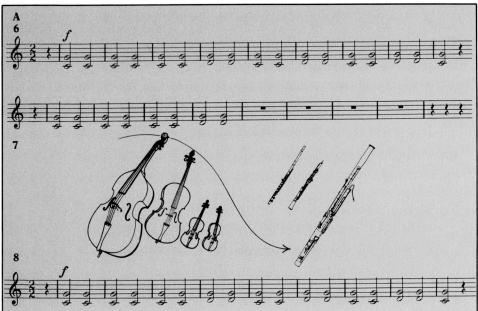

Repetition after a contrasting section creates an ABA, or ternary, form. **Ternary** means having three parts.

- Describe the contrasts between the A and B sections of Lully's "Marche." Identify contrasts in meter, tempo, and tone color.

- Play the A section and the coda of the "Marche" on recorder or keyboard.

A section is duple meter, moderate tempo, uses strings, woodwinds, and brass. The B is triple meter, faster tempo, and uses strings only.

LESSON 6

Section B
5. Follow the dynamic markings as the volume of the music changes.
Section A
6. Follow each measure of the notation in rhythm.
7. Follow the picture of the family of tone color that is heard. (strings then woodwinds)
8. Follow each measure of notation in rhythm.
Coda
9. Follow each measure of notation in rhythm.
• Define ternary form.
• Describe the contrast of meter, tempo, and tone color between the A and B sections.
• Play the A section and coda of the "Marche" on keyboard or recorder.

LESSON 6

4. Introduce the baroque period. Have the students:
• Discuss the information focusing on the musical characteristics of the period.

The Baroque Period (1600–1750)

Royalty, wealthy families, and large churches hired composers of the baroque period to provide music for special occasions or for entertainment. Operas, ballets, and instrumental compositions were written for the world at large. Large religious choral works—Masses and cantatas—were composed for use in churches. For contrasts in tone color composers used a wide variety of instruments such as the organ, violin, flute, oboe, trumpet, and harpsichord.

Most baroque music has steady, rhythmic patterns. Each section of a larger composition conveys a single mood or emotion. Improvements in instruments made more complex music possible. Two of the most famous composers of all time, Johann Sebastian Bach (yō′ hän se-bäs′ tē-än bäкн′) and George Frederick Handel (hän′ del) lived during this period and produced some of the finest examples of baroque music.

Staircase at the Residenz (with frescos by Tiepolo), Würzburg

E X T E N S I O N

• Identify the characteristics of baroque style in ''Marche.'' (steady rhythms, a single mood in each movement, and contrasting tone colors)

Reinforcing the Lesson

Review ''Historical Style Montage'' on page 16 to identify contrasting tone colors.

3 APPRAISAL

The students should be able to:
1. Listen to a composition in duple and triple meter and identify the meters.
2. Demonstrate duple and triple meters using appropriate conducting patterns or movements.
3. Listen to musical examples demonstrating the tone color of brass, woodwind or string families and name, in writing, the tone color.
4. Verbally identify ternary form as a contrasting section followed by a return of the first section.
5. Verbally describe at least three salient musical characteristics of baroque style.

During the baroque period, elaborate styles of architecture, art, and clothing were popular. The exterior scene is of a palace in Vienna, Austria. The interior scene is in Würzburg, West Germany. The musicians in the painting are gathered for a formal portrait.

The Concert. Antonio Domenico Gabbiani

Characteristics of Baroque Music

Steady rhythms

Single mood in each section of a musical composition

Wide variety of instruments used for contrasts in tone
    color and dynamics

The Belvedere. Vienna

23

MORE MUSIC TEACHING IDEAS

Have the students:
1. Play the steady beat on percussion instruments to accompany the B section of ''Marche'' as a contrast to the melodic performance activity in Section A.
2. Listen to ''Spring'' from *The Four Seasons* by Vivaldi, another baroque composer (see page 192).

MAJOR AND MINOR IN TWO STYLES

A Romantic Composition

"Farandole" (fä-rän-dôl') is the final selection in the second *L'Arlésienne* (lär-lā-zē-en') Suite by the French romantic composer Georges Bizet (zhorzh' bē-zā'). A **suite** consists of several individual forms linked together. Bizet wrote the suite as background music for a play called *L'Arlésienne*, or "The Woman of Arles." You may recognize the first of the two themes as the Christmas carol "The March of the Three Kings."

• Listen to "Farandole." Each time you hear a number decide whether you are hearing Theme A or Theme B. 1: A; 2: B; 3: A; 4: B; 5: A; 6: B; 7: A and B

"Farandole" from *L'Arlésienne* Suite No. 2, by Georges Bizet

Georges Bizet (1838–1875), great opera composer, was born in Paris into a family of professional musicians. His father and uncle were singing teachers, and his mother was an excellent pianist. Bizet showed great promise as a musician at an early age. He entered the Paris Conservatory at nine. At nineteen he had won several prizes for piano, organ, and composition.

Although Bizet was a brilliant pianist, his main interest was composing, especially opera. *Carmen* is his best-known work. His music is very melodic with simple orchestral accompaniments. His music for the play *L'Arlésienne* was ignored by the public when it was first presented in 1872. It was not appreciated until the play was revived after his death.

24

LESSON 7

Focus: Major and Minor, Romantic Style

Objectives
To identify major and minor chords
To identify the contrasting sections in a twentieth-century song
To identify the musical characteristics of a romantic composition

Materials
Recordings: "Farandole"
　　　　　Chopin, Etude in E Minor (optional)
　　　　　"Our World"
　　　　　"Marche"
Keyboard, bells, or guitar
Tennis balls
Copying Master 1-1: Listening Map (optional)

Vocabulary
Suite, natural

1 SETTING THE STAGE

Tell the students they will study music in three different styles but with the same basic harmonies.

2 TEACHING THE LESSON

1. Introduce "Farandole." Have the students:

• Listen to "Farandole." As each number is called, write on a sheet of paper which of the themes they hear. (You may wish to use Copying Master 1-1: Listening Map at this time.)

EXTENSION

Theme A of "Farandole" begins with the D minor chord. Theme B begins with the D major chord.

D major chord D minor chord

To play F# (F sharp) on the keyboard, find the black key to the right of F. The symbol ♮ is called a **natural**. It tells you to play F rather than F#. Changing this middle pitch from F# to F changes the D major chord to a D minor chord.

- Play the D minor and D major chords one after the other on keyboard, bells, or guitar to hear the difference between minor and major.

Bizet uses changes between major and minor, and changes in dynamics, to create the romantic style in "Farandole."

- Listen to "Farandole" again. In each section identify the use of major or minor, and changes in dynamics. A: minor, loud; B: major, soft or <

Arles, a city in southern France, was founded almost twenty-five hundred years ago. Many of its ancient buildings have been preserved.

25

- Discuss the information on Bizet and *L'Arlésienne* Suite No. 2.
You may wish to use the following as a basis for further discussion.
Bizet wrote *L'Arlésienne* as background music for a play. Music in theater has many functions. It can set a mood, announce an event, or add a dimension to the plot. Name specific examples of each of the above in movies or television. Discuss some techniques for using music to create a mood or scene.

2. Introduce major and minor chords.
Have the students:
- Discuss the information on the D major and D minor chords.
- Practice playing the chords on keyboard, bells, or guitar to hear the difference.

3. Prepare analysis of "Farandole."
Have the students listen to the recording of "Farandole" again. As each number is called, determine if the themes are presented in major or minor and the appropriate dynamic marking (piano or forte). (You may wish to use Copying Master 1-1: Listening Map at this time.)

SPECIAL LEARNERS

Exceptional students who need visual cues to coordinate visual and reading tasks will benefit from an overhead transparency and individual copies of Copying Master 1-1: Listening Map. As the listening selection is played, pause at the end of each section to allow the students to fill in the chart with the correct responses. Then mark the correct response on the transparency. This will enable the mainstreamed students to coordinate the auditory activity with the visual task.

LESSON 7

4. Introduce the historical and musical characteristics of the romantic period. Have the students:

• Discuss the information focusing on the musical characteristics of the period.

• Summarize the romantic characteristics of "Farandole." (telling a story without words; long complex melodies; prominence of certain instruments; contrasting tone colors; and use of a large orchestra)

The Romantic Period (1830–1900)

Much of the music in movies and on television can be traced back to the kind of music written in the nineteenth-century romantic period. Romantic artists and musicians tried to express their feelings, their outlook, and their hopes and dreams openly. Composers wrote instrumental works that told a story without words. Music became more descriptive, with changes in moods occurring within sections. Long, complex melodies were used to express these moods or emotions. As orchestras became larger and improved instruments were added, tone color became more important than it had been in earlier periods.

Left, the Opéra, Paris, built 1861–75

   Music of the romantic period is very popular today. Many famous romantic works have been used as background music for extremely successful motion pictures. Some of the best known composers of this period were Ludwig van Beethoven (bā′ tō-ven), Franz Schubert (shoo′ bert), Robert Schumann (shoo′ män), Hector Berlioz (ber′ lē-ōz), Frédéric Chopin (shō′ pan), Richard Wagner (väg′ ner), Giuseppe Verdi (ver′ dē), Johannes Brahms (bräms′), Peter Ilyich Tchaikovsky (chī-käv′ skē), and Nicolai Rimsky-Korsakov (rim′ skē kor′ sä-kôv).

26

EXTENSION

COOPERATIVE LEARNING

Have the students form cooperative groups of four. Two readers (one for page 22 and one for page 26), a recorder and a reporter should be assigned in each group. The readers should read page 22 and 26 out loud for the group. Then each group member should write down at least two statements that focus on the similarities and differences between the baroque and romantic musical styles. The group should decide at least four of the most common statements that best describe the differences between baroque and romantic music. The recorder should record the six common statements. The reporter reads

the descriptive statements to the class. Class members should require each cooperative group to provide a rationale as to why they think their statements best describe the differences between baroque and romantic music.

You may wish to vary this activity by having the students read the material and write their statements before you divide the class into groups. The students could then compare lists, choosing several of the most common statements describing the differences between baroque and romantic music.

Florentine Story-teller, Vincenzo Cabianca, MUSEO DELL'ARTE MODERNA, Florence

The Ball, James Tissot, MUSÉE D'ORSAY, Paris

Characteristics of Romantic Music

Changes of mood within sections of a composition

Direct expression of emotions

Long, often complex melodies

Use of large orchestra

Artists of the romantic period often depicted scenes of earlier times.
Top, an imaginary scene of medieval Italy.
Right, women's fashions in the nineteenth century often were quite elaborate.

27

MORE MUSIC TEACHING IDEAS

Have the students:

1. Choose eight to ten selections from current popular music. Listen and identify selections in major and minor.

2. Listen to "Farandole." Pass a tennis ball to the right on the strong beat when the music begins in minor; pass the tennis ball to the left when the music begins in major. (The order is: 1: m; 2: M; 3: m; 4: m, 5: m; 6: m; 7: M)

3. Listen to the Etude in E minor Op. 25, by Chopin, to hear the musical characteristics of the period (see page 199).

LESSON 7

5. Introduce a song in major and minor. Have the students:
• Listen to the repeated and contrasting sections in "Our World" and identify which are major and which are minor.
• Sing "Our World," emphasizing the contrasting sections.

Reinforcing the Lesson

Review "Marche" by Lully, page 18, and compare the major and minor sections.

3 APPRAISAL

The students should be able to:
1. Listen to aural examples of major and minor chords and identify the chords using pencil and paper procedures.
2. While watching the music for "Our World" (with numbered measures) write the measure numbers for the A section repeat and the B contrasting section.
3. Verbally describe at least three salient musical characteristics of romantic style.

A Song in Major and Minor

Key: E♭ major   Starting Pitch: B♭

"Our World" is a twentieth-century song that has sections in both major and minor.

• Listen to the repeated and contrasting sections. You will hear the A section repeat before you hear the B section. Which section is in major and which is in minor? A is in major; B is in minor.
• Sing the song. Be sure to emphasize the contrasting sections.

Scale Tones: E♭ major: *so, la, ta, ti, do re ma mi fa so la ta ti do¹*
G minor: *mi si la ti do¹*

Our World

Piano Accompaniment on page PA 2

Words by Jane Foster Knox
Music by Lana Walter

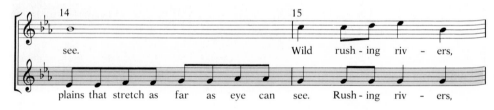

28

E X T E N S I O N

SPECIAL LEARNERS

Students who are slow readers or who have visual impairments may have difficulty following the notation when the song changes from single to double staff format. Prepare an overhead transparency of pages 28–29 of the pupil edition and point to the staff that has the melody. This procedure will enable different learners to follow the order of the song. Mainstreamed students also may need a visual starting cue since "Our World" does not begin on the downbeat.

VOCAL DEVELOPMENT

Have the students sing the pitches of "Our World" on short *doo* sounds to aid rhythmic and melodic accuracy.

SIGNING FOR "OUR WORLD"

In sign language the meaning of the phrase is signed. For example, to "make it so" means to make it happen or succeed; therefore the sign is "succeed."

Think

The index finger points to the brain.

Find

Human Race (People)

Using "P" palms down hands circle alternately in front of the body.

With palm down, index finger and thumb close, as in picking up something.

16 17 *poco rit.* 18 *a tempo* 19 *unison* *mp* 20 *soft and intense*

flash-ing in the sun. Jour-ney just be-gun! What fu - ture will there

flash-ing in the sun. Jour-ney just be-gun! What fu - ture will there

21 no breath 22 23 24 25

be for land and_ air and sea? Liv-ing things like_ you and me?_____

26 27 28 A *mp* 29

I'd like to think a fu - ture hu - man

I'd

30 31

race_____ would find the world a fair and love - ly

like to think a fu - ture hu - man race_____ would

32 33 *mf* 34

place. Lov - ing and car - ing, we can make it so,

find the world a fair and love-ly place. By car - ing we can make it so,

35 36 *rit.* 37 *p* 38 39

shar-ing what we know: lov - ing, we can make it so._____

shar-ing what we know: lov-ing, we can make it so._____

29

Term	Illustration	Description
World		Circle the right "W" forward, down, up and around the left "W" as in the world revolving.
Fair/Lovely		The "O" hand starts at the chin, opens while circling the face, coming back to rest again at the chin.
Loving		With closed fists, cross hands over the heart.
Caring		Place open palms over the heart.
Make It So (Succeed)		Index fingers move up, making two loops, as in moving up the ladder toward success.
Sharing		Move the upright, open-palm of the right hand back and forth across the open, palm-up left hand.
Know		Fingers touch forehead.

LESSON 8

Focus: Synth-Pop Style, Steady Beat

Objectives
To identify a style of popular music
To perform quarter notes and eighth notes
in a rhythm score

Materials
Recordings: ''Head over Heels''
African Sanctus
Drumsticks (or substitutes)
Keyboard, bells, or recorder
Copying Master 1-2 (optional)

Vocabulary
Synth-pop, synthesizer, matched grip

1 SETTING THE STAGE

Tell the students they will be studying a
style of rock music called synth-pop which
uses the synthesizer as the principal instrument.

2 TEACHING THE LESSON

1. Introduce synth-pop style. Have the
students discuss the information on synth-
pop style.
You may use some of the following items as
a basis for further discussion.
1. A synthesizer is a specialized computer
that interprets keyboard inputs in order to
produce musical sounds. Discuss what
kinds of components might be in a synthesizer. (tone generator and amplifier)
2. Does a synth-pop group need different
skills from those of a traditional rock and
roll group? (yes) What kinds of skills? (an
understanding of electronics and sound
engineering) Does this mean that synth-
pop performers need not be musicians?
(no, even synthesizer musicians need an
understanding of basic music principles)

SYNTH-POP: A STYLE OF ROCK MUSIC

Synth-pop is a style of rock music in which the principal instrument
is the synthesizer. **Synthesizers** are electronic keyboards that use
computer technology to imitate the tone color of just about any
musical instrument, or group of instruments. Often a drum machine
provides the steady beat.

The synth-pop style first developed in England. It has a cool,
shimmering tone color that is very different from the sound of
guitar-based bands. Players in many synth-pop bands have had little
formal musical training. Instead, they learned a few basic chords
on the synthesizer and immediately began composing songs.

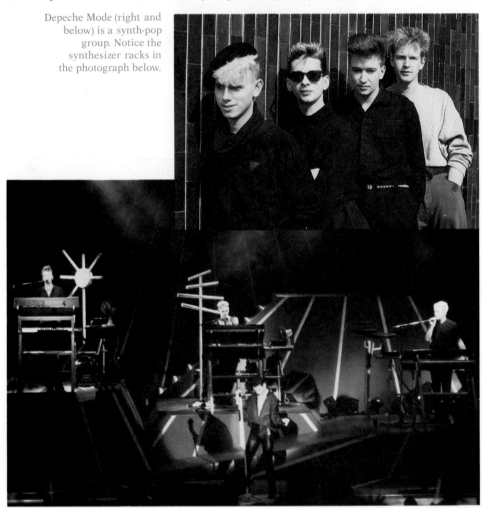

Depeche Mode (right and
below) is a synth-pop
group. Notice the
synthesizer racks in
the photograph below.

30

E X T E N S I O N

CURRICULUM CONNECTION: SCIENCE

Synthesizers—Sound is processed by a
synthesizer in the form of electrical signals.
A keyboard controls the synthesizer's electronic circuits. When a key is pressed, one
signal goes to the *oscillator*, the component
of the synthesizer that determines the pitch
of the note. Another signal tells the *generators* to create their own electrical signals.
The generators control the *filter*, which
modifies the tone quality of the sound, and
the *amplifier*, which adjusts the loudness.
The audio signal begins at the oscillator
and goes through the filter and amplifier
and finally out to the speaker, which produces an audible tone.

In the matched grip, both drumsticks are held in the same position.

2. Introduce rhythmic accompaniment to "Head over Heels." Have the students:
• Prepare to perform the rhythmic patterns by patting the quarter notes and clapping the eighth notes. Make no sound for the rests.
• Learn the matched-grip drumstick position.
• Practice the five patterns, using the matched grip.
• Locate the patterns in the rhythmic accompaniment score to "Head over Heels."

• Practice these patterns with your drumsticks, using the percussion **matched grip.** When you see a quarter rest or an eighth rest, play silently in the air. Stress, or emphasize, the accented notes ($\overset{>}{\downarrow}$).

• Find these patterns in the percussion score to "Head over Heels" on page 33. 1: Introduction and Coda; 2: Refrain 1 and Refrain 2; 3: Introduction and Refrain 1; 4: Verse 1 and Verse 2; 5: Coda

31

LESSON 8

3. Perform a rhythmic accompaniment with the recording of "Head over Heels." Have the students:

• Form six groups, each one playing a section. Each group will pick up from the previous one as each new section begins.

• Play the rhythm accompaniment to "Head over Heels" on page 33. The symbol ⌐—2—⌐ in the score means that you should listen and count for two measures before continuing to play.

 "Head over Heels," by Curt Smith and Roland Orzabal

Below, Roland Orzabal (left) and Curt Smith (right). Right and bottom, Tears for Fears in performance

32

THE COMPOSERS

Curt Smith and **Roland Orzabal**—of the British duo Tears for Fears have known each other since they were at school in Bath, England. They formed their first band when they were nineteen. Their first album, *The Hurting,* was a huge success in England in 1983. Their album *Songs From the Big Chair* made them an international pop success, with songs such as "Shout," "Everybody Wants to Rule the World," and "Head Over Heels." Tears for Fears' music is both moody and uplifting. The complex and exciting dance beat balances the emotional and complex lyrics to fulfill their original goal—to create "music for the body, the heart, and the mind."

Head Over Heels
Rhythm Accompaniment

Introduction

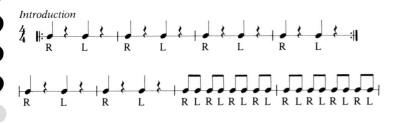

R L R L R L R L

R L R L R L R L R L R L R L R L R L R L

Verse 1   *play 4 times*

R L R L R L R L R L R L R L R L R L R L R L R

Refrain 1

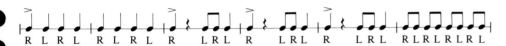

R   R L R   R   R L R   R   R L R   R   R L R   R   R L R   R   R L R

R L R L   R L R L   R   L R L   R   L R L   R   L R L   R L R L R L R L

Verse 2   *play 4 times*

R L R L R   R L R L R   R L R L R   R L R L R

Refrain 2

R   R L R   R   R L R   R   R L R   R   R L R   R   R L R   R   R L R   R L R L   R L R L

Coda

R   L   R   L   R   L   R   L

play 5 times

R   R L R L   L R L R L   R L R L   R L   R L

R   R L R   L   L R L R   L   R   L

R R L R L   L R L R L   R

33

MORE MUSIC TEACHING IDEAS

Have the students perform the melodic accompaniment to "Head over Heels" (Copying Master 1-2) on keyboard, bells, or recorder.

EXTRA HELP

You may wish to use an overhead transparency of pupil page 33 to point to each group and to each section in the accompaniment as it begins.

LESSON 8

• Sing the words to "Head over Heels" along with the recording and play the rhythmic accompaniment.

Reinforcing the Lesson

Review the rhythmic accompaniment to *African Sanctus* on page 8.

3 APPRAISAL

The students should be able to:

1. Identify the tone color of synthesized sound as one of the stylistic characteristics of synth-pop style.

2. Read and perform a rhythmic accompaniment to "Head over Heels" containing quarter notes, quarter rests, and eighth notes.

• Listen once more to "Head over Heels." Sing along with the recording and play a rhythmic accompaniment for the composition.

34

MORE MUSIC TEACHING IDEAS

Have the students list other popular performers whose music is in synth-pop style.

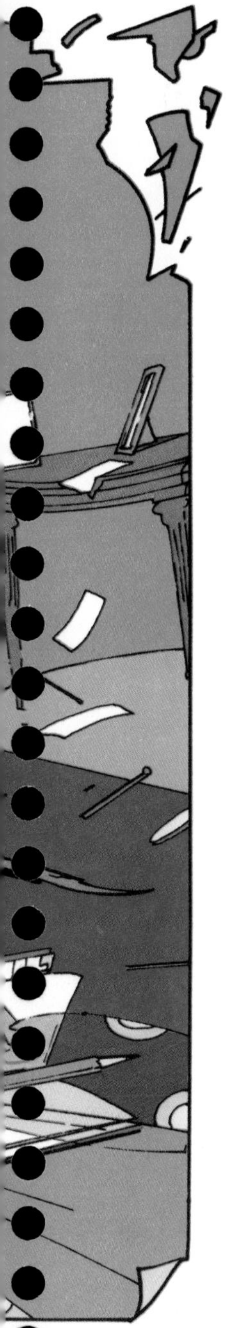

HEAD OVER HEELS

Words and music
by Roland Orzabal
and Curt Smith

1. I wanted to be with you alone
   And talk about the weather
   But traditions I can trace against the child in your face
   Won't escape my attention.
   You keep your distance with a system of touch
   And gentle persuasion.
   I'm lost in admiration could I need you this much?
   Oh you're just wasting my time,
       you're just just just wasting time.

REFRAIN
Something happens and I'm head over heels;
I never find out till I'm head over heels
Something happens and I'm head over heels;
Ah, don't take my heart, don't break my heart don't don't don't
    throw it away. (*First time only*: Throw it away, throw it away.)

2. I made a fire and watching it burn
   Thought of your future
   With one foot in the past now just how long will it last
   No, no, no have you no ambition
   My mother and my brothers used to breathing clean air
   And dreaming I'm a doctor
   It's hard to be a man when there's a gun in your hand
   Oh I feel so. . .(*To Refrain*)

This is my four leaf clover.
I'm on the line, open mind.
This is my four leaf clover.
La la la la la la la la la la la la la la la la la (*Repeat and fade)*

35

REVIEW AND EVALUATION

JUST CHECKING

Objective
To review and test the skills and concepts taught in Unit 1

Materials
Recordings: Just Checking Unit 1
(questions 1, 2, 5, 6, 7, 8, 10)
"Historical Style Montage"
"Run Joe"
"Elements"
African Sanctus
Satto
Unit 1 Evaluation (question 3)
For Extra Credit recordings
(optional)
Keyboard, recorder, or bells
Copying Master 1-3 (optional)
Evaluation Unit 1 Copying Master

TEACHING THE LESSON

Review the skills and concepts taught in Unit 1. Have the students:
• Perform the activities and answer the questions on pages 36–37. (For this review, examples for questions 1, 2, 5, 6, 7, 8, and 10 are included in the "Just Checking Unit 1" recording. Have the students answer these questions first. Then have them answer the other questions in the review, using the recordings in the unit where necessary.)
• Review their answers.
(You may wish to use Copying Master 1-3 at this time.)

 1A, 1B, 2A

CD 1

JUST CHECKING

See how much you remember.

1. Listen to the recording of the steady beat and perform these patterns, patting the quarter notes and clapping the eighth notes.

2. Listen to a section of Lully's "Marche" and decide if the meter is duple or triple. Show your answer by conducting. Is the tempo slow, moderate, or fast? duple; moderate

3. Play the "Ode to Joy" on page 16 on keyboard, recorder, or bells as you listen to the "Historical Style Montage." Decide whether the style period of each version of the "Ode to Joy" is Renaissance, baroque, classical, romantic, or twentieth century. baroque, romantic, twentieth century, Renaissance

4. Perform this pattern as you listen to the verse of "Run Joe" to experience the syncopated calypso style.

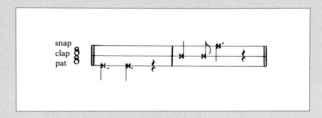

5. Use two movements to show the I and V chords as you listen to the refrain of "Run Joe." Show the chord changes by putting your palms on your desk when you hear the I chord. Put your thumbs up when you hear the V chord.

36

6. Listen to determine whether the style period of each of these compositions is Renaissance, baroque, classical, romantic, or twentieth century. baroque, romantic, classical, twentieth century

7. Listen to a section of Bizet's "Farandole" to determine whether its theme begins in major or minor. minor

8. Listen to determine whether the style of each example is African, synth-pop, Japanese, calypso, or reggae. reggae, Japanese, synth-pop, calypso

9. Listen to "Elements." Raise your right hand to show A sections and your left to show B sections.

10. Listen and identify the instrument family you hear in these excerpts from Lully's "Marche." Show your answer by pointing to the appropriate picture as each number is called.
1. strings only; 2. woodwinds and strings

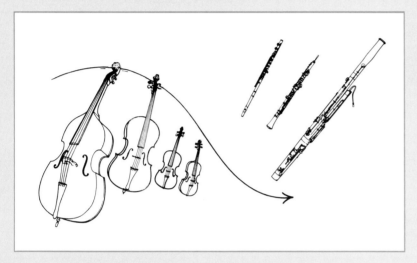

11. Listen to a section of *African Sanctus* and decide if the music sounds more African or more Western. African

12. Listen to a section of *Satto* and show the dynamic changes by clapping the steady beat lightly on the palm of your hand when the music is loud. Tap the beat on the back of your hand when the music is soft.

REVIEW AND EVALUATION

GIVING THE EVALUATION
Evaluation Unit 1 Copying Master can be found in the *Teacher's Copying Masters* book along with full directions for giving the evaluation and checking the answers.

FOR EXTRA CREDIT
You may want to have the students do one of the following activities.
1. Describe how tone color, meter, tempo, and dynamics are used to create contrast in the baroque style of "Marche." (The work is in ABA form. The A sections are in duple meter, slow tempo and use all of the families of instruments. The B section is faster than A, is in triple meter, and uses only the string section of the orchestra.)
2. Binary and ternary form are common in many aspects of our lives. Identify and describe one other object which either contains or is an example of binary form and one which is an example of ternary form. (architecture, buildings, and so on.)

UNIT 2 • OVERVIEW

ELEMENTS OF MUSIC	UNIT 2 OBJECTIVES	Lesson 1 Focus: Duple, Triple, and Quadruple Meter	Lesson 2 Focus: Changing Meter
Dynamics	Identify dynamic changes in a composition		
Tone Color	Identify tone color changes Perform melodic accompaniments on bells, recorder, or keyboard		Perform a melodic accompaniment on bells, recorder, or keyboard
Tempo			
Duration/ Rhythm	**Identify duple, triple, and quadruple meter** **Identify meter changes** **Perform, listen to, and identify irregular meter** in $\frac{5}{4}$ and $\frac{7}{8}$	Identify duple, triple, and quadruple meter by responding to the meter through body percussion, tennis ball activities, and conducting metric patterns Perform meter games by accurately saying and performing the meter patterns Identify duple, triple, and quadruple meter from listening examples Identify changes in meter	Identify changes of duple, triple, and quadruple meter through conducting and movement Listen to, conduct, and perform changing meters in a song Read and perform a melodic accompaniment with rhythmic accuracy Learn to conduct the pattern for $\frac{6}{4}$ Create changing meter patterns
Pitch	Hear, sing songs within a range of B-e'	Sing a song with changing meters	Sing a song with a range of B-e'
Texture	Perform a melodic accompaniment		Read and perform a melodic accompaniment on bells, recorder, or keyboard (d-b)
Form	Conduct a musical composition having a strophic form		Conduct a composition in strophic form
Style	Listen to and discuss the jazz style Discuss nationalism in the romantic style period **Classify musical examples according to style period**	Listen to rhythm use in different musical styles Classify listening examples according to style period	Discuss a contemporary Broadway musical
Reading	Practice known notations Use 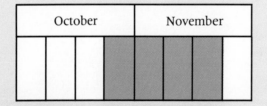	Read ♩, >, ‖: :‖ in $\frac{2}{4}$, $\frac{3}{4}$, $\frac{4}{4}$ Follow body motion score	Sing and play songs using $\frac{3}{4}$, $\frac{4}{4}$, $\frac{6}{4}$, ‖: :‖, ♫, ♩. ♩.

PURPOSE Unit 2: RHYTHM PLAYS A ROLE

In this unit the students will review and/or experience various aspects of rhythm. They will review duple, triple, and quadruple meter and be introduced to some unusual rhythm patterns.

SUGGESTED TIME FRAME

October				November		

FOCUS

- Duple, Triple, and Quadruple Meter
- Changing Meter
- Irregular Meter
- Irregular Meter in Sevens, Jazz

Lesson 3 Focus: Irregular Meter	**Lesson 4** Focus: Irregular Meter in Sevens, Jazz
Follow dynamic changes in a composition	
Follow tone color changes in a composition	Hear instruments in a jazz quartet
Identify, listen to, define, and perform irregular meter Identify meter changes in a composition through body percussion Read and perform a speech chant in $\frac{5}{4}$ meter Perform meter games in $\frac{5}{4}$	Identify, listen to, and perform irregular meter in seven Determine the grouping of twos and threes in a composition with seven beats per measure Tap steady beat while listening to irregular meter Perform a rhythmic ostinato on bells, recorder, or keyboard Play accented beats in $\frac{7}{4}$ meter
Listen to a melody in $\frac{5}{4}$ meter	Read and perform a melodic accompaniment in $\frac{7}{4}$ meter Sing a song with a range of d-e^l
Listen to a jazz composition using irregular meter Discuss nationalism shown through musical style of Modest Mussorgsky Listen to a composition which reflects the romantic style period and uses changing and irregular meters	Discuss jazz style of Dave Brubeck Discuss musicians from the 1950s and 1960s who made unique contributions to popular music
Read body motion score, irregular meters Follow notation in $\frac{2}{4}$, $\frac{3}{4}$, $\frac{5}{4}$, $\frac{6}{4}$	Play ostinato in $\frac{7}{4}$ Sing song in $\frac{7}{8}$

BULLETIN BOARD

Prepare a strip of tagboard with the following label: REGULAR AND IRREGULAR METERS. Place the label centered at the top of the board. Prepare pieces of tagboard with the meter patterns shown. As you move through the unit and discuss the different patterns, have students collect pictures and/or names of similar objects that normally come in groups of twos, threes, fours, fives, or sevens. Display the illustrations alongside the appropriate meter patterns. Some examples might be a pair of socks (2), shamrock leaves (3), the cardinal points (4), the Great Lakes (5), and the seven seas (7).

REGULAR AND IRREGULAR METERS

LESSON 1

UNIT 2

RHYTHM
PLAYS A ROLE

LESSON 1

Focus: Duple, Triple, and Quadruple Meter

Objectives
To identify and distinguish between duple, triple, and quadruple meter in recorded compositions

Materials
Recordings: "Marche"
"Music in Twos"
"Music in Threes"
"Music in Fours"
"Meter Identification
Montage"
"That's What Friends Are
For"
Classroom pitched and unpitched instruments
Tennis balls (one for each student)

Vocabulary
Quadruple meter

1 SETTING THE STAGE
Review conducting "Marche" by Lully on page 18.

M.C. Escher, CORDON ART, Baarn, Holland

39

LESSON 1

2 TEACHING THE LESSON

1. Introduce duple, triple and quadruple meter. Have the students:
• Perform the body percussion in duple meter as shown while listening to "Music in Twos."
• Listen again to "Music in Twos" and perform the body percussion while saying their names as indicated.
• Perform the body percussion in triple meter as shown while listening to "Music in Threes."
• Listen again to "Music in Threes" and perform the body percussion while speaking their names as indicated.
• Perform the body percussion in quadruple meter as shown while listening to "Music in Fours."
• Listen again to "Music in Fours" and perform the body percussion while saying their names as indicated.

Beats can be grouped in sets. The first beat of each group is emphasized.

• Perform this rhythm in duple meter as you listen to the recording.

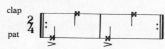

"Music in Twos"

• Listen again, perform the rhythm pattern in duple meter, and play this name game. Each of you, in turn, will say your first name on the accented beat of each measure until everyone has had a turn.

• Perform this rhythm pattern in triple meter as you listen to the recording.

"Music in Threes"

• Listen again, perform the rhythm pattern, and play the name game in triple meter.

• Perform this rhythm pattern in **quadruple meter** as you listen to the recording.

"Music in Fours"

• Listen again, performing the rhythm pattern. Play a variation of the name game in which each of you says your first name on the accented first beat and your last name on the third beat.

40

E X T E N S I O N

- Show duple, triple, and quadruple meter by bouncing a tennis ball on the first beat of each measure. "Change" means to change hands.

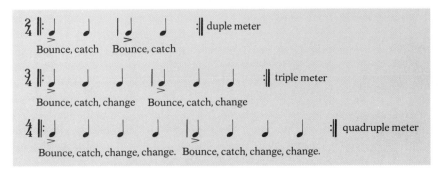

- Show duple, triple, and quadruple by bouncing the ball and then by conducting as you listen to "Meter Identification Montage." duple, quadruple, triple

 "Meter Identification Montage"

This diagram shows the conducting pattern for quadruple meter. The photograph shows how the pattern looks when the conductor faces you.

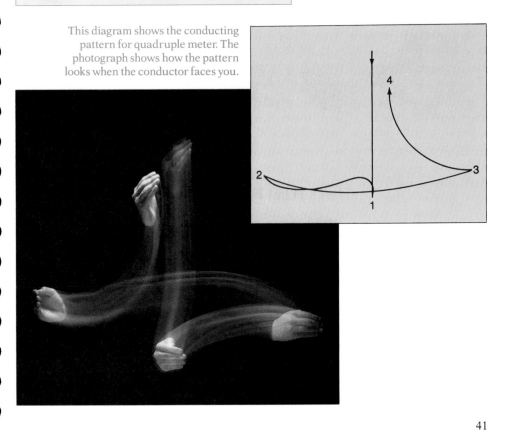

41

2. Introduce tennis ball activity for reinforcing duple, triple and quadruple meter. Have the students practice duple, triple, and quadruple meter by bouncing a tennis ball on the first beat of each measure as indicated. Duple meter is performed as "bounce, catch." Triple meter is performed as "bounce, catch, change" (change hands). Quadruple meter is performed as "bounce, catch, change, change."

3. Introduce conducting patterns to reinforce duple, triple, and quadruple meter. Have the students:

- Review the conducting patterns for duple and triple meters on page 18.
- Examine the conducting pattern for quadruple meter.
- Practice each conducting pattern encouraging the use of two hands.
- Listen to "Meter Identification Montage" and bounce a tennis ball, then conduct, in the appropriate meter with the music.

COOPERATIVE LEARNING

Have the students show duple, triple, and quadruple meters by conducting as they listen to the music. Then working in cooperative groups of four, have the students create their own "Meter Identification Montage" using percussion and pitched instruments. (Encourage the students to use the pentatonic scale or Dorian mode if they know them.) Assign the role of recorder (to write down the order of the meters in the montage) and a conductor. One group may wish to quiz another group by having it determine the order of the meter in the "Meter Identification Montage."

SPECIAL LEARNERS

If a class includes exceptional students who have difficulty with coordination, or have physical handicaps, preplan an alternative activity for the body percussion and tennis ball activities, which emphasize metrical organization. Have these students pat a rhythm instrument on each downbeat. These students also may need a teacher cue for each downbeat.

EXTRA HELP

For beginning experiences with tennis balls, you may want to select two or three students to demonstrate the procedure for the class. Gradually add additional students to the group. You may want to have half the class use tennis balls while others observe. Alternate.

LESSON 1

4. Introduce changing meter. Have the students:

• Follow the score as they listen to "That's What Friends Are For" and notice when the meter changes.

• Sing the song.

Reinforcing the Lesson

Have the students classify the three listening examples from "Meter Identification Montage" according to style periods. Example 1—"Galop" by Igor Stravinsky. Twentieth century because of the emphasis on unusual rhythms and off-beat patterns. Example 2—Sinfonia from Cantata 140 by J. S. Bach. Baroque period because of the steady rhythm and sudden changes in dynamics. Example 3—"Procession of the Nobles" by Nicolai Rimsky-Korsakov. Romantic period because of the large orchestra.

3 APPRAISAL

The students should be able to listen to several musical examples in duple, triple, and quadruple meter and accurately identify the meter.

• Listen to "That's What Friends Are For." Decide when the meter changes. measures 9, 10, 22, 23

• Sing the song.

Key: F major   Starting Pitch: D   Scale Tones: *mi, fa, so, la, ti, do re mi fa so la*

That's What Friends Are For

Piano Accompaniment on page PA 6

Words and music by Carole Bayer Sager and Burt Bacharach

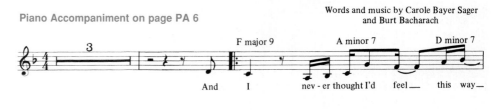

42

EXTENSION

THE COMPOSER

Burt Bacharach—was born in 1928 in Kansas City, where he was raised in a cultured atmosphere. Bacharach studied music at McGill University and studied composition with Darius Milhaud and Henry Cowell. He played jazz piano in nightclubs at the same time. From 1958 to 1961 he was Marlene Dietrich's accompanist. Bacharach is best known for his popular songs, many of which were recorded by singer Dionne Warwick. During the 1960s he teamed up with Hal David to create such timeless songs as "Walk On By," "Raindrops Keep Fallin' On My Head," "What's New, Pussycat?" and "Alfie." "That's What Friends Are For" was written, arranged, and produced by Bacharach and his wife, Carole Bayer Sager.

VOCAL DEVELOPMENT

Have the students emphasize diction (consonant articulation) as a means of experiencing the rhythmic quality of this composition. Also, have them perform selected patterns of short vowels followed by long vowels to assist in achieving rhythmic accuracy, such as

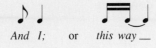

And I;   or   *this way*

Have them find other examples of long and short vowels in the composition.

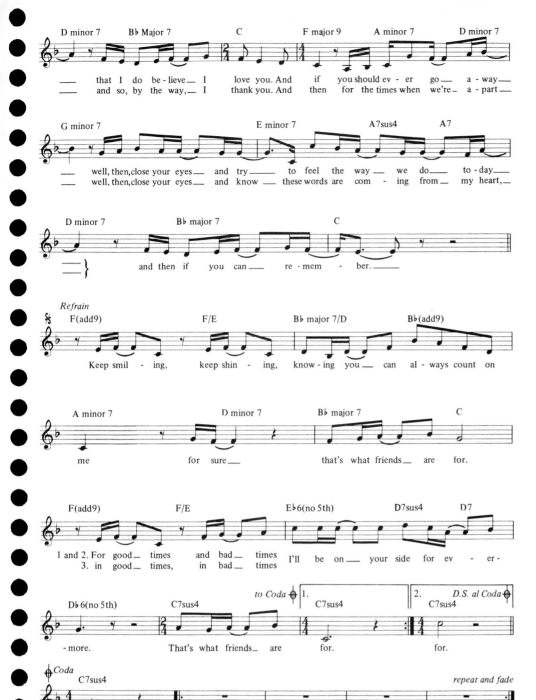

LESSON 2

Focus: Changing Meter

Objectives
To distinguish changes of duple, triple and quadruple meter
To conduct a six-beat pattern
To perform a composition in changing meters

Materials
Recordings: "Love Song"
          "Mix 'Em Up"
          "Meter Identification
            Montage"
Keyboard, recorder, or bells
Tennis balls (one for each student)

1 | SETTING THE STAGE

Tell the students they will be distinguishing changes of duple, triple and quadruple meter, and performing a composition in changing meters.

2 | TEACHING THE LESSON

1. Introduce changing meters. Have the students:
• Listen to "Love Song" and read information on the musical *Pippin*.
• Listen to "Mix 'Em Up" and raise their hands when they hear a change in meter.

CD 2 The musical *Pippin* is set in medieval times. However, because it is largely about young people growing up and learning to face the world around them, it has considerable contemporary appeal. Pippin's father, a character based on Charlemagne, wants his son to become a great warrior. Pippin, on the other hand, dreams of magic shows and miracles. Although Pippin never becomes the great warrior his father desired, he does learn to cope with the realities of being heir to the throne.

• Listen to "Love Song," which contains many changes of meter.

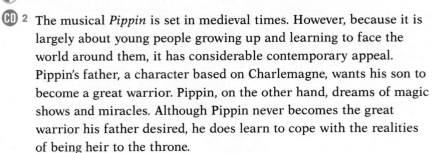 "Love Song" from the musical *Pippin*, by Stephen Schwartz

A scene from the musical *Pippin*.

• Listen to "Mix 'Em Up" and raise your hand when you hear a change from one meter to another.

 "Mix 'Em Up"

44

EXTENSION

THE COMPOSER

Stephen Schwartz—composer and lyricist, was born in New York City in 1948. He studied at the Juilliard School and Carnegie-Mellon University. Schwartz is best known for his musicals. He wrote the music and lyrics to *Godspell*, for which he won the Drama Desk Award, two Grammy Awards, and a gold record. He also wrote the English text for Leonard Bernstein's *Mass*. Schwartz wrote *Pippin* in 1972. During its run on Broadway it won four Tony Awards, among other honors.

• Listen again and show when the composition is in duple, triple, or quadruple meter by conducting the appropriate pattern. duple; quadruple; triple

 CHALLENGE As you listen to "Mix 'Em Up":

Walk forward and conduct in two when you hear duple meter. Stop and conduct in three when you hear triple meter. Stop and clap four beats in a square formation when you hear quadruple meter.

In "Love Song" Stephen Schwartz used meters of three, four, and six beats. Practice conducting the pattern for six beats in a measure.

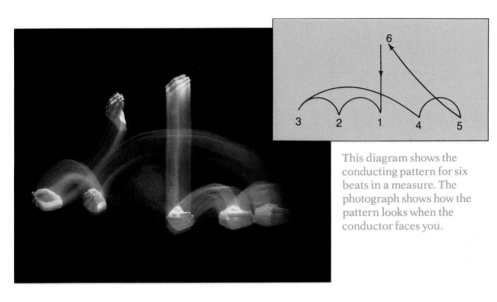

This diagram shows the conducting pattern for six beats in a measure. The photograph shows how the pattern looks when the conductor faces you.

• Look at the first four measures of "Love Song" on page 46 and decide which conducting pattern should be used in each measure. six beats; four beats; three beats; four beats

• Practice conducting the first four measures as you listen to "Love Song."

• Sing "Love Song" (pages 46–47). Play the descant (part tinted in yellow) on recorder, bells, or keyboard.

45

LESSON 2

• Listen again to "Mix 'Em Up" and identify the meter of the selection by conducting the appropriate pattern.
• Listen to "Mix 'Em Up" and respond to the Challenge! by performing the appropriate movement pattern to represent the meter they are hearing.

2. Introduce conducting changing meters. Have the students:
• Practice conducting the beat pattern for six beats in a measure.
• Examine the first four measures of "Love Song" and determine which conducting patterns should be used. (six, four, three, four)
• Practice conducting the first four measures as they listen to the song. (Note that the song is in strophic form so they will have the opportunity to conduct the pattern at least three times.)
• Analyze the conducting patterns for the entire song.

LESSON 2

• Sing the song with the recording and play the descant on keyboard, recorder, or bells.

Reinforcing the Lesson

Review "Meter Identification Montage" on page 41 to identify changes of meter.

3 APPRAISAL

The students should be able to:

1. Listen to "Mix 'Em Up" and with eyes closed, signal when they hear a change in meter.

2. Accurately conduct the changing meters in "Love Song" ($\frac{3}{4}$, $\frac{4}{4}$, and $\frac{6}{4}$).

3. Perform the melodic accompaniment to "Love Song" with rhythmic and melodic accuracy.

Key: E major   **Starting Pitch: F#**   **Scale Tones:** *so, la, ta, ti, do re mi fa so la ta ti do¹*

Love Song

Piano Accompaniment on page PA 10

Words and music
by Stephen Schwartz

Sit-ting on the floor and talk-ing 'til dawn. Can-dles and con-fi-
Pri-vate lit-tle jokes and sil-ly pet names. Lav-en-der soap and
how can you de-fine a look or a touch? How can you weigh a

-den-ces. Trad-ing old be-liefs and hum-ming old songs and
lo-tions. All of the cli-chés and all of the games and
feel-ing? Ta-ken by them-selves, now they don't mean much. To-

low-er-ing old de-fen-ces. Sing-ing a
all of the strange e-mo-tions. Sing-ing a   Love song,   la la la___ la la
-geth-er they send you reel-ing in to a

3rd time cut to Coda ⊕

la la   la___ la la   Love   song,   la la___ la la   la.___

46

E X T E N S I O N

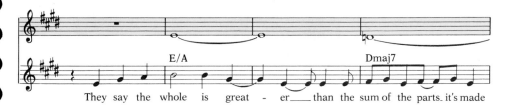

They say the whole is great - er___ than the sum of the parts. it's made

of. Well, if it's true of___ an - y - thing, it's true of love.

D.C. al Coda ⊕

'Cause. Love song, la la___ la la la.___

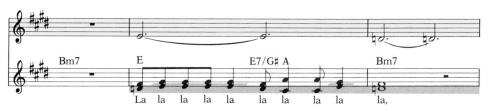

La la la la la la la la la la,

La la la la la la la la la la.

47

MORE MUSIC TEACHING IDEAS

Have the students:

1. Use the tennis ball–bouncing activity to show changing meter while they listen to "Mix 'Em Up."

2. Identify words with two syllables (U-tah) or (base-ball) and three syllables (Ar-kan-sas or bas-ket-ball) and create alternating measures of changing meters.

CURRICULUM CONNECTION: SOCIAL STUDIES

Charlemagne—also known as Charles the Great, was king of the Franks (the ancestors of the modern French people) from 768 to 814. He conquered most of western Europe and ruled as emperor. The arts and literature flourished during his reign. In 806, Charlemagne divided his empire among his three sons, Pepin, Charles, and Louis. Pepin and Charles died soon after, and Louis succeeded his father as emperor. Louis was a weak ruler; his sons warred against him for control of the empire. Finally, a treaty divided the empire into three parts. Without Charlemagne's strong rule, the empire fell into a period of confusion and decline.

LESSON 3

Focus: Irregular Meter

Objectives
To identify, perform, and define irregular meter
To listen to recorded compositions that use irregular meter
To follow changes of meter in a one-line score

Materials
Recordings: *Take Five* pattern
"Goin' Trav'lin'"
Take Five
"Promenade" from *Pictures at an Exhibition*
"Love Song"

Vocabulary
Irregular meter, program music

1 SETTING THE STAGE

Tell the students they will be identifying and performing irregular meters.

2 TEACHING THE LESSON

1. Introduce irregular meter. Have the students:
• Discuss and define irregular meter.
• Listen to the *Take Five* pattern and practice the rhythm pattern that is a combination of triple and duple meter.
• Practice the $\frac{5}{4}$ pattern by patting the accented beats and clapping nonaccented beats while listening again to the *Take Five* pattern.
• Say their first names on the first beat of the measure and their last names on the fourth beat of the measure until every student has said his or her name.

2B IRREGULAR METER
CD 2

Much of the music you have sung and played moves in either duple, triple, or quadruple meter throughout an entire composition. Sometimes composers use changing meter in a repeating pattern to produce **irregular meter.**

This painting by the American artist Romare Bearden illustrates the spirit of jazz.

One Night Stand, Romare Bearden. CORDIER & ECKSTROM GALLERY, NY

A Little Jazz

• As you listen to the *Take Five* pattern, perform this rhythm pattern, which is a combination of triple and duple meter.

Take Five pattern

This same pattern can be written with five beats in each measure with accents on the first and fourth beats.

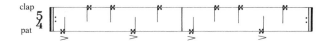

• Listen again. Show this irregular meter by patting your knees on beats 1 and 4 and clapping your hands on beats 2, 3, and 5.
• Continue patting and clapping as you play this variation on the name game. Say your first name on the first beat of your measure and your last name on the fourth beat of your measure.

48

SPECIAL LEARNERS

Prepare an overhead transparency of pupil page 48 if you have mainstreamed students who have difficulty with motor coordination. Some of these students may not be able to coordinate the meter changes. Preplan the lesson so that these students pat or play a rhythm instrument on each downbeat. Exceptional students also may need a teacher cue for each downbeat.

THE ARTIST

Romare (Howard) Bearden (1914–1988)—was an American artist who lived across from the Apollo Theatre in Harlem and was inspired by the great jazz musicians who played there. He made collages with torn paper and paint, and showed his subjects' faces with several angles or colors to suggest African masks.

Traveling in Style

- Perform the pattern in $\frac{5}{4}$ as you recite "Goin' Trav'lin'." Pat the accented beats and make a palms-up motion on each quarter rest.

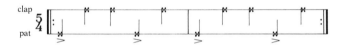

Goin' Trav'lin'

J.K.

Flo - ri - da, New York, Ten - ne - ssee, Maine

When you have been there, Go on to Spain

Nor - way and Swe - den, Ger - ma - ny, France

Stay a while, vis - it, Learn how to dance

Soc - cer and rug - by, Shores and ca - fes

Time to re - turn to Old U. S. A.

- Perform this pattern as you listen to *Take Five.* The composer, saxophonist Paul Desmond, was a member of the Dave Brubeck Quartet.

   *Take Five,* by Paul Desmond, performed by the Dave Brubeck Quartet

49

2. Prepare "Goin' Trav'lin'." Have the students:
- Add to the $\frac{5}{4}$ pattern by patting the accented beat and substitute quarter rests for the claps.
- Perform the $\frac{5}{4}$ pattern as they recite "Goin' Trav'lin'."
- Perform the pat-clap pattern as they listen to *Take Five* by Dave Brubeck.

SPECIAL LEARNERS

Reading "Going Trav'lin'" and performing the body percussion or changing the pattern to sound and silence may be a difficult task for some exceptional students. This activity can be simplified by emphasizing only the accented beats by patting, using instruments, or through participation in only one part of the activity (speech or motion). Prepare an overhead transparency of pupil page 49 to help these students keep track of the words and the accents. For some students to participate in the sound and silence pattern with *Take Five,* a teacher visual cue on each accent will be necessary.

3. Introduce "Promenade" from *Pictures at an Exhibition*. Have the students:
• Read and discuss the information on Mussorgsky.
• Listen to "Promenade" and show the meter changes by pointing to the meter signature in each measure.

Changing Meter and a Change in Style

Changing meter and irregular meter are not unique to jazz. About one hundred years before Paul Desmond wrote *Take Five*, a Russian composer was using these same techniques.

The music of Modest Mussorgsky (mo-dest' mōō-sorg' skē) (1839–1881) reflects his great love for his Russian homeland. He often borrowed folk melodies to use as themes for his works. Sometimes he composed original melodies that sounded like Russian folk tunes.

One of his most famous compositions is *Pictures at an Exhibition*, which he composed in memory of an artist friend, Victor Hartmann. Following Hartmann's death, a number of his paintings were exhibited in a gallery. Mussorgsky decided to compose a collection of musical "pictures" inspired by the paintings. Descriptive music of this type is called **program music**.

Mussorgsky named each section after the painting it represented, for example, "The Gnome," "The Old Castle," and "The Great Gate of Kiev." He composed a "Promenade" theme to introduce the work and to lead the listener from "picture" to "picture" as if strolling through an art gallery. This famous "Promenade" theme makes use of changing and irregular meters.

Although Mussorgsky composed *Pictures at an Exhibition* for piano alone, the French composer Maurice Ravel later arranged the work for full orchestra. It is this orchestral version with its beautiful tone colors that most people hear today.

• Listen to "Promenade" and follow the score on page 51 by pointing to the meter signature changes in each measure.

50

CURRICULUM CONNECTION: HISTORY

Nationalism—the sense of collective identity among the citizens of a country and the promotion of its interests. Examples of nationalism can be found in the arts, as in the case of the "Mighty Handful," a famous group of five Russian nationalistic composers. In the nineteenth century, nationalism developed in tandem with the struggle for democracy. As many European countries were attempting to overthrow monarchs and establish elected governments, the feelings that united the people also inspired loyalty and dedication to the movement. The spirit of reform spread to Russia, and nationalism grew proportionally.

COOPERATIVE LEARNING

Have one of the students write the following term and definition on the board:

Nationalism—the sense of collective identity among the citizens of a country and the promotion of its interests.

Divide the students into cooperative groups of four. Assign the role of reader and recorder in each group. The reader should read page 50 out loud for the group. After the materials have been read, each group member should write down one statement that he or she thinks supports the idea that Mussorgsky was a nationalistic composer. Each member of the group will present his or her statement. The validated examples for the entire group should be listed on a sheet of paper, which is then signed by all of the group members.

"Promenade" from *Pictures at an Exhibition,*
by Modest Mussorgsky

• Listen again and try to determine which instruments are used to create the tone color and dynamics of each section. See notations on score.

Pictures at an Exhibition
Promenade

Modest Mussorgsky

51

• Listen again and try to determine which instruments are used to create the tone color and dynamics of each section.
• Respond to the following:
1. Many composers use folk melodies or create folklike melodies as themes for larger compositions. Why do they use folk tunes instead of melodies they wrote themselves? (To demonstrate a sense of Nationalism and enable the audience to identify with the music.)
2. Name composers besides Mussorgsky who used folk melodies in their music. (Copland: *Appalachian Spring*; Tchaikovsky: Symphony No. 4; Brahms: "Hungarian Dances"; Dvořák: *Slavonic Dances*).
3. How does *Pictures at an Exhibition* reflect the romantic period ideal? (There are many changes of mood within the composition and it reflects expressions of feelings and emotions.)

Reinforcing the Lesson
Review "Love Song," which also has changing meters (pages 46–47).

3 APPRAISAL
The students should be able to:
1. Accurately read and perform a speech canon in $\frac{5}{4}$ meter.
2. Follow changes of meter in a line score to "Promenade."

MORE MUSIC TEACHING IDEAS
Have the students perform the first four measures of "Promenade" on keyboard or bells with the recording.

LISTENING
You may wish to use the Listening Map overhead transparency to help guide the students through the listening selection.

SPECIAL LEARNERS
Prepare an overhead transparency of pupil page 51 if you have exceptional students in the class who have difficulty coordinating auditory and visual skills. Point to the name of each instrument group as the students follow the Listening Map to "Promenade" from *Pictures at an Exhibition.*

LESSON 4

Focus: Irregular Meter in Sevens, Jazz

Objectives
To identify, perform, and define irregular meter in sevens
To read and perform a melodic accompaniment in irregular meter

Materials
Recordings: *Unsquare Dance*
"Samiotissa"
"Promenade" from
Pictures at an Exhibition
Bells, recorder, or keyboard

Vocabulary
Ostinato

1 SETTING THE STAGE

Tell the students they will be studying jazz, which is a twentieth-century popular style.

2 TEACHING THE LESSON

1. Introduce 1950s jazz and Dave Brubeck. Have the students:
• Discuss the information on 1950s jazz and Dave Brubeck.
You may wish to use the following as a basis for extended discussion.
The Dave Brubeck Quartet made a unique contribution to the development of jazz through the use of meters that had been considered unusual in jazz. Name other musicians from the 1950s and 1960s who made unique contributions to popular music. (Chuck Berry, Bill Haley, Jerry Lee Lewis, and many others developed a style known as rock and roll. Bob Dylan used the tone color of folk guitar in developing the style of popular music known as folk rock.)

2B A JAZZ STYLE

CD 2 Unusual meters, rhythms, harmonies, forms, and tone colors have been used in jazz since 1950. You listened to *Take Five*, a composition in $\frac{5}{4}$ meter.

Unsquare Dance, composed by Brubeck, is in $\frac{7}{4}$ meter. The composer writes that this unusual meter makes *Unsquare Dance* "a challenge to the foot-tappers, finger-snappers, and hand-clappers. Deceitfully simple, it refuses to be squared."

These photographs show famous jazz musicians. Right, the Dave Brubeck Quartet; below, Gerry Mulligan; below right, Lionel Hampton (left) and Stan Getz (right).

52

EXTENSION

THE COMPOSER

Dave Brubeck—American jazz pianist and composer, was born in California in 1920 into a family of talented musicians. Brubeck studied with Darius Milhaud and Arnold Schoenberg in Los Angeles. During World War II he played in a military band in Europe. After the war he organized his own jazz band, which became extremely successful. Brubeck brings together elements of jazz and baroque textures in his compositions, which contain a great deal of improvisation.

Above, Dizzy Gillespie;
left, Thelonius Monk

53

2. Introduce meter in sevens. Have the students:
• Practice the rhythm pattern in seven, which is a combination of triple and duple meter.
• Transfer the rhythm pattern to sound and silence by stepping the quarter note and substituting quarter note rests for the claps as they listen to *Unsquare Dance*.
• Identify the meter signature as $\frac{7}{4}$.
• Perform ostinato on keyboard, recorder, or bells with the recording.

Meter in Sevens

• Perform this rhythm pattern, which is a combination of duple and triple meter. Step the accented beat.

This same pattern can be written with seven beats in each measure, with the first, third, and fifth beat accented.

• Step the accented beats and make a palms-up motion on each quarter rest as you listen to *Unsquare Dance*.

• Listen to *Unsquare Dance* again and perform this **ostinato** (äs-tin-ä′ tō), or repeated pattern, on bells, recorder, or keyboard as an accompaniment.

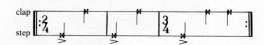

Unsquare Dance, by Dave Brubeck

"Samiotissa" means "girl from Samos." Samos is a Greek island in the Aegean (e-jē′ ən) Sea.

54

Another Meter in Sevens

The Greek song "Samiotissa" (Girl from Samos) is in 7/8 meter. This meter is similar to the meter of *Unsquare Dance*. It has seven beats to a measure. However, in "Samiotissa" different beats are accented. This shift of accent creates a completely different rhythm.

- Listen to "Samiotissa" and tap the steady beat.
- Sing "Samiotissa."

Samiotissa

English version by Stella Phredopoulos
Music by D.A. Vergoni

Sa - mio - tis - sa,   Sa - mio - tis - sa,   You will re-turn to Sa - mos.   Sa -

- mio - tis - sa,   Sa - mio - tis - sa,   Is - land of beau-ty and de - light.

You will come home a - gain to me,   *Sa-mio-tis-sa,* There's mu - sic in the sum-mer night.

You will come home a - gain to me,   *Sa-mio-tis-sa,* There's mu - sic in the sum-mer night.

55

LESSON 4

3. Introduce another meter in sevens.
Have the students:
- Compare the accented beats in *Unsquare Dance* and "Samiotissa."
- Listen to "Samiotissa" and tap the steady beat.
- Sing "Samiotissa."

Reinforcing the Lesson
Review "Promenade" on page 51 for changing and irregular meters.

3 APPRAISAL
The students should be able to:
1. Identify and define rhythm patterns in irregular meters of seven and perform them using body percussion.
2. Accurately read and perform the ostinato melodic accompaniment to *Unsquare Dance.*

MORE MUSIC TEACHING IDEAS

Have the students play the accented beats of *Unsquare Dance* (1, 3, and 5) on percussion instruments.

VOCAL DEVELOPMENT

Have the students perform the following rhythmic and melodic patterns at various pitch levels to expand their vocal range and rhythmic accuracy:

tee   tee tee   tee

tee tee tee tee tee tee tee

REVIEW AND EVALUATION

JUST CHECKING

Objective
To review and test the skills and concepts taught in Unit 2

Materials
Recordings: Just Checking Unit 2
                      Unit 2 Evaluation (question 2)
Recorder, bells, or keyboard
Copying Master 2-1 (optional)
Evaluation Unit 2 Copying Master

TEACHING THE LESSON

Review the skills and concepts taught in Unit 1. Have the students:
• Follow the recorded review with pages 56–57, perform the activities, and answer the questions.
• Review their answers.
(You may wish to use Copying Master 2-1 at this time.)

2B
CD 2

JUST CHECKING

See how much you remember.

1. Listen to the recording and decide if the meter is duple, triple, or quadruple. Show your answers by conducting. duple; quadruple; triple

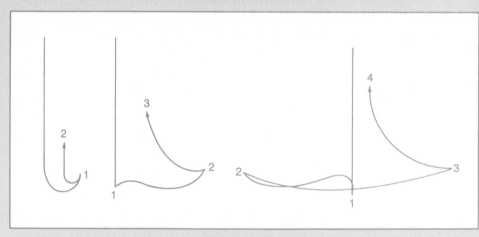

2. Listen to this musical selection, which is an example of changing meters. Identify when the meter changes by conducting the appropriate pattern. The selection begins in duple meter. duple; quadruple; triple

3. Perform this pattern in $\frac{5}{4}$ as you listen to "Goin' Trav'lin' " to review irregular meter.

4. Perform this irregular meter pattern as you listen to *Unsquare Dance.*

56

5. Listen to *Take Five*. Perform a rhythm pattern that shows the meter. $\frac{5}{4}$

6. Play part of the descant accompaniment to "Love Song" below to review changing meter. The recording has an eight-beat introduction.

7. Listen to "Love Song" and show the changes of meter by conducting the first four measures as you listen. The recording has an eight-beat introduction.

8. Clap this pattern as you listen to "Samiotissa" to review irregular meter.

9. Listen to the "Promenade" from *Pictures at an Exhibition* and show the changes of meter by clapping or patting on the first beat of each measure.

57

REVIEW AND EVALUATION

GIVING THE EVALUATION

Evaluation Unit 2 Copying Master can be found in the *Teacher's Copying Masters* book along with full directions for giving the evaluation and checking the answers.

ELEMENTS OF MUSIC	UNIT 3 OBJECTIVES	Lesson 1 Focus: Compound Meter	Lesson 2 Focus: Compound Meters in Combination
Dynamics			
Tone Color	Follow a tone color flow chart Identify tone colors	Read and perform on sticks or claves	
Tempo	Determine tempo relationships in the music Conduct patterns to fit the tempo		Listen for basic beat and tempo relationship in a song with changing meters
Duration/ Rhythm	**Identify, define, perform, and conduct in compound meter** Identify meter changes **Identify polyrhythms**	Identify and define compound meter through body percussion ostinati Read and perform a speech chant in compound meter Determine the order of word rhythms in compound meter music Clap the steady beat (♩.)	Identify, define, and perform compound meter Read and discuss ♩. as the beat Listen to, read, and respond to meter changes Create changing meter patterns
Pitch	Hear, sing songs within a range of G-e♭¹		Listen to and perform a song in a compound meter with a range of G-e♭¹
Texture	Perform a rhythm accompaniment		
Form	Follow a listening map of a composition having the form: Introduction, A, B, Bridge, Improvisation, Bridge, B, Coda		
Style	Listen to a song from a musical and music that combines jazz and classical style Discuss salsa		Listen to and perform a song, in changing meter, from a musical
Reading	Read ♩♫ , ♪♪ , ♩. , ♩. , 𝄽 in ⁶⁄₈ Read ♫♫♫ , ♪ , ♫ , ♪♪♪ , 𝄾 , ♩ , 𝄽 in ⁴⁄₄	Read and perform a speech composition using ♩♫ , ♪♪ , ♩. , ♩. , 𝄽 in ⁶⁄₈	Read compound meter: ¹²⁄₈ , ⁶⁄₈

PURPOSE Unit 3: RHYTHM SETS THE BEAT

In this unit the students will continue to investigate different aspects of rhythm. They will review compound meter and extend their experiences with polyrhythms.

SUGGESTED TIME FRAME

November	December

FOCUS

- Compound Meter
- Compound Meters in Combination
- Compound Meter in Two Contrasting Tempos
- Polyrhythms

Lesson 3 Focus: Compound Meter in Two Contrasting Tempos	**Lesson 4** Focus: Polyrhythms
	Follow a tone color listening map while listening to a composition Identify tone colors through matching pictures
Determine which conducting pattern fits the tempo of the music Listen for basic beat and tempo relationship in a song with changing meters	
Listen to and conduct compound meter in two tempi Listen to, read, and identify meter changes Listen to a composition combining compound and quadruple meter Identify tempo and metric organization of compound meter through body percussion and listening	Identify and perform polyrhythms Perform a polyrhythmic accompaniment Create and perform an original polyrhythmic composition based upon words
Sing a song with a range of B♭ - e♭¹	
	Follow a listening map of a composition (Introduction, A, B, Bridge, Improvisation, Bridge, B, Coda)
Listen to a composition that combines jazz and classical styles Compare two twentieth-century styles	Discuss the salsa style
$\frac{2}{4}$, $\frac{4}{4}$, $\frac{7}{4}$, $\frac{6}{8}$, $\frac{9}{8}$	Follow and play from listening map that uses ♫, ♪, ♫, ♪♪♪, ♩, ♩

BULLETIN BOARD

Prepare a strip of tagboard with the following label: RHYTHMS. Then prepare five marked envelopes containing quarter notes, dotted quarter notes, eighth notes, dotted eighth notes, and sixteenth notes drawn on 3″ × 5″ cards. Hang the envelopes along the bottom of the board. Prepare the rest of the board as shown. As you work through the unit, take a few minutes at the beginning or end of a lesson to have students create a rhythm pattern in $\frac{4}{4}$ meter using any of the notes available in the envelopes. Add that pattern to the board and have students practice it.

When you have completed Lesson 4, on polyrhythms, divide the class into six groups and have the students perform their rhythm patterns simultaneously.

RHYTHMS

LESSON 1

Guigass #4, Victor Vasarely.
VASARELY CENTER, NY

UNIT 3
RHYTHM SETS THE BEAT

58

THE ARTIST

Victor Vasarely (vä-sä-rel′ē) (b. 1908)—was born in Hungary and works in France. He is interested in optical patterns that seem to move, and experiments with geometrical shapes and bright color combinations that give the illusion of three dimensionality or movement. He believes this kind of art is an expression of the geometry found in nature and is thus appealing to all viewers.

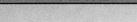
Peacock's Tail, Arman, MARISA DEL RE GALLERY, NY

59

LESSON 1

Objectives
To identify, perform and define compound meter
To perform a speech chant in compound meter

Materials
Recordings: ''Cheers''
            ''Marche''
Sticks and claves

Vocabulary
Dotted quarter note, dotted quarter rest, compound meter

1 SETTING THE STAGE

Tell the students that such familiar songs as ''Row, Row'' and ''Three Blind Mice'' are in compound meter.

LESSON 1

2 TEACHING THE LESSON

1. Introduce compound meter. Have the students:

• Clap the steady beat as they recite "Cheers."

• Transfer the rhythm of the words to sticks or claves while listening to "Cheers."

• Read and discuss information on the system of notation which establishes the dotted quarter note as the basic beat.

• Clap the steady beat as you say this chant.

CHEERS

Cheers for soccer, basketball, volleyball,
Track and rugby, too.
We're for swimming, tennis, and racket ball!
Try them all—one's just right for you.

—*Jane Knox*

• As you listen to "Cheers," play the rhythm of the words on sticks or claves.

 "Cheers," by Jane Knox

In this chant the **dotted quarter note** (♩.) represents the steady beat. The basic dotted quarter-note beat can be divided into threes. The **dotted quarter rest** (𝄽·) represents one beat of silence and can also be divided into threes.

A meter that uses this steady beat might be represented as $\frac{2}{♩.}$ but is usually represented as $\frac{6}{8}$.

60

- Use these words to read these rhythms.

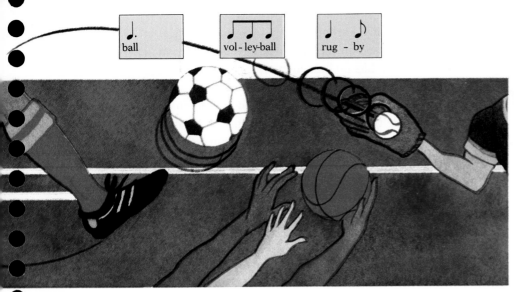

- Pat the steady dotted quarter-note beat as you say the poem.

Meter whose basic beat is subdivided into threes and/or sixes is called **compound meter**. Some compound meters are written as $\frac{6}{8}$, $\frac{9}{8}$, or $\frac{12}{8}$.

61

2. Introduce word rhythms in combination. Have the students:
- Use the words from "Cheers" to read the compound time rhythms.
- Pat the steady dotted quarter note beat as they say the poem.
- Discuss the information on compound meter.

Reinforcing the Lesson
Review the B section of Lully's "Marche" (page 18), which can be conducted in compound meter.

3 APPRAISAL
The students should be able to:
1. Verbally define compound meter and give the time signatures of at least two compound meters.
2. Accurately read and perform a speech chant in compound meter.

COOPERATIVE LEARNING
Place the following rhythm patterns on the board:

1. $\frac{6}{8}$ ♩ ♪ ♩ ♪ | 3. $\frac{6}{8}$ ♩. ♪ |

2. $\frac{6}{8}$ ♫♫ ♫♫ | 4. $\frac{6}{8}$ ♫♫ ♩. |

Have the students pat the steady dotted quarter note beat as they say the poem on page 61. Assist the students in identifying the four separate rhythm patterns (mm. 1, 2, 4, and 8) found in the poem. Repeat each pattern and extend it. Point out that pattern 1 has two uneven sounds per beat; pattern 2 has three even sounds per beat; pattern 3 has one sound on the first beat; and pattern 4 is a combination of three sounds and one sound per beat.

Have the students work in cooperative groups of four to decide on new word rhythms for the four rhythm patterns on the board. The new words should all be from the same category: names of states, counties, automobiles, sports teams, and so on. Assign the role of recorder to notate the word rhythms for each pattern. Appoint a conductor to point to the different rhythm patterns the group is performing. Each cooperative group will perform its newly created word rhythms for the rest of the class.

CURRICULUM CONNECTION: READING

Poetry—Just as music has strong and weak beats, poetry has strong and weak syllables. Like music, poetry often can be organized into divisions of time. One of these divisions, similar to a measure in music, is called a *foot*. A foot contains two or three syllables, which can be stressed (´) or unstressed (˘). Four common types of feet are:

trochaic ´ ˘
iambic ˘ ´
dactylic ´ ˘ ˘
anapestic ˘ ˘ ´

The first line of "Cheers," for example, is composed of two trochaic and two dactylic feet:

Cheérs fŏr sóccĕr, báskĕtbăll, vóllĕybăll.

LESSON 2

Focus: Compound Meters in Combination

Objectives
To identify and perform compound meters in combination

Materials
Recordings: "Cheers"
"Memory"
"Mix 'Em Up"
Tennis balls

1 SETTING THE STAGE
Review "Cheers" on page 60.

2 TEACHING THE LESSON
1. Introduce "Memory." Have the students:
• Discuss the information on the musical *Cats*.
• Listen to the song and raise their hands when changes occur in the meter.

🔊 2B,
3A
💿 2

Imagine a musical set in a garbage dump. Imagine a musical in which the songs are based on the poetry of a Nobel Prize winner. Imagine a musical that has no human characters, only cats. Imagine a musical in which Grizabella, an old and tattered alley cat, finds release from her sorrows and rises to heaven on a discarded automobile tire. Imagine a musical in which story, song, and dance are uniquely combined. You have imagined *Cats*, one of the most successful musicals of the past two decades.

In "Memory," Grizabella wishes her youth and beauty could return. It is probably the most familiar song from *Cats*. "Memory" contains some unusual meters and combinations of meters.

• As you listen to "Memory" notice the changes in meter.

> 🎵 "Memory," from the musical *Cats*, by Andrew Lloyd Webber, Trevor Nunn, and T.S. Eliot

Left, Grizabella, who sings "Memory" in the musical *Cats*. Below, the entire cast of *Cats*. Grizabella is at the far right. This musical has been performed around the world in many languages.

🐈🐈🐈🐈🐈🐈🐈

62

E X T E N S I O N

THE COMPOSER

Andrew Lloyd Webber—British theatrical composer, was born in 1948 into a musical family. His father was the director of the London College of Music, and his mother was a piano teacher. Lloyd Webber learned how to play piano, violin, and French horn at an early age. He later attended Magdalen College, Oxford and the Royal College of Music. Lloyd Webber's first notable musical was *Joseph and the Amazing Technicolor Dreamcoat*, which he wrote when he was 19. His first commercial success came when he was 23 with *Jesus Christ Superstar*, which won seven Tony awards. His list of successes includes *Evita, Song and Dance, Cats, Starlight Express*, and *The Phantom of the Opera*. His *Requiem* was first performed in 1985.

When dotted quarter notes are grouped two to a measure, the meter is represented as $\frac{6}{8}$. When they are grouped four to a measure, the meter is represented as $\frac{12}{8}$.

- Listen to "Memory" again and follow the score on pages 64–65. Pat the basic dotted quarter-note beat for all measures with a meter signature of $\frac{6}{8}$ or $\frac{12}{8}$.
- Listen again and divide the beat into three parts by tapping the following pattern lightly on the palm of your hand for all measures marked with a meter signature of $\frac{6}{8}$ or $\frac{12}{8}$.

- Sing the song. Look for the changing meters as you sing.

Below, a scene from *Cats*

63

2. Introduce unusual meter combinations. Have the students:
- Pat the basic dotted quarter note beat to all measures in $\frac{6}{8}$ or $\frac{12}{8}$ as they listen to "Memory."
- Listen again and subdivide the beat into three equal sounds by tapping lightly on the palms of their hands.
- Sing the song, looking for changing meters in the score.

Reinforcing the Lesson
Review "Mix 'Em Up" on page 44; it also has changing meters.

3 APPRAISAL

The students should be able to listen to the recording of "Memory" and pat the basic dotted quarter note beat or subdivisions of the beat (threes) when cued by the teacher.

MORE MUSIC TEACHING IDEAS
Have the students:
1. Use the tennis ball activity (page 41) to show changing meter while they listen again to "Memory."
2. Identify words with two or three syllables and create alternating measures of changing meters, for example, "It-a-ly," "Swe-den," "Af-ri-ca," "Chi-le," "Pak-is-tan," "Rus-sia."

LESSON 2

B♭ major: *la, ti, do re mi fa fi so la ti do' di' re'* **Memory**   Piano Accompaniment on page PA 14

G♭ major: *fi, so, la, ti, di re mi*

D♭ major: *la, do re mi fa so la ti do' re'*

Words by Trevor Nunn after T.S. Eliot
Music by Andrew Lloyd Webber

Mid - night.___ Not a sound from the pave - ment.___ Has the moon lost her
Mem - 'ry___ All a - lone in the moon - light___ I can smile at the

mem - 'ry?___ She is smil - ing a - lone.___ In the
old days,___ I was beau - ti - ful then.___ I re -

lamp - light the wi-thered leaves col - lect at my feet___ And the
mem - ber the time I knew what hap - pi - ness was,___ Let the

1
wind___ be - gins to moan.

2
mem - 'ry live a -

- gain. Ev - 'ry street lamp seems to beat___ a

fa - tal - is - tic warn - ing. Some - one mut - ters___ and a

poco rit.
street lamp gut - ters___ and soon it will be morn - ing.

a tempo
Day - light.___ I must wait for the sun - rise.___ I must think of a

EXTENSION

VOCAL DEVELOPMENT

Encourage students to use good posture to enhance their breathing for the performance of the long phrases in "Memory." Have the students sing selected phrases on a long *oo* vowel (*loo*) to experience the phrasing, legato, and rhythmic qualities of the melody.

new life___ And I must-n't give in.___ When the dawn comes to-night will be a

mem-o-ry too___ And a new day___ will be - gin.

Burnt out ends of smo - ky days.___ the

stale cold smell___ of morn - ing.___ The street lamp dies, an - o-ther

poco rit.

night is o - ver,___ an - o - ther day is dawn - ing.___

a tempo

Touch me.___ It's so ea - sy to leave me___ All a - lone with the

rall.   *a tempo*

mem - 'ry___ Of my days in the sun.___ If you touch me you'll un-der-stand what

rall.   *a tempo – slightly slower*

hap- pi -ness is.   Look a new day has be - gun.

65

LESSON 3

Focus: Compound Meter in Two Contrasting Tempos

Objectives
To identify, perform and define compound meter in two contrasting tempos
To identify the beat and tempo relationship in a song with changing meters

Materials
Recordings: "Cheers"
"Joyfully Sing," Version 1
"Joyfully Sing," Version 2
"Compound Meter Montage"
"Caprice"
Unsquare Dance (optional)
Tennis balls

1 SETTING THE STAGE

Review "Cheers" on page 60 as an example of compound meter.

2 TEACHING THE LESSON

1. Introduce conducting in compound meter. Have the students:
• Practice conducting the six-beat pattern.
• Listen to "Joyfully Sing," Version 1 as they conduct a slow six-beat pattern.
• Listen to "Joyfully Sing," Version 2 and decide which conducting pattern best fits with the music.
• Discuss the information on conducting compound meter in a slow and fast tempo.

CD 2 "Joyfully Sing" is a folk song about the joy of singing in harmony.

• Listen to Version 1 of "Joyfully Sing." Conduct in a slow six-beat pattern.

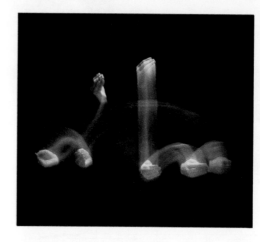

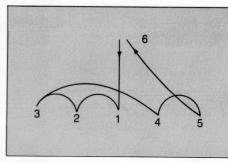

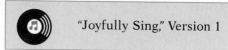
"Joyfully Sing," Version 1

• Listen to Version 2 of "Joyfully Sing," which is performed at a different tempo. Decide which conducting pattern best fits the music. duple meter pattern

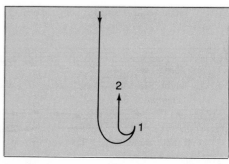

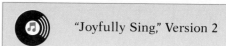
"Joyfully Sing," Version 2

When compound meter is performed at a slow tempo, it is usually conducted in the six-beat pattern. When compound meter is performed at a fast tempo, it is usually conducted in the two-beat pattern.

66

E X T E N S I O N

LESSON 3

Joyfully Sing

Traditional German round
Arr. M.J.

Fa - la -la -la -la - la -la -la - la - la - la,   joy - ful - ly,   joy - ful - ly,

joy - ful - ly,   fa - la -la -la -la - la -la -la - la - la - la,   joy - ful - ly,

joy - ful - ly sing!   Come and lift_____ your   voice   now,

come, sing,   come and sing now, lift your voice_____ in

song!_____   Fa - la -la -la -la - la - la -la - la - la - la,   joy - ful - ly,

joy - ful - ly,   joy - ful - ly,   Fa - la -la -la -la - la - la -la - la - la - la

joy ful - ly,   joy ful - ly sing!   Lis-ten,   lis-ten,   lis-ten to our

coun -ter-point, come sing!_____ We sing, in har-mo - ny   sing.   In

har-mo -ny   sing!   In har-mo -ny   sing!   In har-mo -ny   sing!

67

VOCAL DEVELOPMENT

Build tonal focus and extend the development of breathing and rhythmic accuracy by having students perform ''Joyfully Sing'' without words, using only pure vowels and articulated consonants such as *vee, tee, tah, too.*

LESSON 3

2. Introduce conducting and body percussion patterns for "Joyfully Sing." Have the students:
• Listen to "Joyfully Sing," Version 2 again and identify the changes in meter signatures by deciding which conducting pattern best fits with the music, and show the answer by conducting.
• Perform the body percussion pattern to the steady beat as they listen to "Joyfully Sing."
• Sing the song, looking for the meter changes in the score.
3. Introduce "Compound Meter Montage." Have the students listen to the three examples to decide which conducting pattern best fits with the music, and show the answer by conducting.

Fields surround the village of Kaub, West Germany.

• Listen to "Joyfully Sing" (Version 2) again and identify the changes in meter.

• Perform these rhythm patterns as you listen to "Joyfully Sing" one more time.

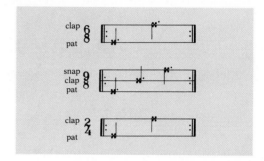

• Sing "Joyfully Sing." Look for the meter changes as you sing.

• Listen to "Compound Meter Montage" and decide which conducting pattern best fits each composition. two-beat pattern; six-beat pattern; two-beat pattern

 "Compound Meter Montage"

68

CLAUDE BOLLING

Claude Bolling was born in Cannes, France, in 1930. He was a child piano prodigy and was studying harmony by the age of twelve. Bolling's interest in jazz also began at an early age. By age fifteen, he was making professional appearances throughout France as a jazz pianist. By the time he was in his mid-twenties, he had become one of the most popular jazz musicians in Europe. He has won several recording industry awards.

Bolling has also received international acclaim as an accompanist-composer. He has worked with such performers as Liza Minnelli, Jerry Lewis, Duke Ellington, and Jean-Pierre Rampal. Bolling has also written scores for dozens of French and American films.

Bolling's Suite for Violin and Jazz Piano is a unique combination of jazz and classical styles. "Caprice," a section of this suite, contains both compound and quadruple meter.

- Listen to this section of "Caprice" and raise your hand when you hear changes in meter.

 "Caprice," from Suite for Violin and Jazz Piano, by Claude Bolling

MORE MUSIC TEACHING IDEAS

Have the students compare "Caprice" from the Suite for Violin and Jazz Piano with Dave Brubeck's *Unsquare Dance.* (*Unsquare Dance:* small ensemble, irregular meter, no change of tempo; "Caprice": small ensemble, compound and quadruple meter, tempo changes between meters.)

LESSON 3

4. Introduce "Caprice," from the Suite for Violin and Jazz Piano by Claude Bolling. Have the students:
• Discuss the information on Claude Bolling and his Suite for Violin and Jazz Piano.
• Listen to the selection from "Caprice" and raise their hands when they hear a change of meter.

Reinforcing the Lesson

Have the students:
• Show the compound and quadruple meter in "Caprice" by bouncing and rolling a tennis ball as indicated by the metrical changes:
Compound $\frac{6}{8}$ (fast tempo); quadruple (moderate tempo); compound $\frac{6}{8}$ (fast tempo).
• Perform the tennis ball activity with the recording.

3 APPRAISAL

The students should be able to:
1. Listen to several examples from "Compound Meter Montage" and match the correct conducting pattern for each example.
2. Read and conduct the meter changes in "Joyfully Sing" in two contrasting tempos. Use appropriate conducting patterns to identify the beat and meter.

LESSON 4

Focus: Polyrhythms

Objectives
To identify, perform, and define polyrhythms
To create and notate a composition using polyrhythms

Materials
Recordings: ''Bachi''
　　　　　''Polyrhythm Montage''
　　　　　''Weather''
Percussion instruments
Pitched or unpitched classroom instruments

Vocabulary
Polyrhythm, salsa

1 SETTING THE STAGE

Tell the students they will be learning about a Latin American musical style called salsa.

2 TEACHING THE LESSON

1. Introduce polyrhythms. Have the students:
• Discuss the information on ''Bachi'' and salsa.
• Listen to ''Bachi'' to hear polyrhythms and the sound of salsa.

PERFORMING POLYRHYTHMS

Polyrhythm is the simultaneous combination of two or more contrasting rhythmic patterns.

"Bachi" is a musical composition that contains *polyrhythms*. The style of "Bachi" is known as *salsa*. Salsa originated in Cuba and spread quickly to the United States. It has the flavor of music from Latin America and Africa, but in addition borrows rhythms and harmonies from blues and rock.

• Listen to "Bachi" to hear polyrhythms and the sound of salsa.

"Bachi," by Clare Fisher

You can accompany melody A of "Bachi" with several different rhythm patterns.

• Practice each new rhythm pattern in the right hand column on page 71.
• Follow the listening guide and perform each new rhythm with the recording.
• In five groups, perform all the rhythm patterns to "Bachi" to create your own polyrhythms.

Rubén Blades (center) is a popular salsa performer.

70

E X T E N S I O N

Bachi
Rhythm Accompaniment and Listening Guide

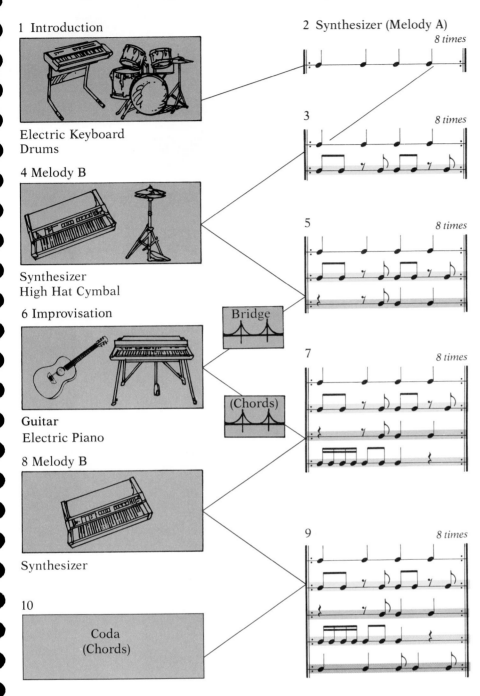

1 Introduction

Electric Keyboard
Drums

4 Melody B

Synthesizer
High Hat Cymbal

6 Improvisation

Guitar
Electric Piano

8 Melody B

Synthesizer

10

Coda
(Chords)

2 Synthesizer (Melody A)   *8 times*

3   *8 times*

5   *8 times*

Bridge

(Chords)

7   *8 times*

9   *8 times*

71

• Practice the individual rhythm patterns in
$\frac{4}{4}$ meter in each repeat of the accompaniment to "Bachi."
• Follow the listening guide and perform each new rhythm with the recording.
• In five groups, perform all the rhythm patterns to "Bachi" to create their own polyrhythms.

LISTENING
You may wish to use the Listening Map overhead transparency to help guide the students through the listening selection.

SPECIAL LEARNERS
Prepare an overhead transparency of pupil page 71 if there are exceptional students in the class who are visually impaired or have difficulty coordinating visual and audio skills. Point to each new section as the students listen to the selection to help these students visually and aurally perceive the components of the selection.

LESSON 4

2. Introduce polyrhythms in different musical styles. Have the students:
• Listen to "Polyrhythm Montage" and match the photo with the music they are hearing. (steel band, *Cats, The Rite of Spring*, African music)
• Discuss each photo.

Listening to Polyrhythms

Polyrhythms are found in many different styles of music. Match the picture with the music you are hearing as you listen to "Polyrhythm Montage." steel band, *Cats, Rite,* African

🎵 "Polyrhythm Montage"

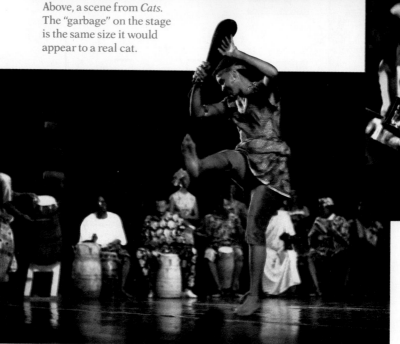

Above, a scene from *The Rite of Spring* in the Joffrey Ballet's re-creation of the original 1913 version

Above, a scene from *Cats.* The "garbage" on the stage is the same size it would appear to a real cat.

Above, a steel band from Trinidad. Left, the Ladzekpo Brothers, an African music and dance ensemble

72

EXTENSION

COOPERATIVE LEARNING

Have the students work in cooperative groups of four to explore the concept of polyrhythms. Each member of the group will create and perform a one-measure ostinato for unpitched or pitched instruments. (Encourage the students to use the pentatonic scale or Dorian mode if they know them.) Each cooperative group will perform its newly created rhythms for the rest of class. Perform the ostinati by starting with one and adding the others in succession. As each ostinato is added, the rhythmic density should become more complex. Assign a student the role of conductor to organize the entrances of the ostinatos.

MORE MUSIC TEACHING IDEAS

Have the students perform the following patterns on percussion instruments to experience polyrhythms.

First bell — High pitch / Low pitch

Second bell — High pitch / Low pitch

Rattle — Against hand / Against knee

High drum (Kagan)

Low drum (Kidi)

Creating Polyrhythms

You can combine words to create different rhythm patterns.

- Read and perform each of the five rhythms in "Weather."
- Perform "Weather" to create polyrhythms.

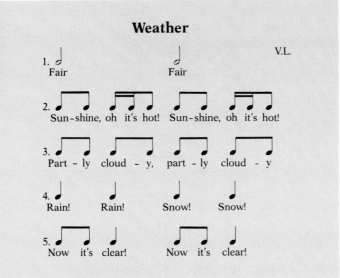

Weather

V.L.

1. Fair   Fair

2. Sun-shine, oh it's hot!   Sun-shine, oh it's hot!

3. Part – ly cloud – y,   part – ly cloud – y

4. Rain! Rain! Snow! Snow!

5. Now it's clear!   Now it's clear!

- Use other words to create compositions with polyrhythms. Here are two examples.

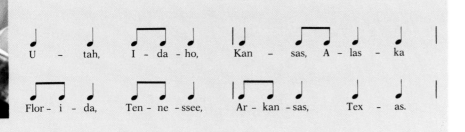

U – tah,   I – da – ho,   Kan – sas, A – las – ka

Flor – i – da, Ten – ne – ssee,   Ar – kan – sas,   Tex – as.

- Choose names of states, classmates, or automobiles to create your own rhythm patterns. Perform the compositions you created for your classmates. Learn and perform the polyrhythms created by your classmates. Mix and match rhythms from different compositions to create additional polyrhythms.

73

3. Introduce creating a polyrhythmic speech composition. Have the students:
- Read and perform each of the five speaking rhythms.
- Form two to five groups and perform "Weather" beginning at different times to experience polyrhythms. ("Weather" can be performed as a round.)

Reinforcing the Lesson

Have the students create their own compositions with polyrhythms as indicated.

3 APPRAISAL

The students should be able to:
1. Identify and verbally define polyrhythm.
2. Perform a polyrhythmic accompaniment to "Bachi" with accuracy.
3. Create and notate an original polyrhythmic composition using word rhythms.

CURRICULUM CONNECTION: SCIENCE

Weather—Meteorologists constantly observe weather conditions around the world. Observation stations measure temperature, humidity, wind direction and speed, and other conditions every hour. Weather balloons with special instruments measure conditions in the atmosphere and transmit data to ground stations. Cameras on satellites take and transmit photographs of cloud patterns and areas of ice and snow on earth. Meteorologists prepare various maps and charts from this information and analyze them to make weather predictions. Forecast maps are also prepared using computers that solve complex formulas to project ahead from current data.

REVIEW AND EVALUATION

JUST CHECKING

Objective
To review and test the skills and concepts taught in Unit 3

Materials
Recordings: Just Checking Unit 3
Unit 3 Evaluation (question 2)
Copying Master 3-1 (optional)
Evaluation Unit 3 Copying Master

TEACHING THE LESSON

Review the skills and concepts taught in Unit 3. Have the students:
• Follow the recorded review with pages 74–75, perform the activities, and answer the questions.
• Review their answers.
(You may wish to use Copying Master 3-1 at this time.)

3B
CD 2

JUST CHECKING

See how much you remember. Listen to the recording.

1. Listen to the steady beat and perform these rhythm patterns individually and then together.

2. Listen to the steady beat and perform these rhythm patterns in $\frac{6}{8}$ meter by clapping as you say the words.

a.
base - ball

b.
track and rug - by

c.
bask-et - ball, vol - ley - ball

d.
just right for you.

74

3. Listen to these recordings and decide if the style of each example is salsa, jazz, or Broadway musical. jazz, Broadway musical, salsa

4. Listen to this excerpt from "Caprice" from Claude Bolling's Suite for Violin and Jazz Piano. Determine if this section is in compound or quadruple meter. Demonstrate your answer by conducting the appropriate pattern. compound meter

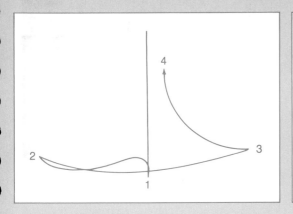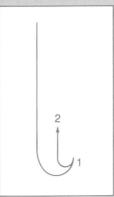

5. Listen to two contrasting selections in compound meter. In which selection does the six-beat conducting pattern fit? In which selection does the two-beat conducting pattern fit? Describe the tempo of each selection. second; first; first: fast; second: slow

6. Listen to the following musical selections and decide which ones contain polyrhythms. Examples 1 and 3

7. Listen to the following musical selections and decide if they are examples of simple or compound meter. simple: Examples 1 and 3; compound: Examples 2 and 4

75

GIVING THE EVALUATION

Evaluation Unit 3 Copying Master can be found in the *Teacher's Copying Masters* book along with full directions for giving the evaluation and checking the answers.

ELEMENTS OF MUSIC	UNIT 4 OBJECTIVES	Lesson 1 Focus: Major Scale, Creating Harmony	Lesson 2 Focus: Repetition of a Musical Idea, Texture
Dynamics			
Tone Color	Perform retrograde on percussion instruments Perform a song on bells or keyboard and classroom instruments	Identify number of singers and accompanying instruments (flute, guitar, hammered dulcimer) Perform accompaniments on keyboard or bells	
Tempo			
Duration/ Rhythm	Clap the rhythm of the melody as a canon Perform rhythms containing meter changes		Clap the rhythm of the melody as a canon Perform a canon with rhythmic accuracy
Pitch	**Learn pitch organization** **Define twelve-tone music** **Perform a tone row and its retrograde**	Identify a D major scale Learn about tonality Develop melodic reading skills Sing a song with a range of A-a	Perform a canon with pitch accuracy Sing a song with a range of d-d'
Texture	Define harmony and consonance **Identify and define poly-phonic, monophonic, and homophonic texture** **Perform melodic accompani-ment**	Define harmony and consonance Play an accompaniment to a melody Identify consonant harmony Play a melodic accompaniment Perform a melodic accompaniment	Define and perform canon Perform a song in unison and as a two-part round Identify and define polyphonic, monophonic, and homophonic texture Analyze the musical texture of a composition Discuss and identify the three textures used in the "Hallelujah" Chorus
Form	Analyze phrase length	Identify and discuss a canon	Identify and discuss an oratorio
Style	Discuss a composer from the baroque period Discuss music of Schoenberg **Identify atonal music composition**		Discuss the composer, George Frederick Handel, from the baroque period Discuss and perform a Korean folk song canon
Reading	Follow listening map using ♪♪♩♩. ♩.♩.♪	Sing and play in ¾ using tie	Follow listening map using ♪♪♩♩. ♩.♩.♪

PURPOSE Unit 4: MELODY

In this unit the students will focus their attention on melody. They will review the major scale and investigate the concept of texture in music. They will be introduced to the twelve-tone row and investigate retrograde as a technique for organizing and developing a melodic pattern.

SUGGESTED TIME FRAME

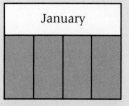

January

FOCUS

- Major Scale, Creating Harmony
- Repetition of a Musical Idea, Texture
- Retrograde Melodies
- Twelve-Tone Music

Lesson 3 Focus: Retrograde Melodies	**Lesson 4** Focus: Twelve-Tone Music
Perform a melody and its retrograde on bells, recorder, or keyboard Perform retrograde on percussion instruments	Perform a tone row on bells or keyboard Perform a song on bells or keyboard with instrumental parts (triangle, finger cymbals, tambourine, or maracas)
	Read and perform rhythms in an atonal composition containing meter changes between $\frac{6}{8}$ and $\frac{9}{8}$ Perform a rhythmic ostinato or body accompaniment to a melody
Read about pitch organization Identify and define retrograde Analyze the pitch organization of a composition	Identify, define, and discuss twelve-tone music Read and perform a twelve-tone row and its retrograde Listen to and perform a song with a range of b-d♭′
Perform two retrograde sound pieces together	
Analyze phrase length Create and perform a retrograde sound piece	
	Discuss expressionism and the musical style of Arnold Schoenberg Create and perform an atonal composition and play in retrograde
Read score using ♫ , ♩ , 𝄽 , ♩ , $\frac{4}{4}$	Read rhythms in $\frac{6}{8}$, $\frac{9}{8}$

BULLETIN BOARD

Prepare a strip of tagboard with the following label: TWELVE-TONE TUNES. Place the label centered at the top of the board. Then on each of twelve pieces of tagboard notate one of the twelve tones of the twelve-tone row presented in Lesson 4 and place them on the board as shown.

Have different students rearrange the notes daily and keep a record of the arrangements. For each arrangement have students create a rhythm pattern that contains twelve notes in any meter.

After lessons 3 and 4, use the note arrangements and rhythm patterns together in any combination to create twelve-tone melodies with retrogrades.

Have the students perform their melodies on keyboard instruments or bells.

TWELVE-TONE TUNES

LESSON 1

UNIT **4**

MELODY

76

LESSON 1

Focus: Major Scale, Creating Harmony

Objectives
To identify the major scale and its use as a basis for melodies
To identify a tonal center
To read and perform a melodic accompaniment with accuracy

Materials
Recordings: "River"
　　　　　　Pachelbel, Canon
Keyboard or bells
Copying Master 4-1 (optional)

Vocabulary
Home tone, tone center, tonal music, tonality, harmony, consonance

1 SETTING THE STAGE

Tell the students they will play a melodic accompaniment to a song.

77

A Song in D Major

- Listen to "River" and decide how many singers and which instruments you hear.   2 singers, steel-string guitar, hammered dulcimer, flute

 "River," by Bill Staines

LESSON 1

2 TEACHING THE LESSON

1. Introduce "River." Have the students:
- Listen to the recording of the song and identify the number of singers (two) and the accompanying instruments. (hammered dulcimer, guitar, flute)
- Sing the song.

River

Words and music by Bill Staines

1. I was born in the path of the win-ter wind, And was raised where the

moun-tains are old._____ The spring-time_____ wa-ters came

danc-ing down, I re-mem-ber the tales they told._____ The

whis-tling_____ ways of my young-er days, Too quick-ly have

fad-ed on by._____ But all of the mem-o-ries

lin-ger still, Like the light in a fad-ing sky._____

78

EXTENSION

SIGNING FOR "RIVER"

It is important to express the mood and fluid qualities of this song with the body, face, and signs. The phrases should be smoothly connected; movement should continue with the sound.

River   Make a "W" for wa-ter close to the mouth then with palms down, left hand behind the right, wiggle the fingers as the hands move to the right. Roll the arms on "rolling old river."

Take Me (Bring [Me])

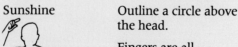 With open palms up, move from left to right in an arc. Hands are not touching.

Sunshine

 Outline a circle above the head.

Fingers are all touching.

Drop down and open as if rays of the sun.

Sing

 Move the hands away from the corners of the mouth in a gesture of singing.

Song (Music)

Extend left arm. The right hand points to the palm of the left hand and makes a series of wavy motions such as a conductor would make.

33 *Refrain*
Riv - er, take me a - long, In your sun - shine

39
sing me your song. Ev - er mov - ing and wind - ing and____

44
free. You roll - ing old riv - er, You chang - ing old riv - er, Let's

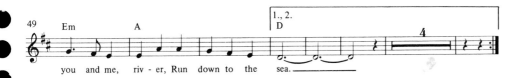

49
you and me, riv - er, Run down to the sea.____

3.
sea.____ Let's you and me, riv - er, Run down to the sea.

2. I've been to the city and back again;
   I've been touched by some things that I've learned,
   Met a lot of good people, and I've called them friends,
   Felt the change when the seasons turned.
   I've heard all the songs that the children sing
   And I've listened to love's melodies;
   I've felt my own music within me rise
   Like the wind in the autumn trees.

   Refrain

3. Someday when the flowers are blooming still,
   Someday when the grass is still green,
   My rolling river will round the bend
   And flow into the open sea.
   So here's to the rainbow that's followed me here,
   And here's to the friends that I know,
   And here's to the song that's within me now;
   I will sing it where'er I go.

   Refrain

79

Winding (Rolling, Moving)

With palms facing and fingers pointing away from the body, the open hands move forward together in a series of curves.

Free

The "F" position hands are crossed at the wrists then un-crossed and opened, moving up and out in an arc.

Changing

With hands in modi-fied "A" position, palms face each other. Twist hands so they reverse posi-tions.

Let

Open hands, palms facing each other move down and up in a scooping motion.

You

Palms up, hands start together then move apart in a sweeping gesture.

Me

Point to the chest with the index finger.

Down to the Sea

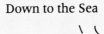

Make a gesture of the river flowing to the sea.

LESSON 1

2. Introduce the D major scale. Have the students:
• Identify the D major scale.
• Give the letter names of the pitches in "River" that begin and end the song.
• Identify the measures which contain the chord symbol D (shown in score).
• Discuss the information on tonality, harmony, and consonance.

The melody of "River" contains the pitches of the **D major scale.**

| D | E | F# | G | A | B | C# | D | D | C# | B | A | G | F# | E | D |
| 1 | 2 | 3 | 4 | 5 | 6 | 7 | 8 | 8 | 7 | 6 | 5 | 4 | 3 | 2 | 1 |

• Give the letter names of the pitches that begin and end the song. D and D
• Which measures contain the chord symbol D? shown in score

The **home tone** D is the focus or **tone center** for "River." When music has a strong tonal center or pitch focus, it is called **tonal music.** It is said to have **tonality.**

When you play or sing two or more pitches together, you are creating **harmony.** Harmonic **consonance** results when the combination of pitches blends.

Right, the North Platte River, Nebraska. Below, the Firth River, Yukon Territory, Canada

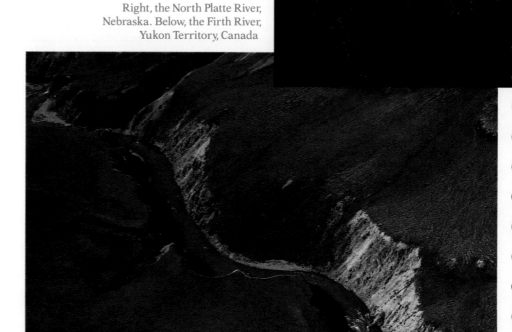

80

E X T E N S I O N

- Play this melodic accompaniment on keyboard or bells with "River." Since it is based on the D major scale, this folklike harmonic accompaniment is **consonant.**

Melodic Accompaniment to "River"

V.L. and M.J.

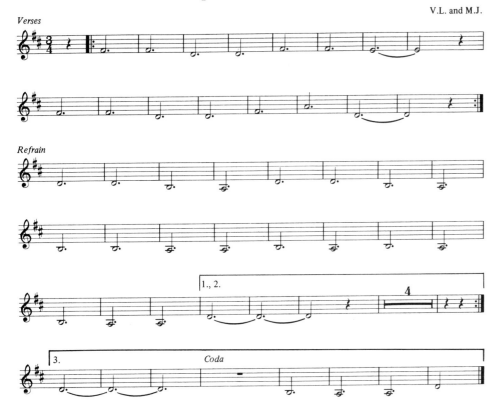

A Melody in D Major

Johann Pachelbel (yō′ hän päКН′ əl-bel) used pitches from the D major scale in his Canon. You may have heard it in commercials and films. The melodies follow one another and, when combined, create harmony.

- Listen to the Canon to hear how Pachelbel used a major scale as a basis for the melodies.

 Canon, by Johann Pachelbel

81

- Play the melodic accompaniment to "River" on keyboard or bells as they listen to the recording.

3. Introduce creating harmony with scale tones. Have the students listen to Pachelbel's Canon to hear how he used a major scale as a basis for the melodies. (You may wish to use Copying Master 4-1 at this time.)

Reinforcing the Lesson

Review tonic and dominant chords on page 11.

3 APPRAISAL

The students should be able to:
1. Identify the major scale of D and its use as a basis for melodies.
2. Identify the tonal center of D major.
3. Read and perform a melodic accompaniment with accuracy.

MORE MUSIC TEACHING IDEAS

Have the students perform melodies to the Canon on keyboard, bells, or other C instruments.

SPECIAL LEARNERS

Students who have reading disabilities may experience difficulty following an overhead transparency of pupil page 81 and playing the melodic accompaniment on bells or recorders. Point out each measure or indicate the beginning of each line.

If the lesson includes Copying Master 4-1, students who have reading disabilities or difficulty tracking may need extra help following and playing the melodies. Point out the beginning of each line on an overhead transparency as it repeats or indicate each measure.

THE COMPOSER

Johann Pachelbel (1653–1706)—was a great German composer and organist. He studied composition, piano, and organ at Nuremberg. Throughout his life he held several important positions as organist, composer, and teacher. Pachelbel was one of the first composers to use major keys to convey happy moods and minor for sad moods in his compositions. Pachelbel was a close friend of the Bach family and taught several members. His keyboard compositions greatly influenced the young Johann Sebastian Bach.

LESSON 2

Focus: Repetition of a Musical Idea, Texture

Objectives
To read and perform a melody as a canon
To identify and describe monophonic, polyphonic, and homophonic texture

Materials
Recordings: Canon
 "Ahrirang"
 "Hallelujah" Chorus
 "Memory"
 "Joyfully Sing"
 "Goin' Trav'lin'"
Rhythm instruments
Copying Master 4-2: Listening Map (optional)

Vocabulary
Canon, texture, monophonic, polyphonic, homophonic, oratorio

1 SETTING THE STAGE
Have the students review Pachelbel's Canon on page 81 as an example of this form.

2 TEACHING THE LESSON

1. Introduce performing a canon.
Have the students:
• Read the information and define canon.
• Learn to sing "Ahrirang" as a canon.
• Attempt the Challenge! and try to perform "Ahrirang" as a canon by clapping the rhythm of the melody without singing it.

Key: G major   Starting Pitch: D   Scale Tones: *so₁ la₁ do re mi so*

CD 2, 3 Performing a Canon

A **canon** is a musical composition in two or more voice parts. A musical phrase is started by one voice and repeated exactly by successive voices, which begin before the first voice has ended. The combination of voices produces harmony.

"Ahrirang" is a Korean folk song about the Ahrirang Pass in the mountains near the city of Seoul.

• Learn to sing "Ahrirang" as a canon.

Ahrirang

Korean folk song
English words by M.S.

Ah - ri - rang, Ah - ri - rang, Ah - ra - ri - yo,_____

Walk - ing o - ver roll ing hills__ of__ Ah - ri - rang.
Time goes ver - y slow - ly far a - way from Ah - ri - rang.

Ⓑ *Verses*

Walk - ing slow - ly to some place__ far,__ far a - way
Back a - gain o - ver tall hills__ of__ Ah - ri - rang

Hop - ing to re - turn a - gain to Ah - ri - rang_____ some day.
Once a - gain re - turn - ing home__ to_____ Ah - ri - rang.

> **CHALLENGE** Try to perform "Ahrirang" as a canon by clapping the rhythm of the melody without singing it.

82

EXTENSION

SPECIAL LEARNERS
If the lesson includes the rhythm clapping Challenge! plan an alternative activity for those students with physical handicaps or motor disabilities. Have the students use rhythm instruments to either keep the steady beat or to play the first beat of each measure. Introduce the necessity for these instruments as a means of insuring success for the class activity.

VOCAL DEVELOPMENT
Strive to have the students experience the sustained quality of "Ahrirang" by emphasizing breath support and the use of sustained vowels. Have the students sing the following at different pitch levels to encourage the expansion of vocal range.

loo   loo   loo loo loo

Musical Texture

Texture in music refers to the way layers of sound are combined. When you sang "Ahrirang" the first time without accompaniment, you sang in unison. Unison singing creates a texture known as **monophonic**, meaning one sound.

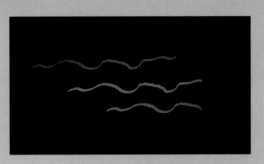

When you sang "Ahrirang" as a canon, you created a texture know as **polyphonic** (po-lē-fo'nik), meaning many voices sounding together.

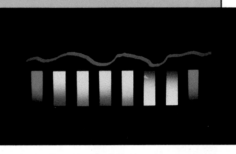

When you sang "River," the melody was in the foreground with accompaniment in the background. This texture is called **homophonic**.

An **oratorio** is a large musical work for solo voices, chorus, and orchestra performed without special costumes or scenery. The "Hallelujah" Chorus from George Frederick Handel's oratorio *Messiah* is one of the most famous choral works in the English language. Handel creates harmonic interest by setting the text in monophonic, polyphonic, and homophonic textures.

The word *hallelujah* is stated and restated by different sections of the chorus almost like a cheering section. Other lines of the text are sung solemnly to emphasize their serious message, and for contrast. The festive quality of the piece is made even more brilliant by the trumpets and timpani. The story is told that at one of the first performances, the English king, George II, was so moved by the music that he stood up to show his approval.

83

LESSON 2

2. Prepare analysis of musical texture. Have the students:
• Discuss the information on monophonic, polyphonic, and homophonic texture.
• Discuss the information on the use of musical texture in the "Hallelujah" Chorus.

COOPERATIVE LEARNING

Using the examples of musical texture found on pupil page 83, have the students work in cooperative groups of three to find examples of monophonic, polyphonic, and homophonic textures in the preceding 82 pages. Within each group, assign a specific category to each student. The student should find an example within the first 83 pages of the text to validate the specific category. Each member of the group will then present his or her example, providing documentation as to how it fits the assigned category. The validated examples for the entire group should be listed on a sheet of paper, which is signed by all the members of the group.

LESSON 2

- Follow the description as they listen to the "Hallelujah" Chorus. When each number is called, write on a sheet of paper the word that best describes the texture they hear. (You may wish to use Copying Master 4-2: Listening Map at this time.)
- Summarize Handel's use of three different textures in this selection.

- Identify the texture you hear when a number is called. The four main themes are shown. See *Teaching the Lesson*.

 "Hallelujah" Chorus from *Messiah*, by George Frederick Handel

Versailles (vair-sī') Cathedral, France, is in the baroque style.

1. Introduction

2. Theme **A**

Hal - le - lu - jah, Hal - le - lu - jah, Hal - le - lu - jah, Hal - le - lu - jah, Hal -

- le - lu - jah,

84

SPECIAL LEARNERS

Students with visual or tracking disabilities may have difficulty following the Listening Map to the "Hallelujah" Chorus. Use an overhead transparency of pupil pages 84–85 and point to each section as it comes up in the recording. This will enable the students to hear the beginning of each theme. Students who have difficulties with aural and visual coordination will benefit from an overhead transparency of Copying Master 4-2. After each number is called, pause to allow the students to choose their response. Then fill in the correct response on the transparency. This will help strengthen aural and visual skills.

3. Theme B

for the Lord God Om - nip - o - tent reign - eth. Hal - le -

- lu - jah, Hal - le - lu - jah, Hal - le - lu - jah, Hal - le - lu - jah,

4. Theme B repeated higher

for the Lord God Om - nip - po - tent reign - eth. Hal - le -

lu - jah! Hal - le - lu - jah! Hal - le - lu - jah! Hal - le - lu - jah!

5. Theme C

The king - dom of this world is be - come

6. Theme D

And He shall reign for ev - er and ev - er

7. "King of Kings and Lord of Lords" is heard in long note values; "forever and ever" is added in shorter note values. Gradually, this moves higher and higher.

8. Theme D repeated

And He shall reign for ev - er and ev - er,

9. "King of Kings and Lord of Lords" is heard in long note values; "forever and ever" is added in shorter note values.

10. The coda ends with four "hallelujahs" followed by a dramatic pause and a final "hallelujah" in very long note values.

85

LESSON 2

3. Introduce George Frederick Handel. Have the students discuss the information on Handel and the *Messiah.*

Reinforcing the Lesson

Review "Memory" (page 62), "Joyfully Sing" (page 66), and "Goin' Trav'lin'" (page 49) and identify the texture of each melody. (homophonic, polyphonic, homophonic)

3 APPRAISAL

The students should be able to:
1. Read and perform a canon with pitch and rhythmic accuracy.
2. Analyze the musical texture of the "Hallelujah" Chorus.

George Frederick Handel, Thomas Hudson. By courtesy of the NATIONAL PORTRAIT GALLERY, London

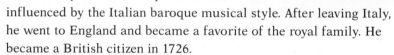

GEORGE FREDERICK HANDEL

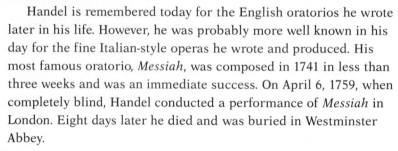

George Frederick Handel (1685–1759) is one of the two most respected and revered musicians of the baroque period. He and Johann Sebastian Bach created musical compositions that brought the baroque period to its peak.

Handel was born in Germany in 1685, and began his formal musical training at the age of eight. In his early twenties he visited Italy and was impressed and influenced by the Italian baroque musical style. After leaving Italy, he went to England and became a favorite of the royal family. He became a British citizen in 1726.

Handel is remembered today for the English oratorios he wrote later in his life. However, he was probably more well known in his day for the fine Italian-style operas he wrote and produced. His most famous oratorio, *Messiah,* was composed in 1741 in less than three weeks and was an immediate success. On April 6, 1759, when completely blind, Handel conducted a performance of *Messiah* in London. Eight days later he died and was buried in Westminster Abbey.

86

EXTENSION

CURRICULUM CONNECTION: SOCIAL STUDIES

Westminster Abbey—officially called the Collegiate Church of St. Peter, is located in Westminster, a borough of London. Originally a monastery, it was rebuilt by Edward the Confessor and dedicated as a church in 1065. In 1245, Henry III tore down most of the church, replacing it with one in the Gothic style. Later monarchs added to the building. All the English kings and queens since William the Conqueror were crowned in the abbey, and eighteen monarchs are buried there. The abbey also houses the tombs and memorials of famous British subjects, including Chaucer, Shakespeare, Handel, T. S. Eliot, and many other authors, musicians, and statesmen.

A NEW WAY TO ORGANIZE A MELODY

Composers use different techniques to create and develop melodies.

- Read "Backward Bill." What repeated word in the poem suggests how a composer might work with a melody? backward

Backward Bill

Backward Bill, Backward Bill,
He lives way up on Backward Hill,
Which is really a hole in the sandy ground
(But that's a hill turned upside down).

Backward Bill's got a backward shack
With a big front porch that's built out back.
You walk through the window and look out the door
And the cellar is up on the very top floor.

Backward Bill he rides like the wind
Don't know where he's going but sees where he's been.
His spurs they go "neigh" and his horse it goes "clang."
And his six-gun goes "gnab," it never goes "bang."

Backward Bill's got a backward pup,
They eat their supper when the sun comes up,
And he's got a wife named Backward Lil,
"She's my own true hate," says Backward Bill.

Backward Bill wears his hat on his toes
And puts on his underwear over his clothes.
And come every payday he pays his boss,
And rides off a-smilin' a-carryin' his hoss.

—Shel Silverstein

Focus: Retrograde Melodies

Objectives
To identify and define retrograde
To perform a retrograde melody with melodic and rhythmic accuracy

Materials
Recordings: "Backward Bill"
"Rhythms in Retrograde"
"Sounds in Retrograde"
"The Web"
Keyboard, bells, or recorder
Percussion instruments

Vocabulary
Retrograde

1 SETTING THE STAGE

Have the students read the words to "Backward Bill" and decide which repeated word suggests how a composer might organize the pitches in a melody.

LESSON 3

1. Introduce retrograde. Have the students:

• Perform "Retrograde in D" on keyboard, recorder or bells.

• Discuss the relationship between measures 1–8 and 9–16.

• Identify and define retrograde.

Day and Night is by the Dutch artist M. C. Escher. Each side of this woodcut is the reverse of the other.

• Perform "Retrograde in D Major" on keyboard, recorder, or bells. The melody in measures 9–16 is a backward version of measures 1–8. The last tone in measure 8 becomes the first tone in measure 9. When a melodic pattern is reversed so that its beginning becomes its end, it is called a *retrograde*.

Retrograde in D major

88

SPECIAL LEARNERS

Mainstreamed students who have reading disabilities or tracking difficulties will benefit from an overhead transparency of pupil page 88. Point to each line or measure as the students play "Retrograde in D" on keyboard, recorder, or bells.

- Compare the pitches of the melody in measures 1–8 with measures 9–16. Are the phrases of equal length? Are the same pitches used in both sections? yes; yes, but in reverse

- Perform "Rhythms in Retrograde."

Rhythms in Retrograde

V.L. and M.J.

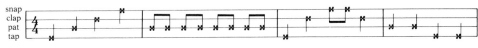

- Choose percussion instruments and perform "Rhythms in Retrograde."
- Perform "Sounds in Retrograde."

Sounds in Retrograde

V.L.

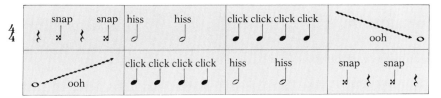

- Perform "Rhythms in Retrograde" and "Sounds in Retrograde" in combination.

> **CHALLENGE** Create, notate, and perform your own retrograde sound piece.

89

- Compare the pitches of measures 1–8 with 9–16 and answer the questions.
2. Introduce rhythms and sounds in retrograde. Have the students:
- Perform "Rhythms in Retrograde" with hand motions and with percussion instruments.
- Perform "Sounds in Retrograde."
- Perform "Rhythms in Retrograde" and "Sounds in Retrograde" in combination.
- Attempt the Challenge! by creating, notating and performing original retrograde sound compositions.

Reinforcing the Lesson
Preview "The Web" on page 91 to experience a musical composition that uses retrograde.

3 APPRAISAL
The students should be able to:
1. Identify and define retrograde
2. Perform a retrograde melody with melodic and rhythmic accuracy.

CURRICULUM CONNECTION: LANGUAGE ARTS

Palindromes—"Retrograde in D" is a musical palindrome—a word, phrase or sentence that reads the same forward or backward. Examples of single-word palindromes, including names, are *pop, refer, Otto,* and *Anna.* One of the best-known palindromes is "Madam, I'm Adam."

Ask students to name a palindrome for each of the following definitions:
1. twelve o'clock (noon)
2. baby dog (pup)
3. part of the face (eye)
4. songs for one singer (solos)
5. signal sent to get help (SOS)
6. highest point (*two words*) (top spot)
Challenge students to think up their own palindromes.

LESSON 4

Focus: Twelve-Tone Music

Objectives
To identify tone row as a kind of pitch organization

To perform a song based on a tone row and its retrograde

Materials
Recordings: "The Web"
Begleitungsmusik zu einer Lichtspielscene (excerpt), Op. 34

Keyboard or bells

Percussion instruments

Vocabulary
Twelve-tone, serial, tone row, atonal, expressionism

1 SETTING THE STAGE
Tell the students they will be learning about a new method of pitch organization used by twentieth-century composers called twelve-tone or serial music.

2 TEACHING THE LESSON
1. Introduce "The Web." Have the students:

• Count all the black and white keys to determine the number of different notes from C to B on the keyboard.

• Discuss information on twelve-tone or serial music.

• Play the original tone row for "The Web" on keyboard or bells.

• Play the retrograde version of the tone row on keyboard or bells.

• Follow the score as they listen and identify the word in the song where the retrograde begins.

CD 3 Twelve-Tone Music

• Count all the black and white keys to determine the number of different pitches from C to B on the keyboard.   7 white keys, 5 black keys, 12 in all

One kind of twentieth-century music is **twelve-tone,** or **serial,** music. In this musical style, the composer organizes all twelve tones in a **row.**

The song "The Web" is based on a twelve-tone row. It also makes use of retrograde. Here is the original tone row upon which "The Web" is based.

• Play this tone row on bells or keyboard.

• Play the retrograde on bells or keyboard.

• Follow the score as you listen to "The Web." Identify the words where the retrograde begins.   "The front is the back."

90

E X T E N S I O N

SPECIAL LEARNERS
Mainstreamed students with visual or tracking disabilities may encounter difficulties in following the score to "The Web" as printed in the student text. Prepare an overhead transparency of "The Web" and point to each specific accompaniment line.

The Web

Key: Twelve-tone   Starting Pitch: E

Words by Susan Lucas
Music by David Ward-Steinman

Piano Accompaniment on page PA 19

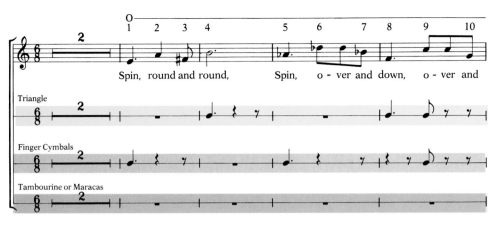

Spin, round and round,   Spin,   o - ver and down,   o - ver and

down. ___ (ow) ___ (n).   The front is the back, the   back is the   front. ___

___ The   end ___ is not   found. ___

- Sing "The Web" or play it on bells or keyboard with the instrumental parts.

LESSON 4

- Notice the letter *O* in measure 3 and the bracket enclosing measures 3–8. (Tell the students that the bracket encloses the *original* organization of twelve tones in the tone row.)
- Notice the letter *R* at the end of measure 8. (Tell the students that this indicates where the original tone row starts being notated in *retrograde*.)
- Point to the places in the retrograde where the notes are written in different rhythms or a different octave than the original, though they remain in the exact reverse order.
- Sing "The Web" or play it on keyboard or bells with the instrumental parts.

CURRICULUM CONNECTION: SCIENCE

Spiderwebs—The spider secretes silk from glands in its abdomen. It begins a web by spinning a single silk thread, which is carried by a breeze until the end catches on a nearby object. The spider then attaches other strands to form an outside frame with connecting "spokes," which meet at the center. Next the spider constructs a loose, temporary spiral, starting at the center and going around to the outside frame. At this point, the spider begins to produce a sticky thread and constructs a final spiral, starting this time at the center and following and removing the earlier spiral. This sticky web traps the insects that the spider uses for food.

LESSON 4

2. Introduce atonal music. Have the students:
• Read and discuss information on atonal music.
• Suggest a reason why the composer of "The Web" chose to use a tone row organization and retrograde techniques. (Because the text is about a web that appears to have no beginning or ending like a tone row. The retrograde reflects the meaning of the words "the front is the back.")
• Create an atonal composition by playing each of the twelve tones without repetition of any tone. Decide on a meter and rhythmic pattern for the melody and reverse its order by playing in retrograde.
• Attempt the Challenge! by adding an instrumental steady beat, a rhythmic ostinato or a body percussion accompaniment to the created melody. Find a way to notate the composition.

In twelve-tone music, all twelve tones are played in the order the composer has chosen until each tone has been used once. The row is deliberately organized so that the melody has no tonal center. When a melody has no tonal center or tonic pitch to which all other tones relate, it is called **atonal.**

- The composer of "The Web" decided to use a tone row to organize the pitches of this song. He also chose to use retrograde. Suggest a reason why he might have done it. to fit the words
- Create your own atonal composition by:

  1. Choosing an order in which to play each of the twelve tones without repetition of any tone to create an atonal melody
  2. Deciding on a meter and a rhythmic pattern for your melody
  3. Reversing the order of the melody, playing it backward, in retrograde

 CHALLENGE Add an instrumental steady beat, a rhythmic ostinato, or a body percussion accompaniment to your melody. Find a way to notate your composition.

Wassily Kandinsky painted *Improvisation XIV* in 1910, about ten years before Arnold Schoenberg introduced twelve-tone music.

92

E X T E N S I O N

THE ARTISTS

Wassily Kandinsky (vä-si-lē kan-din' skē) (1866–1944)—was a Russian painter who also lived in Germany. He thought of painting as a form of personal expression and said that color and line, rather than realistic subjects, were most emotional and inspiring. In *Improvisation XIV* he used vibrant colors and free brush strokes to give the painting its spontaneous, bold style.

Edvard Munch (ed' värd moōnk) (1863–1944)—was a Norwegian artist whose works often show people expressing strong emotions, such as helplessness, isolation, fear, and jealousy. He painted portraits of girls as well as figures in landscapes, and he used intense colors to convey emotions. In *Girls on the Bridge* the deep blues, browns, and grays make the scene sombre and gloomy rather than peaceful or cheery.

Expressionism in Music

Arnold Schoenberg (shən' berg) (1874–1951) is known as one of the leaders of *expressionism* in music. The **expressionist** movement became popular in the early twentieth century. It was a movement in which artists—painters, composers, or authors—tried to produce works that expressed their own feelings about an object or event, rather than depicting the object itself in a realistic manner.

In music this type of creative activity required some new method of dealing with notes, chords, tone colors, and rhythms. Schoenberg first introduced twelve-tone, or serial, music around 1920. His new approach to composing often shocked people. He took away things they expected to hear. Melodies did not always sound "pretty." There were no major or minor harmonies.

- Listen to this example of Schoenberg's work.

Begleitungsmusik zu einer Lichtspielscene (excerpt), Op. 34, by Arnold Schoenberg

Expressionist styles developed in art as well as in music. The painting on the right is a portrait of Arnold Schoenberg, done in 1917. Below, an expressionist painting by the Norwegian artist Edvard Munch.

Girls on the Bridge. Edvard Munch. NATIONAL GALLERY, Oslo

Portrait of Arnold Schoenberg. Egon Schiele

93

3. Introduce expressionism in music.
Have the students:
- Discuss the information on Arnold Schoenberg and expressionism in music.
- Listen to the recording, which is a twelve-tone example of expressionism in music.

Reinforcing the Lesson

Have the students review "Retrograde in D" on page 88 as an example of retrograde motion in a melody.

3 APPRAISAL

The students should be able to:
1. Identify and define the use of tone row in "The Web."
2. Perform a tone row and its retrograde.
3. Create their own tone rows including a retrograde version and perform it with rhythmic and melodic accuracy.

COOPERATIVE LEARNING

Assign the students to cooperative groups of four. Have each group divide into two pairs. One pair will read and discuss the information on page 86, and the other pair will read and discuss the information on page 93. Then both pairs return to the group and teach the information they have learned to the other pair comparing and contrasting the two selections. They may wish to create one question from each page to quiz another group. If the other group can answer the question, that group wins the right to ask a question. If the answer is given by a student in the other group chosen at random, the whole group is rewarded or not depending on whether the answer is correct or incorrect. This encourages group members to be sure everyone knows all the information. The reward could be tangible, such as a snack or extra instrument playing time, or listening to a favorite recording. Another possibility might be listing the names of members of successful groups on a weekly honor roll to be displayed in the classroom.

THE ARTIST

Egon Schiele (ā' gon shē' lə) (1890–1918) —was an Austrian painter who concentrated on conveying emotions rather than portraying things naturally or realistically. In the *Portrait of Arnold Schoenberg*, with its distorted face, harsh brushstrokes, and flat colors, Schiele might have been trying to show Schoenberg's dissonant, unexpected approach to music.

REVIEW AND EVALUATION

JUST CHECKING

Objective
To review and test the skills and concepts taught in Unit 4

Materials
Recordings: Just Checking Unit 4
(questions 1–7)
Unit 4 Evaluation (questions 3, 4)
For Extra Credit recordings (optional)
Bells or keyboard
Copying Master 4-3 (optional)
Evaluation Unit 4 Copying Master

TEACHING THE LESSON

Review the skills and concepts taught in Unit 4. Have the students:
• Perform the activities and answer the questions on pages 94–95. (For this review, examples for questions 1 through 7 are included in the ''Just Checking Unit 4'' recording. Have the students answer these questions first. Then have them answer the other questions in the review.)
• Review their answers.
(You may wish to use Copying Master 4-3 at this time.)

🎵 3B, 4A

💿 2, 3

JUST CHECKING

See how much you remember. Listen to the recording.

1. Listen to the recording and perform these melodies by singing or playing the bells or keyboard. The recording has a four-measure introduction.

a.
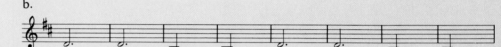

b.

2. The harmony you just performed could best be described as:
atonal and dissonant   tonal and consonant

tonal and consonant

3. Perform or listen to "Ahrirang" as a canon.

4. Listen to the last part of "River" and identify the home tone by humming it or playing it on keyboard, recorder, or bells.

94

5. Listen to a portion of the "Hallelujah" Chorus and determine whether the texture is monophonic, polyphonic, or homophonic. Show your answer by pointing to the diagram that shows the texture as each number is called. polyphonic, homophonic

monophonic	polyphonic	homophonic

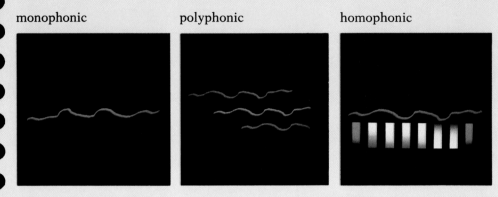

6. Perform the following body percussion to review *retrograde*.

Rhythms in Retrograde

V.L. and M.J.

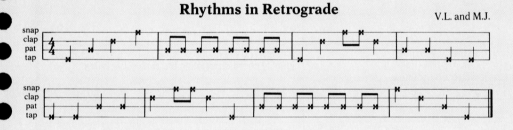

7. Listen to "The Web" to review melodic retrograde. In which measures is the melodic pattern reversed so that its end becomes its beginning? measures 8 to the end

8. On keyboard or bells play the following pitches that make up the twelve-tone row on which the melody of "The Web" is based.

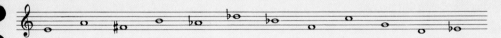

9. Play the retrograde of this tone row on keyboard or bells.

95

REVIEW AND EVALUATION

GIVING THE EVALUATION

Evaluation Unit 4 Copying Master can be found in the *Teacher's Copying Masters* book along with full directions for giving the evaluation and checking the answers.

FOR EXTRA CREDIT

You may want to have the students respond to the following:
Texture in music refers to the way sounds are combined. List one song or other composition you have studied for each of the following textures:
    monophonic ("Ahrirang" in unison)
    polyphonic ("Ahrirang" as a canon; "Hallelujah" Chorus)
    homophonic ("River")
(You may wish to play these recordings to refresh students' memories.)

UNIT 5 • OVERVIEW

ELEMENTS OF MUSIC	UNIT 5 OBJECTIVES	Lesson 1 Focus: Modulation	Lesson 2 Focus: Use of the Blues Scale in Symphonic Music
Dynamics	Identify dynamic changes Determine how dynamics create a mood in the music	Discuss how dynamics affect the music	
Tone Color	Identify bright and dark tone colors Determine appropriate tone colors for a composition	Listen to a composition for flute and orchestra	Listen to and identify instruments Play chord progression on keyboard or bells
Tempo	Determine appropriate tempo for the composition		
Duration/ Rhythm		Create a rhythmic accompaniment	
Pitch	**Listen to and identify key changes** **Define register and modulation** **Identify bitonality**	Listen to and identify key changes Sing two songs with a range of G-d¹ and c♯-b♭¹ Define modulation Follow a score Experience changes of key signature in a score Define register	Create a melody in blues style
Texture	Perform accompaniments in minor tonality **Identify play tonic, subdominant, and dominant chords in C major**	Perform accompaniments in minor Perform a harmonic accompaniment	Identify and define tonic, subdominant, and dominant Identify chord changes in the twelve-bar blues
Form	**Perform the twelve-bar blues progression** Listen to, discuss, and create variations		Perform the twelve-bar blues progression
Style	Sing a song in Spanish Discuss the blues and music by an African American composer **Identify and discuss bitonal music** **Discuss and identify the art song**	Discuss gospel music Sing a Spanish song Read about word painting in music Identify modulation in 3 compositions of contrasting style Discuss the composer Cécile Chaminade	Identify and discuss the blues Discuss the African American composer William Grant Still Discuss and listen to *Afro-American Symphony*, Movement 1
Reading	Read and play ♩. on g, a, b♭, b♮, c	Sing songs in ¾ , 4/4 Read melodic notation g, a, b♭, b♮, c using ♩.	Read chord symbols I IV V Read and play twelve-bar blues

PURPOSE Unit 5: HARMONY

In this unit the students will review and/or experience some techniques composers use to develop melodies and harmonies in their compositions. They will be introduced to the concepts of consonance and dissonance, and will see how composers use changes from major to minor to create shifting moods in their works.

SUGGESTED TIME FRAME

February	March

FOCUS

- Modulation
- Use of the Blues Scale in Symphonic Music
- Harmony—Consonance and Dissonance
- Melody and Harmony

BULLETIN BOARD

Display an enlarged copy of this clock on your bulletin board. Distribute Copying Master 5-1 to the class and/or place the following chart on the chalkboard. (See page 103 for an appropriate time for this activity.)

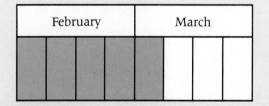

Lesson 3 Focus: Harmony—Consonance and Dissonance	**Lesson 4** Focus: Melody and Harmony
Listen to and identify dynamic changes	Determine the proper dynamics for a composition Identify how dynamics can create a mood
	Determine appropriate tone colors for a composition
	Determine the appropriate tempo for a composition
Listen to and discuss bitonal music	Identify the relationship between text, pitch register, and harmony Create a visual design that reflects musical ideas Discuss the contrasts in major and minor tonality and how they create the mood Identify characteristic themes in popular music
Define, identify, and discuss harmony that is consonant and dissonant	
Listen to, discuss, and create variations Create a variation by changing rhythm, tempo, or style	
Identify and discuss bitonal music Discuss the American composer Charles Ives	Discuss the art song of the romantic period Discuss the musical style of Franz Schubert Listen to determine the mood of a composition
Read melody in $\frac{3}{4}$ Read melodic notation d♭ - f′ Read score	Read and follow the English translation of the original German text of a song

• Each shape on the chart must be filled with one of the numbers shown in parentheses on the clock for that shape. For example, the triangle must be filled with 1⁺ or 2⁻, the circle must be filled with 2⁺ or 3⁻, and so forth.
• All of the numbers 1 through 7 must appear in each vertical column.
• All of the blanks in each vertical column must be filled with all "plus numbers" or all "minus numbers."

Columns 1 and 2 have been filled in, and three other entries have been made to help students out. Column 7 cannot be filled.

When the class has completed the table, tell them to replace all 1s with C, all 2s with D, and so on. Replace every + with a ♯ (sharp), and every − with a ♭ (flat).

Play the pitches in each column.

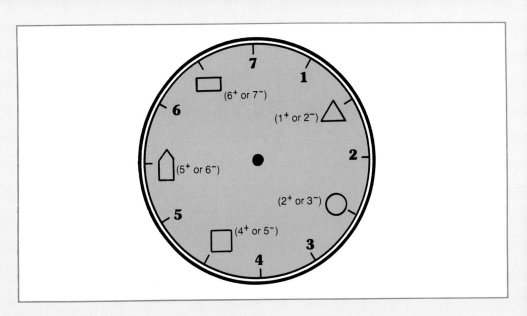

LESSON 1

UNIT **5**

HARMONY

LESSON 1

Focus: Modulation

Objectives
To identify and perform modulation
To perform a melodic accompaniment

Materials
Recordings: "Climbing Up to Zion"
"Mi Caballo Blanco"
Concertino for Flute and
Orchestra
"Run Joe"
"Our World"
Satto
Bells or guitar
Percussion instruments
Copying Master 5-1 (optional)

Vocabulary
Gospel, key, modulation, register

1 SETTING THE STAGE

Tell the students they will be learning about how composers provide musical interest and variety through changing keys.

97

LESSON 1

2 TEACHING THE LESSON

1. Introduce word painting through melody. Have the students:

• Discuss the information on "Climbing Up to Zion" and word painting.

• Follow the different presentations of the melody as they listen to the recording.

• Identify whether the melody sounds higher or lower each time it repeats.

• Sing the melody with the recording.

CHANGING KEYS

Key: C major   Starting Pitch: G   Scale Tones: *so, la, do re mi fa so la do^1 re^1*

Pictures Through Music

The music of the gospel song "Climbing Up to Zion" reflects the meaning of the words.

• Follow the different ways the melody is presented as you listen to the song. Decide whether the melody sounds higher or lower each time it repeats. higher.

> 🎵 "Climbing Up to Zion," by Wintley Phipps

• Sing the melody.

Climbing Up to Zion

Words and music by Wintley Phipps

I'm climb-ing up the rough side of the moun-tain, Climb-ing up to Zi - on to see my Lord. I'm climb-ing up the rough side of the moun-tain, Climb - ing up to Zi - on to see my Lord. I'm climb-ing see my Lord.__ Bro - ther, won't you lis - ten? Oh, yes__ Sis - ter, won't you lis - ten? Oh,__ yes.__ Bro - ther, won't you lis - ten? Oh, yes,__ I'm climb - ing up to Zi - on to see my Lord.

98

E X T E N S I O N

SIGNING FOR "CLIMBING UP TO ZION"

In the opening phrase, "I'm climbing up," move the hands four times as if moving up the rungs of a ladder. Move on the beat on climb/up/rest/rest. Even though the sound stops, the climbing continues throughout the two rests.

Climbing

Curved "V" hands with palms facing each other, moving alternately upward.

Mountain/Zion

See

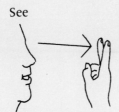

The right hand "A" strikes the back of the left hand "S." Both hands extend upward to show the side of the mountain.

The "V" position moves away from the eyes.

Lord

Right hand "L" moves from the left shoulder to the right hip.

98   UNIT 5

WINTLEY PHIPPS

Wintley Phipps has traveled an unusual path to his career in religious music. He was born in Trinidad, West Indies, but raised in Montréal, Canada. Although familiar with hymns and church music from his early childhood, he did not come into contact with African American gospel music until his college days in Alabama. It was there that he started composing.

After earning a master's degree in divinity, Reverend Phipps knew that he would be devoting his life to church work. His love of music, however, continued. Today, Reverend Phipps both composes and performs his unique multicultural music.

Gospel Music

Gospel music is a type of religious music that originated in the South. It developed in African American Baptist churches during the 1930s, and quickly became more widely known. By the 1940s and 1950s radio stations all over the country played songs by such gospel singers as Rosetta Tharpe and Mahalia Jackson.

Gospel is different from other forms of African American religious music. The composer is usually known. The songs have instrumental accompaniments, and the melodies are complex with nontraditional harmonies. Gospel music, like jazz, has many polyrhythms. Early lyrics were based on the gospels but later became expressions of personal experience.

Gospel music has influenced rhythm and blues and soul music. The foot-stomping frenzy of gospel blended naturally into the intensely expressive soul music of James Brown, Otis Redding, and Ray Charles. A great number of rhythm and blues singers got their start by singing gospel music in church, including Aretha Franklin and Dionne Warwick.

99

LESSON 1

2. Introduce the composer and singer. Have the students discuss information on Wintley Phipps.

3. Introduce gospel music. Have the students discuss the information on the history of gospel music.

Brother

The root sign for male is made by outlining the brim of a hat. Bring index fingers together to indicate "same" or "boy-same," meaning two boys or brothers.

Listen (Hear)

The natural gesture of hearing—open palm behind ear.

Yes

The fist, palm down, nods up and down like a head. Nod once for "Oh," and again for "yes."

Sister

The root sign for female is signed by brushing the cheek toward chin to indicate the bonnet strings of a girl. The index fingers are brought together to show "same" or "girl-same," meaning sister.

TEACHER INFORMATION

Music and You uses the term *African American* when referring to Americans of African descent.

LESSON 1

4. Introduce "Mi Caballo Blanco."
Have the students:
• Listen to the song and decide if it moves to a higher or lower key.
• Review the Spanish text.
• Identify and define modulation.

Changing the Key for Effect

Key: D minor Starting Pitches: A and F
Scale Tones: si, la, ti, do di re mi fa

"Mi Caballo Blanco" is a popular song by Francisco Flores del Campo (frän-sēs' kō flō' res del käm' pō) that describes the devotion of the South American ranchers for their horses. As in "Climbing Up to Zion," the composer moves the melody into different scales, or **keys**, to create an effect.

• Listen and decide if the song moves to higher or lower keys. higher

"Mi Caballo Blanco," by Francisco Flores del Campo

Mi Caballo Blanco

Words and music by
Francisco Flores del Campo

2. En alas de una dicha
   Mi caballo corrió
   En alas de una pena
   El también me llevó.

3. Al Taita Dios le pido
   Y él lo sabe muy bien
   Si a su lado me llama
   En mi caballo iré.

Each section of "Mi Caballo Blanco" is based in a minor key and starts on a different pitch. The change from a section of music based on one scale to a section of music based on another scale is called **modulation.**

100

EXTENSION

CURRICULUM CONNECTION: SOCIAL STUDIES

Ranching—an important industry in Chile, makes up about one-sixth of all Chilean agricultural production. Ranching is located primarily in the Southern Central Valley and has been an important part of Chilean life since the Spanish conquest. Approximately one-fifth of Chile's population lives on ranches. Cowboys in Chile are called *huasos.* They wear wide-brimmed, flat-topped, brown or black hats; short capes called *mantas;* leggings with leather fringes; and high-heeled boots.

MORE MUSIC TEACHING IDEAS

Have the students:
1. Make a list of several "Top 40" popular songs that make use of modulation.
2. Perform a harmonic accompaniment to the first verse of "Mi Caballo Blanco" on bells or guitar.
3. Create a rhythmic accompaniment to "Mi Caballo Blanco."

PRONUNCIATION

1. Es mi caballo blanco
   es mē kä-bä' yō blän' kō
   My horse is white

   Como un amanecer
   kō' mō ōon ä-mä-nä-sär'
   as the dawn,

Siempre juntitos vamos,
s'yem'prä hōōn-tē'tōs vä'mōs
Always do we ride together,

Es mi amigo más fiel.
es mē a-mē' gō mäs f'yel'
he is my most faithful friend.

Mi caballo, mi caballo,
mē kä-bä' yō mē kä-bä' yō
My horse, my horse,

galopando va.
gä-lō-pän'dō vä
goes galloping.

Mi caballo, mi caballo,
mē kä-bä' yō mē kä-bä' yō
My horse, my horse,

100 UNIT 5

• Perform these three melodic accompaniments to "Mi Caballo Blanco." They are based on the D minor, E minor, and F minor scales.

Melodic Accompaniment to "Mi Caballo Blanco"

• Sing the song and perform the accompaniments.

101

• Perform the three melodic accompaniments (to be played in succession with the recording).
• Sing the song with the recording and perform the accompaniments.

se va y se va.
sä vä ē sā vä
just rides and rides.

2. En alas de una dicha
en ä' läs dā ōō' nä dē' chä
On the wings of joy

Mi caballo corrió
mē kä-bä' yō kōr-rē-ō'
my horse ran

En alas de una pena
en ä' läs dā ōō' nä pā' nä
on the wings of grief

El también me llevó
el täm-byen' mā yā-vō'
he carried me too.

3. Al Taita Dios le pido
äl täi' tä dē-ōs' lä pē' thō
I ask my beloved God

Y él lo sabe muy bien
ē el lō sä' bā mōō' ē byen
and he knows it very well

Si a su lado me llama
sē ä sōō lä' thō mä yä' mä
If he calls me to his side

En mi caballo iré.
en mē kä-bä' yō ē-rä'
on my horse I will go.

SPECIAL LEARNERS
Prepare an overhead transparency of pupil page 101 to use when the class sings the song in Spanish and plays the accompaniment. Assign the playing activity to any mainstreamed students who are having difficulty following the Spanish text. Split the class into two groups, assigning one group the singing and the other the playing. Point to the beginning of each line of the melodic accompaniments.

LESSON 1

5. Introduce creating harmonic interest and variety. Have the students:
• Follow the music as they listen to the opening section of the Concertino for Flute and Orchestra.
• Listen again to the recording and decide how the composer uses dynamics and register to create interest and variety.

Creating Variety in Music

Composers use modulation to create interest and variety in their compositions.

• Follow the chart as you listen to the opening section of Concertino for Flute and Orchestra by Cécile Chaminade (se-sēl′ sha-mē-näd′). The theme is stated several times.

 Concertino for Flute and Orchestra, by Cécile Chaminade

1. Statement of theme (key of D major)

2. Statement of theme (key of A major)

3. Statement of theme (key of B♭ major)

4. Statement of theme (key of D major)

• Listen again and decide how the composer uses dynamics and **register,** the high to low range of a voice or instrument, to create interest and variety. soft and loud dynamics; high and low register

102

CÉCILE CHAMINADE

Cécile Chaminade (1857–1944) made her first appearance as a concert pianist at the age of eighteen in her native Paris. She was an illustrious piano soloist and conductor, and traveled widely in France, England, and the United States from 1892 until well into the twentieth century. An active composer as well as performer, Cécile Chaminade is remembered mainly for her elegant piano compositions, many of which she performed in concert.

103

LESSON 1

• Discuss the information on the composer Cécile Chaminade.

Reinforcing the Lesson

Have the students review either "Run Joe" on page 10 to identify tonic and dominant chord changes, "Our World" on page 28 to identify contrasts between major and minor, or *Satto* on page 12 to identify changes in dynamics. (You may wish to have students do the bulletin board activity at this time, in connection with Copying Master 5-1, to review the major scale.)

3 APPRAISAL

The students should be able to:
1. Verbally define modulation and describe how it is used as a compositional device in general and specifically in at least one composition.
2. Identify modulation in three compositions in contrasting styles.
3. Perform a melodic accompaniment to "Mi Caballo Blanco" with rhythmic and melodic accuracy.

LESSON 2

Focus: Use of the Blues Scale in Symphonic Music

Objectives
To perform a twelve-bar blues pattern
To identify the use of the blues scale in a symphonic composition
To identify orchestral tone color

Materials
Recordings: "Hear Me Talking to You"
 Afro-American Symphony,
 first movement
 Variations on "America"
Keyboard or bells

Vocabulary
Blues, twelve-bar blues, subdominant, pizzicato

1 SETTING THE STAGE
Tell the students they will be learning about the style of music called the blues, which was created by African Americans around the turn of the century.

2 TEACHING THE LESSON

1. Review the twelve-bar blues and the blues scale. Have the students:
• Discuss information on the blues.
• Listen to the recording of "Hear Me Talking to You" and identify the instruments that accompany the performance.
• Discuss the information on blues harmony, the subdominant chord, and a twelve-bar blues pattern. (Some twelve-bar blues patterns use a IV chord in the tenth measure.)

THE BLUES—AN AMERICAN STYLE

Playing the Twelve-Bar Blues

The **blues** is a style of music that was created by African Americans around the turn of the century. The words to blues songs are usually about loneliness, sadness, or lost love. The blues has its own scale and chord pattern called the **twelve-bar blues.**

• Listen to early blues singer Gertrude "Ma" Rainey sing "Hear Me Talking to You." Identify the instruments that accompany the performance.
piano, banjo, trumpet, trombone, tuba

 "Hear Me Talking to You," by Gertrude "Ma" Rainey

Blues harmony is based on three chords of the major scale: the tonic (I) chord, the dominant (V) chord, and the chord based on the fourth pitch of the scale called the **subdominant** or **IV chord.** You can play an accompaniment for all traditional blues songs once you learn these three chords.

C D E F G A B C
I   IV V

This twelve-bar accompaniment to "Hear Me Talking to You" shows a twelve-bar blues pattern.

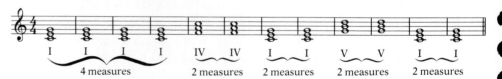

I   I   I   I   IV IV I   I   V   V   I   I
   4 measures   2 measures 2 measures 2 measures 2 measures

104

E X T E N S I O N

THE COMPOSER

Gertrude "Ma" Rainey (1886–1939)— was one of the most significant early female blues singers. Her first public appearance was at age twelve in a talent show in her hometown of Columbus, Georgia. Soon after, she became a cabaret singer and toured with Tolliver's Circus and the Rabbit Foot Minstrels. During the 1920s she organized and toured throughout the South and Mexico with her Georgia Jazz Band. Ma Rainey made her first recording in 1923. Within five years she had made over one hundred recordings with many jazz greats including Louis Armstrong. Rainey is best known for her powerful voice, "moaning" style, and sensitive phrasing. She is also remembered for her lasting influence on Bessie Smith.

- Learn to play the chords in the twelve-bar blues. Then play them with the song.
- Create your own melody and words to go with the twelve-bar blues.

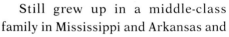

WILLIAM GRANT STILL

William Grant Still (1895–1978) is often referred to as the dean of African American composers. Best known for his music using African American and other American folk songs, he received many awards and honors as the result of his outstanding work.

Still grew up in a middle-class family in Mississippi and Arkansas and was exposed to various styles of popular and classical music, including both opera and blues. From a very early age he heard his grandmother sing hymns, gospel songs, and spirituals. His father, a band leader and cornet player, died while Still was quite young. Later, his stepfather encouraged his musical development by sharing his collection of opera records, taking him to concerts, and providing him with private music lessons.

Still arranged and composed music and directed the band at his college. In 1916 he studied with the French composer Edgar Varèse, further developing his composing skills.

The 1931 premiere of Still's *Afro-American Symphony* by the Rochester Symphony under Howard Hanson was the first performance by a major symphony orchestra of a symphonic work by an African American composer. Later, Still became the first African American to conduct a major American orchestra, the Los Angeles Philharmonic. In 1949 his opera *Troubled Island* was the first composed by an African American to be performed by a major opera company, the New York City Opera. He was also one of the first African American composers to write music for radio, films, and television.

105

LESSON 2

- Learn to play the chord progression of the traditional twelve-bar blues pattern on bells or keyboard. Then play it with the recording. (You may wish to use the keyboard section that begins on pupil page 232 for instruction on the playing of chords.)
- Create their own melody and words to go with the twelve-bar blues.

2. Introduce William Grant Still. Have the students discuss the information on the composer.

CURRICULUM CONNECTION: SOCIAL STUDIES

The blues—is a type of music that was created by African Americans. It grew mainly from work songs and spirituals. But, while spirituals usually have a fast tempo, the blues tempo is generally slow. Most blues songs are sad, but sometimes express a defiant or humorous reaction to trouble.

The blues became popular in the early part of the twentieth century. W. C. Handy and Ferdinand "Jelly Roll" Morton were among the first blues composers. During the 1920s phonograph records helped make the blues more widely known. Two of the best-known blues composer-performers of this period were "Ma" Rainey and her protégée Bessie Smith (c. 1894–1937), the "Empress of the Blues."

LESSON 2

3. Introduce the use of blues in the *Afro-American Symphony*. Have the students:
• Define as a blues melody Theme A of the *Afro-American Symphony*, first movement.
• Discuss the poem that serves as a program for the first movement of *Afro-American Symphony*.
• Identify and name the content of each picture, focusing on the order of the themes and tone color.
• Follow the map as you listen to the recording of Movement I.
• Discuss how the composer achieves unity and variety. (Unity is provided by the repetition of Theme A. Variety is provided through the use of a second theme and changes of tone colors, dynamics and tempo.)

Reinforcing the Lesson

Have the students preview Ives' *Variations on "America,"* page 109, for a very different use of a familiar theme in "classical" music.

3 APPRAISAL

The students should be able to:
1. Perform a twelve-bar blues accompaniment on bells or keyboard, with accuracy, to "Hear Me Talking To You."
2. Identify the composition *Afro-American Symphony* by Still as a composition using the blues scale.
3. Listen to sections or themes from *Afro-American Symphony* that have contrasting tone color and describe the tone color differences.

The Blues in a Symphony

Theme A of the first movement of William Grant Still's *Afro-American Symphony* is based on the twelve-bar blues. The overall mood of the music is one of longing, and is related to this verse of Paul Laurence Dunbar that was later applied to the music.

> All my life long twell de night has pas'
> Let de wo'k come es it will,
> So dat I fin' you, my honey, at last,
> Somewaih des ovah de hill.

• Follow the map as you listen to the first movement of *Afro-American Symphony*. The term **pizzicato** (pit-zi-kä' tō) in boxes 2 and 9 tells the string players to pluck the strings instead of using the bow.

 Afro-American Symphony, First Movement, by William Grant Still

INTRODUCTION

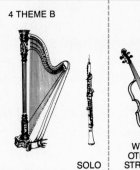

1 THEME A
SOLO

2 THEME A
SOLO
PIZZICATO

3
FULL ORCHESTRA
AND FASTER
THEN

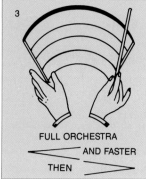

4 THEME B
SOLO
WITH OTHER STRINGS

106

SPECIAL LEARNERS

Students with visual or tracking disabilities may have difficulty following the Listening Map to *Afro-American Symphony*. Prepare an overhead transparency of pupil pages 106 and 107 and point to each section as it comes up in the recording.

LISTENING

You may wish to use the Listening Map overhead transparency to help guide the students through the listening selection.

5 THEME B

WITH OTHER STRINGS

6 THEME B (IN MINOR)

7 THEME A TRANSFORMED

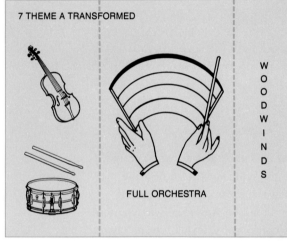

FULL ORCHESTRA

WOODWINDS

8 THEME B (IN MINOR)

9 THEME A

PIZZICATO

WITH WOODWINDS

10 CODA

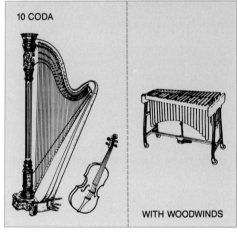

WITH WOODWINDS

107

MORE MUSIC TEACHING IDEAS

Have the students improvise a melody using C, D, E, F, and G with the twelve-bar blues pattern in the key of C.

CURRICULUM CONNECTION: READING

Paul Laurence Dunbar (1872–1906)— African American poet, was best known for his poems on African American life. Dunbar grew up in Dayton, Ohio. After he graduated from high school he compiled a booklet of his verses called *Oak and Ivy* and sold it to passengers riding the elevator he operated. His next book of poems, called *Majors and Minors,* brought him instant recognition. Dunbar's best known collection is called *Lyrics of Lowly Life* which was published in 1896. Dunbar served as an assistant at the Library of Congress for a short period of time. He also appeared as a lecturer at colleges across the country.

LESSON 3

Focus: Harmony—Consonance and Dissonance

Objectives
To identify and perform consonance and dissonance
To identify bitonality

Materials
Recordings: "River"
 "America," Version 1
 "America," Version 2
 Variations on "America"
Keyboard, recorder, bells, or guitar

Vocabulary
Dissonance, bitonal

1 SETTING THE STAGE
Have the students review "River" on page 78 as an example of consonant harmony.

2 TEACHING THE LESSON

1. Introduce consonance and dissonance. Have the students:
• Review the information on consonance on page 80.
• Discuss the information on dissonance.
• Play the first part of "America" on keyboard or bells with the recording of Version 1. (The recording has a four-measure introduction.)
• Identify the harmony in Version 1 as being consonant because there is little or no tension.
• Play the first part of "America" on keyboard or bells with the recording of Version 2. (The recording has a four-measure introduction.) Identify the harmony as dissonant because there is tension or clashing among the pitches.
2. Introduce bitonality. Have the students discuss the information on bitonality.

Consonance and Dissonance

Tones that do not seem to sound as though they go together are called **dissonant**.

• Play the first part of "America" on bells or keyboard with this recording. Does the music sound consonant or dissonant? Why?
consonant; answers will vary

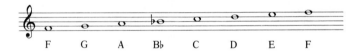

"America," Version 1

• Play the first part of "America" again with the recording of Version 2. Does the music sound consonant or dissonant? Why? dissonant; answers will vary

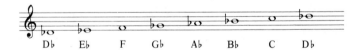

"America," Version 2

The dissonance in harmony in Version 2 of "America" was created by using two different tonal centers or scales at the same time. When music has two tonal centers at the same time, it is called **bitonal**. The bitonal harmony in Version 2 of "America" was written by the twentieth-century American composer Charles Ives as part of a set of variations on the song "America." The variations were written for pipe organ.

The right hand plays harmony based on the F major scale.

F   G   A   Bb   C   D   E   F

The left hand plays harmony based on the Db major scale.

Db   Eb   F   Gb   Ab   Bb   C   Db

108

• Listen to *Variations on "America"* to determine how the composer used different types of harmony, dynamics, and rhythm to create interest and variety.

 Variations on "America," by Charles Ives

1. Introduction: Based on the beginning of the song; phrase "My country, 'tis of thee" most prominent; *ff*

2. "America": Presented in a traditional style; harmony consonant; *pp*

3. First Variation: Melody in bass with continually moving sixteenth notes above melody; *pp*

4. Second Variation: New harmonization of the theme much like the close harmony of a barbershop quartet

5. Interlude: Theme played as a canon; in bitonal harmony

6. Third Variation: Change of rhythm, which produces an effect similar to a calliope; *f*

7. Fourth Variation: Rhythm for theme based in the style of a polonaise, a dance of Poland; now based on a minor scale

8. Interlude: Again uses dissonant bitonal harmony

9. Fifth Variation: Melody played on the keyboard; contrasting line in the pedal part (the lowest part); directions to organists say to play the pedal part as fast as the feet can go

10. Coda: Described by Ives as "in a way a kind of take-off on the Bunker Hill fight."

This work is typical of Ives's strongly original style of music. He takes a recognized melody and treats it in a very creative way.

 CHALLENGE Create your own variations on "America." Change the rhythm, the tempo, or the style.

109

3. Introduce *Variations on "America."*
Have the students:
• Discuss information in preparation for listening to *Variations on "America."*
• Listen to *Variations on "America"* by following the descriptions as each number is called.
• Summarize how Ives used contrasts of harmony, dynamics and rhythm to create interest and variety.
4. Introduce the Challenge! activity.
Have the students create original variations on "America" by changing the rhythm, tempo or style.

COOPERATIVE LEARNING

Have the students turn to page 16 in the text and perform "Ode to Joy" on keyboard, recorder, bells, or guitar. Assign the students to cooperative groups of four to explore the concept of variation, using "Ode to Joy" as the theme. The following variation techniques may provide the students with some models to begin the project:

1. changing from major to minor
2. varying the rhythm
3. changing the tempo
4. varying the dynamics
5. adding a bitonal harmonic accompaniment

Each group should rehearse its variations on "Ode to Joy." Select a conductor to help order the variations and a recorder to develop a simple graph score. Have each group perform its variation for the class.

LESSON 3

5. Introduce the composer. Have the students discuss the information on Charles Ives.

Reinforcing the Lesson

Have the students take a familiar melody such as the "Ode to Joy" and create a bi-tonal accompaniment by using more than one tonality.

3 APPRAISAL

The students should be able to:

1. Verbally define the terms bitonality, consonant harmony and dissonant harmony.
2. Listen to several excerpts from *Variations on "America"* that are clear examples of either consonance or dissonance and accurately match the term to the example.
3. Perform the first six measures of "America" on bells or keyboard as written, while an accompaniment is played that results in either a version that is consonant or dissonant. Identify each with the correct label.

CHARLES IVES

Charles Ives (1874–1954) grew up in a small town in Connecticut where his father was the local bandmaster. He received his early musical training from his father, who encouraged him to experiment with all sorts of sound combinations to "stretch his ears." Ives liked the harsh dissonance created by playing "America" in one key with the right hand at the keyboard and in another key with the left. Doing this at the same time created bitonality.

As a teenager Ives became a church organist, and one can imagine that he enjoyed shocking the congregation by changing the harmonies of familiar songs like "America."

Because he thought his unconventional music was not going to be popular, Ives went into the insurance business. Eventually he founded a successful insurance agency and became very wealthy. However, music remained his first love, and he continued to compose evenings and weekends.

Ives found ideas for his music in the folk and popular music he knew as a boy: hymns, ragtime, village band concerts, church choir music, patriotic songs, and dances. Perhaps it was these sounds that gave him the idea for his *Variations on "America,"* written for pipe organ.

110

TELLING A STORY
THROUGH MELODY AND HARMONY

Franz Schubert's "The Erlking" is one of the finest examples of *art song* romanticism. An **art song** is a composition for solo voice and instrumental accompaniment, usually keyboard. The term *art song* is used to distinguish such songs from folk songs and popular songs. In the text to "The Erlking" the German poet Johann Wolfgang von Goethe (gə(r)′ tə) tells of a father riding on horseback through a storm with his child in his arms. The boy, who is very sick with a high fever, remembers the legend that whoever is touched by the king of the elves, the Erlking, must die.

"The Erlking" has four separate characters. Usually all are sung by one person. Schubert uses a wide range of pitches and contrasts in vocal registers to depict each of the four characters. Contrasts of major and minor tonality also help to identify the characters.

• Listen to the beginning of "The Erlking," and choose one word to describe the mood. Which of these musical characteristics do you think help to express that mood? Answers may vary; minor, loud, fast

   major/minor   soft/loud   fast/slow

   "The Erlking," by Franz Schubert

• Listen to "The Erlking" and follow the translation of the German text.

111

LESSON 4

Focus: Melody and Harmony

Objectives
To identify the relationship between word painting, pitch register and harmony

Materials
Recordings: "The Erlking"
                "Climbing Up to Zion"

Vocabulary
Art song

1 SETTING THE STAGE
Review the romantic period on page 26.

2 TEACHING THE LESSON
1. Introduce the "The Erlking." Have the students:
• Discuss the information on the romantic period and "The Erlking."
• Listen to the beginning of "The Erlking" and decide on one word to describe the mood (anxious, scared, troubled, etc.). Decide which musical characteristics help to express that mood.
• Listen to "The Erlking" and follow the translation of the German text.

**CURRICULUM CONNECTION:
ART**

Have one of the students write the names of the four characters found in Goethe's poem "The Erlking."

   Narrator   Father   Son   Erlking

Review the lesson on "The Erlking," focusing on the musical ideas Schubert used to depict each character. Have the students work in pairs to create a visual design that could be used for the cover of a record jacket for a recording of "The Erlking." Have each cooperative pair share its visual design with the class. Provide an opportunity to render constructive suggestions. Select several of the best designs and display them.

The Erlking

Narrator

1. Who is that riding like the wind through the night?
It is a father, holding his child.
He holds him safely in his arms,
He holds him tightly and keeps him warm.

Father

2. "My son, why do you hide your face so anxiously?"

Son

3. "Father, don't you see the Erlking?
The Erlking with his crown and his train?"

Father

4. "My son, it is a streak of mist."

Erlking

5. "Ah, small boy, come away with me.
We'll play the greatest games with you.
We'll walk by the river, see beautiful flowers.
My mother has fantastic clothes for you."

Son

6. "My father, my father, don't you hear
the Erlking whispering promises to me?"

Father

7. "Be quiet, stay quiet, my child;
the wind is rustling in the dead leaves."

112

EXTENSION

CURRICULUM CONNECTION: LITERATURE

Johann Wolfgang von Goethe (1749–1832)—German author, was one of the most important and influential writers of modern literature. Goethe was born in Frankfurt am Main to a wealthy family. From an early age he was encouraged to study foreign languages, literature, and the fine arts. While studying in Strasbourg, Goethe met philospher Johann Herder. Herder stimulated Goethe's interest in Homer, Shakespeare, ballads, and folk songs. During this time Goethe wrote many poems in a folk-song style, one of which was "The Erlking." Goethe wrote works in every genre. He spent many years writing his masterpiece, *Faust*. He completed it a few months before his death.

Erlking

8. "Ah, fine boy, are you sure you won't come with me?
My daughters will take good care of you.
There'll be parties every night—singing, dancing.
They'll cradle and dance you, and sing you a lullaby."

Son

9. "My father, my father, and don't you see there
the Erlking's daughters in the shadows?"

Father

10. "My son, my son, I see it clearly;
the old willows look so gray."

Erlking

11. "I must have you with me.
If you won't come, then I will use force!"

Son

12. "My father, my father, now he is taking hold of me!
The Erlking has hurt me!"

Narrator

13. The father shudders, he rides swiftly on,
he holds in his arms the groaning child,
he reaches the courtyard weary and anxious;
in his arms the child was dead.

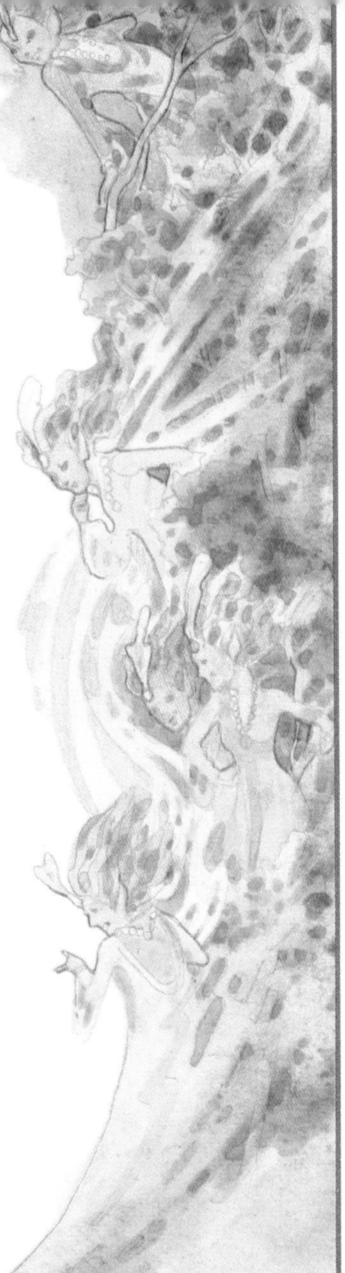

113

LESSON 4

- Listen again to "The Erlking" and respond to the questions.
- Perform the Challenge! activity.

- Listen again to "The Erlking," and answer these questions.

How do dynamics create the mood? Erlking sings softly; other characters more loudly

How does the piano accompaniment set the mood of the story? It conveys the father's urgency, the son's panic, and the Erlking's persuasiveness.

Which character sings in major? Erlking

Why is the remainder of the song in minor? tragic subject

 "The Erlking," by Franz Schubert

 CHALLENGE Think of your favorite songs. Which song seems to use dynamics, accompaniment, and major or minor most effectively to set a mood? Compare this to how Schubert set the mood in "The Erlking." Share your song with your classmates.

Schubert Playing the Piano is by the Austrian artist Gustav Klimt (1872–1918). Klimt chose to paint the scene in a romantic style.

114

EXTENSION

THE ARTIST

Gustav Klimt (goōs' täf klēmt) (1862–1918)—was an Austrian painter. A patron commissioned two scenes, one of them *Schubert at the Piano,* for a place above the doors of the palace music room. The soft, golden light and the delicacy of the figures are romantic in style.

A view of Vienna in Schubert's time

FRANZ SCHUBERT

Franz Schubert, drawing after a water-color by W. A. Rieder

The music of every important composer has something special to offer. In the case of Franz Schubert (1797–1828), it is outstanding melodies, easily remembered for their beauty and simplicity.

Growing up in Austria as the son of a schoolmaster, Schubert received his musical training as a choirboy in the Royal Chapel. Schubert also began a teaching career, but soon abandoned this to devote himself entirely to music.

Schubert composed over six hundred songs for voice and piano, and once composed eight songs in one day. Besides songs, he composed instrumental music including symphonies, chamber music, and solo piano music. Schubert's world-famous "Unfinished" Symphony (so called because it has only two movements instead of the usual four) contains many beautiful melodies. Occasionally Schubert used melodies from his own songs as themes for his instrumental pieces as in the "Trout" Quintet for Piano and Strings and the String Quartet No. 14 in D Minor, known as the "Death and the Maiden" Quartet. Schubert's music also is important in that his style bridges the classical and romantic periods.

115

2. Introduce Franz Schubert. Have the students discuss the information on Schubert. You may wish to use the following item as a basis for extended discussion.

Name other compositions (folk songs, ballads, etc.) that tell a story through the music, and use expressive devices the way Schubert's music does.

Reinforcing the Lesson

Review "Climbing Up to Zion" on page 98 for examples of word painting as an expressive device.

3 APPRAISAL

The students should be able to listen to "The Erlking" and identify the relationship between word painting, pitch register, and harmony.

MORE MUSIC TEACHING IDEAS

Have the students name several cartoon characters and list the characteristics of the music that are used as their themes.

REVIEW AND EVALUATION

JUST CHECKING

Objective
To review and test the skills and concepts taught in Unit 5

Materials
Recordings: Just Checking Unit 5
(questions 3–10)
Unit 5 Evaluation (question 3)
For Extra Credit recordings
(optional)
Recorder, bells or keyboard
Copying Master 5-2 (optional)
Evaluation Unit 5 Copying Master

TEACHING THE LESSON

Review the skills and concepts taught in Unit 5. Have the students:
• Perform the activities and answer the questions on pages 116–117. (For this review, examples for questions 3 through 10 are included in the ''Just Checking Unit 5'' recording. Have the students answer these questions first. Then have them answer the other questions in the review.)
• Review their answers.
(You may wish to use Copying Master 5-2 at this time.)

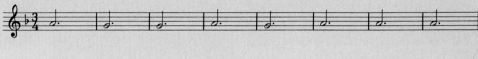

JUST CHECKING

🔊 4B, 5A

💿 3

See how much you remember.

1. Perform this melodic pattern on recorder, bells, or keyboard.

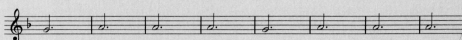

2. Perform this twelve bar blues harmonic progression on bells or keyboard.

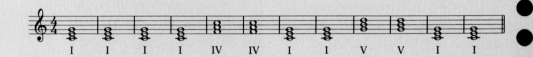

I   I   I   I   IV   IV   I   I   V   V   I   I

3. Listen to part of "Climbing Up to Zion" to review modulation. Decide if the melody sounds higher or lower each time it repeats. higher

4. Listen to a section of the Concertino for Flute and Orchestra and decide how the composer uses dynamics and register to create interest and variety. soft and loud dynamics; high and low register

5. Listen and determine whether the style period for each of these examples is romantic, twentieth century, blues, or gospel. blues, romantic, gospel, twentieth century

6. Listen and determine whether the harmony in each example sounds more consonant or dissonant. consonant, dissonant, consonant, dissonant

116

7. Listen to a section of "Mi Caballo Blanco" and raise your hand when you hear the music modulate.

8. Listen to a section of "Mi Caballo Blanco" and decide if the music modulates to a higher or lower key. *a higher key*

9. As you listen to these examples from "The Erlking," decide which character is singing, based on whether you hear major or minor and the register of the melody. *Erlking*, major, high register; *father*, minor, low register; *son*, minor, high register

10. Listen to Theme A of the *Afro-American Symphony*. Identify the instrumental tone color by naming the picture that best describes what you are hearing. *picture 3*

INTRODUCTION

1 THEME A

SOLO

2 THEME A

SOLO

PIZZICATO

3

FULL ORCHESTRA

4 THEME B

SOLO

WITH OTHER STRINGS

117

GIVING THE EVALUATION

Evaluation Unit 5 Copying Master can be found in the *Teacher's Copying Masters* book along with full directions for giving the evaluation and checking the answers.

FOR EXTRA CREDIT

You may want to have the students respond to the following in a paragraph:

Describe how tone color, melodic register, and major and minor tonalities are used to express the feelings and emotions of the text in "The Erlking." (The music setting of "The Erlking" has four separate characters sung by one voice. Each character has been assigned a specific vocal register—the father is in low register, the Erlking in high register, and so on. The father's voice is assigned a dark tone color while the Erlking is assigned a bright tone color. Only the part of the Erlking is set in major mode. All of the other parts are set in minor mode.) (You may wish to play this recording to refresh students' memories.)

ELEMENTS OF MUSIC	UNIT 6 OBJECTIVES	Lesson 1 Focus: Phrases of Equal Length	Lesson 2 Focus: Phrases of Unequal Length
Dynamics	**Discuss ways in which dynamics affect mood in music** Listen to, identify, and perform contrasting dynamics		Perform a song using contrasting dynamics
Tone Color	Creatively explore tone colors **Perform melodic accompaniment on bells, keyboard, or recorder**	Analyze a composition performed by saxophone and voice	
Tempo	**Discuss ways in which tempo affects mood in music** Identify tempo of a composition		
Duration/ Rhythm	**Perform a rhythmic motive** Perform steady beat Perform music with changing meters	Clap, snap, and step steady beat Identify phrase lengths in popular music	Perform a song with changing meters
Pitch	**Discuss how mode can express the mood of music**		Sing a song with a range of F♯-d¹
Texture	Perform melodic accompaniments	Perform a melodic and harmonic accompaniment on bells, keyboard, or guitar	
Form	**Listen to and identify phrases of different lengths** Identify, create, and perform rhythmic and melodic motives **Identify motive**	Define phrase Listen to, identify, and perform phrases of equal and unequal length Define and perform a harmonic phrase	Listen to and identify phrases of different lengths
Style	Discuss the style of a popular group of the 1980s Discuss musical characteristics of the romantic period and 20th century	Identify musical styles Discuss the pop style of the group Wham!	Listen to and perform songs by popular composers
Reading	Read and play chord pattern Dm Gm B♭ Am throughout a song	Play from melodic notation c-b♭ Read chord symbols Dm Gm B♭ Am	Sing song with changing meters: $\frac{4}{4}$, $\frac{2}{4}$, $\frac{3}{8}$, and *D.S. al Coda*

PURPOSE Unit 6: FORM AND STYLE

In this unit the students will review and extend their knowledge of form. They will explore phrases of equal and unequal length, investigate motives in art and music, discuss strophic form, and experience ballads and art songs.

SUGGESTED TIME FRAME

March				April		

FOCUS

Phrases of Equal Length
Phrases of Unequal Length
Repetition of Motives
Repetition of Sections

Lesson 3 Focus: Repetition of Motives	**Lesson 4** Focus: Repetition of Sections
	Discuss ways in which dynamics can express the mood of a song Listen to and identify dynamics of a song
	Perform accompaniments on bells, recorder, guitar, or keyboard
	Discuss ways in which tempo can influence the mood of a song Listen to and identify the tempo of a song
Perform a rhythmic motive	Create a rhythmic accompaniment
Perform melodic motives on bells, recorder, keyboard, or guitar	Sing a ballad with pitch accuracy Discuss how mode can express the mood of a song Listen to and identify minor mode Sing a song with a range of A-b
	Perform melodic and harmonic accompaniments on bells, recorder, guitar, or keyboard
Identify, define, and perform rhythmic and melodic motives Discuss repetition in paintings and architecture	Define strophic form Listen to, identify and perform a ballad
Discuss the contemporary musical style of Philip Glass Discuss 20th century musical characteristics Define and discuss minimalist music	Identify art song Discuss information on Gordon Lightfoot Discuss the art song and Fanny Mendelssohn Hensel Analyze a German art song Discuss characteristics of the romantic period
Read motives in $\frac{3}{4}$	Read and play accompaniment using pitches g a b c¹ d¹ and chord symbols Am, Em, G, D

BULLETIN BOARD

Have the students collect pictures of buildings, food, fashion, furniture, etc., which illustrate repetition of form, and label them ABA, AAB, ABABA, etc., as appropriate. Using the same illustrations or a different selection, have the students identify the use of motives, listing them and the way they are developed beside each picture.

Dolmen in the Snow, Johann Christian Clausen Dahl,
MUSEUM DER BILDENDEN KÜNSTE, Leipzig

UNIT 6

FORM AND STYLE

118

Three Flags (1958), Jasper Johns. WHITNEY MUSEUM OF AMERICAN ART, NY

Birds of Paradise, Arman. MARISA DEL RE GALLERY, NY

119

LESSON 1

Focus: Phrases of Equal Length

Objectives
To identify and perform phrases of equal length
To perform a melodic and harmonic accompaniment

Materials
Recordings: "Two-Chord Strut"
"Three-Chord Strut"
"Careless Whisper"
"River"
Keyboard, bells, or guitar

Vocabulary
Phrase, harmonic phrase

THE ARTIST

Jasper Johns (b. 1930)—is an American painter and sculptor. Some of his paintings are of numbers, maps, targets, or American flags, because he believes that flat objects are good subjects for paintings, which are also flat. He has made sculptures that are such accurate copies of light bulbs and flashlights that it is very difficult to tell they are not the real thing. In general he is interested in pointing out the most common, popular objects of modern American culture.

LESSON 1

1 SETTING THE STAGE

Discuss the information on phrases. Compare them to sentences, which also are complete thoughts.

2 TEACHING THE LESSON

1. Introduce phrases of equal length.
Have the students:
• Listen to "Two-Chord Strut."
• Clap and snap the two eight-beat phrases as indicated. (Call attention to the two beats of transition in the middle of the piece.)
• Move their hands in an arc to show the length of the phrases.
• Step, stand still, and move their hands in an arc for the two phrases while listening again.
• Listen to "Three-Chord Strut" and change movement patterns as they step each phrase.
2. Introduce phrases in combination.
Have the students:
• Play the melodic accompaniment on keyboard, bells, or guitar while listening to "Careless Whisper."

Phrases can be described as the building blocks of form. A **phrase** is a complete musical idea. Phrases of equal length contain the same number of beats or measures.

As you listen to "Two-Chord Strut":

• Clap the beat to show the length of the first phrase.
• Snap the beat to show the length of the next phrase.
• Move your hands in an arc to show the length of the phrases.

clap   snap

  "Two-Chord Strut,"
by Michael Treni

As you listen to "Two-Chord Strut" again:

• Step the beat to show the length of the first phrase.
• Stand still and move your hands in an arc to show the length of the next phrase.
• Listen to "Three-Chord Strut," and change your movement patterns as you step each phrase.

  "Three-Chord Strut,"
by Michael Treni

In "Two-Chord Strut" and "Three-Chord Strut" most of the phrases are the same length. In the song "Careless Whisper," the composers George Michael and Andrew Ridgeley use layers of phrases of different lengths to create interest and variety.

• Play this melodic accompaniment to "Careless Whisper" on keyboard, bells, or guitar as you listen to the song.

120

E X T E N S I O N

SPECIAL LEARNERS

You may wish to use an overhead transparency of pupil pages 120 and 121 the second time you play "Careless Whisper" for students who have difficulty reading notation. The exceptional students can play the melodic accompaniment on page 120 while the others are playing the harmonic accompaniment on page 121.

MORE MUSIC TEACHING IDEAS

Have the students listen to selected recordings of popular music that use regular phrase structures to determine the number of beats in each phrase.

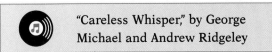 "Careless Whisper," by George Michael and Andrew Ridgeley

- Listen again and play this chord pattern on keyboard, bells, or guitar to accompany the song.

This four-measure chord pattern repeats throughout the song. It establishes a **harmonic phrase** that is sixteen beats long.

- Listen to the opening section of "Careless Whisper." Focus on the number of beats in the phrases performed by the saxophone and the singer.

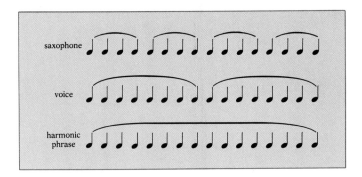

"Careless Whisper" has phrases that are four beats, eight beats, and sixteen beats long. The phrases played on the saxophone are four beats in length. The phrases sung by the lead singer are generally eight beats in length. The harmonic phrase is sixteen beats in length, formed by the four-measure chord patterns.

- As you listen to "Careless Whisper" again, show the three different phrase lengths by moving your hand in an arc from left to right.

121

LESSON 1

- Listen again and play the chord patterns on keyboard, bells, or guitar.
- Identify the patterns as a harmonic phrase.
- Listen to the opening section of "Careless Whisper" (approx. 2 minutes), focusing on the number of beats in the phrases performed by the saxophone and voice. (The saxophone performs four-beat phrases while the voice generally performs eight-beat phrases.)
- Show the three different phrase lengths by moving hands in an arc from left to right.

COOPERATIVE LEARNING

Review the lesson on "Careless Whisper," focusing on the three different phrase lengths. Then have the students work in cooperative groups of four to create a movement routine to show the three phrase lengths. You might tell the students that movement can be shown with only hands, arms, or feet, or a combination. They might also want to use props. Remind the students to be sure that everyone in each group gets a chance to contribute a movement idea. Each group should take into account the abilities of *all* group members; the movement plan should reflect those abilities. Group members should agree that the final product is correct and appropriate in showing phrase lengths. Have the groups practice their movement routines and perform for the class.

SPECIAL LEARNERS

Many different learners may have difficulty understanding abstract symbols and will need a teacher model or cue. Illustrate different phrase lengths on the board or with your arms. Then decide if these learners need additional help in responding to the different phrase lengths while they are listening.

LESSON 1

3. Introduce Wham! Have the students discuss the information on Wham! You may wish to use the following item as a basis for extended discussion.

Discuss the significance of musical groups or performers who have been invited to tour other countries. Despite the vast differences in musical tastes and heritage, how can this type of cultural exchange help to improve relations between nations? (answers will vary)

Reinforcing the Lesson

Review "River" on page 78 and identify phrases of equal length.

3 APPRAISAL

The students should be able to:
1. Show through movement their understanding of regular phrase structures.
2. Perform a melodic and harmonic accompaniment to "Careless Whisper" with accuracy.
3. Identify layers of phrases in "Careless Whisper."

Wham!

George Michael and Andrew Ridgeley of the British group Wham! first met in school in their hometown of Bushey, England. George and Andrew wanted to be pop stars, and in their first group, the Executives, they started writing songs together. Although they were making records as Wham! as early as 1980, they did not produce a top American hit until the release of "Wake Me Up Before You Go-Go" in 1984. Other Wham! hits were "Freedom," "I'm Your Man," and "Christmas."

Wham! achieved international status after the release of "Careless Whisper" in 1985. At the invitation of the Youth Federation of China, Wham! became the first major Western rock band to perform in the People's Republic. Following the release of their third album *Music From the Edge of Heaven*, in 1986, George and Andrew broke up as a duo to follow solo careers.

Wham! in performance.

George Michael and Andrew Ridgeley

122

PHRASES OF DIFFERENT LENGTHS

Key: A major and E major   Starting Pitch: C♯   Scale Tones: See below.

 2A, 3A, 5A

CD 2, 4

In "Careless Whisper" the composers used layers of phrases containing four, eight, and sixteen beats. Each layer was made up of phrases with the same number of beats. In "(Life Is a) Celebration," Rick Springfield uses another technique with phrases to create interest and variety.

• As you listen to "(Life Is a) Celebration," decide if the phrases are all the same length. different lengths

 "(Life Is a) Celebration" by Rick Springfield

• Listen again and move your hand in an arc on each phrase.
• Sing the song.

Scale Tones: A major: *re mi fa fi so la ta ti do¹ re¹ mi¹ fa¹*
E major: *re͵ mi͵ fa͵ so͵ la͵ ta͵ ti͵ do re mi fa so*

"(Life Is a) Celebration"

Words and music by
Rick Springfield

Piano Accompaniment on page PA 20

I was lost on a wind-ing road,_____

I thought that life__ had no-thing left__ to give__

And you came and showed me that just to live_____

was the great-est gift of all. And you showed me

life is a cel-e-bra-tion, and Lord I'm gon-na cel-e-brate.

123

E X T E N S I O N

VOCAL DEVELOPMENT

Rhythmic precision is an important part of the style of "Life is a Celebration." Have the students carefully observe the phrasing markings, and strive for quick, crisp, and clean articulation of vowels and consonants to help capture the performance style of this composition.

LESSON 2

Focus: Phrases of Unequal Length

Objective
To identify phrases of unequal length

Materials
Recordings: "(Life Is a) Celebration"
"Love Song"
"Memory"

1 SETTING THE STAGE

Have the students listen to "(Life Is a) Celebration" and decide if the phrases are all the same length.

2 TEACHING THE LESSON

1. Introduce phrases of unequal length.
Have the students:
• Listen to "(Life Is a) Celebration" again and move their hands in an arc for each phrase.
• Sing the song.

Reinforcing the Lesson

Review "Love Song" on page 46 and "Memory" on page 64 and identify phrases of unequal length.

3 APPRAISAL

The students should be able to identify irregular phrase structures.

THE COMPOSER

Rick Springfield—was born in Sydney, Australia, in 1948. He grew up on army bases in Australia and England. At thirteen Springfield received his first instrument, a guitar. By age sixteen he had organized his first band. In 1972, Springfield moved to the United States to establish a solo career. He appeared as an actor on several major television shows. While he was in the serial "General Hospital," his album *Working Class Dog* became a hit. His eight solo albums have received numerous awards. Springfield wrote "(Life Is a) Celebration" for an episode of the television show "Fame."

LESSON 2

Life is a cel-e-bra-tion, come on now and cel-e-brate, cel-e-brate.

Life is a cel-e-bra-tion, look it's a rev-e-la-tion, so

cel-e-brate now, cel-e-brate life. Cel-e-brate now, cel-e-brate life.

cel-e-brate now, cel-e-brate life. Cel-e-brate now, cel-e-brate life.

Cel-e-brate now, cel-e-brate life.

Cel-e-brate now, cel-e-brate life.

How could I have been so blind, just to think that we were

You came a-long and I was no

liv-ing to die?

lon-ger a-lone,

and you led me to the light.

And you showed me Life is a cel-e-bra-tion, and

124

EXTENSION

SIGNING FOR "(LIFE IS A) CELEBRATION"

Life/Live   Both hands in an "L"
    position move in
unison up the body

Celebration   Both hands hold
   imaginary flags. Wave
them in small circles.

Come   Natural beckoning
   gesture.

Now   The upturned, right-
   angle hands move
down quickly.

Look   The right "V" at the
    eyes turns out so that
the fingertips are
facing out.

124   UNIT 6

Lord, I'm gon - na cel - e-brate. Life is a cel - e - bra - tion,

Life is a cel - e - bra - tion,

cresc.

come on now_ and cel - e-brate, cel - e-brate.

ff

look it's a rev - e - la - tion. So cel - e-brate now, cel - e - brate life.

Cel - e-brate now, cel - e - brate life.

To Coda

Cel - e-brate now, cel - e - brate life. Cel - e-brate now, cel - e - brate life.

Cel - e-brate now, cel - e - brate life. Cel - e-brate now, cel - e - brate life.

D.S. al Coda Coda

Cel - e-brate now, cel - e -

Cel - e-brate now, cel - e -

ff

-brate life. Cel - e - brate, cel - e - brate, cel - e - brate, cel - e - brate,

ff

-brate life. Cel - e - brate, cel - e - brate, cel - e - brate, cel - e - brate,

cel - e -brate, cel - e -brate, cel - e - brate, cel - e - brate life!

cel - e - brate, cel - e -brate, cel - e - brate, cel - e - brate life!

125

Revelation
(Information)

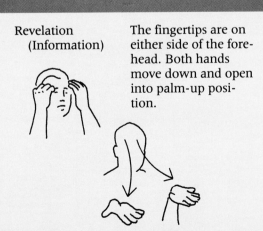

The fingertips are on either side of the fore-head. Both hands move down and open into palm-up posi-tion.

LESSON 3

Focus: Repetition of Motives

Objective
To identify and perform rhythmic and melodic motives

Materials
Recording: "Floe" from *Glassworks*
Keyboard, recorder, bells, or guitar

Vocabulary
Motives, minimalism

1 SETTING THE STAGE

Discuss the information on repetition in architecture and relate it to repetition of motives in music.

EXTENSION

REPETITION: THE BASIS OF FORM

CD 4 Motives in Architecture

When architects design buildings they often repeat small units or shapes such as squares, rectangles, circles, or triangles to create a much larger form. Identify some of the small units used to create the buildings pictured here. Answers will vary.

Below, the chapel at the Air Force Academy in Colorado Springs. Right, the Flatiron Building in New York City. Bottom, Habitat, in Montréal, Canada.

126

Motives in Music

Composers often use repetitions of short musical ideas to develop the form of a composition. These ideas are called *motives*. A **motive** is a short, easily recognized musical unit that keeps its basic identity through many repetitions.

In "Floe" from *Glassworks* by Philip Glass, different motives are used to create a larger form.

- Perform these motives from "Floe" on keyboard, recorder, bells, or guitar.

Motives from "Floe"

- Listen to "Floe" and identify the order in which you hear each motive. 3, 1, 4, 2

 "Floe" from *Glassworks,* by Philip Glass

- Listen again and perform each motive, with the recording, on keyboard, recorder, bells, or guitar.

127

1. Introduce and define *motive*. Have the students:
- Discuss information on motives.
- Perform the motives from "Floe" on keyboard, recorder, bells or guitar.
- Notice that each of these motives is based on the pitches F E D E.
- Listen to "Floe" and identify each new motive as it is introduced by raising their hand.
- Identify the order in which the four motives are introduced.
- Listen again and perform each motive with the recording.

SPECIAL LEARNERS
Use an overhead transparency of pupil page 127 if your class includes students who have difficulty reading notation. Point to the beginning of each line to help the students hear and play each new theme.

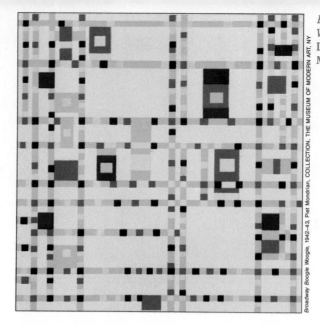

Broadway Boogie Woogie is by the Dutch artist Piet Mondrian.

LESSON 3

2. Introduce motives in visual art.
Have the students:
• Discuss the use of motives in Piet Mondrian's *Broadway Boogie-Woogie.* (repeated square and rectangular shapes give the painting unity)
• Discuss which shape or form serves as a motive for the computer art. (a sphere)

Motives in Art

The use of motives is found in many art forms. The two works shown on this page both use repetition of small forms to create a much larger form. The first, *Broadway Boogie Woogie*, by Piet Mondrian, was inspired by the artist's viewing of the traffic on Broadway from his studio in a nearby skyscraper. He compared the cars and trucks to the rhythms of boogie-woogie. The second work is a piece of computer art. What shape or form serves as a motive for this work? a sphere

128

THE ARTIST

Piet Mondrian (1872–1944) – Dutch painter, is best known for his geometric style. In his paintings he stressed the principle of reducing to horizontal and vertical lines and planes through the use of only white, black, and the primary colors. His art has deeply influenced modern architecture and commercial design. *Broadway Boogie-Woogie* was one of Mondrian's last works. It was inspired by the view of the streets from his New York City studio. His use of small squares creates a playful atmosphere.

Philip Glass and Minimalism

The contemporary composer Philip Glass was born in Baltimore in 1937. Like many composers, he had a traditional musical education. However, he is most noted for his music in the twentieth-century style called **minimalism.**

While studying music in Europe, Glass met the great Indian sitar player Ravi Shankar, who introduced him to Indian classical music. Later, Glass traveled to Morocco and India to study Eastern music first hand. The influence of Eastern music ultimately was reflected in his own music. While he worked to perfect his style back in the United States, Glass took a variety of jobs, including moving furniture, doing carpentry, and driving a cab. About the same time, he met several painters and sculptors who influenced his work. Their method was to emphasize one aspect of visual art (for example, color or texture) to create the greatest possible effect with the least possible means. Glass adapted this method to his music, in combination with characteristics of the Eastern music he had studied.

Minimalist music does not imitate the sound of Eastern music. However, it does contain some of the same techniques, such as repetition of short rhythmic and melodic patterns. This emphasis on repetition is the basis of all minimalist music. In contrast, other Western musical styles emphasize melody or harmony. Young audiences in particular have found Glass's blend of rock realism and Eastern mysticism appealing.

"Floe" is a typical example of the minimalist style. In it, Glass achieves his effects with only a few repeated rhythmic and melodic ideas. By using orchestral instruments—especially the brasses—in unusual ways, Glass creates the tone qualities that are characteristic of minimalist music.

3. Introduce Philip Glass and minimalism. Have the students discuss the information on Philip Glass and minimalism. You may wish to use the following item as a basis for extended discussion.

Philip Glass has composed some of the most exciting contemporary music in the world. After he demonstrated that his new musical ideas were worthwhile, his audiences grew and he again began to receive financial grants and commissions. One of his commissioned works was the music that accompanied the lighting of the torch at the 1984 Olympics. Discuss the meaning of *commissioned.* ("made to order") What are the benefits of this type of an assignment? (The composer knows he/she will be paid for work done.) What are some of the hazards? (The commissioner may not like the finished product; the work may not be exactly to the composer's liking.) (answers will vary)

Reinforcing the Lesson

Have the students create new motives on the pitches used in the "Floe" examples (D, E, F and A) and perform them on keyboard, recorder, bells, or guitar with the recording.

3 APPRAISAL

The students should be able to:
1. Identify repetition in architecture and paintings.
2. Identify and perform motives found in "Floe."
3. Identify the use of motives in minimalist music and certain art forms.

129

LESSON 4

Focus: Repetition of Sections

Objectives
To identify and perform a composition in strophic form
To identify the characteristics of a ballad
To identify the musical characteristics of art song

Materials
Recordings: "The Wreck of the Edmund Fitzgerald"
"Schwanenlied"
"The Erlking"
Keyboard, recorder, or bells

Vocabulary
Ballad, strophic form

1 SETTING THE STAGE

Have the students review the definition of art song on page 111.

2 TEACHING THE LESSON

1. Introduce repetition of sections.
Have the students:
• Discuss the information on ballad, strophic form, and "The Wreck of the Edmund Fitzgerald."
• Listen to "The Wreck of the Edmund Fitzgerald" and follow the story.
• Perform the melodic accompaniment to "The Wreck of the Edmund Fitzgerald" on keyboard, recorder, or bells.

The Ballad

A **ballad** is a narrative poem or song. The ballad is one of the oldest forms of poetry and one of the oldest kinds of music. Its beginnings are almost impossible to trace, partly because the earliest composers of ballads probably could not read or write. The ballad form apparently was established by 1400. Ballads were passed down by word of mouth from generation to generation. European settlers brought their ballads to the New World, besides composing new ones. Some surviving ballads from the 1500s and 1600s were sung in much the same way as we sing them now.

In his ballad "The Wreck of the Edmund Fitzgerald," the composer and singer Gordon Lightfoot tells of the sinking of a giant ore carrier. Seven different verses, all set to repetitions of the same melody and harmony, describe the loss of the *Edmund Fitzgerald* and her twenty-nine crew members in a raging Lake Superior storm in November 1976.

"The Wreck of the Edmund Fitzgerald" is a ballad set in *strophic form*. **Strophic form** repeats the same melody or section of music with each new verse or stanza of text.

• Listen to "The Wreck of the Edmund Fitzgerald" and follow the story.

 "The Wreck of the Edmund Fitzgerald," by Gordon Lightfoot

• Perform the melodic accompaniment to "The Wreck of the Edmund Fitzgerald" on keyboard, recorder, or bells.

130

E X T E N S I O N

SPECIAL LEARNERS
Use an overhead transparency of pupil page 131 if there are any students in the class who have difficulty reading notation. Point to the beginning of each line as the students play the melodic accompaniment to "The Wreck of the Edmund Fitzgerald."

MORE MUSIC TEACHING IDEAS
Have the students create a rhythmic accompaniment to "The Wreck of the Edmund Fitzgerald."

The Wreck of the Edmund Fitzgerald

Words and music by
Gordon Lightfoot

Melodic
Accompaniment

Am	Em
G	D	Am
Am	Em
G	D	Am

1. The leg-end lives on from the Chip-pe-wa on down of the
With a load of iron ore twenty-six thou-sand tons more than the

big lake they called "Git-chee Gu-mee."
Ed-mund Fitz-ger-ald weighed emp-ty,

The lake, it is said, nev-er__ gives up her dead when the
that good ship and true was a__ bone to be chewed when the

skies of No-vem-ber turn gloom-y.__
"Gales of No-vem-ber" came ear-ly.__

song continues on next page

131

LESSON 4

VOCAL DEVELOPMENT

Have the students substitute *loo* for each of the syllables to enhance the qualities of legato style, breath support, and vocal tone associated with this folk song. Emphasis can be placed on the boy's changing voice by having the boys vocalize, using the following pattern:

Loo_____

Continue down to

COOPERATIVE LEARNING

Assign the students to cooperative groups of four. Have each group divide into two pairs. One pair will read and discuss the information on page 111, and the other pair will read and discuss the information on page 130. Then both pairs return to the group and teach the information they have learned to the other pair, comparing and contrasting the two songs. They may wish to create one question from each page to ask another group. If the other group can answer the question, that group wins the right to ask a question. You may wish to use some of the reward strategies referred to on page 93.

LESSON 4

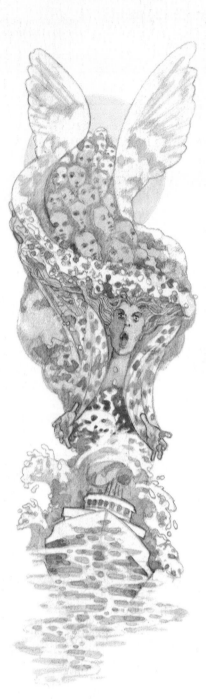

2. ≈≈≈

The ship was the pride of the American side
coming back from some mill in Wisconsin.
As the big freighters go it was bigger than most
with a crew and good captain well seasoned,
concluding some terms with a couple of steel firms
when they left fully loaded for Cleveland.
And later that night when the ship's bell rang,
could it be the north wind they'd been feelin'?

3. ≈≈≈

The wind in the wires made a tattletale sound
and a wave broke over the railing.
And ev'ry man knew as the captain did too
'twas the witch of November come stealin'.
The dawn came late and the breakfast had to wait
when the Gales of November came slashin'.
When afternoon came it was freezin' rain
in the face of a hurricane west wind.

4. ≈≈≈

When suppertime came the old cook came on deck
sayin', "Fellas, it's too rough t' feed ya."
At seven P.M. a main hatchway caved in;
he said, "Fellas, it's bin good t' know ya!"
The captain wired in he had water comin' in
and the good ship and crew was in peril.
And later that night when 'is lights went outta sight
came the wreck of the Edmund Fitzgerald.

5. ≈≈≈

Does anyone know where the love of God goes
when the waves turn the minutes to hours?
The searchers all say they'd have made Whitefish Bay
if they'd put fifteen more miles behind 'er.
They might have split up or they might have capsized;
they may have broke deep and took water.
And all that remains is the faces and the names
of the wives and the sons and the daughters.

6. ≈≈≈

Lake Huron rolls, Superior sings
in the rooms of her ice-water mansion.
Old Michigan steams like a young man's dreams;
the islands and bays are for sportsmen.
And farther below Lake Ontario
takes in what Lake Erie can send her,
and the iron boats go as the mariners all know
with the Gales of November remembered.

7. ≈≈≈

In a musty old hall in Detroit they prayed,
in the "Maritime Sailors' Cathedral."
The church bell chimed 'til it rang twenty-nine times
for each man on the Edmund Fitzgerald.
The legend lives on from the Chippewa on down
of the big lake they call "Gitchee Gumee."
"Superior," they said, "never gives up her dead
when the Gales of November come early!"

GORDON LIGHTFOOT

Canadian singer Gordon Lightfoot was born in 1938 in Ontario. His first musical experience was singing in his church choir. He went to Westlake College of Music in Los Angeles where he studied music theory. He later learned to play the guitar and began to experiment with folk music. It was Bob Dylan's socially conscious music that inspired Lightfoot to write and record his first album, *Lightfoot*.

Lightfoot has enjoyed widespread popularity as a singer and guitarist since the early 1970s with tuneful, easy-to-sing hits such as "Sundown" and "If You Could Read My Mind." His clear, warm voice is the perfect vehicle for his ballads about everyday people and their lives. Lately he has concentrated on writing collections of songs illustrating and praising Canadian life. Like the masterful epic "The Wreck of the Edmund Fitzgerald," most of Lightfoot's songs feature only guitar and voice, allowing him to emphasize the story line and mood.

133

LESSON 4

2. Introduce the composer. Have the students discuss the information on Gordon Lightfoot.

CURRICULUM CONNECTION: SOCIAL STUDIES

Ballads—The ballad is one of the oldest surviving forms of poetry and music. The earliest ballad composers were professional musicians, as well as poets, clergymen, and nobles. Gradually the lower classes became familiar with ballads and began to use them for telling stories and news. These ballads were passed orally from generation to generation. Sixteenth-century ballads were simple compositions; nineteenth-century ballads were complex romantic songs. Appalachia and the Midwest have produced hundreds of mountain and cowboy ballads. The ballad reemerged in popular culture in the 1950s and 1960s with such singers as the Weavers, Bob Dylan, and Joan Baez composing and performing songs of social protest.

LESSON 4

3. Introduce the art song. Have the students:
• Discuss the information on art song.
• Listen to *"Schwanenlied"* and read the English translation of the German text as each number is called, and answer the question.
• Decide which musical characteristics help to express the mood of the song.

4. Introduce the composer. Have the students discuss the information on Fanny Mendelssohn Hensel.
You may wish to use the following item as a basis for extended discussion.

During the nineteenth century women were not expected to follow the same kinds of careers they do today. How might this have affected Fanny Mendelssohn's pursuit of a career in music? (Answers will vary.)

Reinforcing the Lesson

Have the students review "The Erlking" on page 111 as another example of art song. Compare the way the texts, harmonies, dynamics, and pitches create contrast and variety.

3 APPRAISAL

The students should be able to:
1. Identify a song in strophic form.
2. Identify and perform a ballad by singing and accompanying "The Wreck of the Edmund Fitzgerald."
3. Identify the musical characteristics used to create mood "*Schwanenlied.*"

An Art Song

The art song was one of the most important forms of the romantic period. These songs usually combine a solo voice with piano accompaniment. Through poetry and music, art songs express a particular mood or idea, often with deep emotion. Like "The Wreck of the Edmund Fitzgerald," "Schwanenlied" (shvän' en-lēd) is in strophic form. "Schwanenlied" was composed by Fanny Mendelssohn Hensel. The text was written by Heinrich Heine (hīn' riKH hī' nə) (1797–1856), one of the greatest German poets.

• Listen to "Schwanenlied," and read the English translation of the German text on page 135. Decide on a word to describe the mood of the text. sorrowful

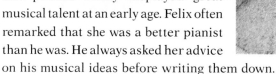

 "*Schwanenlied,*" by Fanny Mendelssohn Hensel

Fanny Mendelssohn Hensel

Fanny Mendelssohn Hensel (1805–1847), German composer and pianist, was the oldest of four children in an extremely talented family. Her grandfather was a well-known philosopher, and her brother Felix also became a renowned composer and pianist. Fanny displayed great musical talent at an early age. Felix often remarked that she was a better pianist than he was. He always asked her advice on his musical ideas before writing them down.

Fanny published only five collections of songs and a piano trio during her lifetime. In fact, her early works were published under Felix's name. Queen Victoria's favorite Mendelssohn song, "*Italien,*" actually was written by Fanny. Her art songs, such as "*Schwanenlied,*" reveal many characteristics of the romantic period, such as direct expression of emotions and long, complex melodies.

134

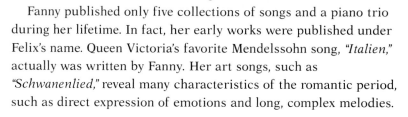

EXTENSION

CURRICULUM CONNECTION: LITERATURE

Heinrich Heine (1797–1856)—was one of the most popular writers of German literature. He was born in Düsseldorf, the eldest son of Jewish parents. He was mainly taught by French priests, and he became deeply influenced by French liberalism. In 1831 he moved to Paris and lived there for the rest of his life. In his writings, Heine tried to bring about greater understanding between the French and German people. One of his poetry collections, *Buch der Lieder* ("Songbook") was set to music by Schubert and Schumann.

MORE MUSIC TEACHING IDEAS

Have the students list important twentieth-century women composers. (Answers will vary; encourage students to name popular music performers and groups.)

Schwanenlied (Swan's Song)

Verse 1

Es fällt ein Stern herunter aus seiner funkelnden Höh,
A star falls down from its sparkling heights.

das ist der Stern der Liebe, den ich dort fallen seh.
That is the star of love that I see falling.

Es fallen von Apfelbaume, der weissen Blätter so viel,
So many white leaves fall from the apple tree

es kommen die neckenden Lüfte, und treiben damit ihr spiel.
The teasing breezes come and playfully use them for their games.

Verse 2

Es singt der Schwan im Weiher, und rudert auf und ab,
The swan sings in the pond and glides back and forth,

und immer leiser singend, taucht er ins Fluthengrab.
And ever so softly singing he dips into the deep watery grave.

Es ist so still und dunkel, verweht ist Blatt und Blüth,
It is so still and dark, leaves and blossoms have disappeared.

der Stern ist knisternd zerstoben, Verklungen das Schwanenlied.
The star's brilliance is gone. The swan's song has died away.

Which of these musical characteristics express the mood of
"Schwanenlied"? slow; minor; mostly soft
slow or fast   major or minor   mostly loud or mostly soft

135

REVIEW AND EVALUATION

JUST CHECKING

Objective
To review and test the skills and concepts taught in Unit 6

Materials
Recordings: Just Checking Unit 6 (questions 4–9)
"Floe"
"The Wreck of the Edmund Fitzgerald"
"Careless Whisper"
Unit 6 Evaluation (question 2)
For Extra Credit recordings (optional)
Keyboard, recorder, bells, or guitar
Copying Master 6-1 (optional)
Evaluation Unit 6 Copying Master

TEACHING THE LESSON

Review the skills and concepts taught in Unit 6. Have the students:

• Perform the activities and answer the questions on pages 136–137. (For this review, examples for questions 4 through 9 are included in the "Just Checking Unit 6" recording. Have the students answer these questions first. Then have them answer the other questions in the review, using the recordings in the unit where necessary.)

• Review their answers.

(You may wish to use Copying Master 6-1 at this time.)

 5A, 5B

CD 4

JUST CHECKING

See how much you remember. Listen to the recording.

1. Listen to the steady beat and perform these motives on keyboard, recorder, bells, or guitar. Perform with "Floe."

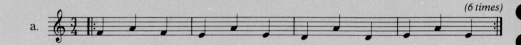
(6 times)

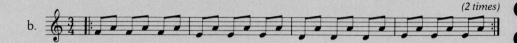
(2 times)

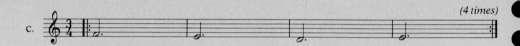
(4 times)

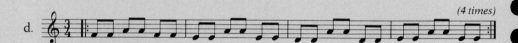
(4 times)

2. Perform this melodic accompaniment on bells, recorder or keyboard. Perform with "The Wreck of the Edmund Fitzgerald."

136

3. Perform this melodic accompaniment on keyboard, bells, or recorder. Perform with "Careless Whisper."

4. Listen to a portion of "The Wreck of the Edmund Fitzgerald" and determine if the form is strophic or ternary. strophic

5. Listen to a portion of "(Life Is a) Celebration" and show the regular and irregular phrase structure by moving your hand in an arc.

6. Listen to "*Schwanenlied*" and decide whether the composition is in major or minor. minor

7. Show the three phrase lengths in "Careless Whisper" by moving your hands in an arc from left to right.

8. Name some musical characteristics that express the mood of "*Schwanenlied.*" slow and mostly soft, minor

9. Listen to a portion of "The Wreck of the Edmund Fitzgerald" and determine if the song is in major or minor. minor

137

REVIEW AND EVALUATION

GIVING THE EVALUATION

Evaluation Unit 6 Copying Master can be found in the *Teacher's Copying Masters* book along with full directions for giving the evaluation and checking the answers.

FOR EXTRA CREDIT

You may want to have the students respond to the following:

Discuss some of the techniques composers use to develop a theme. (repetition of motives, rhythmic alteration, melodic alteration, change of textures, change of tone color, change of register)

(You may wish to play recordings to refresh the students' memories.)

ELEMENTS OF MUSIC	UNIT 7 OBJECTIVES	Lesson 1 Focus: Classical Symphony	Lesson 2 Focus: Development of a Musical Idea
Dynamics	Follow dynamics from a listening map Listen to and identify contrasting dynamics		Follow dynamics of a symphony from a listening map
Tone Color	Listen to and identify the orchestra	Listen to a symphony orchestra	Listen to a symphony orchestra
Tempo	Perform a free form composition keeping a steady tempo		
Duration/ Rhythm	**Identify rhythmic motives** **Define *legato* and *staccato* articulation**	Locate, identify and perform rhythmic motives following a listening map Perform rhythmic motives by using body movement Define *legato* and *staccato* articulation	Identify, perform, and create rhythmic motives
Pitch	Follow a melodic listening map Create a melodic motive Identify pitch levels and major/minor tonality Read and perform spoken music		Sing a song with a range of e-d' Perform a melody on bells, recorder, and keyboard Perform and create a melodic motive Listen to and identify levels of pitch
Texture			
Form	**Discuss and identify motives** **Discuss sonata allegro form** **Listen to and identify free form** Discuss, create, and perform a composition in free form	Identify rhythmic and melodic motives Analyze and discuss repeated motives as a unifying device	Define development Define and discuss sonata allegro form Discuss the symphony
Style	**Identify musical characteristics of the classical and neoclassical style period** **Identify program music**	Discuss characteristics of the classical period Identify composers of the classical period	Discuss neoclassical style
Reading	Read *staccato* and *legato* patterns:	Read rhythms in $\frac{2}{4}$ Recognize *staccato* and *legato* Read score Follow listening map	Follow listening map

PURPOSE Unit 7: ELEMENTS OF FORM

In this unit the students will extend their concept of form. They will develop an awareness of the use of motives and will investigate the classical aesthetic principles of unity, variety, and clarity. They will define and experience sonata allegro form, be introduced to program music, and investigate free form.

SUGGESTED TIME FRAME

April			May		

FOCUS

Classical Symphony
Development of a Musical Idea
Program Music
Free Form

Lesson 3 Focus: Program Music	Lesson 4 Focus: Free Form
Identify the contrasting dynamics of a composition	
	Read and perform a composition for spoken chorus
Identify major/minor tonality	
Listen to and identify themes in a composition	Identify, listen to, define, discuss, create, and perform a composition in free form
Identify, define, and listen to program music Define absolute music <mark>Create program music</mark>	Discuss creative developments in 20th century art
Follow listening map	Read contemporary score in $\frac{6}{8}$

BULLETIN BOARD

Have the students collect or create representations of realistic and abstract art to demonstrate the differences between organized and free forms. Clearly display and label the two groups and add to each as the students move through the unit, for example: pictures of clarity, form and order (eighteenth-century gardens, buildings, etc.) to illustrate the classical period; those telling a story to illustrate program music; and some twentieth-century abstract forms to represent free form.

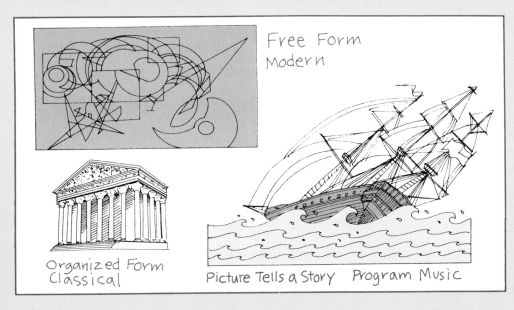

Free Form
Modern

Organized Form
Classical

Picture Tells a Story   Program Music

UNIT **7**

ELEMENTS
OF FORM

138

Still Life with Fruit Bowls, Carafe, and Fruit. Paul Cézanne. LOUVRE, Paris

View from Wind River Mountains, Wyoming. Albert Bierstadt. THE MUSEUM OF FINE ARTS, Boston

139

LESSON 1

Focus: Classical Symphony

Objectives
To develop awareness of the use of a motive
To identify legato and staccato
To explore aspects of the classical period and its aesthetic principles of unity, variety and clarity
To listen to a complete movement of a symphony

Materials
Recordings: "Beethoven Seventh Motive Montage"
Beethoven, Symphony No. 7, Second Movement
Mozart, Quintet for Clarinet and Strings in A Major, Fourth Movement (optional)

Vocabulary
Legato, staccato

1 SETTING THE STAGE

Tell the students they will learn about new ways to use themes and motives in music.

THE ARTISTS

Albert Bierstadt (bēr′ stät) (1830–1902) —was born in Germany and grew up in the United States. He painted romanticized panoramas of the American West, such as the *View from Wind River Mountains*. He was very successful because many people of his time had not seen the scenery of the West, and he was considered one of the greatest American landscape painters of the time.

Paul Cézanne (se′ zän) (1839–1906)—was a French painter who aimed to see objects as spheres, cylinders, cones, and other basic forms. He painted very slowly, so he liked to paint apples because they did not move or rot quickly.

UNIT 7   **139**

LESSON 1

2 TEACHING THE LESSON

1. Introduce the motives in the second movement of Beethoven's Seventh Symphony. Have the students:

• Perform each of the rhythmic motives from Symphony No. 7 using pats, claps, and snaps.

• Analyze melodies a, b, and c and identify which of the rhythm motives 1, 2, and 3 goes with each melody, (1, b; 2, a; 3, c)

Identifying Motives

The second movement of Ludwig van Beethoven's Symphony No. 7 is based on repetition of rhythmic and melodic motives.

• Perform these rhythmic motives by patting the quarter notes, pat-sliding the tied notes, clapping the eighth notes, and snapping the triplets with alternating hands.

Each of the following melodies uses one of the rhythmic motives you have performed.

• Identify the melody that uses rhythmic motive 1, motive 2, and motive 3. 1,b; 2,a; 3,c

140

EXTENSION

SPECIAL LEARNERS

Prepare an overhead transparency of pupil page 140 if there are students in the class who have difficulty reading notation. Point to each beat when the students play motives 2 and 3 together. This will enable the students to coordinate the two rhythm patterns. You may also wish to split the class into two groups, assigning a line to each.

- Listen and match the rhythmic motives 1, 2, or 3 with recorded examples a, b, and c from the second movement of the Seventh Symphony. 1, b; 2, a; 3, c

Beethoven Seventh Motive Montage

Which of the melodies in the Beethoven Seventh Motive Montage sounded smooth and connected? *a*

Which of the melodies sounded detached and crisp? *b* and *c*

Music that sounds smooth is said to be performed **legato** (le-gä′ tō). Music that sounds detached and crisp is said to be performed **staccato** (stä-kä′ tō). Notes to be played or sung staccato are written this way: ♪ or ♩ .

Symphony orchestras often consist of over a hundred musicians. These two photos show the Boston Symphony Orchestra in performance.

LESSON 1

- Listen to the Beethoven Seventh Motive Montage and match rhythmic motives 1, 2, or 3 with recorded examples a, b, and c. (1, b; 2, a; 3, c)

2. Introduce legato and staccato. Have the students:
- Identify which term is appropriate for the melodies in the Beethoven Seventh Motive Montage.
- Discuss the differences between the terms legato and staccato, with emphasis on using the terms in the discussion.
- Identify examples of legato and staccato in popular tunes of today. (answers will vary)

COOPERATIVE LEARNING

Place the following articulation markings on the board:

⌢   ....

After identifying and reviewing legato and staccato, have the students work in cooperative groups to find examples with the first six units of the text of melodies that contain legato and staccato. Each student in the cooperative groups should find an example within the designated portion of the text to validate the specific category. Each member of the group will then present his or her example, providing documentation as to how it fits the assigned category. The validated examples for the entire group should be listed on a sheet of paper, which is then signed by all of the group members.

SPECIAL LEARNERS

You may wish to use an overhead transparency of pupil pages 140 and 141 if there are students in the class who have difficulty coordinating visual and audio skills. After each melody, pause to allow the students to choose the correct response. Then mark the correct response on the overhead transparency.

LESSON 1

3. Introduce identifying motives in a listening map. Have the students:

• Listen to the first portion of the second movement of Beethoven's Symphony No. 7 and point to each repetition of the motive on the map.
• Locate rhythmic motives 2 and 3.
• Listen to the entire second movement and point to the rhythmic motives as they follow the map.

Identifying Motives in a Listening Map

• Listen to the first portion of the second movement of Beethoven's Symphony No. 7. When you hear rhythmic motive 1 (♩ ♫ | ♩ ♩), find it on the map.

 Symphony No. 7, Second Movement, by Ludwig van Beethoven

• Examine the map. Find rhythmic motive 2 (♩ ♩ | ♩) and rhythmic motive 3 (♫ ♫).
• Follow the map as you listen to the second movement of Beethoven's Symphony No. 7.

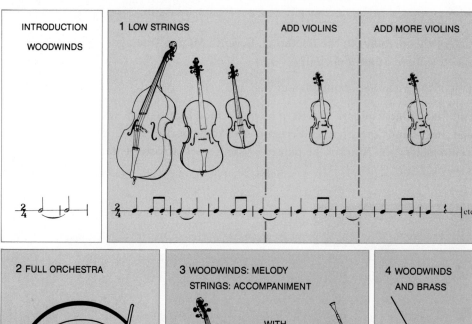

INTRODUCTION
WOODWINDS

1 LOW STRINGS   ADD VIOLINS   ADD MORE VIOLINS

2 FULL ORCHESTRA

3 WOODWINDS: MELODY
STRINGS: ACCOMPANIMENT
WITH

4 WOODWINDS
AND BRASS

STRINGS

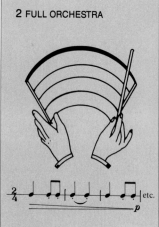

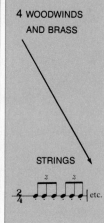

142

5 STRING BASSES: MELODY (PIZZICATO)

WOODWINDS
AND STRINGS:
ACCOMPANIMENT

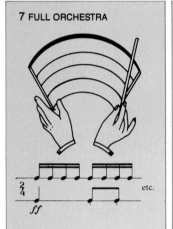

6 POLYPHONY

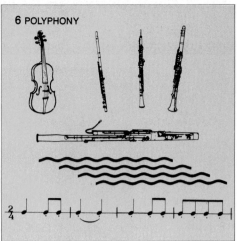

7 FULL ORCHESTRA

ff   etc.

8 WOODWINDS: MELODY

STRINGS: ACCOMPANIMENT

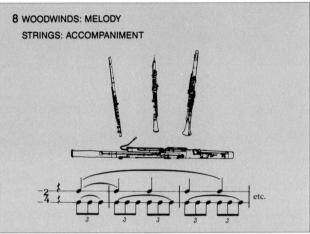

etc.

9 CODA

STRINGS (PIZZICATO) AND
WOODWINDS

WITH

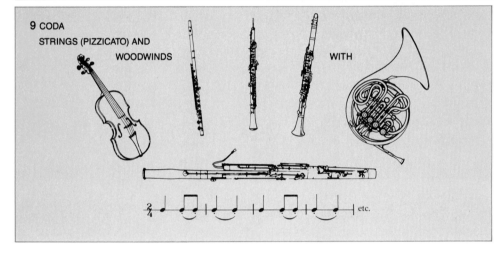

etc.

THE COMPOSER

Ludwig van Beethoven (1770–1827)—great German composer, was born in Bonn. He showed great promise on both the violin and piano at an early age. By age twelve he was publishing his keyboard compositions. In 1792 Beethoven moved to Vienna, where he studied composition with Haydn and Salieri. Beethoven began to lose his hearing by the late 1790s. As he lost his hearing, he began to withdraw from his friends and became extremely suspicious and sensitive. Many of his greatest works, such as the Ninth Symphony, were written when he was almost completely deaf. The Seventh Symphony was also written during this period. The first performance was at a benefit concert for wounded Austrian soldiers on December 8, 1813.

LESSON 1

4. Review the classical period. Have the students:
• Discuss the characteristics of the classical period.
• Examine the pictures from the period.
• Define and identify Beethoven as being a bridge composer. Evidence used to support this should be his life dates (1770–1827) and a combination of both classical and romantic characteristics present in the ABA structure of the second movement. (romantic: drama, intense expression; classical: repetition, variety, balance and unity)

Reinforcing the Lesson

Review motives in music (pages 127–129) and compare the ways Beethoven and Glass incorporate motives in their compositions.

3 APPRAISAL

The students should be able to:
1. Find, identify, and perform motives found in the second movement of Beethoven's Seventh Symphony.
2. Analyze and discuss repeated motives as a unifying device.
3. Identify and define the expressive markings of legato and staccato as contained in the second movement of Beethoven's Seventh Symphony.
4. Define and discuss the artistic principles of unity, variety, balance, and clarity as found in the classical period.

Artists of the classical period often depicted scenes of ancient Greece and Rome.

Countryside of Arcadia. Nicolas Poussin. LOUVRE, Paris

The Classical Period (1750-1830)

The characteristics of music from the classical period are charm, delicacy, and gracefulness. Melodies generally are short and tuneful. Beneath this seeming simplicity there are often deeper feelings; however, these feelings are usually understated. A single section of a classical work can have contrasting moods, and dynamic changes include crescendo and decrescendo. Classical composers wrote operas and concertos, as did the earlier baroque composers. They also established some new musical forms, the symphony and the string quartet.

The orchestra of today developed during this period in musical history. Great composers of the classical period include Haydn (hī′ dən) and Mozart (mōt′ särt). Early works of Beethoven are often considered to be classical in style. However, Beethoven is credited by most musicians with ushering in the next great period in musical history, the romantic period.

144

The Pantheon, Paris

Characteristics of Classical Period Music

Changes of mood within
sections of a composition
Dynamic changes including
crescendo and decrescendo
Short, tuneful melodies
Controlled feelings or emotions
Emphasis on unity and balance

Hippocrates Refusing the Presents of Artaxerxes. Anne-Louis Girodet-Trioson. FACULTÉ DE MEDECINE, Paris

Above,
architects of
the classical
period often
were
influenced by
Greek and
Roman styles.
Left, this
painting
illustrates a
scene from the
life of
Hippocrates,
the ancient
Greek "father
of medicine."

145

MORE MUSIC TEACHING IDEAS

Have the students listen to the fourth
movement of Mozart's Quintet for Clarinet
and Strings in A Major, K. 581 (page 194),
an example of the classical style.

LESSON 2

Focus: Development of a Musical Idea

Objectives
To identify and perform techniques of development
To identify and define sonata allegro form

Materials
Recordings: Beethoven, Symphony No. 7, Second Movement
Prokofiev, *Classical Symphony*, First Movement
Keyboard, recorder, or bells

Vocabulary
Development, rhythmic motive, melodic motive, symphony, sonata allegro form, introduction, exposition, recapitulation, neoclassical

1 SETTING THE STAGE

Review the repetition of rhythmic and melodic motives in the second movement of Beethoven's Symphony No. 7, pages 142–143.

2 TEACHING THE LESSON

1. Introduce repetition in visual art. Have the students compare the different shapes and forms in Arthur Dove's painting *Clouds and Water*.

CD 4 **Repetition in Art**

Arthur Dove's painting *Clouds and Water* is made up of simple curved shapes that are repeated and contrasted. The waves in the water are repeated in the shapes of the mountains and clouds. Contrast is provided by the different colors of the water, land, and sky. The sails on the three boats provide additional contrasts of color and movement. Each area of the painting is an adaptation, expansion, contraction, alteration, or elaboration of a basic curved shape.

• Compare the different shapes and forms in the painting.

Clouds and Water. Arthur G. Dove. THE METROPOLITAN MUSEUM OF ART, NY

146

Transforming a Musical Idea

Key: F major   Starting Pitch: F
Scale Tones: *ti do re mi fa so la*

Like the artist who painted *Clouds and Water,* a composer may decide to adapt, expand, contract, alter, or elaborate a musical idea. This transformation of a musical idea is known as **development.**

Because the melody of "America" is well known, you can probably remember how different parts of the song sound. This should enable you to explore some of the techniques composers use to develop a musical idea.

• Sing through one verse of "America." Use the lyrics to help you keep track of each measure while you are singing.

America

Words by Samuel F. Smith
Music by Henry Carey

How many times does the rhythmic pattern ♩ ♩ ♩ | ♩. ♪ ♩ appear in the song? 4

The rhythmic pattern you just identified is called a **rhythmic motive.**

• Perform the beginning of "America."

• Create your own rhythmic motives by changing the rhythm of one measure.

You have just altered the rhythm of the melody.

147

LESSON 2

2. Introduce transformation of a musical idea. Have the students:
• Discuss the information on development, or transformation, of a musical idea.
• Sing through one verse of "America."
• Count the number of times the rhythmic motive of measures 1 and 2 appears in the song.
• Perform the beginning of "America."
• Create their own rhythmic motives by changing the rhythm of one measure.

LESSON 2

- Perform "America" on keyboard, recorder or bells.
- Create a new melodic motive by performing measures 1 and 11 together.
- Create further motives by combining other measures of the song.
- Perform measures 7 and 8, then 9 and 10, and decide if the latter two measures are higher or lower than the former. Decide if they have the same or different rhythm patterns.
- Discuss the different techniques which can be used to develop a musical idea.

- Perform "America" on keyboard, recorder, or bells.
- Perform measure 1 and then measure 11.

My coun-try   from ev - 'ry___

You have just created a **melodic motive** from portions of "America."

- Create your own melodic motives by combining other measures of the song.
- Perform measures 7 and 8, then perform measures 9 and 10.

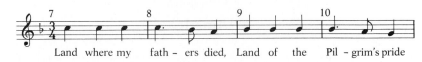

Land where my   fath - ers died, Land of the   Pil - grim's pride

Do measures 9 and 10 sound higher or lower than measures 7 and 8? lower

Do they have the same or different rhythm patterns? same

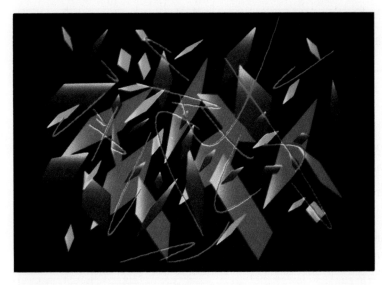

Although the diamond shapes in this computer art are turned at different angles, you can still recognize their basic form.

You can use any of these techniques, along with many others, to develop a musical idea:

> Altering rhythms
> Altering melodies
> Creating rhythmic and melodic motives

148

SPECIAL LEARNERS

Use an overhead transparency of page 147 if there are students in the class who have difficulty reading notation. Point or call out each measure while the students perform the melody to "America."

Organization in the First Movement of a Symphony

The symphony as a musical art form emerged during the classical period. A **symphony** is a long orchestral work organized into four movements. The first movement is almost always in what is called *sonata allegro form*. **Sonata allegro form** consists of three sections much like ABA form.

The A section sometimes begins with a foreshadowing of the musical ideas to come. This is called the *introduction* and is followed by the presentation of two or more musical ideas or themes. These themes are often contrasting in nature. The presentation of the themes is called the *exposition*. The B section is developmental. Here the themes presented in the exposition are adapted, expanded, contracted, altered, and elaborated. The composer uses a variety of techniques to transform the original musical ideas. The last section of sonata allegro form is the *recapitulation* in which the composer restates each of the themes. This section sometimes ends with a summary called the *coda*.

The following diagram depicts sonata allegro form graphically.

A	B	A
Exposition	Development	Recapitulation
(Ideas stated)	(Ideas transformed)	(Ideas restated)
Themes A and B introduced	Themes A and B developed	Themes A and B restated

Twentieth-century composer Sergei Prokofiev (ser-gā′ prō-kof′ yəf) (1891–1953) wrote his first symphony in the style of the classical period. The symphony is referred to as **neoclassical** since it exhibits all the characteristics of a classical symphony but was written almost a century after the close of that musical period.

The first movement of Prokofiev's Symphony No. 1 in D Major, or *Classical Symphony,* is an excellent example of sonata allegro form.

149

3. Introduce development in the first movement of a symphony. Have the students:
• Discuss the information on the symphony and sonata allegro form.
• Discuss the information on Sergei Prokofiev.
You may wish to use the following as a basis for extended discussion.

Prokofiev is famous for his use of humor in music. How does he use this talent in the first movement of his *Classical Symphony*? (He uses twentieth-century techniques to exaggerate the eighteenth-century forms.) Describe some other ways to show humor in music. (surprises, abrupt changes in pace, use of unusual instruments and unusual combinations of instruments, and so on)

THE COMPOSER

Sergei Prokofiev (1891–1953)—was a leading Soviet composer. Prokofiev was born in the Ukraine and received his first musical training from his mother, an amateur pianist. At thirteen he entered the St. Petersburg Conservatory where he studied composition with Rimsky-Korsakov. He graduated in 1914, receiving the Anton Rubinstein Prize—a grand piano. In 1918 he left Russia and spent sixteen years in France, Germany, and the United States. In 1934 Prokofiev returned to Russia, where he composed most of his major works. The *Classical Symphony* was written early in his career and was first performed in the spring of 1918. In this work he re-created the formal style popular in the eighteenth century while using many twentieth-century techniques.

LESSON 2

4. Introduce the listening map. Have the students follow the listening map of the first movement of Prokofiev's *Classical Symphony* while listening to the music.

Reinforcing the Lesson

Have the students take familiar melodies and experiment with creating techniques for developing a musical idea. (change of rhythm, change of register)

3 APPRAISAL

The students should be able to:
1. Identify and perform examples of developmental techniques on keyboard, recorder or bells.
2. Identify and define sonata allegro form.
3. Accurately follow a listening map of the *Classical Symphony*.

• Follow the listening map of the first movement of Prokofiev's *Classical Symphony,* as you listen to the music.

 Classical Symphony, First Movement, by Sergei Prokofiev

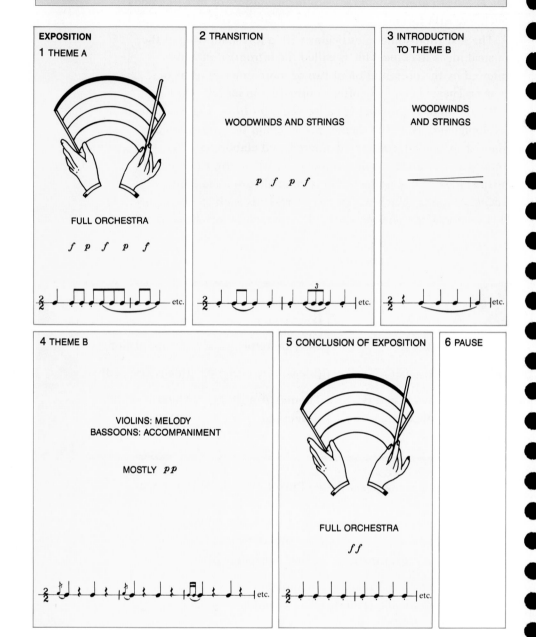

150

E X T E N S I O N

SPECIAL LEARNERS

Prepare an overhead transparency of pupil pages 150 and 151 if the class includes students who have difficulty with abstract musical notation or have visual tracking disabilities. Pause after each call number and point to the different thematic motives. This will enable the students to better understand sonata allegro form.

LISTENING

You may wish to use the Listening Map overhead transparency to help guide the students through the listening selection.

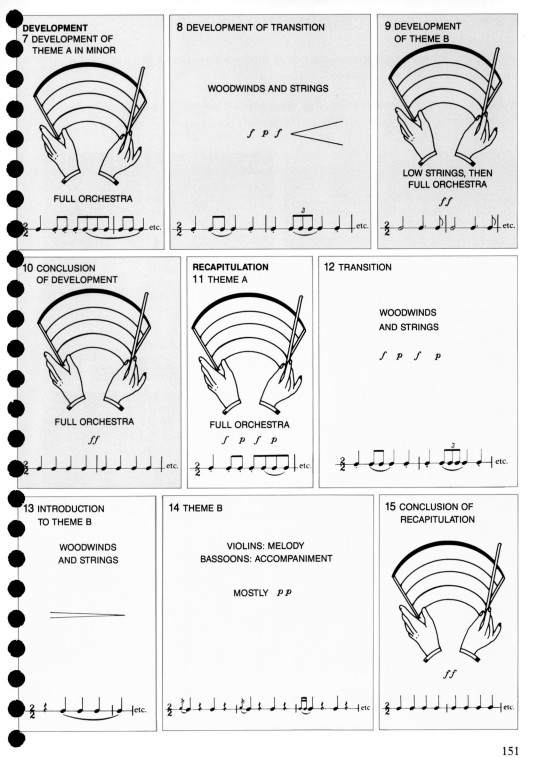

DEVELOPMENT
7 DEVELOPMENT OF THEME A IN MINOR
FULL ORCHESTRA

8 DEVELOPMENT OF TRANSITION
WOODWINDS AND STRINGS
f p f

9 DEVELOPMENT OF THEME B
LOW STRINGS, THEN FULL ORCHESTRA
ff

10 CONCLUSION OF DEVELOPMENT
FULL ORCHESTRA
ff

RECAPITULATION
11 THEME A
FULL ORCHESTRA
f p f p

12 TRANSITION
WOODWINDS AND STRINGS
f p f p

13 INTRODUCTION TO THEME B
WOODWINDS AND STRINGS

14 THEME B
VIOLINS: MELODY
BASSOONS: ACCOMPANIMENT
MOSTLY *pp*

15 CONCLUSION OF RECAPITULATION
ff

151

MORE MUSIC TEACHING IDEAS

Have the students examine other art forms that are neoclassical in style. (for example, the Lincoln Memorial in Washington, D.C.)

LESSON 3

Focus: Program Music

Objectives
To identify and define program music
To listen to a composition based on a story

Materials
Recordings: "The Erlking"
"The Wreck of the Edmund Fitzgerald"
"Program Music Example" ("The Steel Foundry" by Mossolov)
"Marche"
Wellington's Victory Theme Montage
Wellington's Victory
"The Birth of Kijé" (optional)
"The Wedding of Kijé" (optional)
"April Rain Song" (optional)

Percussion instruments, keyboard, recorder, guitar, and bells

Vocabulary
Absolute music

1 SETTING THE STAGE

Review "The Erlking" (page 111) and "The Wreck of the Edmund Fitzgerald" (page 130), both of which represent pictures through music and are a kind of program music.

2 TEACHING THE LESSON

1. Introduce program music. Have the students:
• Discuss the information on program music.
• Examine the pictures and imagine what the music might sound like for each.

PROGRAM MUSIC

Sounds can be used to convey simple or complex ideas. They can also be organized to depict images or scenes.

• Before listening to music related to one of these scenes, imagine what the music for each picture might sound like.

• Listen to the music and select the scene that is most like the music. factory scene

 Program Music Example

152

E X T E N S I O N

The terms below describe some of the musical characteristics of pitch, rhythm, and tone color that helped you select the scene. Which characteristics helped you make your choice?

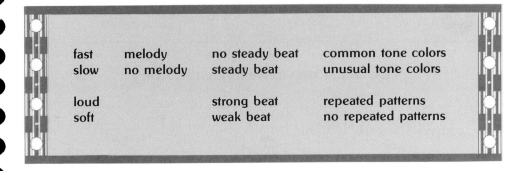

fast	melody	no steady beat	common tone colors
slow	no melody	steady beat	unusual tone colors
loud		strong beat	repeated patterns
soft		weak beat	no repeated patterns

The term *program music* is often used to describe musical works that tell a story, describe an action or event, paint a picture, or create an impression. The term is used in contrast to **absolute music**, music which attempts to do none of those things.

Program music was a popular style of the nineteenth century. People were interested in poetry, prose, mythology, history, and current events. They especially enjoyed hearing musical interpretations of those interests. Composers often used literature or history as a guide for developing their music.

Wellington's Victory by Ludwig van Beethoven is an example of program music that depicts a dramatic battle in 1813 between the French and British armies.

You may recognize three of the main themes in *Wellington's Victory*. The first theme, representing the British army, is "Rule Britannia." This theme is often used in films or on television to represent the British people. The second theme, "Marlborough," represents the French army and is best known to small children as "The Bear Went Over the Mountain." The last popular theme heard is "God Save the King," which uses the same melody as our own patriotic song "America."

• Listen to the three main themes used by Beethoven in *Wellington's Victory*.

 Wellington's Victory Theme Montage

153

• Listen to "Program Music Example" and select the scene which is most like the music.
• Discuss the terms used to describe musical characteristics.
2. Introduce *Wellington's Victory*. Have the students:
• Discuss information on program and absolute music. Compare examples of the two. (e.g., "Marche" by Lully, "The Erlking" by Schubert)
• Discuss the information on *Wellington's Victory*.
• Listen to the three main themes used by Beethoven in *Wellington's Victory*.

CURRICULUM CONNECTION: SOCIAL STUDIES

History—*Wellington's Victory* was written to celebrate the Duke of Wellington's victory over Napoleon's armies at Vittoria in 1813. Beethoven was ask to write a composition to celebrate the victory by Johann Mälzel, the inventor of the modern metronome. Mälzel thought that the piece with such easily recognizable themes as "Rule Britannia" and "God Save the King" would be well received in both Vienna and England. The piece, also known as the "Battle Symphony," was originally written for the Panharmonicon, a mechanical instrument intended to reproduce the sound of an entire orchestra. The first performance of the piece took place on December 8, 1813, at a benefit for wounded Austrian soldiers.

LESSON 3

3. Introduce the listening map to *Wellington's Victory*. Have the students follow the listening map as they listen to the recording of *Wellington's Victory*.

Reinforcing the Lesson

Identify examples of program music from popular music of today. (answers will vary)

3 APPRAISAL

The students should be able to:
1. Identify and define program music.
2. Follow a listening guide to *Wellington's Victory*.

 As you listen to *Wellington's Victory*, follow the listening map. You can determine the losers because the theme representing the defeated army is played in minor and at a soft dynamic level.

Wellington's Victory, by Ludwig van Beethoven

Listening Map to *Wellington's Victory*

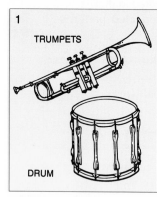

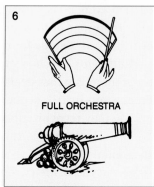

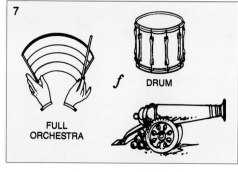

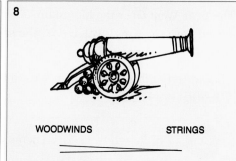

154

SPECIAL LEARNERS

Prepare an overhead transparency of pupil pages 154 and 155 if there are students in the class who have difficulty coordinating visual and audio skills. Point to each call number to help the students clearly identify each theme. This will enable the students to better understand the concept of program music.

MORE MUSIC TEACHING IDEAS

Have the students listen to "The Birth of Kijé" and "The Wedding of Kijé" from Prokofiev's *Lieutenant Kijé Suite* (page 204), another example of program music.

LISTENING

You may wish to use the Listening Map overhead transparency to help guide the students through the listening selection.

9

WOODWINDS   STRINGS

10

VICTORY!

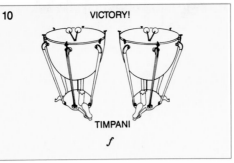

TIMPANI

f

11

"GOD SAVE THE KING"

p

12

VICTORY!

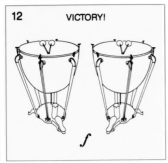

f

13

"GOD SAVE THE KING"

p f p f p f p f p f p f p f p f

14

STRINGS

FRENCH HORN

OBOE

so

‖: mi   fa   :‖

15

POLYPHONY
STRINGS

16

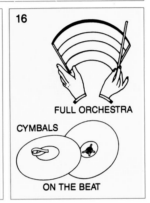

FULL ORCHESTRA

CYMBALS

ON THE BEAT

17

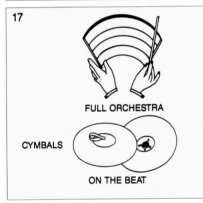

FULL ORCHESTRA

CYMBALS

ON THE BEAT

18

STRINGS, THEN

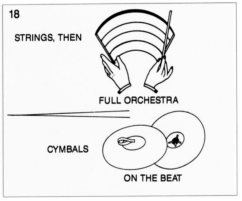

FULL ORCHESTRA

CYMBALS

ON THE BEAT

155

MORE MUSIC TEACHING IDEAS

Have the students read "April Rain Song" by Langston Hughes. Create a composition using classroom instruments to depict the images in the poem.

April Rain Song

Let the rain kiss you.
Let the rain beat upon your head with
    silver liquid drops.
Let the rain sing you a lullaby.
The rain makes still pools on the sidewalk.
The rain makes running pools in the gutter.
The rain plays a little sleep-song on our
    roof at night—and I love the rain.

—Langston Hughes

LESSON 4

Objectives
To identify and define free form
To perform a composition in free form
To create a composition in free form

Materials
Recording: "A Marvelous Place"
Percussion instruments, keyboard, recorder, guitar, bells
Ice cream or other sticks (at least eight)

Vocabulary
Free form

1 SETTING THE STAGE

Discuss the art shown and look for characteristics of twentieth-century style.

2 TEACHING THE LESSON

1. Introduce twentieth-century styles in music. Have the students discuss the information on creative developments in the twentieth century.

6A
CD 4

CREATIVITY IN THE TWENTIETH CENTURY

Creativity in Art

The creative principles of balance, unity, control, and variety were extremely important during the baroque, classical, and romantic periods. Some artists of the twentieth century have continued the traditions of the past. To others creativity has been characterized by a search for new ideas and new sounds.

● Examine the contemporary works of art pictured on these pages. Which works illustrate the experimentation of the twentieth century? Which works illustrate the principles emphasized during earlier style periods?
  Moore, Picasso, Cornell; Valerio

Street View, James Valerio, FRUMKIN/ADAMS GALLERY, NY, Collection of Dr. Larry and Marlene Milner

Artists of the twentieth century have created art in many styles. The painting above is by the American artist James Valerio. The sculpture at right is by the English artist Henry Moore.

Family Group, Henry Moore, THE TATE GALLERY, London

156

E X T E N S I O N

THE ARTIST

Henry Moore (1898–1986)—was an English sculptor whose works are large stone figures. He used holes or openings in the stone to create a sense of mass. Many of Moore's sculptures are designed to stand outdoors.

Three Musicians. Pablo Picasso. PHILADELPHIA MUSEUM OF ART

Pablo Picasso painted *Three Musicians* (left) in 1921. Joseph Cornell created his "pantry ballet" just for fun.

A Pantry Ballet (for Jacques Offenbach). Joseph Cornell. THE NELSON-ATKINS MUSEUM OF ART, Kansas City, MO

157

THE ARTIST

Pablo Picasso (pä'blō pē-käs' sō) (1881–1973)—was born in Spain and worked in France. He was a pioneer in many styles of painting during his lifetime, and was one of the most famous painters of the twentieth century. In one of his styles, Picasso painted more than one side of his subject and put pieces of the many views together in overlapping geometric shapes. In the *Three Musicians,* for example, three musicians are visible and are portrayed in an original combination of shapes.

LESSON 4

2. Introduce a composition in free form. Have the students:
• Discuss the information on the structure of "A Marvelous Place."
• Examine the score and identify the six events whose order can change in each performance. (all lines except the beginning and the ending)
• Listen to the music and follow the score in preparation for performing this composition.

A Composition in Free Form

"A Marvelous Place" is a composition for speaking chorus. The score for this composition looks unusual because it is in *free form*. A composition is in **free form** when the order of the individual sections of the piece can change from one performance to the next. "A Marvelous Place" contains six events that can be performed in any order.

• Examine the score and identify the six events which can change.
• Listen to the recording and follow the score to get ready to perform this composition.

 "A Marvelous Place"

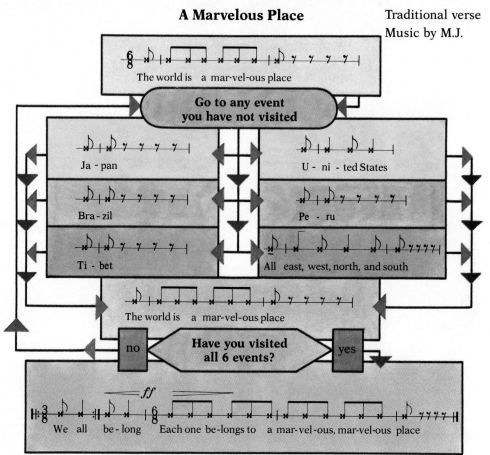

A Marvelous Place

Traditional verse
Music by M.J.

158

repeat gradually louder until all parts are performing

Creating Free Compositions

Free composition is not new. Composers in different style periods have experimented with giving up their power to make decisions about melody, harmony, tone color, and form. In 1751, William Hayes, an English composer, wrote *The Art of Composing Music by a Method Entirely New, Suited to the Meanest Capacity*. He described a method in which a small paint brush is dipped in ink. The brush then is shaken over music paper so that the ink falls on the staff lines. The ink splatterings then become the note heads. The classical composer Wolfgang Amadeus Mozart created music in which melodies were to be played in an order determined by a spinning dial, such as you see at carnivals.

Here are several suggestions to help you create free compositions. What is free about each of these compositional techniques? Answers will vary.

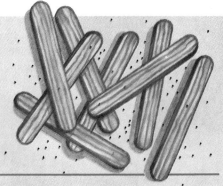

Stick Melody
1. Choose eight pitches.
2. Assign each pitch a number.
3. Number eight sticks.
4. Drop the sticks and read from left to right to determine the order of pitches to be performed.

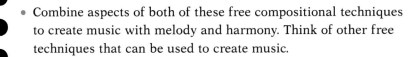

Telephone Harmony

A	0
B'	1'
C	2
:	
B'	8,
C'	9

1. Choose ten pitches
2. Assign each pitch a number. (0–9)
3. Select 3 ten-digit phone numbers.
4. Write each as a pitch pattern.
   2 1 2 - 7 0 2 - 7 8 9 6
   C B C - A'A C - A'B'C'G
5. Perform the three patterns at the same time to produce harmony.

• Combine aspects of both of these free compositional techniques to create music with melody and harmony. Think of other free techniques that can be used to create music.

159

3. Prepare creating free-form compositions. Have the students:
• Discuss the information on creating free-form compositions.
• Create musical compositions using the free compositional procedures indicated.

Reinforcing the Lesson
Have the students think of other free techniques which can be used to create music. (telephone numbers, license plates, addresses, letters of a name)

3 APPRAISAL
The students should be able to:
1. Identify and define free forms as used in twentieth-century compositions.
2. Read and perform the free-form composition "A Marvelous Place."
3. Create and perform a composition in free form.

SPECIAL LEARNERS
If the class includes different learners, split the class into small groups. Make sure each group is a mixture of exceptional and regular learners. Clarify the expectations and directions for creating a free composition.

REVIEW AND EVALUATION

JUST CHECKING

Objective
To review and test the skills and concepts taught in Unit 7

Materials
Recordings: Just Checking Unit 7
           (questions 1, 3, 5, 6)
           Unit 7 Evaluation (question 2)
           For Extra Credit recordings
           (optional)
Copying Master 7-1 (optional)
Evaluation Unit 7 Copying Master

TEACHING THE LESSON

Review the skills and concepts taught in Unit 7. Have the students:

• Perform the activities and answer the questions on pages 160–161. (For this review, examples for questions 1, 3, 5, and 6 are included in the "Just Checking Unit 7" recording. Have the students answer these questions first. Then have them answer the other questions in the review.)

• Review their answers.
(You may wish to use Copying Master 7-1 at this time.)

5B, 6B
CD 4

JUST CHECKING

See how much you remember. Listen to the recording.

1. Listen to the steady beat and perform these rhythm motives by patting the quarter notes, pat-sliding the tied notes, clapping the eighth notes, and snapping the triplets with alternating hands.

2. Identify the melody below that uses rhythm motive 1, motive 2, or motive 3 above.   1,b: 2,c; 3,a

3. Listen to this section of the second movement of Beethoven's Symphony No. 7 and decide whether the articulation is legato or staccato. staccato

160

4. Which of the following defines legato? Which defines staccato? a, staccato; b, legato

   a. detached and crisp
   b. smooth and connected

5. Listen to this section of the *Classical Symphony,* by Sergei Prokofiev. Identify the different sections of the exposition section by pointing to the descriptions on the listening map.

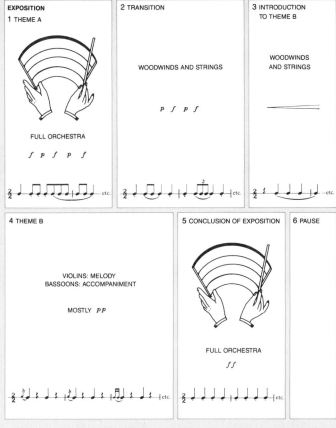

6. Listen to this version of the "America" melody. It is an example of: alteration of rhythm

   alteration of rhythm   creating a motive

7. Which of the following describes free form? a

   a. order of sections can change b. order stays the same

161

GIVING THE EVALUATION

Evaluation Unit 7 Copying Master can be found in the *Teacher's Copying Masters* book along with full directions for giving the evaluation and checking the answers.

FOR EXTRA CREDIT

You may want to have the students respond to the following:

Describe how Beethoven used tone color, legato, staccato, and rhythmic motives to create unity and contrast in the second movement of his Symphony No. 7. (The work is in ABA form. The A sections have a basic string tone color. The B section features woodwinds and strings. The A sections and the B section have contrasting rhythmic motives. While the A section is *mostly* staccato, the B section is *mostly* legato.)

(You may wish to play recordings to refresh the students' memories.)

ELEMENTS OF MUSIC	UNIT 8 OBJECTIVES	Lesson 1 Focus: Traditional Instruments Used in Nontraditional Ways	Lesson 2 Focus: New Tone Colors
Dynamics	Listen to, identify, and perform contrasting dynamics		
Tone Color	**Discuss traditional and nontraditional tone colors** **Perform vocal tone colors** **Listen to prepared piano and steel band** **Identify new sounds from found objects** **Identify synthesizer**	Discuss information on percussion instruments Discuss ways in which composers experiment with new tone color Create new instruments	Follow a contemporary tone color score Experience new tone colors produced on traditional instruments Read and perform vocal tone colors Experiment with tone colors on piano Discuss ways to produce new sounds from voices and traditional instruments
Tempo	Read and perform sounds at different tempos		
Duration/ Rhythm	**Read and perform a rhythm score**	Read and perform a rhythmic accompaniment Read and perform a rhythm score with drumsticks	
Pitch	**Read and perform pitch sounds from a score**		Read and perform new pitch sounds from a score Read and perform pitches on Autoharp
Texture			
Form			
Style	**Discuss the pipe organ and synthesizer** **Identify composer Vangelis** Discuss composers **Discuss ways to produce new sounds from voices and traditional instruments** Discuss the electronic revolution	Discuss the fact that percussion instruments were used in ancient times	
Reading	Read and play rhythm scores for contemporary music using ♬♬ , ♫ , ♩ , ♪ , 𝄾 , ▬	Read sticking patterns (R, L) and rhythm scores Read contemporary score	Read contemporary score and contemporary voice notation

PURPOSE Unit 8: TONE COLOR IN DIFFERENT STYLES

In this unit the students will investigate twentieth-century musical innovations. They will experience traditional instruments used in nontraditional ways as well as new tone colors produced by recently developed electronic instruments. They will listen to a traditional romantic composition as it was originally composed for piano, as it was later orchestrated, and as it sounds performed on a synthesizer. They will hopefully extend their understanding and appreciation of many forms and styles of music of yesterday and today.

SUGGESTED TIME FRAME

May			June			

FOCUS

Traditional Instruments Used in Non-traditional Ways
New Tone Colors
Comparing Traditional and Twentieth-Century Tone Colors
Prepared Piano
Electronic Tone Colors
Recycling Sound (Found Objects)

Lesson 3 Focus: Comparing Traditional and Twentieth-Century Tone Colors	Lesson 4 Focus: Prepared Piano	Lesson 5 Focus: Electronic Tone Colors	Lesson 6 Focus: Recycling Sound (Found Objects)
		Listen to and identify contrasts in dynamics	Perform dynamic contrasts in a composition using sound sources
Discuss the tone color of the pipe organ Listen to and describe traditional and nontraditional tone colors Compare the tone color of keyboard instruments from two style periods (synthesizers, pipe organ)	Listen to and identify instruments Listen to tone colors of prepared piano Discuss the parts of a piano and the types of tones produced Create new tone colors on piano	Listen to and identify contrasts in tone color Listen to and discuss music performed electronically on synthesizer	Identify the use of new sound sources from found objects Listen to and identify traditional and found objects used in composition Listen to and identify tone color of steel drums Create melodies on pitches of found objects
			Perform different tempos in a composition using source sounds
Discuss the pipe organ of the baroque period Listen to J.S. Bach's baroque organ music Discuss the synthesizer of the 20th century Perform movements to a 20th-century composition Discuss the 20th-century Greek composer Vangelis	Discuss the musical style of John Cage and use of the prepared piano Perform a composition on a prepared piano	Discuss the electronic revolution of the 20th century and its effect on music Discuss the Japanese composer Isao Tomita Listen to and discuss a work by Milton Babbitt	Listen to music performed by found objects Create a composition using found objects Discuss American composer Harry Partch
Follow contemporary music movement score	Read prepared piano score in $\frac{4}{4}$ using a *ritardando*		

BULLETIN BOARD

Have the students collect pictures of musical instruments, both traditional and modern, label them, and display them on the bulletin board in either of two categories: TRADITIONAL and TWENTIETH CENTURY.

TWENTIETH CENTURY

TRADITIONAL

UNIT 8

TONE COLOR IN DIFFERENT STYLES

Guitar: Paris (1912, early), Pablo Picasso, COLLECTION, THE MUSEUM OF MODERN ART, NY

162

E X T E N S I O N

LESSON 1

Focus: Traditional Instruments Used in Nontraditional Ways

Objectives
To perform a rhythmic accompaniment
To play percussion instruments in non-traditional ways

Materials
Recordings: "Tone Color Montage"
    Heaven and Hell, Part 2
Drumsticks
Pitched and unpitched classroom instruments

1 SETTING THE STAGE

Tell the students they will be learning to identify new ways of creating sound developed by twentieth-century composers.

Quartet, Ben Shahn, Private Collection

163

THE ARTIST

Ben Shahn (shän) (1898–1969)—was an American painter who often portrayed controversial subjects such as labor movements, race relations, and atomic warfare. He painted strong figures of common people, such as the musicians in *Quartet*. He wanted his figures and his direct style to communicate his interest in social justice to his viewers.

LESSON 1

1. Introduce creating sounds. Have the students:

• Read information about composers experimenting with new ways of creating sounds.

• Listen to "Tone Color Montage." As each number is called follow and listen as old instruments produce tone colors in new ways. (1, prepared piano; 2, electric bass guitar, slapped; 3, violin, struck with wood part of bow; 4, vocal sounds; 5, gong, played with a bow)

• Examine the pictures and examine how new tone colors were created.

Creating Sounds

Musicians have often explored new ways to create sound. Twentieth-century musicians have continued to experiment with tone color. They have developed new instruments. They have also experimented with unusual ways to play traditional instruments. The musicians in these pictures are creating new tone colors.

• Listen to these examples of traditional instruments producing musical sounds in new ways.

"Tone Color Montage"

164

Percussion Instruments

Percussion instruments are among the oldest musical instruments in the world. Ancient writings, drawings, carvings, and sculptures show percussion instruments in a variety of settings.

Percussion instruments are generally used to establish or maintain the beat. Many musical compositions feature strong, repeated rhythms on percussion instruments.

* Read and practice each pattern with your drumsticks using the matched grip. Use your right hand (R) and left hand (L) as indicated.

This Greek vase is about twenty-five hundred years old. The god of music, Apollo, is shown at left. The woman at right is playing an ancient percussion instrument.

Apollo and the Muses. Greek Attic lekythos. LOUVRE. Paris

165

2. Introduce percussion instruments.
Have the students:
* Discuss the information on percussion instruments.
* Practice the rhythmic patterns with drumsticks using the matched grip. Use right and left hands (R and L) as indicated.

LESSON 1

3. Introduce performing a rhythmic accompaniment. Have the students:
• Listen to *Heaven and Hell,* Part 2.
• Read and perform the rhythmic accompaniment using the matched grip.

Performing a Rhythmic Accompaniment

Vangelis (van-je′ lis), a Greek composer, created the theme music for the Academy Award-winning film *Chariots of Fire.* The rhythms you have performed can be played as an accompaniment to *Heaven and Hell,* Part 2, another of his compositions.

• Listen to the recording of *Heaven and Hell,* Part 2. Read and perform the rhythmic accompaniment with your drumsticks using the matched grip.

 Heaven and Hell, Part 2 by Vangelis

Accompaniment to *Heaven and Hell*, Part 2

166

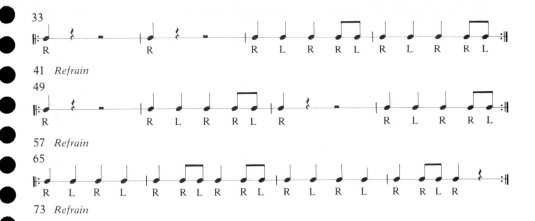

33

R   R   R   L   R   R L   R   L   R   R L

41 *Refrain*

49

R   R   L   R   R L   R   R   L   R   R L

57 *Refrain*

65

R   L   R   L   R   R L R   R L   R   L   R   L   R   R L R

73 *Refrain*

VANGELIS

The Greek composer Vangelis was born in Athens in 1943. He is basically a self-taught musician. As a child he studied the piano and later the pipe organ. His interest in the variety of sounds that could be produced by the pipe organ led Vangelis to its modern equivalent, the synthesizer. The possibilities of producing both traditional and non-traditional sounds attracted him.

Vangelis performed with the Greek rock band Formynx. Political pressures led him to leave Greece and settle in Paris. He composed soundtracks for many European films and television documentaries.

The synthesizer has enabled Vangelis to use many new sounds. He finds this instrument the best means of expressing his musical ideas. He has composed, produced, and performed on over forty record albums.

167

LESSON 1

4. Introduce the composer. Have the students discuss the information on the Greek composer Vangelis.

LESSON 1

5. Introduce new percussion sounds.

Have the students:

• Read the information about new ways percussionists use their drumsticks to produce new tone colors.

• Experiment with their drumsticks to produce new tone colors as indicated, observing the notation.

• Read and practice the patterns in the percussion score to *Heaven and Hell,* Part 2, and perform as indicated with the recording.

Reinforcing the Lesson

Have the students select a classroom instrument which they would like to investigate. List the many different ways sound can be produced on this instrument. Describe the type of sound produced. (Answers will vary.)

3 APPRAISAL

The students should be able to:

1. Perform a rhythmic accompaniment to *Heaven and Hell*, Part 2.

2. Read and perform traditional and non-traditional drumstick patterns with rhythmic accuracy.

New Percussion Sounds

Sometimes percussionists use their instruments in new or different ways. In this example, the drumsticks are used in different ways to create new tone colors. The symbol ✗ means "hold the drumsticks in the air and tap them lightly together." The symbol ✗→ means "hold the drumsticks in the air, tap them together, then slide one over the other as shown in this photograph."

• Read and practice these patterns with your drumsticks.

Refrain

• Perform these patterns as you listen to *Heaven and Hell*, Part 2 again. Use this order:

A–B–C–D–E–D–E–D–C–D

168

EXTENSION

MORE MUSIC TEACHING IDEAS

Have the students create a new instrument. Use this instrument as an accompaniment to a familiar musical selection.

COOPERATIVE LEARNING

Have the students read "Dreams" on page 15. Review the information on using traditional instruments in new ways on pupil page 168. Assign the students to work in cooperative groups of four. Each group should create a sound composition to accompany a reading of the poem. The sound piece should use traditional classroom pitched and unpitched instruments in new and different ways. A second aspect of the project might be to create special notation to indicate the new sounds. Appoint one student to be the recorder to prepare a simple line score. Another student will be the conductor, one the reader, and one the discussion leader who will lead the evaluation process. Have each group practice its sound

piece and perform for the entire class. On another day, you may want to have the groups exchange scores.

You may want to have the groups use different poems for this activity.

PERFORM WITH NEW TONE COLORS

Notation

The tone colors of "Misty, Moisty Morning" are produced by using traditional instruments in new ways. The composer used some special notation to indicate these new sounds.

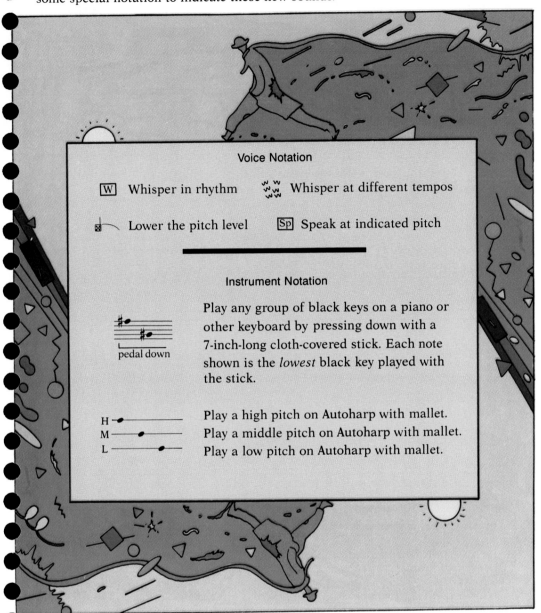

Voice Notation

| W | Whisper in rhythm | ᴡᴡᴡ | Whisper at different tempos |

Lower the pitch level   Sp   Speak at indicated pitch

Instrument Notation

pedal down — Play any group of black keys on a piano or other keyboard by pressing down with a 7-inch-long cloth-covered stick. Each note shown is the *lowest* black key played with the stick.

H — Play a high pitch on Autoharp with mallet.
M — Play a middle pitch on Autoharp with mallet.
L — Play a low pitch on Autoharp with mallet.

169

LESSON 2

Focus: New Tone Colors

Objectives
To perform a vocal composition using non-traditional notation
To identify the use of new tone colors in a twentieth-century vocal composition

Materials
Recordings: "Our World"
   "Misty, Moisty Morning"
   Saint Luke Passion
Piano, Autoharp, recorder, bells, guitar, percussion instruments

1 SETTING THE STAGE
Have the students review "Our World" (page 28), which has traditional tone colors and notation.

2 TEACHING THE LESSON

1. Introduce performing with unusual tone colors. Have the students:
• Discuss information on the special notation used by the composer of "Misty, Moisty Morning" to designate unusual sounds.
• Focus on the notation and practice each example in preparation for performing the composition.

LESSON 2

• Perform "Misty, Moisty Morning" to experience music with unusual vocal tone colors.

Misty, Moisty Morning

Traditional text
Music by M.J.

170

E X T E N S I O N

VOCAL DEVELOPMENT

Have the students expand the expressive qualities of the voice by encouraging the use of correct breathing, posture, vowels, and diction in performing "Misty, Moisty Morning." Have them experience speaking, singing, and whispering portions of the text to assist in "feeling" the difference in the use of the vocal instrument.

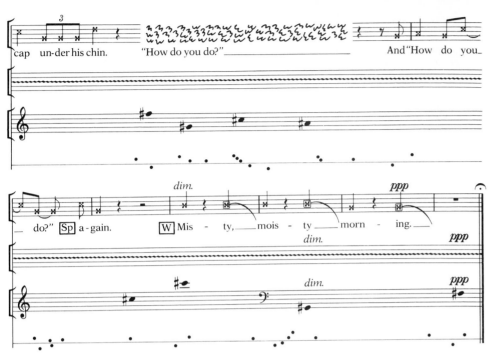

Other New Tone Colors

Krzysztof Penderecki (kris' tof pen-de-re' skē) is a contemporary
Polish composer who draws novel sounds from voices and
traditional instruments. He also was one of the first composers to
experiment with sounds such as saws cutting wood and paper
rustling, as well as unusual vocal effects. His *Saint Luke Passion*
was an immediate success after its premiere in 1966.

- Listen to part of the *Saint Luke Passion*. Listen for singers
  hissing, shouting, and whispering, and for percussive effects
  produced by voices in the chorus.

 Saint Luke Passion by Krzysztof Penderecki

171

2. Introduce other new tone colors.
Have the students:
- Discuss information on the composer
Krzysztof Penderecki.
- Listen to part of the *Saint Luke Passion*,
paying particular attention to the special
effects produced by voices in the chorus.

Reinforcing the Lesson

Have the students create a new accompaniment to a traditional song, for example,
"Our World" (page 28), using unusual
tone colors.

3 APPRAISAL

The students should be able to:
1. Read and perform "Misty, Moisty
Morning" with rhythmic, melodic and
vocal tone color accuracy.
2. Identify the use of new tone colors in a
twentieth-century vocal composition.

LESSON 3

Focus: Comparing Traditional and Twentieth-Century Tone Colors

Objectives
To compare the tone color of keyboard instruments from two contrasting style periods
To move to a twentieth-century electronic composition

Materials
Recordings: Toccata and Fugue in D Minor
"Alpha" from *Albedo 39*
Ensembles for Synthesizer
Composition for Synthesizer

1 SETTING THE STAGE

Tell the students they will be learning to identify the tone color of the electronic instruments known as synthesizers.

2 TEACHING THE LESSON

1. Introduce the pipe organ. Have the students:
• Discuss information on the pipe organ.
• Listen for the sound of the instrument in the Toccata and Fugue in D Minor.

CD 5 Pipe Organ

During the baroque period (1600–1750) the pipe organ was a popular instrument. It could produce a wide variety of sounds.

• Listen for the sound of the pipe organ.

Toccata and Fugue in D Minor, by Johann Sebastian Bach

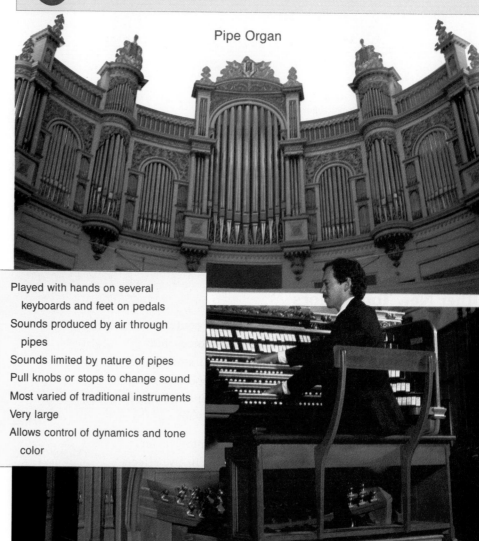

Pipe Organ

Played with hands on several
   keyboards and feet on pedals
Sounds produced by air through
   pipes
Sounds limited by nature of pipes
Pull knobs or stops to change sound
Most varied of traditional instruments
Very large
Allows control of dynamics and tone
   color

172

Synthesizer

The Greek composer Vangelis first composed for the pipe organ. He later became interested in the synthesizer because of its even greater tone color possibilities. He composed "Alpha," from his *Albedo 39*, for the synthesizer.

• Listen and describe the traditional and nontraditional sounds.

 "Alpha," from *Albedo 39*, by Vangelis

Ensembles for Synthesizer takes advantage of other tone color possibilities.

• Listen for the many sounds of the synthesizer.

 Ensembles for Synthesizer by Milton Babbitt

Synthesizer

Usually played with hands on one or more keyboards

Sounds produced by electronic components

Sounds limited only by composer's imagination

Buttons and knobs change sounds

Most flexible of nontraditional instruments

Generally small and compact

Allows almost total control of tone color, pitch, rhythm, and dynamics

173

2. Introduce the synthesizer. Have the students:
• Discuss information on the tone colors of "Alpha."
• Listen to the recording of "Alpha" and describe the traditional and nontraditional sounds.
• Identify the many sounds of the synthesizer as they listen to *Ensembles for Synthesizer*.
• Discuss similarities between the synthesizer of the twentieth-century and the pipe organ of the baroque period.

LESSON 3

3. Introduce movement to sounds of the twentieth century. Have the students:
• Examine the pictures of dance movements.
• Describe the movements shown in each picture as short and choppy, long and sustained, or high and low.
• Practice each movement.
• Listen to "Alpha" again and perform each movement in order with the music.

Reinforcing the Lesson

Preview page 180 and listen to *Composition for Synthesizer* by Milton Babbitt as a further example of an electronically generated work by this composer.

3 APPRAISAL

The students should be able to:
1. Compare the tone color resources of the baroque pipe organ and the twentieth-century synthesizer.
2. Identify and perform movement gestures based on line drawings to "Alpha."

Moving to Sounds of the Twentieth Century

These pictures show contemporary dance movements.

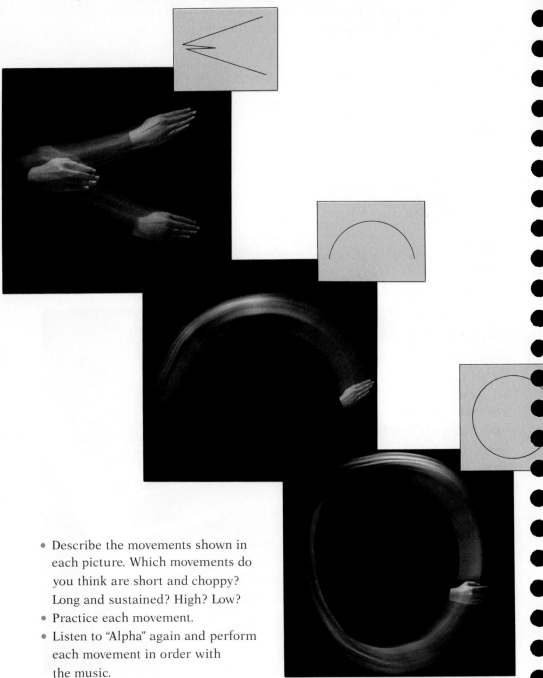

• Describe the movements shown in each picture. Which movements do you think are short and choppy? Long and sustained? High? Low?
• Practice each movement.
• Listen to "Alpha" again and perform each movement in order with the music.

174

NEW SOUNDS FROM A FAMILIAR INSTRUMENT ◯ 7A ⊙ 5

What Is It?

Sometimes familiar instruments can produce new or different tone colors.

- Listen to this music. Try to identify the instrument or instruments you hear.

> *The Perilous Night*, by John Cage

The instrument you heard is a **prepared piano**. Pianos can be prepared in several ways. Items made of wood, metal, or rubber can be placed on or between the strings of the piano. Other piano sounds are produced when the performer strums the strings inside the piano or uses a mallet to hit the wood of the piano. It all depends what sounds the composer wants produced.

John Cage, an American composer, developed the idea of the prepared piano and used it in his compositions to produce different tone colors.

175

EXTENSION

Focus: Prepared Piano

Objective
To create a composition for prepared piano

Materials
Recordings: *The Perilous Night*
  "Eraser Piano Tees"
  Suite for Percussion
Piano, facing class with front panels off, both top and bottom. (If a grand piano, the lid should be raised so class can gather around.)
Two golf tees
Two rubber erasers (ink or pencil)

Vocabulary
Prepared piano

1 SETTING THE STAGE
Tell the students they will be introduced to compositions that develop new ways of creating sound from a piano.

2 TEACHING THE LESSON
1. Introduce new sounds from a familiar instrument. Have the students:
- Listen to *The Perilous Night* and identify the instrument they hear.
- Discuss the information on the prepared piano and the composer John Cage.

THE COMPOSER
John Cage—American experimental composer, was born in Los Angeles in 1912. He studied composition with Adolph Weiss and Henry Cowell, and also attended Arnold Schoenberg's classes at the University of California. Cage's 1951 work *Music of Changes* for piano was the first well-known twentieth-century *aleatory*, or chance, music. Aleatory music contains elements of chance or unpredictability, with some or all choices in performance determined by the player. Cage also developed the "prepared piano." The preparation consists of placing screws, coins, rubber bands, and other objects on the piano strings to change the tone color of individual keys. Cage is a lecturer and performer, and encourages his audiences to participate in his presentations.

LESSON 4

2. Introduce the piano. Have the students:
• Move to the area around the piano. (You may wish to divide the class into two or more groups.)
• Experiment with the tone color options of the piano as indicated.

Inside the Piano

A piano has many parts: keyboard, pedals, hammers, strings.
You can look inside a piano to see how the parts work together.

• Observe the hammers. What do they do? strike the strings

• Place your hand across a group of strings. Play the keys for these strings. What happens to the tone? becomes muffled

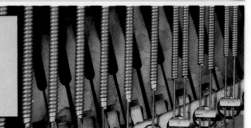

• The thickness of the strings and the number of strings related to each key affect the sound produced by the key. Locate the thickest strings. What kind of tone do their keys produce? low

• Locate the keys that use three strings; two strings; one string. What kind of tones do these keys produce? high, middle, low

• Find the pedals. What is the purpose of each? Left—softer tone, middle—sustains low tones, right—sustains all tones

176

**CURRICULUM CONNECTION:
SOCIAL STUDIES**

The piano—In about 1709, Bartolommeo Cristofori of Florence designed the first piano in an attempt to create an instrument that was capable of playing loud and soft. First described as a "harpsichord with soft and loud," the instrument later was called the pianoforte. During the late 1700s and the 1800s several instrument makers improved on Cristofori's invention. John Broadwood of London created a piano with a louder and richer tone. Sebastien Érard of Paris perfected the mechanics for rapid repetition of a note. Alpheus Babcock of Boston invented the cast-iron frame, which could stand the stress of thicker strings and greater tension. In 1855 Steinway and Sons incorporated all the many improvements to create the modern piano.

Performing on a Prepared Piano

"Eraser Piano Tees" is a prepared piano composition written for eight prepared notes.

- Prepare four low notes on the piano by using two large rubber erasers. Place each eraser between two sets of low strings.

- Prepare four middle range notes (near middle C) by using four golf tees. Place each tee between the two strings for each middle range note.

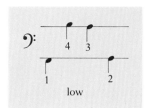

- Use your prepared piano notes to play this composition. The pitches are numbered from the lowest to highest.

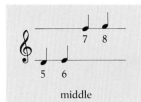

Eraser Piano Tees

Dorothy Gail Elliott

177

3. Introduce performing a prepared piano composition. Have the students:
- Discuss the information in preparation for notating and performing "Eraser Piano Tees."
- Prepare the piano as indicated.
- Perform "Eraser Piano Tees" from the notation.

Reinforcing the Lesson
Preview page 181 and listen to *Suite for Percussion* as an example of both traditional and nontraditional instruments being used as sound sources.

3 APPRAISAL
The students should be able to:
1. Identify a prepared piano composition.
2. Create and perform a prepared piano composition from notation.

MORE MUSIC TEACHING IDEAS
Have the students experiment with the piano to produce new sounds.
1. Depress C E G without making any sound. Then strum the center section of piano strings with fingers or a pick. This was a technique Henry Cowell used in his *Aeolian Harp*.
2. Tap on the case of the piano at various spots. Use hard rubber-tipped mallets to protect the finish of the piano. Try to create at least five different sounds.

LESSON 5

Focus: Electronic Tone Colors

Objectives
To identify and define electronic tone colors used by twentieth-century composers
To listen to a composition performed with three different tone colors
To identify Milton Babbitt as a twentieth-century composer of electronic music

Materials
Recordings: "Alpha" from *Albedo 39*
"Promenade Montage"
Composition for Synthesizer

1 SETTING THE STAGE

Review the information on the synthesizer on page 173 and listen to "Alpha" from *Albedo 39*.

2 TEACHING THE LESSON

1. Introduce the electronic revolution. Have the students discuss the information on electronic musical instruments.

Electronic Musical Instruments

Electronic musical instruments were developed in the twentieth century. In 1927 Leon Theremin (ther′ e-min), a Russian musician, invented the first electronic musical instrument, the Theremin. To control the pitch, the player moves his or her hands toward or away from vertical and horizontal antennas. In 1928 Maurice Martenot (mär-te-nô′), a French musician, invented the Ondes Martenot (ônd′ mär-te-nô′), the ancestor of the synthesizer.

At top, Theremin players must wear special tight-fitting clothes. Even the rustle of fabric will change the pitch of the Theremin. Above, synthesizers include many electronic components.

178

The electronic revolution moved quickly in music. By the late 1950s, many studios for electronic music were in operation. They were equipped with sound generators, filters, mixers, and recorders.

With the invention of the transistor and then the integrated circuit the technology to create and manipulate electronic sound became easier to use and less expensive. Synthesizers, units that combined sound generators, sound modifiers and a keyboard in a single control system appeared. The Moog and Buchla synthesizers were complete electronic studios. Today simplified units are available to the general public at moderate prices.

Above, the Moog synthesizer was developed by Robert Moog in the 1960s. Below left, Tomita has created electronic versions of much "classical" music.

One Composition — Several Styles

Pictures at an Exhibition by Modest Mussorgsky was composed for the piano alone. The French composer Maurice Ravel arranged the work for full orchestra. In 1975, the Japanese composer Isao Tomita created an electronic version.

- Listen to "Promenade" from *Pictures at an Exhibition* in piano, orchestral, and electronic versions. Compare. In which version is the contrast of dynamics and tone color most obvious? Which version do you find most interesting? Why? Answers will vary.

 "Promenade Montage"

179

2. Introduce one composition in several styles. Have the students:
- Discuss the information on the different versions of Mussorgsky's "Promenade."
- Listen to the "Promenade" in piano, orchestral and electronic versions.
- Compare and discuss which version displays the most obvious contrasts of dynamics and tone color, and decide which version they find most interesting. (answers will vary)

LESSON 5

3. Introduce other electronic music.
Have the students:
• Discuss the information on Milton Babbitt and his *Composition for Synthesizer*.
• Follow the description of the first part of the work as they listen to the recording. You may wish to use the following items as a basis for extended discussion.
1. In the development of electronic musical instruments, is it a necessary prerequisite to be a musician? Why? (Yes; musical knowledge needed to create compositions on electronic instruments.)
2. How did the synthesizer get its name? Think of another name by which this instrument might have been called. Justify your choice. (The music is created by synthesis; sound processor: the instrument processes sound as a word processor does words.)

Reinforcing the Lesson

Have the students identify popular musicians of today who use synthesizers. (e.g., Tears for Fears; other answers will vary)

3 APPRAISAL

The students should be able to:
1. Identify and define electronic tone colors used by twentieth-century composers.
2. Listen and compare three tone color versions of "Promenade" from *Pictures at an Exhibition*.
3. Identify Milton Babbitt as a twentieth-century composer of electronic music.

More Electronic Music

Milton Babbitt has long been a composer of electronic music. His control of sound is evident in *Composition for Synthesizer*, composed in 1960–1961. The synthesizer produces pitches and rhythms from directions provided by the composer. This work presents sounds with an evenness and a speed only possible through electronics.

 Composition for Synthesizer, by Milton Babbitt

As you listen to this composition follow this description:
1. Two gonglike sustained chords. A staccato melody.
2. Two sustained chords. Two staccato melodies.
3. One sustained chord. Two high staccato melodies with a low, legato melody.

Milton Babbitt, distinguished contemporary American composer, was born in Philadelphia in 1916. He received his early musical training in Jackson, Mississippi, and went on to study at New York University and Princeton University. He later became a professor of music at Princeton, where he also taught mathematics.

Babbitt began a program of electronic music at Princeton and Columbia universities, working with the newly developed synthesizer. He helped create the Columbia–Princeton Electronic Music Center, which became a haven for experiments in electronic music. Babbitt has also written many books and articles on music and musicians. His theories about mathematics and music and his innovations with the synthesizer have influenced the musical thinking of many young American composers.

180

E X T E N S I O N

COOPERATIVE LEARNING

Have the students form cooperative groups of three members or pairs. Each member or pair should read either page 167, 171, or 180. Then the students should return to the group and teach the information they have learned to the rest of the group members. If each group member or pair writes down three main points about the composer, the group can use these facts to create test questions. This time, you may want to collect one question from each group, put all the questions together into a test, and give the test during the next class period. Each group's grades should be combined to give a group grade. Any group achieving above a certain percentage correct can be rewarded in the ways suggested on page 93.

Found Objects

⊕ 7A
ⓒⓓ 5

Composers sometimes search for new sound sources when traditional musical instruments are not able to produce all the sounds that they want. *Suite for Percussion*, by Lou Harrison, uses both traditional percussion instruments and new sound sources. His new sources include **found objects**, or everyday objects.

• Listen for both traditional instruments and found objects you think were used.

Suite for Percussion, by Lou Harrison

181

LESSON 6

Focus: Recycling Sound (Found Objects)

Objectives
To identify the use of new instruments from found objects
To create an improvisation using found objects
To identify the tone color of steel drums

Materials
Recordings: *Suite for Percussion*
Steel band music
Harry Partch on *Spoils of War*
Classroom objects suitable as sound sources

Vocabulary
Found objects

1 SETTING THE STAGE

Tell the students they will be learning to create sound from new sources found in the classroom.

2 TEACHING THE LESSON

1. Introduce found objects. Have the students:
• Discuss the information on found objects as new sources of sound.
• Listen to *Suite for Percussion*, by Lou Harrison, and identify both the traditional instruments and the found objects they think were used in the composition. (Answers may vary. *Suite for Percussion* uses the following: traditional instruments—bells, timpani, snare drum, gong, tom-tom, chimes, triangle, bass drum; found objects—automobile brake drums, lengths of plumbers' pipes, galvanized washtubs, glass bowls.)

EXTENSION

THE COMPOSER

Lou Harrison—American avante-garde composer, was born in Oregon in 1917. Like John Cage, he studied with Henry Cowell and attended Arnold Schoenberg's classes at the University of California. In 1943 he moved to New York City, where he became a music critic for the *New York Herald-Tribune*. He has also taught at Black Mountain College and San José State College. In 1961 he went to the Orient to study Japanese and Korean rhythmic structures and modalities. Harrison also tried his luck as an instrument maker. He invented new principles for clavichord construction as well as a process for direct composing on a phonograph disc. Through his composing Harrison has sought new sources of sound production.

LESSON 6

2. Prepare to create a recycled sound composition. Have the students:

- Discuss the information on creating new sound compositions using found objects.
- Work in small groups to identify classroom objects that would be good sound sources.
- Experiment with the new instruments and discover one short sound and one sustained sound.
- Use the suggestions listed as they create their own compositions.
- Perform their compositions several different ways, and tape record different performances.
- Decide which performance demonstrates the most contrast, and which is the most interesting. (answer will vary)

3. Introduce unusual instruments. Have the students:

- Discuss the information on steel drums.
- Listen to the recording of steel band music.
- Listen for the tone color of the steel drums as they pat or clap the steady beat while listening to the recording.

Your Own Recycled Sound Composition

You and your classmates can create your own compositions using new sources for sound. It is more fun to work in small groups.

1. Work with your group to identify classroom objects (found objects) that would be good sound sources.
2. Experiment with your new instruments. Discover one short sound and one sustained sound.
3. To create unity, play one instrument continuously throughout the composition.
4. Plan a definite beginning and a definite ending.
5. Plan a definite order for different players.
6. To create variety, use three or four different instruments for contrast. Use silence, different dynamics, different tempos, and different pitches. Try different combinations.
7. Perform your composition several different ways.
8. Tape-record different performances of your composition.
9. Decide which of your performances demonstrates the most contrast. Which one is the most interesting?

Unusual Instruments

After World War II, the United States Navy left many large, empty oil containers in the West Indies. These fifty-gallon steel containers inspired the people of the West Indies to create their own special instruments. The oil containers were cut and hammered into steel drums. Groups of steel drum players formed bands with their own unique tone color.

- Listen for the tone color of the steel drums as you pat or clap the steady beat.

 Steel Band Music

182

CURRICULUM CONNECTION: SOCIAL STUDIES

Steel band music—is created with a combination of homemade instruments. Some of the instruments used are steel drums of various sizes and timbres, "chit-chats" (maracas), scratch sticks, and "cutters" (brake drums from Model T Fords). The steel drums provide all the melody and have a range of four octaves. They are played by striking the hammered sides with the fingertips or a rubber-tipped mallet. This creates a marimbalike sound that is slightly flat or sharp. Steel band music has become popular in the United States. The 10th Naval District Steel Band is one of the more well-known bands.

Creating New Instruments

Harry Partch (1901-1973), an American experimental composer, inspired others with his creative ideas. He also invented original instruments for special effects.

• Listen to learn about his composition *Spoils of War* and the unique instruments used in it.

Harry Partch on *Spoils of War*

Below is a list of "instruments" used in *Spoils of War.* Which ones are not familiar to you?

7 brass artillery casings
Pernambuco block (type of wood block)
4 cloud chamber bowls (12-gallon glass bottles cut in half and hung as bells)
2 tuned bamboo rods
Wood block
Guiro (ribbed gourd)
3 "wang guns"

Harry Partch built this instrument and named it *Spoils of War.*

Many modern composers feel free to use any sounds that have the qualities they like. What found instruments might you use to improvise music?

183

---

4. Introduce inventing new instruments. Have the students:
• Discuss the information on the experimental composer Harry Partch.
• Listen to the composer discuss his *Spoils of War* and play the instruments.
• Identify the parts of *Spoils of War.*
• Decide what instruments they might use to improvise a music piece similar to the Partch composition.

Reinforcing the Lesson

Have the students create an original accompaniment to any folk or traditional song, using found objects as sound sources.

3 APPRAISAL

The students should be able to:
1. Identify the basic properties of the tone color of new instruments created from found objects.
2. Create an improvised composition using the basic properties of found objects.
3. Identify the tone color of steel drums.

MORE MUSIC TEACHING IDEAS

Have the students choose twelve pitched found objects that will give the twelve tones of a tone-row with different timbres and improvise a short composition. (Have some students play a few unpitched instruments to keep the beat.)

THE COMPOSER

Harry Partch (1901–1974)—was a remarkable self-taught American composer. He began his work by experimenting with instruments that could produce fractional intervals, and in the process devised a 43-tone scale. He published his findings in a book, *Genesis of a Music.* Partch invented and built his own instruments and trained musicians to play them. His *Spoils of War* was named for the military scrap it contains. Some of his other instruments are kitharas with 72 strings and harmonic canons with 44 strings. Partch also was interested in American folk life. He traveled across the country during the Depression, collecting folk expressions and graffiti, which he used as texts in his compositions.

REVIEW AND EVALUATION

JUST CHECKING

Objective
To review and test the skills and concepts taught in Unit 8

Materials
Recordings: Just Checking Unit 8 (questions 1–6, 9–11) "Alpha" Unit 8 Evaluation (question 3) *For Extra Credit* recordings (optional)
Drumsticks
Copying Master 8-1 (optional)
Evaluation Unit 8 Copying Master

TEACHING THE LESSON

Review the skills and concepts taught in Unit 8. Have the students:
• Perform the activities and answer the questions on pages 184–185. (For this review, examples for questions 1 through 6 and 9 through 11 are included in the "Just Checking Unit 8" recording. Have the students answer these questions first. Then have them answer the other questions in the review, using the recordings in the unit where necessary.)
• Review their answers.
(You may wish to use Copying Master 8-1 at this time.)

 7A, 7B

CD 5

JUST CHECKING

See how much you remember. Listen to the recording.

1. Listen to the steady beat and perform these rhythms on drumsticks using the matched grip.

2. Listen to a portion of the *Saint Luke Passion* and identify the unusual vocal effects. hissing, shouting, chanting, speech

3. Listen to excerpts of three versions of "Promenade" and describe the contrasts of dynamics and tone color. answers will vary

4. The unique tone color of this ensemble is produced on homemade instruments. Name the instrument. steel drums

184

5. Perform these vocal sounds with the recording of "Misty, Moisty Morning."

6. Listen to this selection and tell whether the tone color is created by a pipe organ or a synthesizer. synthesizer

7. Listen to "Alpha" from *Albedo 39* by Vangelis. Use appropriate contemporary dance movements with this piece.

8. Name and describe two unusual instruments or familiar instruments used in unusual ways. Answers will vary.

9. Listen and identify the selection you hear. Choose from the titles below. c
   a. Toccata and Fugue in D minor
   b. "Alpha" from *Albedo 39*
   c. *Heaven and Hell*, Part 2
   d. "Promenade" from *Pictures at an Exhibition*
   e. *The Perilous Night*

10. Listen to a portion of *The Perilous Night* and describe how the composer used a traditional instrument to produce different tone colors. John Cage prepared the piano by placing wood, metal, and rubber objects between the strings of the piano.

11. Listen to a portion of *Spoils of War* and describe several of the original instruments Harry Partch invented. cloud chamber bowls, tuned bamboo rods, brass artillery casings, "wang gun"

185

REVIEW AND EVALUATION

GIVING THE EVALUATION

Evaluation Unit 8 Copying Master can be found in the *Teacher's Copying Masters* book along with full directions for giving the evaluation and checking the answers.

FOR EXTRA CREDIT

You may want to have the students answer the following question. Vangelis has had very little formal training. What skills might be necessary for a composer of electronic music in comparison to a more traditional composer? (some knowledge of traditional music is necessary; knowledge of computers, resources of the synthesizer)

YEAR-END REVIEW

Objective
To review the skills and concepts taught throughout Grade 8

Materials
Recording: Year-End Review (questions 1–4, 7–10)
Keyboard or bells

TEACHING THE LESSON

Review the skills and concepts taught in Grade 8. Have the students:
• Perform the activities and answer the questions on pages 186–187. (For this review, examples for questions 1 through 4 and 7 through 10 are included in the ''Year-End Review'' recording. Have the students answer these questions first. Then have them answer the other questions in the review.)
• Review their answers.

YEAR-END REVIEW

🌐 7B
💿 5

1. Listen to determine whether the style of each example is African, synth-pop, Japanese, calypso, or reggae. reggae, Japanese, synth-pop, calypso

2. Listen to "Elements" and determine whether the form of the selection is AB or ABA. AB

3. Listen to this musical selection, which is an example of changing meters. Identify when the meter changes by conducting the appropriate pattern. The selection begins in duple meter. duple; triple; duple

4. Listen to this excerpt from "Caprice" from Claude Bolling's Suite for Violin and Jazz Piano. Determine if this section is in compound or quadruple meter. Demonstrate your answer by conducting the appropriate pattern. compound meter

5a. Play the following pitches on keyboard or bells that make up the twelve-tone row on which the melody of "The Web" is based.

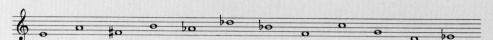

b. Play the retrograde of this tone row on keyboard or bells.

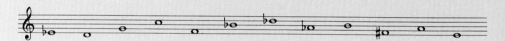

6. Perform this twelve-bar blues harmonic progression on bells or keyboard.

I   I   I   I   IV   IV   I   I   V   V   I   I

186

7a. Listen to a section of "Mi Caballo Blanco" and raise your hand when you hear the music modulate.

b. Listen to a section of "Mi Caballo Blanco" and decide if the music modulates to a higher or lower key. a higher key

8. Listen to *"Schwanenlied"* and decide whether the composition is in major or minor. minor

9. Listen to this section of Symphony No. 1 by Sergei Prokofiev. Identify the different parts of the exposition section by pointing to the descriptions on the listening map.

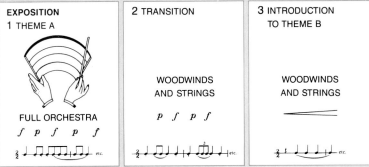

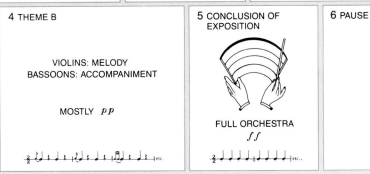

10. Listen and identify the selection you hear. Choose from the titles below. c

    a. Toccata and Fugue in D minor
    b. "Alpha"
    c. *Heaven and Hell,* Part 2
    d. "Promenade" *(Pictures at an Exhibition)*
    e. *The Perilous Night*

187

WESTERN MUSICAL STYLES

WESTERN
MUSICAL
STYLES

Francesco Veracini

188

Chopin Playing the Piano in Prince Anton Radziwill's Salon at Berlin, Siemiradski

189

WESTERN MUSICAL STYLES

Renaissance: *O Care, thou wilt despatch me*, by Thomas Weelkes

Materials
Recording: *O Care, thou wilt despatch me*

TEACHING THE LESSON

Introduce Renaissance musical styles.
Have the students:
• Discuss the information on the madrigal.
• Discuss and define homophonic and polyphonic musical textures.
• Listen to *O Care, thou wilt despatch me* and identify the two moods the composer portrays. How does the music depict his unhappiness? How does it depict the joy he hopes to find in music? (long note values; short note values)
• Compare madrigals with today's popular music. What do both have in common? (short; performed by small groups; same music for each verse; lyrics can be about love or events of the day; can be performed by amateurs or professionals)

RENAISSANCE

CD 5 *O Care, thou wilt despatch me*, by Thomas Weelkes

One of the most popular forms of vocal music in the Renaissance was the **madrigal** (mad′ ri-gəl). Madrigals were written in polyphonic style, usually for five singers. They generally were short works, simple in structure. The lyrics were taken from both great literature and popular poetry. Like the popular songs of today, most madrigals were about love, happy or unhappy. Other topics included politics and issues of the day. Most madrigals were in **strophic** form, with each verse being sung to essentially the same music. This made madrigals easy to learn.

Vocal music was especially popular in the Renaissance, which is often called the "Golden Age of Singing." Church music was sung by professional, all-male choirs, but madrigals were sung by both men and women. Madrigals were performed at social gatherings and as home entertainment. Usually one performer sang each part, sometimes accompanied by recorders, lutes, or viols playing the same music.

In *O Care, thou wilt despatch me*, the English composer Thomas Weelkes looks to music to cheer him up.

> O Care, thou wilt despatch me,
> If music do not match thee.
> Fa la la la la la la.
> So deadly dost thou sting me,
> Mirth only help can bring me.
> Fa la la la la la,
> Fa la la la la la.

• Listen for the two moods the composer portrays. How does the music depict his unhappiness? How does it depict the joy he hopes to find in music? long note values; short note values

 O Care, thou wilt despatch me, by Thomas Weelkes

• Compare madrigals with today's pop music. What do both have in common? both short; performed by small groups; same music for each verse; lyrics could be about love, or events of the day; both

190

E X T E N S I O N

THE COMPOSER

Thomas Weelkes (1576?–1623)—was an English composer and organist. Little is known about his early life. He received a degree in music from Oxford University and was for a time organist at Chichester Cathedral. Weelkes wrote a great deal of church music and also instrumental works, but it is his madrigals for which he is best remembered. Besides showing a remarkable union of melody and text, many of these songs contain harmonies and chord progressions that were well ahead of their time. For this, Weelkes is considered one of the greatest English madrigalists.

MORE MUSIC TEACHING IDEAS

Have the students:
1. Compare the text of *O Care, thou wilt despatch me* with texts of songs from other periods and identify how different periods treat the same idea. (See pages 343, 357.)
2. Perform compositions containing homophonic and polyphonic sections. (See pages 330, 343.)
3. Listen to examples of unaccompanied choral singing and identify similarities and differences in vocal tone color. (See pages 340, 355.)
4. Create a text that has a similar meaning to that of *O Care, thou wilt despatch me*.

You may wish to use this selection in conjunction with:
European-Western Styles, pp. 16–17
Performing a Canon, p. 82

During the Renaissance, people enjoyed singing and playing music together. The instruments shown in these paintings include viols (early members of the violin family), lutes, recorder, and a type of portable harpsichord.

Hearing, Abraham Bosse

Group with Lute Player and Three Musicians on the Terrace of a House, unknown 16th-century artist

191

WESTERN MUSICAL STYLES

General Characteristics

1. Emphasis on unaccompanied polyphonic choral music sometimes based on Gregorian chant melodies
2. In polyphonic music, equal importance given to each voice
3. Carefully controlled consonance and dissonance
4. Rhythms often very complex and frequently changing
5. Dance music usually homophonic and instrumental (recorders and so on)
6. The beginning of music for solo instruments, such as the lute

Form Alternation of polyphonic and homophonic sections determined by the text in vocal music; dances usually in binary form

Tone Color Unaccompanied voices, instruments of the Renaissance

WESTERN MUSICAL STYLES

Baroque: "Spring" (First Movement) from *The Four Seasons*, by Antonio Vivaldi

Materials
Recordings: "Spring"
"Marche" (optional)

TEACHING THE LESSON

Review the baroque musical style. Have the students:
• Review the information about baroque style on pages 22–23.
• Discuss the information on "Spring" and the concerto.

1B, 8A

CD 1, 5   **"Spring" (First Movement) from *The Four Seasons*, by Antonio Vivaldi**

The **concerto** (kôn-cher′tō) was one of the most important instrumental forms used in the baroque period. The term *concerto* comes from the Italian word *concertare* (kôn-cher-tä′ re), which suggests a friendly argument or contrasting forces. In a concerto, one instrument or group of instruments is set against the orchestra.

The Four Seasons is a group of violin concertos written around 1725 by the Italian baroque composer Antonio Vivaldi (än-tō′ nē-ō vi-väl′ dē) (1675-1741). Each concerto is accompanied by a poem, also written by Vivaldi, describing that season. This is a very early example of **program music,** music that tells a story or describes a scene.

One of the musical characteristics emphasized in the baroque concerto was *contrast.* In a style typical of the baroque, Vivaldi used two contrasting groups of instruments, contrasting melodies, and abrupt contrasts of loud and soft.

Rialto Bridge. Canaletto. GALLERIA CORSINI, Rome

Vivaldi was born in Venice and lived most of his life there. This painting by the Italian artist Canaletto (1697–1768) shows Venice as it looked during Vivaldi's lifetime.

"Spring" begins with the main theme played by everyone. Sections of a concerto played by everyone are called **ritornello** (ri-tôr-ne′ lō). The contrasting sections, called **episodes,** are played by the solo players. The music played suggests musical descriptions of spring, such as birds singing, murmuring waters, lightning and thunder.

192

E X T E N S I O N

THE COMPOSER

Antonio Vivaldi (1678–1741)—was born in Venice. He studied violin with his father, who was a professional musician. When Vivaldi was fifteen he entered the priesthood, and was ordained in 1703. A year later he became the music director at the Ospedale della Pietà, a conservatory in Venice. Many of his vocal works were written for the students there. Vivaldi also composed many successful operas. But his chief fame rests on his instrumental music, in particular his violin concertos. *The Four Seasons,* early examples of program music, are the first four in a series of twelve violin concertos called *The Contest Between Harmony and Invention.* Each season's concerto is accompanied by a descriptive poem, also written by Vivaldi.

THE ARTIST

Canaletto (1697-1768)—was an Italian painter best known for his scenes of 18th-century Venice. His paintings are colorful and show the famous buildings that lined the main canals of Venice. Canaletto first worked as a painter of theater scenery in his father's studio. Many of his paintings of Venice were commissioned by English visitors.

Each picture represents musical sounds. The term *concertino* (kôn-cher-tē′ no) refers to the solo instrument or instruments. *Tutti* (tōō′ tē) refers to all the instruments together.

- Which pictures are similar? Which are different? *like:* pictures 1, 3, 4, 5, 7, 9; pictures 2, 8; *different:* 6

- Listen to "Spring" and notice the contrasts in tone color, themes, and dynamics. Follow the map as you listen.

- Describe the sound of the baroque orchestra. What instruments are used? What keyboard instrument can you hear throughout the concerto? stringed instruments; harpsichord

"Spring" (First Movement), from *The Four Seasons*, by Antonio Vivaldi

Listening Map of "Spring" (First Movement) from *The Four Seasons*

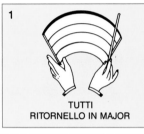

1 TUTTI RITORNELLO IN MAJOR

2 SOLO AND CONCERTINO BIRD CALLS

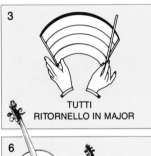

3 TUTTI RITORNELLO IN MAJOR

4 TUTTI A MURMURING STREAM

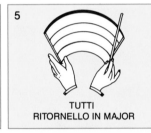

5 TUTTI RITORNELLO IN MAJOR

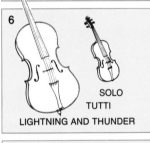

6 SOLO / TUTTI LIGHTNING AND THUNDER

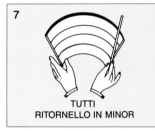

7 TUTTI RITORNELLO IN MINOR

8 SOLO AND CONCERTINO BIRDS RETURN AFTER THE STORM

9 SOLO, CONCERTINO, AND TUTTI RITORNELLO IN MAJOR

193

WESTERN MUSICAL STYLES

- Prepare to listen by identifying the musical sounds represented by each picture. Which pictures are similar and which are different?
- Listen to the recording, following the map. Notice the contrasts in tone color, themes, and dynamics as they listen.
- Describe the sound of the baroque orchestra (small size with strings predominant).
- Determine what instruments were used in this recording. (strings, harpsichord)

General Characteristics
1. Development of instrumental music in the form of the concerto
2. Steady rhythms and repetition of rhythmic motives and patterns
3. Sudden changes in dynamics
4. Contrasts of solo and tutti
5. Contrasts of textures

Form Based on contrasts between solo and tutti, episode and ritornello

Tone Color Homogenous instrumental sound in string concertos; clearly defined individual lines or voices in polyphonic compositions

MORE MUSIC TEACHING IDEAS
Have the students:
1. Compare "Spring" with other compositions in baroque style. ("Marche" by Lully, page 18)
2. Perform compositions that use contrasts of dynamics and tone color. (instrumental accompaniment to "Marche")
3. Listen to examples of compositions in baroque style.
4. Create a sound composition that uses contrasts of tone color and dynamics.
5. Analyze popular music of today and identify characteristics similar to those of "Spring."

You may wish to use this selection in conjunction with:
European-Western Styles, pp. 16–17
Moving to Sounds of the Twentieth Century, p. 174

LISTENING
You may wish to use the Listening Map overhead transparency to help guide the students through the listening selection.

WESTERN MUSICAL STYLES

Classical: Quintet for Clarinet and Strings in A Major, K. 581 (Fourth Movement), by Wolfgang Amadeus Mozart

Materials
Recording: Quintet for Clarinet and Strings (fourth movement)

TEACHING THE LESSON

Review the classical style. Have the students:
• Read about classical style on pages 144–145.
• Discuss the information on Mozart's Quintet for Clarinet and Strings, focusing on the theme and variation form used in the fourth movement.
• Listen to the recording, reading the description for each section. Notice the contrast between staccato and legato.

General Characteristics

1. Strict use of form
2. Clarity, order, and refinement
3. Straightforward, predictable harmonies
4. More subtle phrasing, dynamics, and orchestration than baroque style
5. Short and tuneful melodies

Form ABA, sonata, theme and variations

Tone Color Development of the orchestra as we know it today

6 Quintet for Clarinet and Strings in A Major, K. 581, Fourth Movement, by Wolfgang Amadeus Mozart

Compositions for small groups of instruments are called **chamber music** because they are designed to be performed in rooms (chambers) rather than concert halls. Like **symphonies** (works for full orchestra), chamber works are in several movements.

For the fourth and final movement of his Clarinet Quintet, Wolfgang Amadeus Mozart (volf' gäng ä-mä-dā' ōōs mōt' särt) decided to write a theme with six variations and a **coda,** or conclusion. The theme itself is a very simple one, which Mozart varies in several ways. For example, he shows off the instruments' abilities to change from major to minor, or to play **legato** (lā-gä' tō, smoothly) or **staccato** (stä-kä' tō, detached). For contrasting tone color, Mozart even leaves out the clarinet entirely in one variation.

• Listen to the music and read the description on page 195. Notice the contrast between staccato and legato sections.

> Quintet for Clarinet and Strings in A Major, K. 581, Fourth Movement, by Wolfgang Amadeus Mozart

EXTENSION

THE COMPOSER

Wolfgang Amadeus Mozart (1756–1791)—was born in Salzburg, Austria. His great talent was evident very early; his father took him and his older sister Nannerl on tours all across Europe. Mozart's father, an excellent musician, gave Wolfgang solid musical training. Wolfgang also studied with Johann Christian Bach. In 1781 Mozart settled in Vienna. He wrote operas, symphonies, chamber music, piano music, sacred music, and many other works, all unsurpassed in melodic beauty and expressiveness.

MORE MUSIC TEACHING IDEAS

Have the students:
1. Compare the Quintet for Clarinet and Strings to other compositions in classical style ("Ode to Joy," page 16).
2. Perform compositions that use variations on a basic melodic idea.
3. Listen to other examples of theme and variations form in classical style.
4. Create a theme and variations as indicated on page 109.
5. Analyze popular music of today and identify characteristics similar to those of the Quintet for Clarinet and Strings (answers will vary).

You may wish to use this selection in conjunction with:
European-Western Styles, pp. 16–17
Repetition and Identifying Motives, pp. 140–141
Repetition and Development, pp. 146–151

1. *Theme:* Cheerful, staccato theme is played and immediately repeated. The second part of the theme, momentarily legato, leads right back to the first (staccato) part, and this is repeated.
2. *Variation 1:* Clarinet, legato, has a new tune as strings play the staccato basic theme. This continues into Part 2 of the theme.
3. *Variation 2:* Strings agitated, but melody soars when clarinet enters. In Part 2 the agitation continues.
4. *Variation 3:* A change to minor gives a melancholy quality to the theme. This entire variation is played by strings only.
5. *Variation 4:* Rapid passages in clarinet accompany a return to the jolly mood of the theme in the strings.
6. *Adagio (Variation 5):* Change to a slow tempo is introduced by a series of chords and descending passages on the clarinet. Strings play yet another variation on the theme, joined by a wistful song on the clarinet, and this segment is repeated. The second part of the theme has the clarinet dominating, then giving in to the strings, and this segment also is repeated. A short, legato passage leads to:
7. *Allegro (Variation 6):* Another treatment of the basic theme. A coda of four chords brings this music to a strong conclusion.

Below, a typical chamber music concert during Mozart's time. Right, the child Mozart (at the keyboard) with his father and sister.

Mozart as a Child, with his Father and Sister, Carmontelle, MUSÉE CONDÉ Chantilly

The Concert, Augustin de Saint Aubin

195

WESTERN MUSICAL STYLES

Romantic: "Un bel dì vedremo" from
Madama Butterfly, by Giacomo Puccini

Materials
Recordings: *"Un bel dì vedremo"*
"The Erlking" (optional)
"Schwanenlied" (optional)
"The Wreck of the Edmund Fitzgerald" (optional)

TEACHING THE LESSON

Introduce the romantic style. Have the students:
• Discuss the information on the opera *Madama Butterfly*.
• Read the description and musical analysis of the aria *"Un bel dì vedremo."*

"Un bel dì vedremo," from *Madama Butterfly*, by Giacomo Puccini

Opera is one of the most exciting of all musical forms, for it offers not only music, but also dramatic action, scenery, costumes, interesting stories and, often, unusual lighting effects. An opera performance, therefore, is a special event.

Madama Butterfly, by the Italian composer Giacomo Puccini, is one of the most popular operas ever written. Puccini's characters are understandable and human.

Madama Butterfly is another name for Cio-Cio-San (chō′ chō-sän), a young Japanese woman who marries an American naval officer, Lieutenant Pinkerton. She plans to devote her life to this marriage, but to Pinkerton, it is just a temporary fling until he meets and marries the American woman of his dreams. Butterfly remains true, but Pinkerton, while in America, marries someone else. When Butterfly realizes that Pinkerton has deserted her, she kills herself.

Butterfly sings the famous **aria** (ä′ rē-ä, solo song) *"Un bel dì vedremo,"* while she still believes Pinkerton will come back to her. She tells her servant, Suzuki, that one beautiful day Pinkerton will return, and she describes everything she thinks will happen.

The powerful opening melody of this aria occurs again near the end of the song, making a kind of ABA form. Butterfly's belief that Pinkerton will return to her is reflected in the straightforward melody. Near the end of her song, the music becomes more insistent as she talks herself and her servant into believing that what she says actually will come to pass.

As you listen to this selection, you will notice that the composer has provided several changes of mood and tempo to illustrate the situations Butterfly describes. Puccini's melody is strong at the beginning when Pinkerton's return is described, but becomes gentler as Butterfly tells of her own reactions to the situation. She will stay where she is, waiting anxiously for Pinkerton to find her, almost unable to control her emotions. The first melody returns as she describes their first meeting. The aria reaches its peak near the end as Butterfly tries to assure Suzuki that Pinkerton will, indeed, return.

196

E X T E N S I O N

THE COMPOSER

Giacomo Puccini (1858–1924)—Italian composer, is considered one of the world's great operatic composers. As a child he showed no leaning or special talent for music, but entered music school at his mother's insistence. Indifference soon turned to enthusiasm. While Puccini was studying composition at the Milan Conservatory one of his teachers persuaded him to enter a one-act opera competition. Although his opera did not win, it attracted the attention of influential people, one of whom commissioned Puccini to write a second opera. This work was a failure, but his next effort, *Manon Lescaut*, was a success. The operas that followed won international fame. Among these, *La Bohème, Tosca, Madama Butterfly*, and *Turandot* remain very popular.

Right, poster advertising a 1906 production of *Madama Butterfly*. Below and page 198, Renata Scotto in the Metropolitan Opera production. Below is the wedding scene; on page 198, *"Un bel dì vedremo."*

197

WESTERN MUSICAL STYLES

• Listen to the recording, following the Italian words and the translation. Notice how Puccini's music reflects Butterfly's hopes and feelings.

General Characteristics of Romantic Music

1. Changes of mood within sections of a composition
2. Definite expressions of feelings and emotions
3. Melodies often long and complex
4. Extreme modulations
5. Program music as important as absolute music
6. Virtuosity emphasized and technique developed
7. New status of the artist as a creative personality, in contrast to formerly being regarded as an employee of the church or court

Characteristics of Romantic Operas

Form Through composed, often reflecting the feelings and emotions behind the words

Tone Color Larger orchestras, with newly improved instruments added

• Follow the Italian words and their translation as you hear them. Notice how Puccini's music reflects the hopes and feelings to which Butterfly refers.

Un bel dì, vedremo
Levarsi un fil di fumo
Sull'estremo confin del mare.
E poi la nave appare.
Poi la nave bianca
Entra nel porto,
Romba il suo saluto.
Vedi? È venuto!
Io non gli scendo incontro. Io no. Mi metto là sul ciglio del colle e aspetto, e aspetto gran tempo e non mi pesa la lunga attesa.
E uscito dalla folla cittadina un uomo, un picciol punto s'avvia per la collina.

Chi sarà? Chi sarà? E come sarà giunto che dirà? Che dirà? Chiamerà Butterfly dalla lontana. Io, senza dar risposta me ne starò nascosta un po' per celia, e un po' per non morire al primo incontro, ed egli alquanto in pena chiamerà, chiamerà: "Piccina mogliettina olezzo di verbena" i nomi che mi dava al suo venire.

Tutto questo avverrà, te lo prometto.

Tienti la tua paura, io con sicura fede l'aspetto.

One fine day, we shall see
A thread of smoke rising
Over the horizon
And then the ship will appear.
Then the white ship
Enters the harbor.
Her salute thunders out.
You see? He has come!
I don't go down to meet him. Not I. I stand on the brow of the hill and wait, and wait a long time and do not weary of the long watch.
Out of the city crowds there comes a man—a tiny speck—who makes his way toward the hill.
Who can it be? Who can it be? And when he arrives what will he say? What will he say? He will call Butterfly from the distance. I, without answering, will stay hidden partly for fun, and partly so as not to die at the first meeting. And he, a little troubled, will call, he will call: "My little wife, my sweet-scented flower"—the names he used to call me when he came.
All this will come to pass, I promise you.

Keep your fears: I, with unshakeable faith, will await him.

 "Un bel dì vedremo," from *Madama Butterfly*, by Giacomo Puccini

198

E X T E N S I O N

MORE MUSIC TEACHING IDEAS

Have the students:
1. Compare *"Un bel dì vedremo"* with other compositions in romantic style ("The Erlking," p. 111; *"Schwanenlied,"* p. 134).
2. Perform selections in which the music reflects the feelings and mood of the words ("The Wreck of the Edmund Fitzgerald," p. 130).
3. Listen to other examples of romantic vocal music in which the music reflects the feelings and ideas of the words.
4. Analyze popular music of today and identify characteristics similar to those in *"Un bel dì vedremo."*

You may wish to use this selection in conjunction with:
European-Western Styles, pp. 16–17
Story Through Song, pp. 130–135
Telling a Story, pp. 111—115

Étude in E Minor, Opus 25, No. 5, by Frédéric Chopin

1B, 8B
CD 1, 6

Polish composer Frédéric Chopin specialized in writing music for the piano. Among his finest works, which include waltzes, sonatas, and many other pieces, are his **études**. *Étude* means "study," and an étude's purpose is to help students with technical playing problems. Chopin's études are more than just studies, however, because they are important musical selections in their own right. Chopin played several of them in his concerts, and many pianists do so today.

Of the more than two dozen études that Chopin composed, the Étude in E Minor, Opus 25, No. 5, is particularly impressive. Its opening section (A) is mainly staccato and is played at a fast tempo. The middle section (B) offers an expressive legato, in a slower tempo. When the A section returns, its staccato idea brings to mind the strong contrast that exists between the three sections of this work. Chopin includes a coda (ending section) with chords and a melodic trill at the close.

- Listen to the Étude in E Minor and raise your hand when you hear the contrasting B section.

- How does the étude show unity and variety? unity: A section repeated; variety: contrasting B section

Étude in E Minor, Opus 25, No. 5, by Frédéric Chopin

Frédéric Chopin, Eugène Delacroix, LOUVRE, Paris

Chopin often played private concerts in the homes of the nobility.

Chopin Playing the Piano in Prince Anton Radziwill's Salon at Berlin, Siemiradski

199

WESTERN MUSICAL STYLES

Étude in E Minor, Opus 25, No. 5, by Frédéric Chopin

Materials
Recordings: Étude in E Minor
"Farandole" (optional)

TEACHING THE LESSON

Introduce piano music of the romantic era. Have the students:
- Discuss the information on Frédéric Chopin and the étude.
- Read the description and musical analysis of Étude No. 5.
- Listen to the recording and indicate the beginning of the contrasting B section by raising their hands.
- Identify how the Étude shows unity and variety. (unity: A section repeated; variety: contrasting B section)

Characteristics of Étude in E Minor

Form ABA; small forms and miniatures popular, especially for solo instruments

Tone Color Importance of the piano as a solo instrument

EXTENSION

MORE MUSIC TEACHING IDEAS
Have the students:
1. Compare the Étude in E Minor with other romantic compositions ("Farandole," p. 24).
2. Listen to other examples of romantic music in which there are changes of mood within a single composition.
3. Analyze popular music of today and identify characteristics similar to those in the Étude in E Minor.

You may wish to use this selection in conjunction with:
European-Western Styles, pp. 16–17
Characteristics of the Romantic Period, pp. 26–27

THE ARTIST
Eugene Delacroix (de-lä-krwä') (1798-1863)—was a French painter important in the Romantic movement. The subjects of many of his paintings were inspired by the writings of William Shakespeare, Dante, Lord Byron, and Sir Walter Scott. He particularly liked to paint exciting, violent, or exotic scenes, including battles and lion hunts. He was also known as a portrait painter, and among his subjects was Frédéric Chopin.

THE COMPOSER
Frédéric Chopin (1810–1849)—Polish composer and pianist. He began studying piano when he was six and gave his first public performance at the age of eight. By this time he had already begun to compose. After finishing his studies at the Warsaw Conservatory, Chopin left Poland and eventually settled in Paris. Chopin is one of the few composers who wrote almost exclusively for solo piano. In his use of the rhythms of Polish folk dances such as the mazurka and the polonaise, he was one of the first nationalistic composers. He was a master of small forms, such as the waltz, nocturne, and prelude. His études brought the study of technical problems to the level of great art. Today Chopin is regarded as one of the most influential composers of piano music.

WESTERN MUSICAL STYLES

Twentieth Century: "Infernal Dance,"
from *The Firebird*, by Igor Stravinsky

Materials
Recordings: "Infernal Dance"
"Misty, Moisty Morning"
(optional)
Saint Luke Passion (optional)
Suite for Percussion (optional)
Steel Band Music (optional)
Harry Partch on *Spoils of War*
(optional)

TEACHING THE LESSON

Introduce twentieth-century music.
Have the students:
• Discuss the information on *The Firebird* and the "Infernal Dance."
• Listen to the recording and read the description for each number.

General Characteristics of Twentieth-Century Music

1. Use of many different styles and types of music
2. Experimentation with new sounds and combinations of instruments (as in *Spoils of War*, by Harry Partch, on page 183)
3. Extreme dissonance (as in *Variations on "America,"* by Charles Ives, on page 108), extending to atonality
4. Abandonment of standard melodic formulas (as in *Saint Luke Passion*, by Krzysztof Penderecki, on page 171)
5. Development of new tonal systems, such as serialism (as in "The Web" on page 91)

Characteristics of "Infernal Dance"

Form Determined by the composer

Tone Color Large orchestra; use of persistent rhythms and dramatic effects

---

Infernal Dance, from *The Firebird*, by Igor Stravinsky

Through movement, ballet can express feelings that would be difficult or impossible to say in words. Some ballets are story ballets. Stravinsky's *The Firebird* is one of the finest story ballets of the twentieth century. Based on a Russian folk legend, it tells of Prince Ivan. He discovers a magic garden whose inhabitants are under the spell of an evil king named Kastchei (käs-chā′ē). With the help of the enchanted firebird, Ivan breaks the spell. This releases, among the others, the girl he marries, and all ends happily.

In the Infernal Dance, Stravinsky describes the King Kastchei's evil power through ominous-sounding themes, abrupt changes of instruments and dynamics, and strong rhythms. One can imagine, just by listening to this music, Kastchei's menacing gestures and his domination of the scene, even without seeing his actions on stage.

• Listen to the music and read the description below.

 "Infernal Dance" from *The Firebird*, by Igor Stravinsky

1. Loud chord—brasses and bassoons present ominous theme; theme is repeated.
2. Xylophone joins the proceedings.
3. A flowing melody in the strings.
4. Xylophone alternates with other instruments.
5. Smoother melodic ideas in strings and other instruments, soft and loud.
6. Entire orchestra plays the smoother idea at a loud dynamic level.
7. Suddenly soft, though the scary mood continues.
8. Theme (soft) punctuated by xylophone.
9. Crescendo built with shorter, faster notes.
10. Brasses alternate with other instruments.
11. Faster tempo builds a peak; music ends with one loud chord, then a soft chord.

200

E X T E N S I O N

THE COMPOSER

Igor Stravinsky (1882–1972)—Russian-born composer. As a young man Stravinsky studied law, but eventually turned to music. Stravinsky first became famous when he composed three ballets in Paris between 1909 and 1913. The first two—*The Firebird* and *Petrushka*—were easy to listen to and quickly became popular. The third, *The Rite of Spring*, was so unconventional that the audience rioted at the first performance. In the 1920s Stravinsky wrote in a neoclassical style with a twentieth-century flavor (*Symphony of Psalms*). At the outbreak of World War II Stravinsky moved to the United States. Stravinsky's innovations and versatility have greatly influenced twentieth-century music.

MORE MUSIC TEACHING IDEAS

Have the students:
1. Compare the "Infernal Dance" with other twentieth-century compositions ("Misty, Moisty Morning," and *Saint Luke Passion*, pp. 169–171; Recycling for Sound, pp. 181–183).
2. Listen to compositions that use traditional instruments in experimental ways ("Misty, Moisty Morning," pp. 170–171).
3. Create compositions that use traditional instruments in experimental ways (Create a Sound Composition, p. 14)
4. Analyze popular music of today and identify characteristics similar to those in the "Infernal Dance."

You may wish to use this selection in conjunction with:
European-Western Styles, pp. 16–17
New Sounds from a Familiar Instrument, pp. 175–177

"Tonight," from *West Side Story*, by Leonard Bernstein and Stephen Sondheim

🌐 4B, 5B, 8B

💿 3, 4, 6

When *West Side Story* opened on Broadway in 1957, it was quite different from other musical plays of the time. In it, the story of Romeo and Juliet was transplanted to New York's West Side and given a contemporary flavor by the use of popular music styles.

The plot of *West Side Story* concerns two street gangs, the Jets and the Sharks, each of which wants to rule the neighborhood. At the beginning of the story Tony, formerly a member of the Jets, has quit the gang and taken a job in hopes of bettering his life. One night at a dance Tony meets Maria, a Puerto Rican girl. They fall in love. But Maria and Tony's romance is doomed from the start. Maria is the sister of Bernardo, the leader of the Sharks, and is engaged to Bernardo's friend Chino. Despite this the two lovers meet secretly. In a scene reminiscent of the famous balcony scene in *Romeo and Juliet* they sing the beautiful duet "Tonight" on the fire escape outside Maria's apartment.

The two rival gangs plan a rumble (fight) to determine who will rule the neighborhood. Tony tries unsuccessfully to stop the fight and make peace between the two gangs. Bernardo and Tony's best friend Riff fight as everyone else watches. The rules for the fight specify no weapons, but knives are drawn and Bernardo kills Riff. In a grief-stricken rage, Tony takes Riff's knife and kills Bernardo. The gang members scatter as the police arrive.

Anita, Bernardo's girlfriend, learns the outcome of the rumble and goes to Maria to break the news about Bernardo to her. Maria is only concerned about Tony. Angrily, Anita tells her that Tony killed Bernardo. Maria is sorrowful, but is determined to forgive Tony.

Tony and Maria make plans to go away together. When Maria is delayed she sends Anita with a message for Tony. Anita goes to the store where Tony works and encounters some of the Jets. They know she is Bernardo's girlfriend and taunt her. Enraged, Anita gives

201

E X T E N S I O N

WESTERN MUSICAL STYLES

"Tonight," from *West Side Story*, by Leonard Bernstein and Stephen Sondheim

Materials
Recordings: "Tonight"
　　　　　　"The Erlking" (optional)
　　　　　　"Schwanenlied" (optional)

TEACHING THE LESSON

Introduce twentieth-century styles.
Have the students:
• Discuss the information on *West Side Story* and "Tonight."

THE COMPOSER

Leonard Bernstein—American composer and conductor, was born in Lawrence, Massachusetts, in 1918. He studied at Harvard, the Curtis Institute in Philadelphia, and Tanglewood. In 1943 he became an assistant conductor with the New York Philharmonic. Later that year he rose to fame when he substituted for Bruno Walter, who was ill. In 1958 Bernstein became the principal conductor of the New York Philharmonic, the first American ever to hold that post. Bernstein is an equally gifted composer of both classical and popular music. He has written a series of successful musicals, including *On the Town* (1944), *Candide* (1956), and *West Side Story* (1957). Bernstein is also a fine lecturer on music, with his televised series of Young People's Concerts in the 1950s.

WESTERN MUSICAL STYLES

• Listen to the recording, focusing on the story line, and read the description for each number.
• Describe the different kinds of music the composer provides for each character or group, and how he may have decided on it. (answers will vary)

Characteristics of "Tonight"

Form Partner song

Tone Color Use of vocal tone color, range, and register to reflect mood and feelings

them a different message for Tony: Chino found out about Tony and Maria, and killed her.

Tony, numb with grief, goes looking for Chino. But Chino finds Tony first, and shoots him in revenge for Bernardo. Maria finds Tony lying in the street. She cradles him in her arms as he dies. United by tragedy, the rival gangs finally make an effort at peace and jointly carry Tony's body away as Maria follows.

West Side Story contains solos, duets, instrumental sections, and ensembles (music in which several people sing at the same time). If several actors were to talk at the same time, the audience would not be able to understand them. However, in music, two or more things can happen at once, and the results will still be understandable. This ensemble, entitled "Tonight," has several different ideas going on at the same time: Maria and Tony express their love for each other; Anita looks forward to an evening of fun; and the opposing gangs plot the rumble that is about to take place.

• Follow the story line in "Tonight" by reading the descriptions.

1. *Jets:* "The Jets are gonna have their day tonight."
   Sharks: "We're gonna hand them a surprise tonight."
   Brief, jazzy introduction, Jets and Sharks in a fast tempo, with a strong rhythmic accompaniment.

2. *Anita:* "Anita's gonna get her kicks tonight."
   Introduced by brief, jazzlike pattern; same melody that was sung by Jets and Sharks, but sung as a solo.

3. *Tony:* "Tonight, tonight."
   A new melody is introduced; rhythmic accompaniment here is more subdued for this soaring, smoother tune, which depicts Tony and Maria's love for each other.

4. *Maria* continues Tony's melody of "Tonight."

5. *Jets:* "The Jets are comin' out on top tonight."
   Strong accompaniment returns, illustrating the warlike mentality of the gangs.

6. *Maria* sings "Tonight" with short comments in the background by the *Jets,* the *Sharks, Tony,* and *Anita.* Each melody is different from the others, even though they are all sung at the same time. The quintet reaches an exciting conclusion.

• Decide how the composer provides different music for each character or group. answers will vary

202

THE LYRICIST

Stephen Sondheim—American composer and lyricist, was born in New York City in 1930. He studied with the lyricist Oscar Hammerstein II and the composer Milton Babbitt. Sondheim's first major work was with Leonard Bernstein on *West Side Story.* The first musical for which he wrote both music and lyrics was *A Funny Thing Happened on the Way to the Forum* (1962), based on the comedies of the Roman author Plautus. Sondheim's shows are notable for their complex melodies, witty lyrics, and sophisticated plots. Other Sondheim shows include *Company* (1970), *Follies* (1971), *A Little Night Music* (1973), *Sweeney Todd* (1979), *Sunday in the Park with George* (1984), and *Into the Woods* (1987).

MORE MUSIC TEACHING IDEAS

Have the students:
1. Compare "Tonight" with other dramatic vocal compositions ("The Erlking," pp. 111–115; "*Schwanenlied,* " pp. 134–135).
2. Perform selections in which the music reflects the feelings and mood of the words.
3. Create compositions in which the music reflects the feelings and mood of the text (Create a Sound Composition, page 14).
4. Analyze popular music of today and identify characteristics similar to those in "Tonight." (answers will vary)

You may wish to use this selection in conjunction with:
European-Western Styles, pp. 16–17
Story Through Song, pp. 130–135
Telling a Story, pp. 111–115

These scenes are from the film of *West Side Story*. Above, the rumble. Tony (Richard Beymer) is facing forward. Left, Anita (Rita Moreno) and some friends on the roof of their apartment building.

"Tonight," quintet from *West Side Story*, by Leonard Bernstein and Stephen Sondheim

Maria (Natalie Wood) and Tony declare their love in this "wedding" scene.

203

WESTERN MUSICAL STYLES

Lieutenant Kijé Suite, by Sergei Prokofiev

Materials
Recordings: "The Birth of Kijé"
          Wellington's Victory (optional)
          "The Wreck of the Edmund
          Fitzgerald" (optional)
          "Rainbow Writing" (optional)
          "Dreams" (optional)
          "Bravado" (optional)
          "The Wedding of Kijé"
Copying Master W-1: Listening Map (optional)

TEACHING THE LESSON

Introduce twentieth-century styles.
Have the students:
• Discuss the information on the *Lieutenant Kijé Suite.* (You may wish to review the information on Prokofiev on page 149 of the Teacher's Edition.)
• Identify the "Kijé" theme.
• Listen to the first movement of the suite and identify the instruments that Prokofiev uses to convey the idea of Kijé's military service. (brass and percussion)
• Continue following the story line.
• Identify themes 2 and 3.

Lieutenant Kijé Suite, by Sergei Prokofiev

Lieutenant Kijé (kē' jā) was a Russian film for which Sergei Prokofiev (ser' gā prō-kō' fē-ev) composed the score. The story of *Lieutenant Kijé* is a humorous one, set in the nineteenth century. One day the czar of Russia is looking at military reports and misreads the name *Kijé* in an account of a heroic deed. When the czar asks questions about Lieutenant Kijé, his advisors are afraid to tell him that he has made a mistake. Consequently they proceed to make up a life story for the imaginary Lieutenant Kijé.

In the first movement of the suite, "The Birth of Kijé," a solo cornet theme decribes Kijé's birth and some of his supposed military exploits. A separate theme is used to represent Kijé himself. This theme reappears in later movements of the suite whenever Kijé is present.

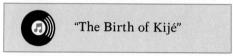

• Listen to the first movement of this suite and identify the instruments that Prokofiev uses to convey the idea of Kijé's military service. **brass and percussion**

"The Birth of Kijé"

The advisors continue their story, and in the second movement of the suite, "Romance," Kijé falls in love. A "love song" theme is played by string bass, cello, and tenor saxophone. This is followed by themes from Kijé's wedding and the celebration afterward.

204

E X T E N S I O N

CURRICULUM CONNECTION: VISUAL ARTS

Motion Pictures—The 1934 film *Lieutenant Kijé* was the first film for which Sergei Prokofiev wrote the score. Later Prokofiev adapted an orchestral suite from this music. He conducted the first performance of the suite in Paris in 1937. Since then the *Lieutenant Kijé Suite* has become part of orchestra repertoires around the world. Other films for which Prokofiev wrote music include *Alexander Nevsky* (1938) and *Ivan the Terrible* (1942–45).

MORE MUSIC TEACHING IDEAS

Have the students:
1. Compare the *Lieutenant Kijé Suite* with other programmatic selections (*Wellington's Victory,* pp. 153–155).
2. Perform selections in which the music reflects the feelings and mood of the words ("The Wreck of the Edmund Fitzgerald," pp. 131–132).
3. Create compositions that are programmatic in nature (Create a Sound Composition, p. 14)
4. Analyze film music of today and identify characteristics similar to those of *Lieutenant Kijé.* (program music)

You may wish to use this selection in conjunction with:
European-Western Styles, pp. 16–17
Program Music, pp. 152–155

A scene from
the 1934 film
Lieutenant Kijé

• Listen to the third movement and identify which theme is heard as each number is called. (You may wish to use Copying Master W-1: Listening Map at this time.)
• Discuss the end of the story.

Characteristics of *Lieutenant Kijé Suite*
Form Suite

Tone Color Use of unusual tone colors, range, and register to reflect mood and feelings

Prokofiev uses these two themes in the third movement, "The Wedding of Kijé," to describe the relationship between the stately ceremony (Theme 2) and the celebration (Theme 3). Kijé's theme (Theme 1) also is heard throughout.

• Listen and identify which theme you hear for each number. No. 1: Theme 2; No. 2: Theme 3; No. 3: Theme 1; No. 4: Theme 3; No. 5: Theme 2; No. 6: Theme 3; No. 7: Theme 2

 "The Wedding of Kijé"

The advisors describe more of Kijé's deeds to the czar. Their plan backfires when the czar is so interested that he asks to meet Kijé! The advisors must do something quickly. They tell the czar that Kijé has died and has been buried with full military honors.

In the fifth and last movement, "The Burial of Kijé," Prokofiev uses many of the themes from the earlier movements to remind the audience of Kijé's life. Then the solo cornet returns with the opening theme as the hero is laid to rest.

205

WESTERN MUSICAL STYLES

"Ev'ry Time I Feel the Spirit," an African American spiritual, arranged by William Dawson

Materials
Recordings: ''Ev'ry Time I Feel the Spirit''
''Run Joe'' (optional)
Keyboard or bells

TEACHING THE LESSON

Introduce arrangement as a musical technique. Have the students:
• Discuss the information on arranging a melody.
• Discuss the information on William Dawson and ''Ev'ry Time I Feel the Spirit.''

"Ev'ry Time I Feel the Spirit," an African American spiritual, arranged by William Dawson

Some musicians **arrange** rather than compose music. In arranging, a musician takes an existing composition and resets it for a different combination of musical resources. For example, a work for two voices may be rearranged for two clarinets.

One of the challenges an arranger faces is not to let the arrangement overpower the unique qualities of the original music. "Ev'ry Time I Feel the Spirit" illustrates William Dawson's sensitive feeling in preserving the characteristics of spirituals in his choral arrangements.

William Dawson, composer, arranger, and conductor

William Dawson, born at the turn of the century, has arranged many African American spirituals. By creating arrangements, he has made it possible for choirs to perform this exciting and expressive music. As choir director at Tuskeegee Institute in Alabama, Dawson has shared his arrangements with people throughout the United States and Europe.

"Ev'ry Time I Feel the Spirit" is one of William Dawson's best-known choral arrangements. He uses strongly syncopated rhythms, contrasts between group and solo singing, and the improvised quality of the choral parts to create an exciting musical setting.

Learn the melody before you listen to a performance of "Ev'ry Time I Feel the Spirit" by the Brazeal Dennard Chorale.

206

EXTENSION

THE ARRANGER

William Dawson—African American composer, arranger, and trombonist, was born in Anniston, Alabama, at the turn of the century. He left home at thirteen to enter the Tuskeegee Institute in Alabama. After graduation he continued his studies at the Horner Institute for Fine Arts in Kansas City, and at the American Conservatory in Chicago, where he received his master's degree. He played first trombone with the Chicago Civic Orchestra before returning to Tuskeegee as choir director. Dawson is well known as a composer and arranger. Among his own compositions is the three-movement *Negro Folk Symphony*.

Key: E♭ major   Starting Pitch: E♭   Scale Tones: *do re mi so la do'*

- Perform the melody by singing it or playing it on keyboard or bells.

Ev'ry Time I Feel the Spirit

African American Spiritual

Ev - 'ry time I___ feel the spi - rit___ Mov - in' in my heart___ I will pray;   Yes; ev-'ry

time I___ feel the spi - rit___ Mov - in' in my heart___ I will pray.___

- Listen to the Brazeal Dennard Chorale perform "Ev'ry Time I Feel the Spirit."

"Ev'ry Time I Feel the Spirit"

The Brazeal Dennard Chorale of Detroit, Michigan, specializes in performing music by African American composers and arrangers. Named after its conductor, the group has performed many concerts in the Detroit area as well as in Michigan and Ohio.

The Brazeal Dennard Chorale. Mr. Dennard is at the lower right.

207

WESTERN MUSICAL STYLES

- Perform the melody of "Ev'ry Time I Feel the Spirit" by singing it or playing it on keyboard or bells.
- Listen to the recording.
- Discuss the information on the Brazeal Dennard Chorale.
- Summarize the information on arranging a melody.

General Characteristics

1. Folk style is characterized by simple melody, harmony, and phrasing
2. Rhythms sometimes very syncopated, as in "Ev'ry Time I Feel the Spirit"

Form Strophic (same music, different words)

Tone Color Choral ensemble of soprano, alto, tenor, and bass

MORE MUSIC TEACHING IDEAS

Have the students:
1. Compare "Ev'ry Time I Feel the Spirit" with other folk songs and spirituals ("Run Joe," p. 10).
2. Listen to other selections in a folk or spiritual style.
3. Analyze popular music of today and identify characteristics similar to those in "Ev'ry Time I Feel the Spirit." (answers will vary)

You may wish to use this selection in conjunction with:
European-Western Styles, pp. 16–17
Major and Minor in Two Styles, pp. 24–29

CURRICULUM CONNECTION: SOCIAL STUDIES

The spiritual—is a type of folk song that is usually religious. Developed by African American slaves, spirituals are songs of yearning. Spirituals are characterized by variations in meter and intonation, and sometimes by the use of call-and-response patterns. Some spirituals are sorrow songs ("Nobody Knows the Trouble I've Seen") or shouts ("Give me that Old-Time Religion). The first spiritual to be published was "Roll, Jordan, Roll" in 1867. However, it was not until the tour of the Fisk Jubilee Singers in 1871 that the world really became familiar with this music.

MUSIC OF THE WORLD'S CULTURES

208

209

MUSIC OF THE WORLD'S CULTURES

Focus: Cultures of the World Interact

Objectives
To identify and define the combining of characteristics of different cultures
To identify the presence of different cultures in music and architecture
To play accompaniments to music combining the characteristics of different cultures

Materials
Recordings: *Kogoklaras*
             "Come On Baby Dance with Me"
Guitar or keyboard
Drumsticks or other percussion instruments

1 SETTING THE STAGE

Discuss the text at the top of the page. (Emphasize that culture is the product of the people of a society.)

2 TEACHING THE LESSON

1. Identify characteristics of different cultures. Have the students examine and describe the Western and Egyptian influences in the architectural example. (Western: use of steel and glass; Egyptian: influence of the pyramid.)

9A THE INFLUENCE OF WORLD CULTURES

Musicians, dancers, authors, architects, and sculptors get their ideas from many different sources. They are often influenced by the cultural traditions of other countries.

Sometimes the characteristics of other cultures are obvious. At other times cultural influences may be more difficult to identify. The College Life Insurance headquarters buildings have characteristics of contemporary styles and the styles of ancient Egypt.

- Identify the contemporary characteristics of these buildings. use of steel and glass
- Identify the ancient Egyptian characteristics. pyramid shape

Left, the pyramids at Giza, Egypt. Below, the College Life Insurance Headquarters, Indianapolis, Indiana.

210

Mixing Musical Cultures

In this first section you will listen to music that mixes the characteristics of music of the United States with characteristics of the music of another culture. Some ways musicians do this are to combine instruments, rhythm, melodies, or harmonies of both cultures.

Kogoklaras (kō-gō-klä' räs) is one example of this mix. It combines characteristics of Indonesian music and music of the United States.

Right and below, dancers from the island of Bali, Indonesia. The dancers must practice for years to master these difficult techniques.

- Listen and identify musical characteristics of Indonesia and the United States. Indonesian instruments U.S.: prepared piano

Kogoklaras, by Vincent McDermott

211

2. Introduce aspects of different musical cultures. Have the students discuss how musical compositions can also merge different ideas together to create something new.

3. Listen to identify aspects of different musical cultures. Have the students:
• Identify characteristics of the Indonesian and Western musical cultures while listening to *Kogoklaras.* (Indonesia: Indonesian instruments; U.S.: prepared piano)
• Discuss how effectively the musical traditions of these two cultures are merged: "Is the composition musically interesting?"

4. Discuss the influence on Western music of other music. Have the students:
• Discuss the text at the top of the page.
• Listen for characteristics of Indian music and music of the United States in ''Come On Baby Dance with Me.''

5. Introduce the accompaniment to "Come On Baby Dance with Me." Have the students:
• Practice the rhythm on percussion instruments.
• Read and identify the notes of the chord.
• Practice the chords on guitar or keyboard.
• Form two groups and play the rhythm and chords with the recording.
• Respond to the Challenge! by playing the melody or the ostinati with the recording.

Reinforcing the Lesson

Discuss the fact that different cultures have different traditions in general, and different musical traditions in particular. Because of increased interactions between different cultures, musical compositions of one culture can be influenced by the music of other cultures.

3 APPRAISAL

The students should be able to:
1. Verbally define characteristics of architecture and music that combine elements from different cultures.
2. Identify non-Western influences on architecture and music of the United States.
3. Perform an accompaniment accurately on percussion, and keyboard or guitar.

American and Indian Cultures Interact

Other cultures, including that of India, have influenced the music of the United States. Shakti, a musical group from the United States, combines Indian traditional music and instruments with rock style instruments of the United States in "Come On Baby Dance With Me."

• Listen for characteristics of Indian music and music of the United States.

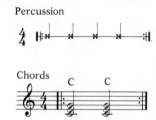 "Come On Baby Dance With Me," performed by Shakti

You can learn these instrumental parts to perform accompaniments to "Come On Baby Dance With Me."

• Practice each part before performing with the recording.

Percussion

Chords

• Form groups. One group should play the percussion part with drumsticks or other percussion instruments. The other group should play the chords on guitar or keyboard.

CHALLENGE Try playing these melodic patterns to "Come On Baby Dance With Me."

Melody

Ostinati

212

MORE MUSIC TEACHING IDEAS

Have the students identify elements from other cultures, other than architecture, that exist in our environment. (Clothing and food are evident.)

THE MUSIC OF INDIA

The Hall of Public Audience, Agra, India

"Come On Baby Dance With Me" is a combination of Indian music and music of the United States. Next you will hear Indian concert music. Like Western jazz, Indian concert music is improvised. In some Indian music, one pitch, called a *drone*, is repeated in such a way that it is sounding continuously. This drone pitch provides a background for the creation and performance of rhythmic and melodic patterns. In *Madhu Kauns*, (mä' dōō käns), the pitch D-flat (the black key to the left of D on the keyboard) is repeated as the drone.

5B, 9A

CD 4, 6

• Listen for the D-flat drone in *Madhu Kauns*.

 Madhu Kauns

• Play D-flat at the proper time on keyboard or bells as you listen again.

Rhythm patterns in Indian music usually are longer than those in Western music. Instead of two, three, or four beats to a group, Indian rhythm patterns can have ten, twelve, fourteen, or sixteen beats. These patterns are repeated and used as a basis for improvisation.

• Perform the steady beat on percussion instruments with *Madhu Kauns*.
• Next play the D-flat drone and the steady beat with the recording.

CHALLENGE Try playing this rhythm pattern to *Madhu Kauns*.

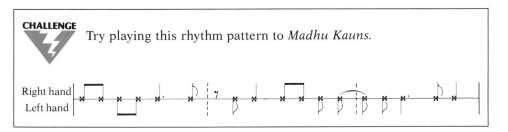

213

Focus: The Music of India

Objectives
To develop knowledge of repetition and tone color in Indian music
To introduce the sitar
To play music in an Indian style

Materials
Recordings: "Floe"
              Madhu Kauns
Bells or keyboard
Drumsticks, drums, or other unpitched percussion instruments

Vocabulary
Drone, sitar

1 SETTING THE STAGE

Review "Floe," page 127, and remind students that Philip Glass was influenced by the use of repetition in Indian classical music.

2 TEACHING THE LESSON

1. Introduce India and repetition as found in Indian music. Have the students:
• Discuss repetition in Indian music as presented in the text.
• Listen to *Madhu Kauns* and indicate the repeated pitch, D-flat, by raising their hands when they hear that pitch.
2. Perform the drone pitch and rhythm of Indian music. Have the students:
• Play D-flat on keyboard or bells with the recording.
• Discuss the information on rhythm patterns in Indian music.

MUSIC OF THE WORLD'S CULTURES

- Perform the steady beat on percussion instruments with *Madhu Kauns*.
- Form two groups to practice and perform the steady beat and the D-flat drone pitch using appropriate instruments.
- Perform with the recording.
- Respond to the Challenge! by playing the rhythm pattern with the recording.

3. Introduce and listen to the sitar.
Have the students:
- Discuss the text and picture of the sitar.
- Listen to the sound of the sitar in *Madhu Kauns*.

Reinforcing the Lesson

Discuss traditional Indian music and its use of repetition.

3 APPRAISAL

The students should be able to:
1. Distinguish repetition of rhythm and drone pitch in Indian music.
2. Identify and describe the sitar.
3. Perform rhythm and drone pitches to Indian music accurately.

Tone Colors in the Music of India

The melody of *Madhu Kauns* is performed on a *sitar* (si' tär). The sitar is a twenty-six-stringed instrument somewhat like a lute. The performer uses six of these strings to play a melody. The rest of the strings vibrate when the melody is played, resulting in a continuous layer of sound.

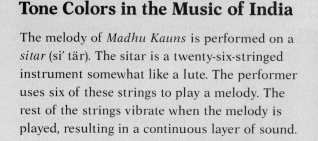

Top, girls from northern India. Above, Ravi Shankar (center), a world-famous sitar player. The other performers in his ensemble play the tambura (right), a stringed instrument that produces the drone pitches, and the tabla (left), drums.

- Listen again to *Madhu Kauns* and focus on the sound of the sitar.

 Madhu Kauns (excerpt)

The sitar melodies combine with the drone pitch and repeated rhythms played on hand drums to give Indian music its distinctive sound.

The traditional music of India is performed in concert settings. Members of an Indian audience are familiar with the repeated rhythms. As they listen they frequently move their hands silently in time to the rhythm. How is this different from the way an audience in the United States might respond? applause, shouts of "Bravo!" and so on

214

EXTENSION

MORE MUSIC TEACHING IDEAS

Have the students:
1. Discuss the reaction of audiences in the United States to different types of musical events, such as orchestral concerts, music videos, school assemblies, and so on.
2. Identify the use of repetition in familiar music compositions.
3. Find compositions in Western music that use the sitar, for example, music of the Beatles from the mid-1960s.

CURRICULUM CONNECTION: SOCIAL STUDIES

India—a large country in southern Asia. It is the second largest country in the world in population. India has one of the great ancient civilizations, dating back to 2500 B.C. Its total present-day area is about 1,246,880 square miles, a little more than one-third the size of the forty-eight contiguous United States. Its capital city is New Delhi.

Xylophone ensembles are popular in many parts of Africa. These performers are members of the Senufo tribe from the Ivory Coast.

Xylophone ensembles are popular in many parts of Africa. These performers are members of the Senufo tribe from the Ivory Coast.

MUSIC OF MALI

In the African nation of Mali, *xylophone ensembles* frequently perform complex rhythmic and melodic patterns. Xylophones in an ensemble can vary. Sometimes other instruments perform with the xylophones, for example, guitar, metal clappers, drums, or voice.

Musicians in a xylophone ensemble perform rhythms in several different ways. They can repeat just one rhythm pattern or alternate between patterns. They can echo a pattern that another musician has just played or create new patterns.

• Listen to *Kondawele*, a piece from Mali.

 Kondawele (excerpt)

You can use these rhythms to create a percussion ensemble in the style of those found in Mali.

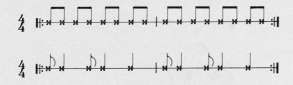

• Perform both lines of rhythm. Use different melodic and percussion instruments for each line.
• Notice how the sound of your ensemble changes when you use different instruments. Try other combinations of instruments.

215

EXTENSION

CURRICULUM CONNECTION: SOCIAL STUDIES

Mali—a large republic in western Africa. Half of Mali is covered by the Sahara desert. The rest of the country is rolling grassland. During the Middle Ages areas of present-day Mali formed part of three great black empires that controlled important African trade routes. In this period the city of Timbuktu flourished as a center of wealth and learning. In the late nineteenth century what is now Mali became a French colony known as French Sudan. When it gained complete independence in 1960, French Sudan changed its name to the Republic of Mali. Mali is about 478,000 square miles in area. Its capital city is Bamako.

9A
CD 6

MUSIC OF THE WORLD'S CULTURES

Focus: The Music of Mali

Objectives
To develop knowledge of instruments and tone colors in the music of Mali
To perform in a percussion ensemble similar to those found in Mali
To distinguish tone color changes in a percussion instrument ensemble

Materials
Recording: *Kondawele* (excerpt)
Orff instruments, bells, or other melodic percussion objects (pans, pan lids, metal objects, and so on)
Drumsticks, drums, or other rhythmic percussion objects

Vocabulary
Xylophone ensemble

1 SETTING THE STAGE

Introduce Mali, xylophone, and xylophone ensemble. Have the students discuss the text at the top of the page and the instruments in the picture. Then have them listen to *Kondawele*.

2 TEACHING THE LESSON

1. Play percussion instruments in an ensemble. Have the students:
• Identify melodic (pitched) and rhythmic (non-pitched) percussion instruments.
• Read the rhythmic notation for each line, saying the note values but not playing them.
• Practice the rhythm of each line on melodic, then rhythmic, percussion instruments.
• Form two groups with a combination of melodic and rhythmic percussion instruments to each line. Perform both lines at the same time.
2. Identify and discuss changing the ensemble sound. Have the students:
• Recognize and use words to describe the changes in sound when different combinations of instruments perform. (brighter, darker, light, heavy, and so on)

Reinforcing the Lesson
Summarize and discuss rhythmic and tonal characteristics of music from Mali.

3 APPRAISAL

The students should be able to:
1. Perform rhythm patterns characteristic of the music of Mali accurately in a percussion instrument ensemble.
2. Recognize tone color changes in performances of a percussion ensemble.

MUSIC OF THE WORLD'S CULTURES

Focus: Music of Gambia and Zimbabwe

Objectives
To develop a knowledge of instrumental and vocal tone colors in the music of Gambia and Zimbabwe
To listen to the kora and mbira
To play music similar to Zimbabwean music

Materials
Recordings: *Kelefa ba*
             Cedo
             Chemutengure
Bells or keyboard
Unpitched percussion instruments

Vocabulary
Kora, griot, mbira

1 SETTING THE STAGE
Tell the students they will be learning about two new different kinds of African music.

2 TEACHING THE LESSON

1. Examine the rhythmic complexity of *Kelefa ba.* Have the students:
• Discuss the text.
• Listen to *Kelefa ba* and recognize the changing rhythmic complexity as the number of parts is varied.
• Practice the three rhythm patterns.
• Form three groups and perform two of the patterns together, then all three.
• Perform *Kelefa ba,* paying attention to the rhythmic changes.

The Sounds of Gambia

Rhythmic variety is characteristic of traditional music from the African country of Gambia. *Kelefa ba* (ke-le′ fä bä) is an example of this style of music. Each of its rhythm parts is different from the others. When they are performed together, the result is a rhythmically complex and constantly changing musical sound.

• Listen to *Kelefa ba* to hear this rhythmic variety.

 Kelefa ba

• Practice each of these rhythm patterns on unpitched percussion instruments.

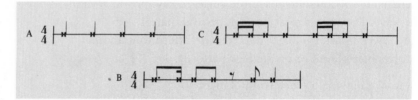

• Compare the rhythm patterns. Which has mostly short note values? Mostly long note values?
• Form three groups. Listen to the changing rhythmic sound as two groups perform two of the rhythm patterns at the same time. Have the third group add the third part.
• Perform the rhythm patterns with the recording of *Kelefa ba.* Listen for the changes in rhythm.
• Practice this melodic pattern on keyboard or bells. Play it with *Kelefa ba.*

• Form four groups to perform the three rhythm patterns and the melodic pattern with *Kelefa ba.*

216

Instrumental and Vocal Sounds of Gambia

Some Gambian music is performed by a solo voice and a stringed instrument called a *kora* (kô' rä). The kora, a kind of harp-lute, comes in several sizes with from five to twenty-one strings. A small metal disk with metal rings attached produces a rasping sound when the performer plucks or strums the strings.

Throughout West Africa, professional musicians are called *griots* (grē' ō). In Gambia, griots are very important, because one of their roles is to record the history of the Gambian people. They pass this history on through their music. In contrast, people of Western cultures write books to record their history. The griots compose songs to comment on historical events.

• Listen to *Cedo* (kā' dō), a Gambian history, to hear the tone color of the kora.

Cedo

Koras are made in many sizes, from small (left) to large (below). *Cedo* is played on a large kora.

217

2. Learn and perform an accompaniment to *Kelefa ba*. Have the students:
• Practice the melodic pattern on keyboard or bells.
• Form four groups, three to play the rhythm patterns and one to play the melodic pattern.
• Perform the rhythm patterns, then the melodic pattern, with the recording.
• Perform both with the recording.

3. Introduce and discuss the kora and griots. Have the students:
• Discuss the kora, and speculate on what it might sound like.
• Discuss griots and their role in Gambian society and relate this to folk songs that tell stories in the United States.
• Listen to and distinguish the buzzing sound of the kora in *Cedo*.

CURRICULUM CONNECTION: SOCIAL STUDIES

Gambia—a small country in western Africa that lies along the banks of the Gambia River, extending inland from the Atlantic Ocean for about two hundred miles. Once a British crown colony, Gambia gained its independence in 1965 and became a republic in 1970. Gambia is only about four thousand square miles in area, approximately twice the size of the state of Delaware. Its capital is Banjul.

4. Listen to the use of the voice in Gambian music. Have the students:
• Listen and distinguish the quality of the voice singing in *Cedo*.
• Summarize the sound of the voice in Gambian music.
5. Introduce Zimbabwe and examine how the voice is used in Zimbabwean music. Have the students:
• Discuss the material on Zimbabwe and the voice.
• Listen and distinguish the quality of the voice singing in *Chemutengure*.
• Compare and summarize the sound of the voice in Gambian and Zimbabwean music. (Even though they are countries in different parts of Africa, their singing styles are similar.)
• Compare the differences between the music of the two countries.

The melody in *Cedo* is performed by a singer.

• Listen to *Cedo* again. Identify which of these words best describe the quality of the voice: light or heavy; rough or smooth; strong or weak. heavy, rough, strong

Cedo

In this Ivory Coast village, boys of the Yaou tribe listen as a storyteller recounts a tribal legend.

Instrumental and Vocal Sounds of Zimbabwe

Zimbabwe, an African country, is about thirty-five hundred miles southwest of Gambia. The two countries have many cultural differences. However, in their music, the use of voice is similar.

• Listen to *Chemutengure* (che-mōō-ten-gōō′ re) and identify which of these words best describe the quality of the voice: light or heavy; rough or smooth; strong or weak. heavy, rough, strong

 Chemutengure

Although the voice is used similarly in the music of Zimbabwe and Gambia, the music of these two countries differs in other ways. For example, Gambian music uses stringed instruments, while in Zimbabwe the *mbira* (m′ bē′ rä) is very important.

218

The mbira is found in many African cultures. Recently, it has become popular in Western musical styles.

The mbira is a melodic instrument. It has a wooden frame with metal tongs attached. The performer plays the mbira by pulling down or plucking each tong, causing it to vibrate. A dried gourd serves to amplify the sound, much like the body of a guitar. In other African cultures, the mbira is called the *sansa, likembe, budongo,* or *kalimba.*

In Zimbabwe, the mbira is used in many different musical ways. It can be used as a solo instrument to express personal feelings. Frequently it is used in religious settings. At other times it accompanies songs of love or politics.

Chemutengure is a composition for the mbira and the voice. Both perform the same melody but at different times.

• Listen to *Chemutengure* again and follow the melody.

• Practice this accompaniment to *Chemutengure,* then play it with the recording.

The mbira also has been used in American music. Both jazz and popular music groups have included its traditional sounds. Some performers have even used an electrified version.

219

MUSIC OF THE WORLD'S CULTURES

6. Introduce the mbira and its use in Zimbabwean music. Have the students:
• Examine the picture and discuss the material on the role of the mbira in Zimbabwean music.
• Discuss using an instrument and music for spiritual, political, and expressive reasons.

7. Listen to and perform music from Zimbabwe. Have the students:
• Listen to the melody while following the score with the recording of *Chemutengure.*
• Learn and practice the accompaniment on keyboard or bells.
• Perform the accompaniment with the recording.
• Discuss the information on the use of the mbira in American music.

Reinforcing the Lesson

Summarize the similarities and differences between how voices and instruments are used in Gambian and Zimbabwean music. Have the students:
• Identify and discuss the similarities in the musical traditions of both cultures.
• Identify and discuss the differences in the musical traditions of both cultures.

3 APPRAISAL

The students should be able to:
1. Identify and describe the sound of the voice in Gambian and Zimbabwean music.
2. Identify and describe the kora and the mbira.
3. Perform an accompaniment to Zimbabwean music accurately on pitched percussion instruments.

MORE MUSIC TEACHING IDEAS

Have the students:
1. Distinguish different uses of the voice in music performed in the United States.
2. Identify other cultures in which history is passed down through music.

CURRICULUM CONNECTION: SOCIAL STUDIES

Zimbabwe—an independent republic in southeast Africa. Zimbabwe's beautiful scenery includes the famous Victoria Falls on the Zambezi River along its northern border. From the 1890s until the 1960s Zimbabwe, then called Rhodesia, was under British rule. In 1965 the Rhodesian government declared its independence from Great Britain, the first colony to do so since the American colonies declared their independence in 1776. The Rhodesian government underwent many changes over the next fifteen years. In 1980 Great Britain recognized the country's independence, and Rhodesia's name was officially changed to Zimbabwe.

MUSIC OF THE WORLD'S CULTURES

Focus: The Music of Turkey

Objectives
To develop knowledge of instruments and tone colors in Turkish music
To introduce the ney

Materials
Recording: *Taksim in Mode Segah*
Keyboard, recorder, or bells

Vocabulary
Ney, ornaments

1 SETTING THE STAGE
Listen to *Taksim in Mode Segah* to experience the scale and the sound of the ney.

2 TEACHING THE LESSON

1. Introduce Turkey and discuss the ney. Have the students:
• Examine and discuss the text and the picture of the ney.
• Discuss Turkey and the Middle East.

2. Introduce a scale from Turkey. Have the students:
• Play the scale shown on bells, keyboard, or recorder.
• Listen again to *Taksim in Mode Segah,* which is based on this scale.
• Recognize the sound of the ney.

THE MUSIC OF TURKEY

The *ney* (nā) is a flutelike wind instrument used in the music of Turkey and other countries of the Middle East. It is a hollow cane tube with six finger holes in front and one in back. Unlike the flute, which is held horizontally, the ney is held at an angle when it is played.

The classical music of Turkey is performed on the ney. In this music the performer frequently performs long solos. Sometimes a ney performance includes drums and stringed instruments. The ney is associated with a religious sect, and is played during certain religious services.

The ney is popular throughout the Middle East.

• Play this Turkish scale on keyboard, recorder, or bells. (B-sharp and C are the same key on a keyboard.)

• Listen to *Taksim* (täk' sim), or improvisation, *in Mode Segah.* It is performed on the ney. This piece is based on the scale you just played, which is called mode *segah* (sā' gä).

 Taksim in Mode Segah

220

The ney performer plays along melodic lines that are frequently improvised, or made up on the spot. Single tones of the scale are used as centers around which melodies are developed. In this example, each white note is the center of a melody, or tonal center.

Many times a performer uses *ornaments* with a melody. **Ornaments** are added notes that decorate a basic melody.

• Listen to *Taksim in Mode Segah* again. Try to hear each melodic line and its tonal center. Notice the ornaments the performer adds to the melody, and the long pauses.

Turkey has long been a meeting place between Europe and Asia. These ruins of a fortification are on the Mediterranean coast at Üçagiz near Kale.

221

MUSIC OF THE WORLD'S CULTURES

3. Recognize the ney and its music.
Have the students:
• Discuss music performed on the ney. Examine the notation and identify the center tones. (Center tones are those tones on which a performer bases a melodic improvisation. In this example center tones are shown as whole notes.)
• Discuss ornaments and their relationship to music. (An ornament is a form of decoration not basic to an object; in music, added notes ornament a melody or musical idea).
• Listen for ornaments in *Taksim in Mode Segah*. Emphasize the presence of center tones, long pauses, and ornaments in additional listenings.

Reinforcing the Lesson
Summarize the use of the ney in Turkish music.

3 APPRAISAL
The students should be able to:
1. Identify and describe the ney, a Turkish woodwind instrument.
2. Listen to and identify tone colors in Turkish music.

CURRICULUM CONNECTION: SOCIAL STUDIES

Turkey—located in both western Asia and southeastern Europe. European Turkey and Asian Turkey are separated by a strait called the Bosporus. Turkey is approximately three hundred thousand square miles in area, which is slightly larger than the state of Texas. Its capital city is Ankara.

MUSIC OF THE WORLD'S CULTURES

Focus: The Music of Japan

Objective
To develop knowledge of instruments and tone colors in Japanese music

Materials
Recording: *Sambaso*

Vocabulary
Nagauta, kabuki, o-tsuzumi, ko-tsuzumi, taiko, shamisen, bue

1 SETTING THE STAGE

Introduce Japan, the nagauta ensemble, and its instruments. Have the students discuss the text at the top of the page.

2 TEACHING THE LESSON

1. Introduce the percussion instruments of the nagauta ensemble. Have the students recognize the effect on pitch when the performer squeezes the laces on the ko-tsuzumi (pitch changes).

2. Introduce the sounds of a nagauta ensemble. Have the students:
• Discuss the shamisen and the bue.
• Listen to the recording of *Sambaso* with call numbers. Read the description by each number as it is called. Listen for percussion sounds in the music. Listen for the sounds of the shamisen and bue.

Reinforcing the Lesson

Compare the nagauta ensemble to the xylophone ensembles of Mali, page 215. Contrast the number and kinds of instruments and the circumstances in which each ensemble would perform.

9B THE MUSIC OF JAPAN

CD 6

In Japan the *nagauta* (nä′ gä-ōō-tä) ensemble is used to accompany a popular form of operalike drama called *kabuki* (kä′ bōō-kē). The nagauta ensemble is similar to the xylophone ensemble of Mali in that it contains percussion instruments as well as pitched instruments. However, the nagauta ensemble performs only in very formal concert settings to accompany the kabuki plays.

The nagauta ensemble contains three different drums: the *o-tsuzumi* (ō′ tsōō-zōō-mē), the *ko-tsuzumi* (kō′ tsōō-zōō-mē), and the *taiko* (tī′ kō). The o-tsuzumi and ko-tsuzumi are doubleheaded laced drums. The player holds the drum on the shoulder and plays it with the other hand. The performer can make the pitch of the ko-tsuzumi high or lower by squeezing the laces while striking the head of the drum. The taiko also is double headed and laced, but is hung from a frame and played with sticks.

The nagauta ensemble also includes two pitched instruments. One is a stringed instrument, the *shamisen* (shä′ mē-sen), and the other, the *bue* (bōō′ ā), is a wind instrument.

• Listen to *Sambaso* (säm′ bä-sō). Follow the description of the music.

Above, the nagauta To-On-Kai in performance. In the front row are one bue, three o-tsuzumi or ko-tsuzumi, and one taiko. The shamisen players in the upper row are awaiting their turn.

 Sambaso

1. Ko-tsuzumi and taiko are heard; voice; drum calls; music becomes faster.
2. Vocal solo; drum calls are heard.
3. The bue is heard, along with the shamisen.
4. The shamisen presents an ascending pattern, then a melodic pattern.
5. Shamisen and bue continue melody; music gradually becomes faster.
6. Bue and drum calls are heard.

222

EXTENSION

CURRICULUM CONNECTION: SOCIAL STUDIES

Japan—is an island country located off the northeast coast of Asia. Four large islands and thousands of smaller islands make up the country. The four main islands are Hokkaido, Honshu, Kyushu, and Shikoku. Japanese culture dates back many thousands of years. One of the great industrial nations of the world, Japan is approximately 141,000 square miles in area. Its capital is Tokyo.

MUSIC OF THE WORLD'S CULTURES

3 **APPRAISAL**

The students should be able to:
1. Identify the nagauta of Japan.
2. Identify and describe instruments in the nagauta ensemble.

Some scenes of Japan.
Opposite page,
umbrellas drying after
painting at a factory.
This page, top, a
shamisen player. Above,
Himeji Castle, near
Osaka, the most famous
medieval Japanese
castle. Left, a festival
scene at Sapporo, on
Hokkaido island.

223

MUSIC OF THE WORLD'S CULTURES

Focus: The Music of Indonesia

Objectives
To develop knowledge of instruments and tone colors in Indonesian music
To introduce the gamelan
To play music in a gamelan style

Materials
Recording: *Hudan Mas*
Unpitched percussion instruments
Orff instruments, bells, handbells, keyboard, or other pitched percussion objects (pans, pan lids, metal objects, and so on)

Vocabulary
Gamelan

1 SETTING THE STAGE

Discuss the text at the top of the page and the instruments in the photo.

2 TEACHING THE LESSON

1. Introduce Indonesia, gamelan, and gamelan ensemble. Have the students:
• Discuss the information on the gamelan.
2. Perform rhythms in gamelan style. Have the students:
• Discuss sharing rhythms. (*Sharing* is used here to specify notes on the same notation line which a performer omits. These notes are then performed, or shared, by another performer, either with the same or with a different tone color.)
• Read the rhythmic notation, saying the note values without clapping them.
• Clap the rhythm.
• Identify partners and decide which notes will be shared.

E X T E N S I O N

CURRICULUM CONNECTION: SOCIAL STUDIES

Indonesia—a country of more than three thousand islands located in the southwestern Pacific Ocean. The main islands include Sumatra, Java, and Celebes. Indonesia is approximately 580,000 square miles in area, virtually the same size as Alaska. Its capital city is Jakarta.

THE MUSIC OF INDONESIA

The Sound of the Gamelan

You heard a combination of Indonesian music and the music of the United States in *Kogoklaras* on page 211. This section concentrates on Indonesian sound alone.

The *gamelan* (gä' me-län) is the traditional instrumental ensemble of Indonesia. The ensemble consists of gongs and metallophones, rhythmic drums, flute, and stringed instruments. Some of the gongs play melodies, and others set the meter of the music.

A gamelan from Bali, Indonesia, with gongs, metallophones, and drums. The flute player is near the upper right-hand corner.

In Indonesia, the gamelan accompanies dance, drama, and puppet theatre. Although other types of musical ensembles are common in Indonesia, the gamelan is the most important. There are many different kinds of gamelans, and each kind uses a slightly different set of pitches. Some ensembles perform with five pitches and some use seven. Others use as few as four.

The sound of each instrument in the gamelan has a distinctive quality. As performers repeat rhythmic patterns, the sound joins with others to create layers of sound.

224

Perform in Gamelan Style

One type of gamelan rhythm develops when the musicians read the same line of rhythm. Instead of performing all of the notes, however, they alternate with other ensemble members to share the notes of the rhythm pattern. The interlocking sounds of their instruments creates an interesting rhythmic and melodic quality.

- Clap this gamelan rhythm.

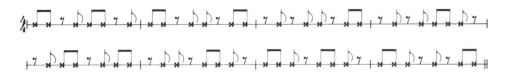

- Perform in gamelan style with a partner:

1. Each of you should clap or pat every *other* note of the rhythm pattern. Listen closely to the change in the sound of the rhythm as you alternate.
2. You and your partner should each choose an unpitched percussion instrument.
3. Perform the rhythm pattern on percussion instruments. Alternate the notes.

Melodic patterns on pitched instruments also are part of gamelan music. Some patterns are based on a four-pitch scale:

- Perform a two-pitch gamelan-style melodic pattern with a partner:

1. Each of you should choose one pitch on a bell set, handbell set, xylophone, keyboard, or any pitched object.
2. With your partner, decide which pitch will be played first.
3. Perform the rhythm pattern at the top of the page. Alternate with your partner so that you each play every other note. Listen closely to the change in the sounds as you alternate the two pitches.

225

- Perform, listening closely to the change in sound from when one person clapped the entire rhythm.
- Share the rhythm on percussion instruments.

3. Introduce the four-note scale and perform melodic patterns in gamelan style. Have the students:
- Examine and discuss the four-note scale. (Emphasize the difference from our traditional twelve-pitch scale and the lack of half steps.)
- Identify a partner and share rhythms on pitched percussion instruments.
- Perform the rhythms, listening closely to the change in sound.

4. Create new gamelan-style sounds. Have the students:
- Choose pitched and unpitched instruments.
- Compose and perform additional rhythm patterns on these instruments.

Reinforcing the Lesson

Have the students:
1. Preview *Hudan Mas* on page 226 to hear the layering of sounds in gamelan music.
2. Compare the use of different scales and instruments in the music of Indonesia and Turkey, pages 220–221.

3 APPRAISAL

The students should be able to:
1. Identify and describe the gamelan, an instrumental ensemble from Indonesia.
2. Perform accurately on percussion instruments in gamelan style.

MORE MUSIC TEACHING IDEAS

Have the students find examples of percussion and wind instruments from other countries.

MUSIC OF THE WORLD'S CULTURES

Focus: A Western Composer Uses Non-Western Ideas

Objectives
To introduce sources of musical ideas
To become familiar with the composer Claude Debussy and how he used ideas inspired by gamelan music
To perform a gamelan melody using stratification
To listen to melodic stratification in gamelan music
To listen to non-Western influences in Western music

Materials
Recordings: *Hudan Mas*
          ''Pagodes''
Bells or keyboard

Vocabulary
Stratification, impressionism

---

1 SETTING THE STAGE
Review the two-pitch pattern from the previous lesson.

2 TEACHING THE LESSON

1. Introduce borrowing musical ideas and melodic stratification. Have the students:
• Discuss borrowing musical ideas. (This practice is of long standing. Composers borrow not only from other sources but also from some of their own compositions. This practice was especially common prior to the mid-nineteenth century.)
• Discuss stratification.

BORROWING MUSICAL IDEAS

One composer who was deeply influenced by music of another culture was Claude Debussy (klôd də-byu-sē). The aspect of Indonesian music that most interested Debussy was the layering of sound. **Stratification** occurs when layers of melody or sound are heard.

Stratification occurs not only in music but also in nature. These layered rice terraces are on Luzon, in the Philippines.

• Practice this gamelan melody on keyboard or bells.

• Form several groups and perform the melody in stratification. Each group should perform the melody at a different tempo.

The melody you just performed is from *Hudan Mas* (hoo' dän mäs), a musical work from the island of Java in Indonesia.

• Listen to *Hudan Mas* to hear the layers of sound.

 Hudan Mas

226

CLAUDE DEBUSSY

Claude Debussy (1862–1918) was one of the greatest French composers. Debussy was born in a suburb of Paris and was encouraged to play the piano at an early age. He entered the Paris Conservatory when he was eleven and studied there for eleven years. Debussy created a musical style known as *impressionism*. During his years in Paris he became acquainted with impressionist painters such as Claude Monet, whose works brought out the effects of light and color on nature. He created a style of music that used different harmonies and exotic rhythms to evoke delicate and mysterious moods.

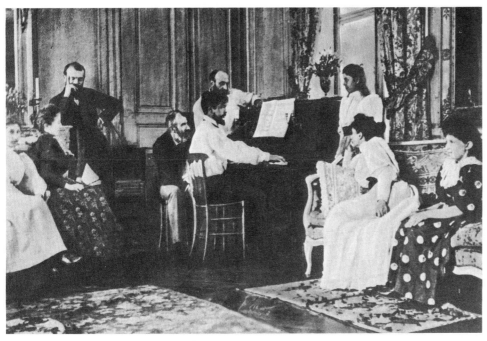

This photo shows the young Debussy playing the piano in a private home in Paris.

227

MUSIC OF THE WORLD'S CULTURES

2. Perform a melody in stratification. Have the students:
• Say the names of the notes without playing the notes.
• Practice the gamelan melody on bells or keyboard.
• Play the gamelan melody together at the same tempo.
• Form two groups. Each group performs the melody in a different tempo. (Make the tempos as different as possible the first time they do this.)
• Form three or more groups and perform the melody, each group playing at a different tempo.

3. Listen to *Hudan Mas*. Have the students listen to *Hudan Mas* and hear the melody they just performed in stratification.

4. Introduce Claude Debussy. Have the students discuss the text. (Emphasize Debussy's classical training at the Paris Conservatory, and his interest in music from another culture.)

5. Introduce "Pagodes." Have the students identify and discuss the gamelan characteristics Debussy used in *"Pagodes."*

6. Prepare the students for listening to "Pagodes" with call numbers. Have the students listen as you play each numbered

MUSIC OF THE WORLD'S CULTURES

melody below on the piano several times until the students can recognize the melodies when played at random.

Debussy's *"Pagodes"*

At the international Paris Exposition in 1889, Debussy had the opportunity to hear a gamelan ensemble from Java, one of the Indonesian islands. He was fascinated by the sounds of this exotic music. A different gamelan ensemble performed at the 1900 Paris Exposition. Again Debussy was intrigued by the music. The rhythms and melodies he heard challenged Debussy to include some of their characteristics in his own music.

Debussy wrote *"Pagodes"* (pä-gôd′, "pagodas") in 1904, some years after he had heard the gamelan music that influenced this piano composition. Instead of imitating a gamelan ensemble, he included characteristics of gamelan music. He used scales that were not commonly found in Western music. He changed the rhythms of the melodies and added ornamental pitches to them. He also created layers of sound by having more than one melody sounding at the same time.

* Listen to *"Pagodes"* to hear how Debussy was influenced by gamelan music. Read the descriptions.

 "Pagodes," by Claude Debussy

A Section
1. Low gonglike pitches; melody 1; melody 1 with melody 2 below; altered melody 1 with melody 3 below; short melody 4
2. Altered melody 3, using high and low registers; altered melody 1; tempo slows down slightly

B Section
3. Melody 5; melody 1 reappears in part with melody 6 (very loud)
4. Melody 5 (lower); trills

A Section
   Low gonglike pitches; melody 1; melody 1 with melody 2 below; altered melody 1 with melody 3 below; short melody 4
5. Melody 3, using high and low registers; melody 6 (very loud)

Coda
   Melodies 1, 2, and 6, one after the other, with fast, high notes and low, soft gonglike pitches accompanying, to the end

228

MORE MUSIC TEACHING IDEAS
Have the students:
1. Create melodies and perform them on bells or keyboard using stratification.
2. Find other examples of musical compositions that contain mixtures of different musical cultures.

Many peoples of the Far East have built pagodas. Left, below, and bottom, Borobudur Pagoda, on the island of Java, Indonesia

Left, Schwedagon Pagoda, in Rangoon, Burma

229

MUSIC OF THE WORLD'S CULTURES

7. Listen to the gamelan characteristics in "Pagodes." Have the students listen to the recording of "Pagodes" with call numbers. Read each description as each number is called. Listen for melodic stratification and other characteristics of gamelan music.

Reinforcing the Lesson

Discuss the concept of borrowing non-Western musical ideas for use in Western music. (You may wish to mention other composers who incorporated nontraditional ideas into their music, such as Bartók, Schoenberg, Stravinsky, Varèse, and other composers active after World War I.)

3 APPRAISAL

The students should be able to:
1. Identify Claude Debussy and explain how he used gamelan techniques in his music.
2. Perform a gamelan melody accurately on bells or keyboard.
3. Recognize stratification in gamelan music and in music by Claude Debussy.
4. Define melodic stratification.

MUSIC OF THE WORLD'S CULTURES

LOOKING BACK

Objective
To review the skills and concepts taught in Music of the World's Cultures

Materials
Recording: Looking Back
Percussion instruments
Copying Master M-1 (optional)

TEACHING THE LESSON

1. Review the skills and concepts taught in Music of the World's Cultures. Have the students:
• Follow the recorded review with pages 230–231, perform the activities, and answer the questions.
• Review their answers.
(You may wish to use Copying Master M-1 at this time.)

LOOKING BACK

See how much you remember.

1. Perform these rhythms from Mali and Indonesia on a percussion instrument with the recording.

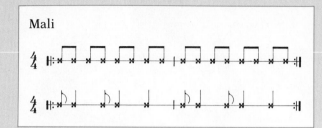

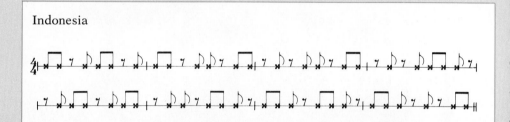

2. Pat the steady beat as you listen to *Madhu Kauns.*

230

3. Listen and identify the country of origin for each musical example.
   a. Japan or Turkey   Japan
   b. India or Mali   Mali
   c. Indonesia or Zimbabwe   Zimbabwe

4. Listen to this excerpt from *Kogoklaras* and identify the two cultures that contributed to this music. Indonesia and U.S.

5. Listen and identify the instruments you hear in these excerpts of music from three different cultures.
   a. xylophone ensemble or ney   xylophone ensemble
   b. kora or gamelan   gamelan
   c. nagauta ensemble or sitar   nagauta ensemble

6. Listen and decide which of these examples contain repetition. yes; no; no

7. Listen to a portion of *Sambaso* and identify the instrument families you hear. strings, woodwinds, percussion

8. Listen to a recording of a gamelan and describe the texture you hear. As performers repeat rhythmic patterns, the sound joins with others to create layers of sound.

9. Listen to a portion of *Cedo* and identify the tone colors in this musical example. Identify the country where you might find this musical style. vocal, kora; Gambia

231

MUSIC OF THE WORLD'S CULTURES

The piano was invented about 1720 and developed into the familiar instrument of today during the first half of the nineteenth century. The pipe organ had its roots in ancient Greece. The electronic organ was invented in the mid-1900s.

Keyboard instruments of today include pianos, organs, and synthesizers, which were developed during the 1960s. Today's synthesizers enable players to produce an almost unlimited variety

232

Detail from *Harpsichord*, Johann Christoph Weigel

of sounds, even the sounds of other instruments. Through rhythm units (drum machines), sequencers (recording devices), and a variety of tone colors, the synthesizer has become more complex.

Keyboard instruments are used by many popular music groups.

Notice the many sizes and shapes of the keyboards shown here. The arrangement of black and white keys is always the same.

233

KEYBOARDS OF TODAY

Focus: Learning to Play Keyboard Instruments

Objective
To develop performance skills on the keyboard

Materials
Recordings: "Dream of Dreams"
"Harmonic Repetition Montage"
"Twelve-Bar Blues"

Vocabulary
Chord, twelve-bar blues

1 SETTING THE STAGE

Have the students:
• Discuss the information on the keyboard.
• Become familiar with the sizes and shapes of keyboards.

KEYBOARDS OF TODAY

2 TEACHING THE LESSON

1. Introduce learning to play keyboard instruments. Have the students:
• Listen to two selections to hear the sounds of different keyboard instruments.
• Discuss the information on keyboard basics.
• Locate each set of two black keys up and down the keyboard.
• Locate and identify the notes C, D, and E.
• Locate each set of three black keys up and down the keyboard.
• Locate and identify the notes F, G, A, and B.

• Listen to these two selections to hear the sounds of different keyboard instruments.

 "Dream of Dreams," by Joe Sample

 "Harmonic Repetition Montage"

The keyboard has sets of white and black keys. Center yourself in front of the keyboard and find each set of *two* black keys up and down the keyboard. C is always the white key to the left, D is the white key in the middle, and E is the white key to the right of the two black keys. Middle C is the C that is closest to the center of the keyboard.

Each set of *three* black keys is a reference point for finding F, G, A, and B. F is always the white key to the left, G and A are the white keys in the middle, and B is the white key to the right of the three black keys.

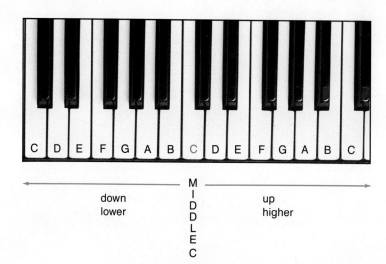

234

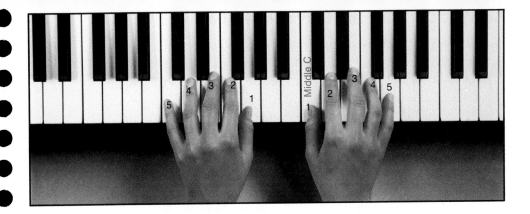

These hands show how the fingers are numbered for the keyboard. Notice that both thumbs are numbered *1*.

You can learn to play chords on the keyboard. **A chord** consists of three or more pitches played together. The twelve-bar blues is a common chord progression, or pattern, used in popular music.

To start you can play one pitch at a time.

- Find pitches C, F, and G on your keyboard. Use the fingers of your right hand as shown.

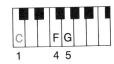

Right hand

- Play the following pitches along with the recording of the twelve-bar blues.

$\frac{4}{4}$
CCCC   CCCC   CCCC   CCCC

FFFF   FFFF   CCCC   CCCC

GGGG   FFFF   CCCC   CCCC

 "Twelve-Bar Blues," by Michael Treni

- Play the same pitches again with the twelve-bar blues, this time using the fingers of your left hand as shown.

Left hand

235

2. Introduce finger numbers for both hands and the chord sequence for the twelve-bar blues. Have the students:
- Discuss the information on chords and the twelve-bar blues.
- Identify the pitches C, F, and G.
- Read and play C, F, and G with the right hand following the twelve-bar blues sequence. Use proper fingering and play each pitch for four beats.
- Play the pattern twice with the recording. (The recording has a four-measure introduction and a coda.)
- Read and play C, F, and G with the left hand following the twelve-bar blues sequence. Use proper fingering and play each pitch for four beats.
- Play with the recording.

KEYBOARDS OF TODAY

3. Introduce the C, F, and G chords.
Have the students:
• Understand the meaning of a chord.
• Learn how the notes of a chord are arranged by skips.
• Learn to play the C, F, and G chords.

Learning to Play the C, F, and G Chords

You can play the C chord on the keyboard.
• Start with the left hand and play C with your fifth finger.
  Skip up one white key to the right and use your third finger. You should now be on E with your third finger.
  Skip up another key and use your thumb. You should now be on G with your thumb.
  Play all three notes at the same time.

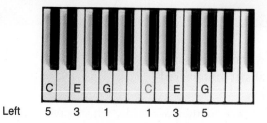

Left   5   3   1   1   3   5   Right

You have just learned to form and play the C chord.
• Now play the C chord with your right hand. Your thumb will be on C, your third finger will be on E, and your fifth finger will be on G.

You can play the F chord.
• Start with your left hand.
  Your fifth finger should be on F.
  Skip up one white key to the right. You should be on A with your third finger.
  Skip up another key and use your thumb. You should be on C with your thumb. Play all three notes together.
• Again, try the chord with your right hand, using your first, third, and fifth fingers.

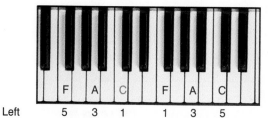

Left   5   3   1   1   3   5   Right

236

You can play the G chord.

- Start with your left hand.
  Your fifth finger should be on G.
  Skip up one white key to the right. You should be on B with your third finger.
  Skip up another key and use your thumb. You should be on D with your thumb. Play all three notes together.
- Again, try the chord with your right hand, using your first, third, and fifth fingers, the same fingers you used for the C and F chords.

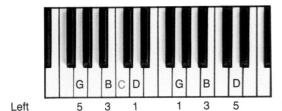

Left   5   3   1   1   3   5   Right

Now that you can play C, F, and G chords with either your left or right hand you can play the twelve-bar blues chord progression.

Many musicians play chords from chord charts. The following chord chart shows the 12 measures or bars of the twelve-bar blues. Three slashes after each chord's letter name indicate that the chord is to be played on every beat of each four-beat measure.

Twelve-Bar Blues

$\frac{4}{4}$ C/// C/// C/// C///
F/// F/// C/// C///
G/// F/// C/// C///

- Play along with the recording of the twelve-bar blues.

 CHALLENGE
Play the twelve-bar blues with both hands.

237

- Discuss the information on chord charts.
- Practice playing the C, F, and G chords following the twelve-bar blues sequence. Play on every beat of the measure using either the left or right hand.
- Play the pattern twice with the recording. (The recording has a four-measure introduction and a coda.)

Reinforcing the Lesson
Respond to the Challenge! by playing the twelve-bar blues with both hands.

3 APPRAISAL
The student should be able to:
1. Identify sets of two and three black keys on the keyboard.
2. Identify the pitches C, D, E, F, G, A, and B on the keyboard.
3. Read and perform the C, F, and G chords using the twelve-bar blues sequence.

KEYBOARDS OF TODAY

Focus: Reading Steps and Skips

Objective
To learn to read and play steps and skips on the keyboard

Vocabulary
Staff, stepwise, skipwise

1 SETTING THE STAGE

Review the information on skips, page 236.

2 TEACHING THE LESSON

Introduce reading steps and skips at the keyboard. Have the students:

• Discuss the information on reading music at the keyboard.
• Discuss the information on reading steps.
• Read and perform the exercises as indicated.

The pitches on the keyboard are notated on the **staff** as shown in the following diagram. Pitches can be notated either on lines or in spaces.

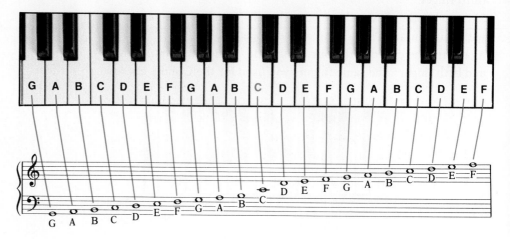

Pitches in the treble clef usually are played with the right hand. Pitches in the bass clef usually are played with the left hand.

Reading Steps

When a melody moves *up or down* on the keyboard from one white key to the next without skipping any notes in between, it is said to move **stepwise**. The steps from one key to the next are notated on the staff as either *line to space* or *space to line*.

• Place the third finger of your left hand on G in the bass clef. Play A, the next note to the right (up), with your second finger. You have moved up a step. Play B, the next note to the right (up), with your thumb. You have moved another step.

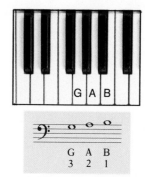

238

- Read and play these patterns of steps in the bass clef. Say the names of the notes before you play them and again as you play them. Notice the upward and downward motion of each melody.

1.					2.					3.					
F	E	D	E	F	F	G	A	G	F	F	G	A	G	F	E	F
1	2	3	2	1	3	2	1	2	3	3	2	1	2	3	4	3

- Place the thumb (finger 1) of your right hand on G in the treble clef. Play A, the next note to the right (up), with your second finger. You have moved up a step. Play B, the next note to the right (up), with your third finger. You have moved up another step.

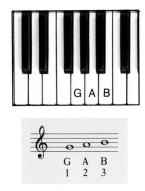

- Read and play these patterns of steps in the treble clef. Say the names of the notes before you play them and again as you play them. Notice the upward and downward motion of each melody.

1.					2.					3.					
B	A	G	A	B	C	D	E	D	C	C	B	A	B	C	D	C
3	2	1	2	3	1	2	3	2	1	3	2	1	2	3	4	3

239

- Read and play the patterns of steps in the bass clef.
- Read and play the patterns of steps in the treble clef.
- Describe the direction of the step, for example, step up, step down.

KEYBOARDS OF TODAY

- Discuss the information on reading skips.
- Learn to play a broken C chord in the bass clef as indicated.
- Learn to play a broken F chord in the bass clef (using the chart on page 238 if necessary).
- Read and play the practice patterns in the bass clef.
- Learn to play a broken F chord in the treble clef as indicated.
- Learn to play broken C and G chords in the treble clef (using the chart on page 238 if necessary).
- Read and play the practice patterns in the treble clef.
- Learn to play broken C, F, and G chords in both clefs, then create and play practice patterns for each chord (using the chart on page 238 if necessary).
- Describe the direction of the skip, for example, skip up, skip down.

Reinforcing the Lesson

Have the students play C, E, and G together with the left hand to hear the C chord. Then have them play F, A, and C together with the right hand to hear the F chord.

3 APPRAISAL

The students should be able to read and perform melodies containing steps and skips in the bass and treble clefs.

Reading Skips

When a melody moves *up or down* from one note to the next and skips some notes, it is said to move **skipwise**. When you skip one key on the keyboard it is notated on the staff as either *line to line* or *space to space*.

- Play C with the fifth finger of your left hand. Skip a key up to the right and play E with finger 3. Skip another key up to the right and play G with finger 1.

- Read and play these patterns of skips in the bass clef. Say the names of the notes before you play them and again as you play them. Notice the upward and downward motion of each melody.

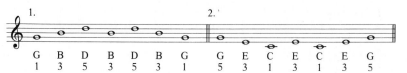

- Play F with the first finger of your right hand. Skip a key up to the right and play A with finger 3. Skip another key up to the right and play C with finger 5.

- Read and play these patterns of skips in the treble clef. Say the names of the notes before you play them and again as you play them. Notice the upward and downward motion of each melody.

1.
G	B	D	B	D	B	G
1	3	5	3	5	3	1

2.
G	E	C	E	C	E	G
5	3	1	3	1	3	5

240

THE TWELVE-BAR BLUES

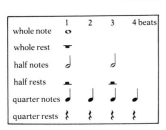

	1	2	3	4 beats
whole note	o			
whole rest				
half notes				
half rests				
quarter notes				
quarter rests				

This chart shows the relationships between notes and rests, or silences, of different durations.

- Read and play this blues progression. Practice each part separately before playing them together.
- Perform this progression with the twelve-bar blues.

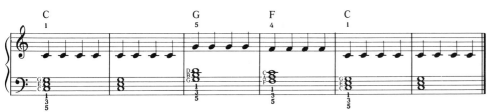

- Play these right hand melodies with the chord sequence. Pattern 1 contains steps. Patterns 2 and 3 contain skips.
- Choose pattern 1, 2, or 3. Play it with the twelve-bar blues. Be sure to play each chord enough times to fit the twelve-bar blues progression.

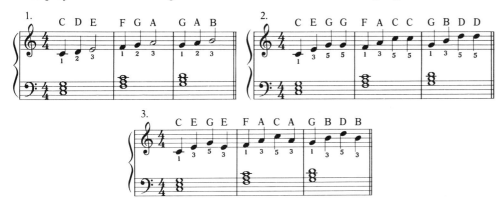

241

KEYBOARDS OF TODAY

Focus: Reading Music at the Keyboard

Objective
To read and play a blues progression on the keyboard

Materials
Recording: "Twelve-Bar Blues"

1 SETTING THE STAGE
Review the twelve-bar blues sequence in both the right and left hands.

2 TEACHING THE LESSON
Perform the twelve-bar blues. Have the students:
- Practice and then perform the twelve-bar blues sequence with the recording.
- Vary the right hand melody by reading and playing melodic patterns 1–3. (Inform the students that the starting note of each right hand melodic pattern is the root of the chord below.)

KEYBOARDS OF TODAY

- Practice and then perform the twelve-bar blues sequence with the recording.
- Vary the left hand by reading and playing melodic patterns 1–3. (Inform the students that the starting note of each left hand melodic pattern is the root of the chord above. Remind the students to play the melodic patterns the correct number of times to fit the sequence of the progression.)

Reinforcing the Lesson

Have the students create their own improvisation by combining alternate right and left hand patterns while performing the twelve-bar blues. (Encourage the students to refer to the patterns on these pages.)

3 APPRAISAL

The students should be able to read and perform melodies containing steps and skips in the bass and treble clefs using a twelve-bar blues sequence.

You can read and play this blues progression. Note that the chords are in the treble clef, and the melodic patterns are in the bass clef.

- Practice each part separately. Play the chords with your right hand. Play the melody with your left hand. Then play both parts together.
- Perform with the twelve-bar blues.

- Play these left hand melodies with the chord sequence. Pattern 1 measures contain steps and skips. Pattern 2 measures contain steps. Pattern 3 measures contain skips. Notice that when the chord changes to F or G, the beginning note of the left hand melodic pattern changes to F or G.
- Choose pattern 1, 2, or 3. Play it with the twelve-bar blues. Be sure to play each chord enough times to fit the twelve-bar blues progression.

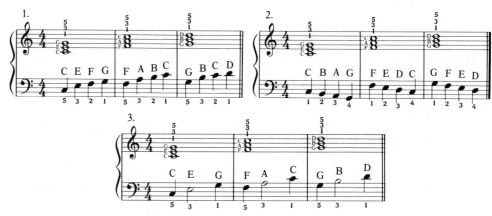

 CHALLENGE Create your own melodies by combining right and left hand patterns to play with the twelve-bar blues.

TRIADS

The chords you have been playing are based on skips. The three notes are called a **triad**. The bottom note of the chord or triad is called the **root**, the middle note is called the **third**, and the top note is called the **fifth**.

Each measure of melodic pattern 1 below begins on the root, each measure of pattern 2 begins on the third, and each measure of pattern 3 begins on the fifth of each chord.

Two eighth notes (♫) have the same duration as one quarter note (♩).

• Find the starting pitch of each melodic pattern before you play each chord change.

Roots: C F G

Thirds: E A B

Fifths: G C D

• Play the twelve-bar blues with each pattern.

243

KEYBOARDS OF TODAY

Focus: Reading Triads

Objective
To read and play triads on the keyboard

Materials
Recording: "Twelve-Bar Blues"

Vocabulary
Triad, root, third, fifth

1 SETTING THE STAGE
Review the definition of chords, page 235.

2 TEACHING THE LESSON
Introduce the triad. Have the students:
• Discuss the information on the construction of a triad.
• Practice finding the starting pitch and finger number of melodic patterns 1–3. (Inform the students that pattern 1 begins on the root, pattern 2 begins on the third, and pattern 3 begins on the fifth.)
• Read and perform melodic patterns 1–3.

Reinforcing the Lesson
Have the students play the twelve-bar blues sequence with melodic patterns 1–3. (Remind the students to play the melodic pattern the correct number of times to fit the sequence of the progression.)

3 APPRAISAL
The students should be able to define, read, and play triads at the keyboard.

KEYBOARDS OF TODAY

Focus: Reading Seventh Chords

Objective
To read and play seventh chords on the keyboard

Materials
Recording: "Twelve-Bar Blues"

Vocabulary
Seventh, flat

1 SETTING THE STAGE

Review the definition of chords, page 235, and tell the students that a chord can consist of more than three pitches.

2 TEACHING THE LESSON

Introduce the seventh chord. Have the students:

• Discuss the information on the construction of seventh chords.
• Examine this version of the twelve-bar blues and identify which measures contain a seventh chord. (measures 4 and 9)
• Practice the chords in the left hand and observe the fingering indicated.
• Examine right hand melodic patterns 1–3.
• Practice finding the starting pitch and finger number of each melodic pattern. (Inform the students that pattern 1 begins on the root, pattern 2 begins on the third, and pattern 3 begins on the fifth.)
• Practice each melodic pattern.

Reinforcing the Lesson

Have the students play the twelve-bar blues sequence with melodic patterns 1–3. (Remind the students to play the melodic pattern the correct number of times to fit the sequence of the progression.)

3 APPRAISAL

The students should be able to:
1. Define the seventh chord.
2. Read and perform chords and melodies that contain the seventh degree of the scale.

SEVENTH CHORDS

The triads you have been playing contain three pitches. When a chord contains four pitches, the fourth pitch is usually one skip above the fifth. It is the seventh scale tone above the root, called the **seventh**.

• Look at this version of the twelve-bar blues and identify which measures contain chords with four pitches or seventh chords.
• Play the left hand part shown.
B♭ (**B-flat**) is the black key to the *left* of B.

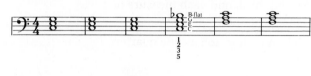

Melodic pattern 1 begins on the root, pattern 2 begins on the third, and pattern 3 begins on the the fifth of each chord. E♭ (E-flat) is the black key to the left of E.

• Name the starting pitch of each melodic pattern. Refer to the chart on page 241 if necessary.
• Play each pattern with the twelve-bar blues.

244

"Several Shades of Blue"

The keyboard selection "Several Shades of Blue" uses the twelve-bar blues progression and several of the melodic patterns you have learned.

• Follow the suggestions in Part I through Part IV to prepare to play "Several Shades of Blue."

Part I: Play the individual notes in each measure all at the same time to form the chord.

Part II: Practice playing fingers 1, 2, and 5 in the right hand on all notes of the chord (Example 1). Later add finger 3 to form a four-note chord (Example 2).

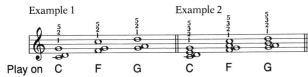

Part III: Practice moving the left hand from the root to the fifth.

Part IV: Practice with descending quarter notes (Example 1) and then add the root in the right hand (Example 2).

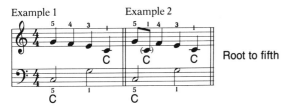

The mark ◁==== stands for **crescendo** (kre-shen' dō), meaning to play gradually louder. The mark ====▷ stands for **decrescendo** (dā' kre-shen-dō), meaning to play gradually softer. The term **simile** (sim' i-lē) means you should continue to follow the marks for crescendo or decrescendo.

245

KEYBOARDS OF TODAY

Focus: Reading Music at the Keyboard

Objective
To read and perform a song based on the twelve-bar blues sequence

Materials
Recording: "Several Shades of Blue"
Guitar, bass, or bells (or synthesizer)
Classroom percussion instruments

Vocabulary
Crescendo, decrescendo, simile

1 SETTING THE STAGE
Review the twelve-bar blues sequence, page 235.

2 TEACHING THE LESSON
Introduce "Several Shades of Blue."
Have the students:
• Observe the suggestions in Part I through Part IV before reading and performing "Several Shades of Blue."
• Discuss the information on the dynamics used while performing the piece.

KEYBOARDS OF TODAY

- Listen to the recording of "Several Shades of Blue."
- Read and perform "Several Shades of Blue."

Several Shades of Blue

- With a group, perform "Several Shades of Blue" by:
  1. playing the root of each chord on guitar, bass, or bells (or synthesizer)
  2. improvising a percussion accompaniment on classroom instruments
  3. playing along with the rhythm section of your keyboard

If you are using a synthesizer with a sequencer, record the root of each chord on your sequencer and replay in repeat mode. Change the keyboard voice on your synthesizer and play along with the sequencer.

247

KEYBOARDS OF TODAY

Reinforcing the Lesson
Have the students form a group and perform "Several Shades of Blue" using the suggestions.

3 APPRAISAL
The students should be able to read and perform "Several Shades of Blue" based on the twelve-bar blues sequence.

KEYBOARDS OF TODAY

Focus: A New Chord Pattern

Objective
To read and perform chords and melodies on the keyboard

Materials
Recording: "New Chord Pattern"

Vocabulary
Tie, sharp

1 SETTING THE STAGE
Review the C, F, and G chords.

2 TEACHING THE LESSON
Introduce the new chord pattern.
Have the students:
• Listen to the recording of the pattern.
• Identify the new chords in this progression.
• Practice the chord changes.
• Perform the chords with the recording.
• Practice finding the starting pitch of melodic patterns 1–3.
• Discuss the information on the tie and the sharp.

Reinforcing the Lesson
Have the students read and perform melodic patterns 1–3 with chords.

3 APPRAISAL
The students should be able to read and perform the new chord progression accurately.

A NEW CHORD PATTERN

There are some new chords in this progression. They are shown in both the treble and the bass clef.

• Practice these chords.

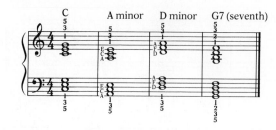

• Find and name the starting pitch of each melodic pattern below before you play it. C, E, G

In pattern 2, two notes of the same pitch are connected by a curved line called a **tie**. Hold that pitch for the *combined* value of the two notes. In pattern 3, F♯ (**F-sharp**), D♯ (**D-sharp**), and G♯ (**G-sharp**) are the black keys to the *right* of F, D, and G, respectively.

• Play this chord progression with each melodic pattern.

Start on the highest pitch of the chord

248

RESHAPING CHORDS

The pitches of a chord can be rearranged to make changes between chords smoother. This is called **revoicing**. It makes transitions from chord to chord sound smoother. It is important to remember that the names of chords do not change when they are revoiced.

- Practice this revoiced chord progression with the left hand.

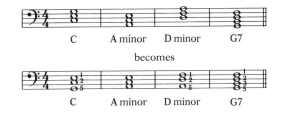

- Create your own melodic pattern in the right hand to play with the left hand chords. Use melodic patterns you have already learned.

- Practice this revoiced chord progression with the right hand.

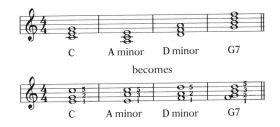

- Create your own melodic pattern in the left hand to play with the right hand chords. Use melodic patterns you have already learned.

"Blue Heart"

"Blue Heart" contains parts of the chord progressions you have learned, along with several of the melodic patterns you have learned. The **fermata** (𝄐) in the last measure tells you to hold those notes slightly longer than usual.

- Practice patterns 1 and 2 before you perform "Blue Heart."

249

KEYBOARDS OF TODAY

Focus: Reshaping Chords

Objective
To read and perform chords and melodies on the keyboard

Materials
Recording: "Blue Heart"
Guitar, bass, or bells (or synthesizer)
Classroom percussion instruments

Vocabulary
Revoicing, fermata

1 SETTING THE STAGE
Review the C, D minor, F, and G chords.

2 TEACHING THE LESSON

1. Introduce reshaping chords. Have the students:
- Discuss the information on reshaping chords.
- Practice the revoiced chord progression with the left hand.
- Create their own melodic patterns for the right hand to go with the chord progression.
- Practice the revoiced chord progression with the right hand.
- Create their own melodic patterns for the left hand to go with the chord progression.

2. Introduce "Blue Heart." Have the students:
- Practice patterns 1 and 2 in preparation for reading and performing "Blue Heart."

EXTENSION

MORE MUSIC TEACHING IDEAS
Revoice the chords in the twelve-bar blues sequence.

KEYBOARDS OF TODAY

- Listen to the recording of "Blue Heart."
- Read and perform "Blue Heart."

Reinforcing the Lesson

Have the students form their own groups and perform "Blue Heart" as indicated.

3 APPRAISAL

The students should be able to:

1. Perform a revoiced chord progression with the right and left hands.
2. Read and perform "Blue Heart" accurately.

Blue Heart

L.H.

- With a group, perform "Blue Heart" by:
  1. playing the root of each chord on guitar, bass, or bells (or synthesizer)
  2. improvising a percussion accompaniment on classroom instruments
  3. playing along with the rhythm section of your keyboard

If you are using a synthesizer with a sequencer, record the root of each chord on your sequencer and replay in repeat mode. Change the keyboard voice on your synthesizer and play along with the sequencer.

250

ANOTHER FAMILIAR CHORD PROGRESSION

🔊 10A
💿 7

This chord progression uses chords from the twelve-bar blues. It is frequently found in popular music.

● Practice the chord changes before you play this progression.

● Practice the left hand melodic patterns below. Find the starting pitch of each measure before you play it. All patterns: Measure 1, C; Measure 2, F; Measure 3, G

Fine (End)

Da Capo al Fine
(Go back to the beginning and play to Fine)

The **natural** sign (♮) cancels a previous sharp or flat in the same measure.

 Reverse the parts so that the right hand plays the melodic patterns while the left hand plays the chords.

251

KEYBOARDS OF TODAY

Focus: A Familiar Chord Progression

Objective
To read and play new chords and melodies on the keyboard

Materials
Recording: "Another Familiar Chord Progression"

Vocabulary
Natural

1 SETTING THE STAGE
Review the C, D minor, F, and G chords.

2 TEACHING THE LESSON

1. Introduce the new chord progression. Have the students:
● Listen to the recording.
● Identify the chords in this progression.
● Practice the chord changes.
● Practice the right hand chords and then add the root in the left hand.
● Perform the chord progression with the recording.
● Practice the left hand part in melodic patterns 1–3.
● Play the right hand chords with each left hand part.
● Perform melodic patterns 1–3 with the recording.
● Respond to the Challenge! by reversing the right hand and left hand parts.

Reinforcing the Lesson
Have the students improvise their own melodies to this chord progression.

3 APPRAISAL
The students should be able to read and perform a familiar chord progression accurately.

KEYBOARDS OF TODAY

Focus: Performing an Accompaniment

Objective
To read and perform a keyboard accompaniment to a song

Materials
Recording: "Mama Don't 'Low"
Guitar, bass, or bells (or synthesizer)
Classroom percussion instruments

1 SETTING THE STAGE

Review the G and C chords.

2 TEACHING THE LESSON

Introduce "Mama Don't 'Low." Have the students:
• Sing the song.
• Play the second measure of pattern 2 and identify it as the new chord D major.
• Practice the patterns in preparation for playing the accompaniment.
• Observe correct fingerings.

CD 7 **"Mama Don't 'Low"**

You can play the American folk song "Mama Don't 'Low" as a solo or with other keyboard instruments or guitars.

• Sing the song first to become familiar with it.

Mama Don't 'Low
American folk song
(arr. P.W.)

The keyboard accompaniment to "Mama Don't 'Low" is based on chords G major and C major, which you have learned, and new chord D major.

• Practice these patterns before you perform "Mama Don't 'Low."

252

Notice that the music has a new meter signature: $\frac{2}{4}$. In $\frac{2}{4}$ meter, the the quarter note has the steady beat, with two beats in each measure.

- Pat the steady beat and clap the eighth notes to prepare for playing "Mama Don't 'Low."

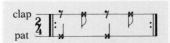

Keyboard Accompaniment to "Mama Don't 'Low"

You can also play this accompaniment with the version for guitar on page 263.

- With a group, perform "Mama Don't 'Low" by:
  1. playing the root of each chord on guitar, bass, or bells (or synthesizer)
  2. improvising a percussion accompaniment on classroom instruments
  3. playing along with the rhythm section of your keyboard

If you are using a synthesizer with a sequencer, record the root of each chord on your sequencer and replay in repeat mode. Change the keyboard voice on your synthesizer and play along with the sequencer.

253

KEYBOARDS OF TODAY

- Discuss the information on $\frac{2}{4}$ meter.
- Practice the rhythm pattern, using body percussion.
- Sing the song as they perform on the keyboard.
- Form two groups. Have one group perform the accompaniment on the keyboard while the other group performs on guitar (see pages 262–263).

Reinforcing the Lesson

Have the students form their own groups and perform "Mama Don't 'Low" as indicated.

3 APPRAISAL

The students should be able to accurately perform a keyboard accompaniment to a song.

PLAYING
THE
GUITAR

Listen to these compositions for guitar. How do they sound alike?
How do they sound different?

 Concerto in D Major for Guitar and Orchestra, Third Movement,
by Antonio Vivaldi

254

EXTENSION

from *Presentation in the Temple*, Vittore Carpaccio, ACCADEMIA, Venice

"Hickory Hollow," performed by Banks and Shane

255

PLAYING THE GUITAR

Focus: Playing the Guitar

Objectives
To identify the parts of the guitar and electric bass
To read and play simple accompaniments on guitar and/or electric bass

Materials
Recordings: Concerto in D Major for Guitar and Orchestra, Third Movement
"Hickory Hollow"
"Drunken Sailor"
Guitars
Electric basses and amplifiers (optional)
Keyboard

Vocabulary
Fret, strum, open string, tablature, chord diagram

1   SETTING THE STAGE
Introduce the guitar. Have the students:
• Discuss the photographs.
• Identify and discuss the types of instruments represented in the pictures.
• Listen to and compare the two recordings.

THE ARTIST

Vittore Carpaccio (vē-to're kär-pä' chō) (ca.1455-ca.1526)—was an Italian painter. His work reflects the style of Venetian painting in his time, which emphasized the colors and textures of rich cloth, marble, and other materials. He painted many scenes of Venice as settings for religious figures.

EXTRA HELP

If your class is unable to complete Lesson 1 in one session, you may wish to teach pages 254–257 as one lesson, pages 258–260 as two lessons, and page 261 as a fourth lesson.

PLAYING THE GUITAR

2 TEACHING THE LESSON

1. **Introduce or review the parts of the guitar and electric bass.** Have the students:
• Discuss the information given.
• Identify and compare the parts of the guitar and electric bass.

PARTS OF THE GUITAR

In this section you will learn to play strum patterns, chords, and bass parts on the guitar. The four lowest strings of the six-stringed guitar can be tuned to the same pitches as the four strings of the electric bass. You can play bass parts on either instrument.

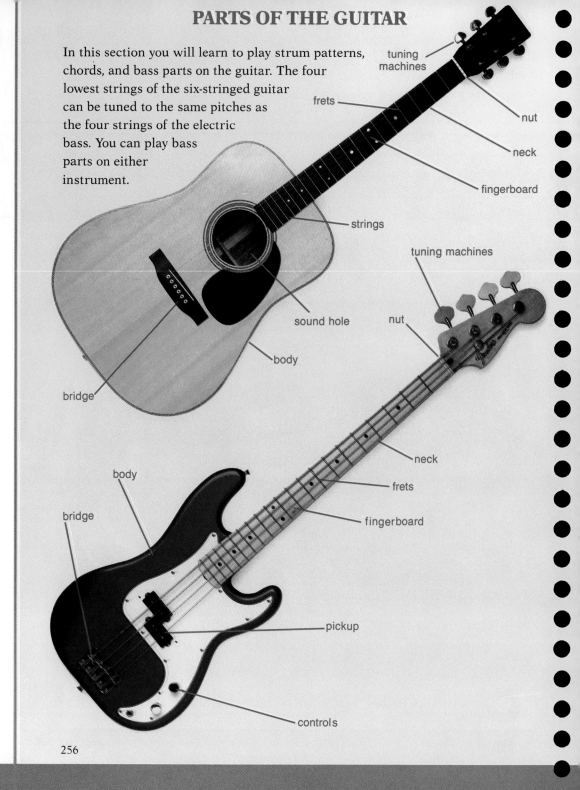

tuning machines

frets

nut

neck

fingerboard

strings

tuning machines

sound hole

nut

body

neck

bridge

frets

body

fingerboard

bridge

pickup

controls

256

TUNING YOUR GUITAR

The tuning most often used for guitar and bass is pictured here as it relates to the keyboard. The four strings of the electric bass are tuned to the same pitches (one octave below) as the four lowest strings on a six-stringed guitar.

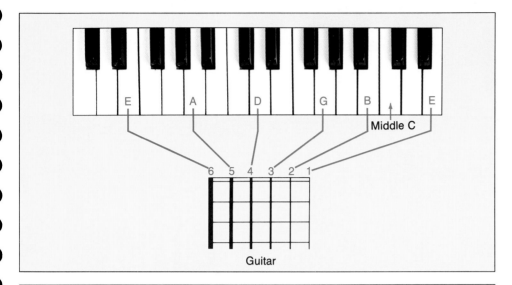

Guitar

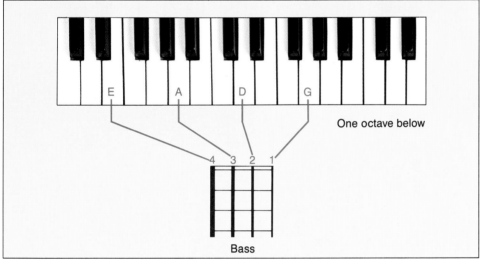

Bass

You can use two alternate tunings for some of the songs in this section. You will find these tunings, as well as chord frames for the songs, on pages 276–277.

257

PLAYING THE GUITAR

2. Introduce or review tuning the guitar and electric bass. Have the students:
• Discuss the tuning diagrams and identify the strings on the guitar and electric bass.
• Compare the string arrangements of the guitar and electric bass.
• Tune their instruments as they are able.

PLAYING THE GUITAR

3. Introduce or review holding and playing the guitar and electric bass. Have the students:
• Discuss the photos of proper playing positions.
• Discuss the left-hand position and the order of left-hand fingering.
• Identify the meaning of *fret*.
• Discuss the right-hand position. (Some students may prefer to use a pick when playing the electric bass.)
• Identify the symbol for down strum and practice the down strum on the guitar.
• Identify the symbol for up strum and practice the up strum on the guitar.

Left-Hand Position

Place the pad of your left thumb in the center back of the guitar neck. Curve your fingers over the strings, keeping your palm away from the neck. The fingers are numbered from the index finger (1) to the little finger (4). Your fingers **fret**, or press down, the strings for single notes or to form chords.

Right-Hand Position

Curve the fingers and **strum**, or brush down across the strings with your fingernails. A down strum is indicated by this sign ⊓.

Brush up across the strings with your thumbnail for an up strum (∨).

258

Strum Patterns for Guitar

Practice these rhythm patterns on **open** (unfretted) strings, or with any chords you already know. Play the downward (⌐) and upward (v) strums where indicated.

READING A BASS PART IN TABLATURE

Bass parts for either the six-stringed guitar or the electric bass can be written in *tablature*. **Tablature** is a picture of the guitar strings divided into measures of music.

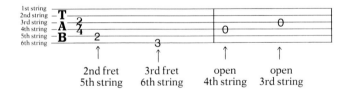

2nd fret   3rd fret   open   open
5th string 6th string 4th string 3rd string

• Perform the rhythm patterns at the top of the page, using the down and up strums.
4. Introduce reading a bass part in tablature. Have the students:
• Discuss the information on tablature.

PLAYING THE GUITAR

• Discuss and compare the note durations and tablature symbols.
• Practice the short tablature sample at the bottom of the page.

The six lines represent the six strings of the guitar. The numbers on the line indicate the frets. An *O* indicates an open, or unfretted, string. In some tablature the rhythms are shown above the fret numbers. Here the rhythm is

More commonly, tablature symbols are used. They are shown with their equivalents in staff notation. The fret number is written inside the note head. The fret number replaces the note head for dotted quarter notes, quarter notes and eighth notes. The rests are the same as in staff notation.

NAMES	STAFF NOTATION	TABLATURE SYMBOLS
whole note	o	2 (just the number)
dotted half notes	♩. ♩·	②. ②·
half notes	♩ ♩	② ②
dotted quarter notes	♩. ♩·	2. 2·
quarter notes	♩ ♩	2 2
eighth notes	♪ ♪	2 2
eighth notes	♫ ♫	2 2 2 2

This is how the symbols look in tablature.

Unless otherwise indicated, the left hand fingering is the same number as the fret.

260

PLAYING CHORDS

A chord diagram or frame shows where to place your left fingers on the fingerboard to fret, or form, a chord. The number in the circle indicates which finger to use. The circle shows you where your finger belongs. An **X** means that a string is not played.

- Practice the E minor and D major chords and the accompaniment patterns for "Drunken Sailor." Then play them with the song.

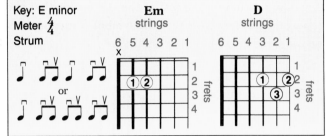

Drunken Sailor

Traditional

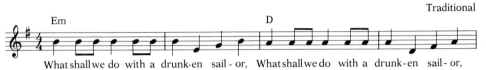

Em — What shall we do with a drunk-en sail - or, What shall we do with a drunk-en sail - or,

Em — What shall we do with a drunk-en sail - or, Ear - lye in the morn - ing?

Refrain Way, hey, and up she rises, (*3 times*)
Earlye in the morning.
2. Throw him in the longboat till he's sober, (*3 times*)
Earlye in the morning.
3. Pull out the plug and wet him all over, (*3 times*)
Earlye in the morning.

ADD A BASS PART

You can play a bass part for this song on the four lowest strings of a six-stringed guitar or on the electric bass. The top line shows the part in staff notation.

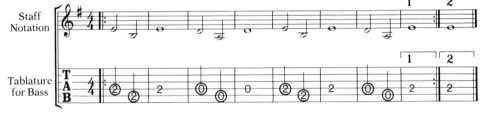

Staff Notation

Tablature for Bass

261

PLAYING THE GUITAR

5. Introduce or review playing chords and strum patterns on the guitar. Have the students:
- Discuss the information on playing chords and fret positions.
- Examine the diagrams for the E minor and D major chords and practice playing them on the guitar.
- Practice the chords with the strums indicated.

6. Introduce "Drunken Sailor." Have the students:
- Sing "Drunken Sailor."
- Sing the song again, playing the proper chord on the downbeat of each measure.
- Play "Drunken Sailor" with the two-chord accompaniment.

7. Introduce the bass accompaniment for "Drunken Sailor." Have the students:
- Examine the tablature for the bass accompaniment.
- Practice playing the bass part.

Reinforcing the Lesson

Have the students form two groups and perform both accompaniments with "Drunken Sailor."

3 **APPRAISAL**

The students should be able to:
1. Identify the different parts of the guitar and electric bass.
2. Read and play simple two-chord and bass accompaniments to "Drunken Sailor."

MORE MUSIC TEACHING IDEAS

You may wish to use the D minor tuning on page 277 for this song.

EXTRA HELP

If some students are unable to play the strum patterns for this song or any other song in this section, have them strum down on the proper chord on the downbeat of each measure.

PLAYING THE GUITAR

Focus: Alternating Bass Patterns

Objective

To read and play simple alternating bass patterns on the guitar

Materials

Recording: "Mama Don't 'Low"
Guitars
Electric basses and amplifiers (optional)
Keyboard

Vocabulary

Bass pattern

1 SETTING THE STAGE

Review fret positions, playing chords, and the down strum.

2 TEACHING THE LESSON

1. Introduce playing alternating bass patterns. Have the students:

• Identify the bass (lowest) notes in familiar chords, such as E minor and D major. (Note that the bass note will not always be the root.)

• Discuss the alternating bass patterns and examine the diagrams of the G, G7, D7, and C chords.

• Fret each chord and identify the bass note in each.

• Practice each chord, using alternating bass, in $\frac{2}{4}$ meter. Then practice changing from one chord to the next: G to G7, G7 to C, C to G, G to D7, and D7 to G.

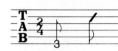

Bass patterns involve playing the lowest notes of a chord separately from the other notes. In "Mama Don't 'Low," the chords are G major, G7, D7, and C major.

To play a bass pattern, first fret the chord. Then pluck *only* the single bass note shown in the tablature. Follow that with a downward strum on the rest of the strings for that chord. Then repeat the pattern. Note that the symbol ⨍ means the strum should be the same duration as an eighth note. For the G major chord:

1. Fret the chord
2. Pluck *only* this string with your right thumb

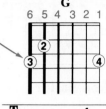

The left hand fingering for G and G7 chords is *not* the same as the fret number. The left hand fingering is shown in parentheses above the tablature.

3. Strum down on the remaining strings

Note that the G7 chord has the same bass note as the G major chord.

• Fret the D7 chord, pluck the fourth string bass note, and strum all the strings *except* the sixth string.

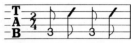

• Fret the C major chord, pluck the fifth string bass note, and strum all the strings except the sixth.

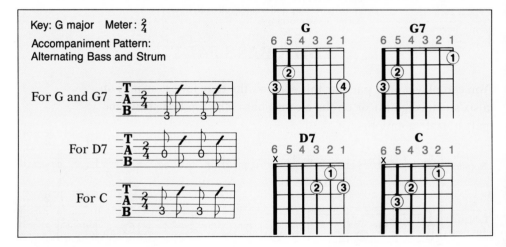

Key: G major   Meter: $\frac{2}{4}$
Accompaniment Pattern: Alternating Bass and Strum

For G and G7

For D7

For C

262

E X T E N S I O N

Mama Don't 'Low

Key: G major   Starting Pitch: G   Scale Tones: *so, la, ti, do re ma mi so*

American folk song (arr. P.W.)

1.)
2.) Ma-ma don't 'low   no   { gui - tar   play-in' round   here,_____
3.) G   { ban - jo   pick-in' round   here,_____
(2)   { har - mo - niz-in' round   here,_____

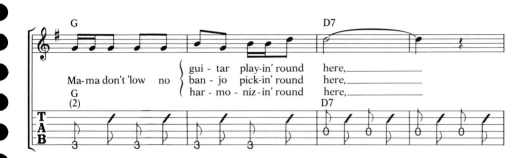

Ma-ma don't 'low   no   { gui - tar   play-in' round   here,_____
G   { ban - jo   pick-in' round   here,_____
(2)   { har - mo - niz-in' round   here,_____

I   don't care what   Ma-ma don't 'low, Gon-na   { play   my gui - tar   an - y - how,
G   G7   { pick   my ban - jo   an - y - how,
(2)   (2)   { har - mo-nize songs   an - y - how,

Ma-ma don't 'low   no   { gui - tar   play-in' round   here._____
G   { ban - jo   pick-in' round   here._____
(2)   { har - mo - niz-in' round   here._____

263

PLAYING THE GUITAR

2. Play the alternating bass pattern.
Have the students:
• Sing the song, playing the proper chord on the downbeat of each measure.
• Sing the song again, playing the alternating bass accompaniment.
• Form two groups. Group I strums the chords on the beat while Group II plays the alternating bass pattern.

Reinforcing the Lesson
Have the students form three groups to play the chords, the alternating bass pattern, and the keyboard accompaniment on page 253.

3 APPRAISAL
The students should be able to read and play a simple alternating bass pattern as an accompaniment to ''Mama Don't 'Low.''

MORE MUSIC TEACHING IDEAS
Some students may want to improvise a bass part to ''Mama Don't 'Low'' on guitar or electric bass.

PLAYING THE GUITAR

Focus: Bass Runs

Objective
To read and play simple bass runs on the guitar

Materials
Recordings: "Mama Don't 'Low"
              "The Wabash Cannonball"
Guitars
Electric basses and amplifiers (optional)

Vocabulary
Bass run

1 SETTING THE STAGE
Review alternating bass by forming two groups, with one group strumming on the beat while the other plays the alternating bass and strum pattern to "Mama Don't 'Low." Then switch parts if students are able.

2 TEACHING THE LESSON
1. **Introduce the bass run.** Have the students:
- Review the G, C, and D7 chords.
- Define and discuss a bass run and examine the bass runs shown.
- Practice playing these bass runs.

BASS RUNS

10B

CD 7 A **run** is a stepwise pattern of notes that connects two chords in a song. Runs can be played on the six-stringed guitar. Each note in a run is played individually, usually in an even rhythm. The symbol means the strum should be the same duration as a quarter note.

To play Bass Run 1:
1. Fret and play the bass note and the chord in the previous measure.
2. With your right thumb, pluck the single notes shown in the tablature. Change the left hand fingers as necessary.
3. Fret and play the next bass note and chord.

Play Bass Run 2 in the same way:

- Practice these runs until they sound smooth, then play them where they are indicated in "The Wabash Cannonball."

Notice that in this song, the bass notes for each chord alternate.

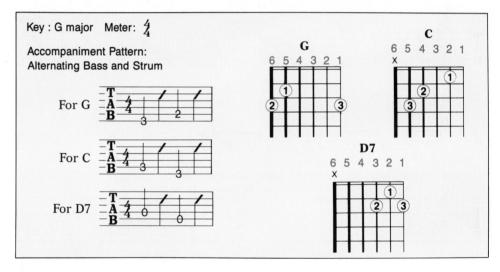

264

E X T E N S I O N

MORE MUSIC TEACHING IDEAS
You may wish to use the D major tuning on page 276 for this song. (Note that the bass runs cannot be played in this tuning.)

Key: G major   Starting Pitch: D   Scale Tones: *fa, so, la, ti, do re mi so*

The Wabash Cannonball

Traditional

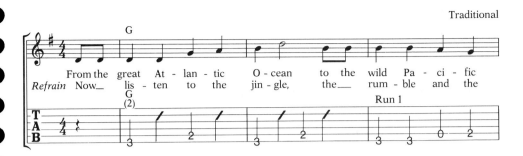

From the great At-lan-tic O-cean to the wild Pa-ci-fic
Refrain Now__ lis-ten to the jin-gle, the__ rum-ble and the

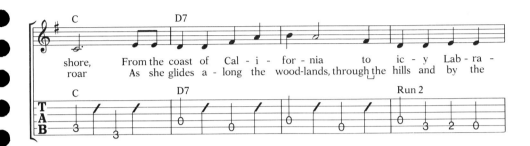

shore, From the coast of Cal-i-for-nia to ic-y Lab-ra-
roar As she glides a-long the wood-lands, through the hills and by the

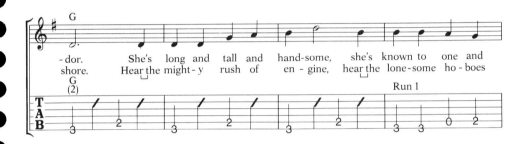

-dor. She's long and tall and hand-some, she's known to one and
shore. Hear the might-y rush of en-gine, hear the lone-some ho-boes

all, that heav'n-ly com-bin-a-tion, the Wa-bash Can-non-ball.
call As they trav-el a-cross the coun-try on the Wa-bash Can-non-ball.

265

PLAYING THE GUITAR

2. Introduce "The Wabash Cannonball." Have the students:
• Sing "The Wabash Cannonball."
• Practice the G, C, and D7 chords with the song. Play the proper chord on the downbeat of each measure.
• Sing the song, playing the bass runs as they are able.
• Form two groups. Group I practices strumming the chords on the beat while Group II practices the bass runs.

Reinforcing the Lesson
Have the students perform "The Wabash Cannonball," combining the strummed accompaniment with the bass runs.

3 APPRAISAL
The students should be able to read and play simple bass run patterns as an accompaniment to "The Wabash Cannonball."

MORE MUSIC TEACHING IDEAS
Some students may want to improvise a bass part to "The Wabash Cannonball" on guitar or electric bass.

PLAYING THE GUITAR

Focus: The Slide

Objective
To read and play a simple slide on the guitar or electric bass

Materials
Recording: "The Wreck of the Edmund Fitzgerald"
Guitars
Electric basses and amplifiers (optional)

Vocabulary
Slide

1 SETTING THE STAGE

Review the E minor, D, and G chords, with students taking turns playing alternating bass and bass run patterns with these chords.

2 TEACHING THE LESSON

1. Introduce the slide. Have the students:
• Define a slide and discuss the three steps for playing one.
• Examine the tablature, on this page and in the song, that indicates a slide.
• Practice playing this slide on the guitar or electric bass. Observe that in this song it always occurs at the same time as the G chord.

2. Introduce the A minor chord and strum patterns. Have the students:
• Examine the diagram and identify the bass in the A minor chord.
• Practice playing the A minor chord.
• Practice playing all the chords with the strum patterns shown.

CD 4 A **slide** is a kind of slur in which you fret two different pitches but pluck the string only once. The bass part in this song has a slide, on the sixth string. To play a slide:

1. Fret the string with the left hand finger indicated.
2. Pluck that string with your right thumb.
3. *At the same time*, slide the left hand finger up or down to the second fret number indicated. You will hear the pitch move up or down, too.

For example, to play, start on the second fret and slide to the third fret.

In this bass part for "The Wreck of the Edmund Fitzgerald," most of the left hand fingerings are *not* the same as the fret numbers. The left hand fingerings are shown in parentheses above the tablature.

This song is in a new meter, ¾, with *three* beats to a measure.

The song contains one new chord: A minor.

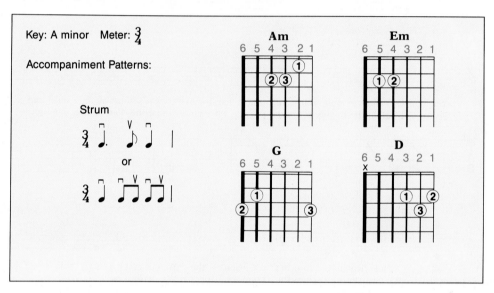

• Play "The Wreck of the Edmund Fitzgerald" with the bass part. Then play it again with the chord accompaniment.

266

MORE MUSIC TEACHING IDEAS
You may wish to use the D minor tuning on page 277 for this song.

The Wreck of the Edmund Fitzgerald

Key: Dorian mode on A   Starting Pitch: E   Scale Tones: *la, re mi fi so la ti*

Words and music by Gordon Lightfoot

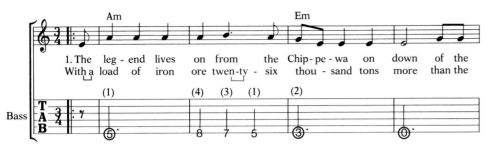

1. The leg - end lives on from the Chip- pe - wa on down of the
With a load of iron ore twen-ty - six thou - sand tons more than the

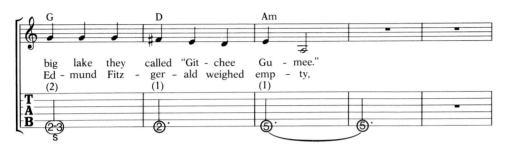

big lake they called "Git - chee Gu - mee."
Ed - mund Fitz - ger - ald weighed emp - ty,

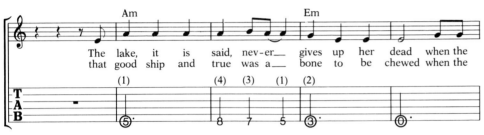

The lake, it is said, nev-er__ gives up her dead when the
that good ship and true was a__ bone to be chewed when the

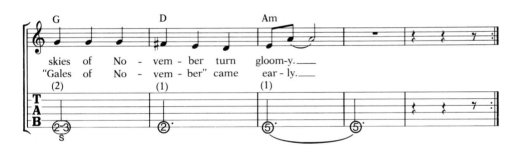

skies of No - vem - ber turn gloom-y.___
"Gales of No - vem - ber" came ear - ly.___

You will find the rest of the verses to this song on page 132.

267

---

3. Review "The Wreck of the Edmund Fitzgerald." Have the students:

- Sing the song.
- Sing the song again, playing the proper chord on the downbeat of each measure.
- Form two groups. Group I practices strumming the chords on the beat while Group II practices the bass accompaniment to the song, paying close attention to the bass slide on the G chord.

Reinforcing the Lesson

Have both groups perform "The Wreck of the Edmund Fitzgerald." Then switch parts if the students are able.

3 APPRAISAL

The students should be able to read and play simple slides in the bass part of the accompaniment to "The Wreck of the Edmund Fitzgerald."

PLAYING THE GUITAR

Focus: Playing the Blues

Objective
To read and play a simple blues shuffle pattern on the guitar

Materials
Recording: "Worried Man Blues"
Guitars
Electric basses and amplifiers (optional)

Vocabulary
Blues shuffle

1 SETTING THE STAGE
Review the C, D, and G chords, with the students taking turns playing alternating bass and bass run patterns.

2 TEACHING THE LESSON

1. Introduce the blues. Have the students:
• Discuss the information on playing the blues. (You may wish to review the information on pages 104–105, and page 105 of the Teacher's Edition.)
• Examine the blues rhythm pattern.
• Practice playing the blues rhythm on the G, C, and D chords.

2. Introduce playing the blues shuffle. Have the students:
• Discuss the information on playing the blues shuffle.
• Examine the diagrams for root chords and chords with the added sixth.
• Practice playing the G and G6 chords, the C and C6 chords, and the D and D6 chords, using the blues rhythm pattern.

PLAYING THE BLUES

One basic rhythm pattern for the blues is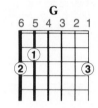

count: 1   2   3   4

• Play it with a relaxed swing of long and short sounds.

• Practice this rhythm with the G, C, and D chords. You can play an accompaniment to "Worried Man Blues" using the rhythm pattern shown above.

The Blues Shuffle

The **blues shuffle** pattern combines the rhythm you have learned with two alternating chords, a root chord, and the same chord with an added tone, called the sixth.

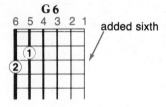

Play the root chord (G, C, or D) on the first and third beats of the measure. Play the sixth chord (G6, C6, or D6) on the second and fourth beats of the measure. You need to move only one finger back and forth to make the change from one chord to the other.

• Play the blues shuffle with these chords from "Worried Man Blues."

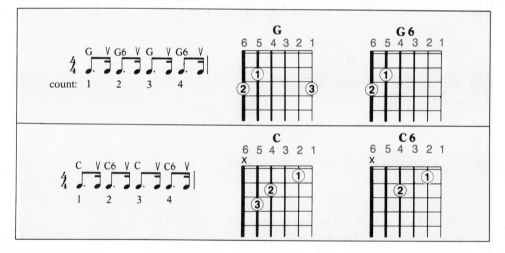

268

E X T E N S I O N

MORE MUSIC TEACHING IDEAS
You may wish to use the D major tuning on page 276 for this song.

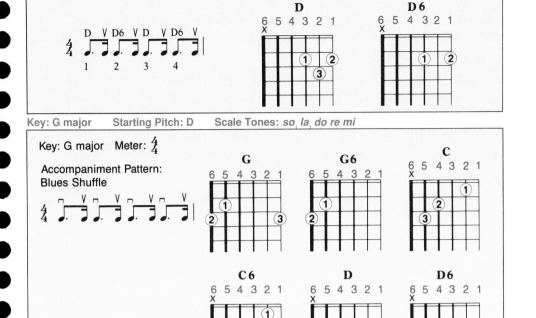

Key: G major   Starting Pitch: D   Scale Tones: *so la do re mi*

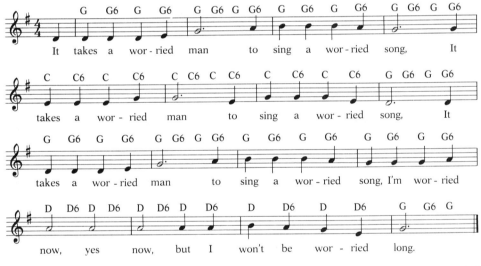

Worried Man Blues

Traditional

| G | G6 | G | G6 | G | G6 | G | G6 | G | G6 | G | G6 | G | G6 | G | G6 |

It takes a wor-ried man   to sing a wor-ried song,   It

| C | C6 | C | C6 | C | C6 | C | C6 | C | C6 | C | C6 | G | G6 | G | G6 |

takes a wor-ried man   to sing a wor-ried song,   It

| G | G6 | G | G6 | G | G6 | G | G6 | G | G6 | G | G6 | G | G6 | G | G6 |

takes a wor-ried man   to sing a wor-ried song, I'm wor-ried

| D | D6 | D | D6 | D | D6 | D | D6 | D | D6 | D | D6 | G | G6 | G |

now,   yes   now,   but I won't be wor-ried long.

269

PLAYING THE GUITAR

3. Introduce "Worried Man Blues."
Have the students:
• Sing "Worried Man Blues."
• Practice the blues shuffle as they sing the song again.
• Perform "Worried Man Blues" with the guitar accompaniment.

Reinforcing the Lesson

Some students may want to compose their own blues songs to perform with the blues shuffle, or use it as an accompaniment to blues songs they already know.

3 **APPRAISAL**

The students should be able to read and play simple blues shuffle patterns on the guitar as an accompaniment to "Worried Man Blues."

MORE MUSIC TEACHING IDEAS

Some students may wish to improvise bass patterns to "Worried Man Blues" by playing only the lowest note of each chord on the guitar or electric bass.

PLAYING THE GUITAR

Focus: The Hammer-On

Objective
To read and play a hammer-on

Materials
Recording: "Follow the Drinkin' Gourd"
Guitars
Electric basses and amplifiers (optional)

Vocabulary
Hammer-on

1 SETTING THE STAGE
Review the E minor, G, and D chords. Practice the up and down strums with these chords.

2 TEACHING THE LESSON

1. Introduce the hammer-on. Have the students:
• Discuss the information on the hammer-on.
• Examine the tablature for the hammer-on on this page and in the bass accompaniment to the song.
• Practice the hammer-on on the guitar or electric bass, following the steps outlined. Continue until it sounds smooth.

2. Introduce the B minor and A chords and the strum patterns. Have the students:
• Examine the diagrams for these chords.
• Practice playing the B minor and A chords, using the down and up strums.
• Practice all the chords, playing the strum patterns shown.

THE HAMMER-ON

7 In a **hammer-on**, you pluck an open string, then fret it, to play two pitches. The bass part to this song includes a hammer-on. To play this hammer-on:

1. Pluck the open fourth string with your right thumb.
2. *Quickly* fret ("hammer") the second finger of your left hand onto the second fret of the fourth string. You will hear two pitches. The second pitch lasts for the rest of the measure.

• Practice the hammer-on until it sounds smooth, then play it where it is indicated in the song.

"Follow the Drinkin' Gourd" was a kind of map in song for slaves who wanted to escape to the North. The "Drinkin' Gourd" was the Big Dipper, which points to the North Star. The "old man" was a sailor who had a wooden leg. He led the way along the riverbank.

The song contains two new chords: B minor and A.

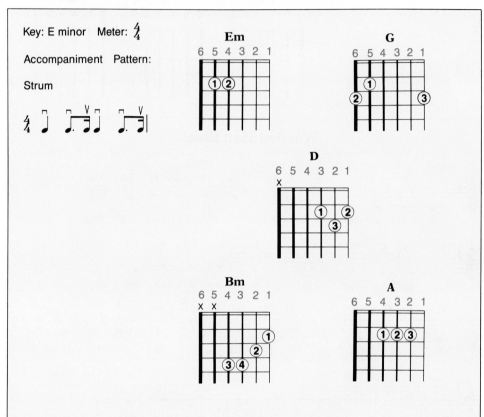

270

Key: E minor   Starting Pitch: E   Scale Tones: *mi, so, la, ti, do re mi*

Follow the Drinkin' Gourd

Traditional

Em

Verse 1. When the sun comes back and the first quail calls,_____
2. Now the riv-er bank-'ll make___ a might-y good road;_____ The
3. Now the riv - er ends___ be - tween two hills;_____

G   D

Fol - low_____ the Drink-in' Gourd._Then the Old Man is a-wait-in' for to
dead trees___ will show you the way. And the left___ foot, peg - foot,_
Fol - low_____ the Drink-in' Gourd._ And_ there's an-oth-er riv - er on the

Em   Bm   Em   Bm   Em

car - ry you to free-dom, Fol - low the Drink - in' Gourd.
trav - el - in'_____ on, _____ Fol - low the Drink - in' Gourd.
oth - er_____ side, _____ Fol - low the Drink - in' Gourd.

A   Em   A

Refrain Fol - low_____ the Drink - in' Gourd,_ Fol - low_____ the

Em   G   D

Drink - in' Gourd,_ For the Old Man is a - wait - in' for to

Em   Bm   Em   Bm   Em

car - ry you to free-dom, Fol - low the Drink - in' Gourd.

Verse

Bass

Refrain

271

PLAYING THE GUITAR

3. Introduce "Follow the Drinkin' Gourd." Have the students:
• Sing the song, strumming the proper chord on the downbeat of each measure.
• Listen to or sing the song, strumming on the guitar as they are able.
• Form two groups. One group plays the chords in the strum pattern while the other plays the bass accompaniment, paying close attention to the hammer-ons.

Reinforcing the Lesson

Combine the groups and perform the song. Then switch parts if the students are able.

3 APPRAISAL

The students should be able to read and play the hammer-on as they accompany "Follow the Drinkin' Gourd."

PLAYING THE GUITAR

Focus: Interpreting the Mood of a Song

Objective
To play a guitar accompaniment in a manner that reflects the mood of a song

Materials
Recording: "The Ghost Ship"
Guitars
Electric basses and amplifiers (optional)

1 SETTING THE STAGE

Review the E minor, A, C, D, and G chords, with students practicing the down and up strums on each chord. Practice playing the bass notes of the chords on the guitar or electric bass.

2 TEACHING THE LESSON

1. Introduce the B7 chord. Have the students:
• Examine the diagram for this chord.
• Practice playing the chord, using the down and up strums.

2. Introduce the strum patterns for "The Ghost Ship." Have the students:
• Examine the strum patterns.
• Practice the strum patterns, first with the chords they know, then with the B7 chord.

3. Introduce "The Ghost Ship." Have the students:
• Listen to "The Ghost Ship," paying close attention to the mood of the song.
• Discuss the mood of the song (spooky, scary) and the kind of accompaniment that would be most appropriate.
• Sing "The Ghost Ship," using their voices to create an appropriate mood.
• Sing the song again, strumming the proper chord on the downbeat of each measure of verse 1, the refrain, and verse 2.

10B

SETTING THE MOOD OF A SONG

CD 7 Try to catch the mood of "The Ghost Ship" as you play the guitar part or the bass part. This song has one new chord: B7.

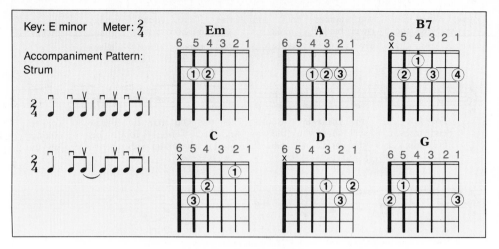

The Ghost Ship

Words and music by
Don Besig and Nancy Price

1. Now lis-ten well as a tale I tell of a night I shook with fear. We were sail-ing west on the o-pen sea, head-in' home from a long, long year. I was stand-ing

272

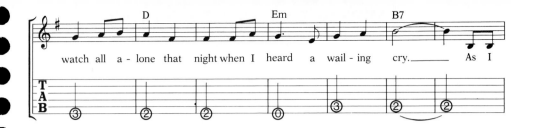

watch all a-lone that night when I heard a wail-ing cry.____ As I

strained to see what the sound could be, some-thing flashed and caught my eye.____

Refrain

____ And the cold wind blew,____

____ and the cold wind blew.____

2. 'Twas then I spied off the starboard side a strange, mysterious sight.
   I froze with fear as it drifted near like a ghost in the dark of night.
   I could see a sail on a broken mast and deserted decks below.
   From all around came a mournful sound, but I saw not a living soul!

3. Well, I held fast to the forward mast as the ship moved slowly on.
   And I watched that way 'til the break of day, when I knew that it fin'lly
      had gone.
   Oh, they laughed and joked as I told my tale to the captain and the men.
   But the story's true, I can promise you, and it's sure to happen again.

273

PLAYING THE GUITAR

4. Prepare the accompaniment for "The Ghost Ship." Have the students:
• Practice the strum patterns and chord changes. Try to capture the mood of the song.
• Examine and practice the bass part to the song, interpreting the mood as best they can.
• Form two groups. One group plays the strum patterns while the other plays the bass part. Combine the two parts, using their ideas for interpreting the mood of the song.

Reinforcing the Lesson

Have the students perform "The Ghost Ship," combining the two guitar parts to create an appropriate mood for the song. Then switch parts if they are able, and try a different interpretation of the song. Compare the two versions.

3 APPRAISAL

The students should be able to play guitar and bass accompaniment in a style that accurately reflects the mood of "The Ghost Ship."

PLAYING THE GUITAR

Focus: Arpeggio

Objective
To read and play arpeggios on the guitar

Materials
Recording: "River"
Guitars
Electric basses and amplifiers (optional)

Vocabulary
Arpeggio

1 SETTING THE STAGE

Review the D, G, B minor, C, A, and E minor chords, with students practicing alternating bass and bass run patterns with these chords as they are able.

2 TEACHING THE LESSON

1. Introduce the arpeggio. Have the students:
• Discuss the information on the arpeggio and define it.
• Examine the tablature for the arpeggios.
• Practice the arpeggio pattern for each chord.
2. Review "River." Have the students:
• Sing the song. Compare the mood of this song with that of "The Ghost Ship" or another song in this section.
• Listen to the song or sing it again, playing the proper chord on the downbeat of each measure (and on the proper beat in measure 43).
• Sing the song again, playing the arpeggio accompaniment as they are able.
• Perform the song with the guitar accompaniment. Try to capture the mood of the song.

AN ARPEGGIO ACCOMPANIMENT
Key: D major   **Starting Pitch: D**   **Scale Tones:** *so, la, do re mi fa so*

An **arpeggio** is a chord whose notes are played one at a time, rather than all at once.

To play an arpeggio:

1. Fret the chord.
2. Pluck the strings indicated, one at a time and in rhythm, with your right hand fingers. Finger numbers for the right hand are shown in parentheses *below* the arpeggio. They are the same as for the left hand.

• Practice these arpeggios. Notice that the bass note changes from the fourth to the fifth to the sixth string. The upper strings remain the same for all the chords.

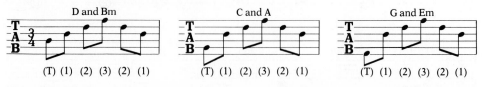

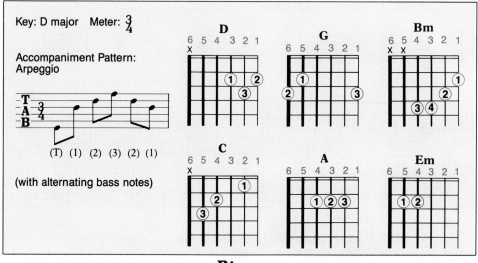

River

Words and music by Bill Staines

Verse

I was born in the path of the win-ter wind, And was raised where the moun-tains are old. The spring-time wa-ters came

274

EXTENSION

MORE MUSIC TEACHING IDEAS
Some students may want to improvise a bass accompaniment for this song on the guitar or electric bass.

11 G   D   Bm   A   G   D

danc - ing down, I re - mem - ber the tales they told. _____ The

17 D   G   D

whis - tling ___ ways of my young - er days, Too quick - ly have

22 Bm   C   A   D

fad - ed on by. _____ But all of the mem - o - ries

27 G   D   Bm   A   G   D

lin - ger still, Like the light in a fad - ing sky. _____

33 *Refrain*   D   G   A   D

Riv - er, take me a - long, In your sun - shine

39 G   A   Em   A

sing me your song, Ev - er mov - ing and wind - ing and __

44 D   Em   D   Em   D

free. You roll - ing old riv - er, You chang - ing old riv - er, Let's

49 Em   A | 1., 2. D   4

you and me, riv - er, Run down to the sea. _____

| 3. D   Coda   G   A   *ritard.*   D

sea. _____   Let's you and me, riv - er, Run down to the sea.

2. I've been to the city and back again;
I've been touched by some things that I've learned,
Met a lot of good people, and I've called them friends,
Felt the change when the seasons turned.
I've heard all the songs that the children sing
And I've listened to love's melodies;
I've felt my own music within me rise
Like the wind in the autumn trees.

Refrain

3. Someday when the flowers are blooming still,
Someday when the grass is still green,
My rolling waters will round the bend
And flow into the open sea.
So here's to the rainbow that's followed me here,
And here's to the friends that I know,
And here's to the song that's within me now;
I will sing it where'er I go.

Refrain

275

PLAYING THE GUITAR

Reinforcing the Lesson

Have the students form two groups. One group strums the chords on the beat while the other plays the arpeggio patterns. Perform "River," combining the two guitar parts to create an appropriate mood for the song.

3 APPRAISAL

The students should be able to read and play arpeggios on the guitar as an accompaniment to "River."

PLAYING THE GUITAR

Alternate Tunings

This section is provided for those teachers who may wish to teach D tuning. As the students tune their guitars to D major or D minor, point out that the fourth and fifth strings of the six-stringed guitar and the second and third strings of the electric bass do not have to be retuned.

When the students have retuned their guitars, have them examine the chord diagrams and practice playing these chords. Introduce the bar chord. When the students are familiar with the new chord fingerings, they can accompany "The Wabash Cannonball," "Worried Man Blues" (both in D major), "Drunken Sailor," and "The Wreck of the Edmund Fitzgerald" (both in D minor).

ALTERNATE TUNING: D MAJOR

You can use this tuning to play "The Wabash Cannonball" and "Worried Man Blues."

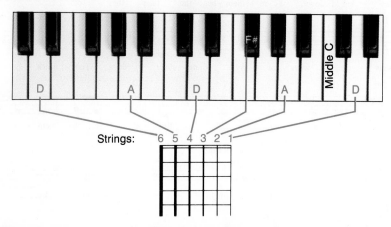

Strings: 6 5 4 3 2 1

"The Wabash Cannonball"

To play the alternating bass and strum with your right hand, pluck the sixth string with your right thumb for all three chords, then strum the rest of the strings. Omit the bass runs in this tuning. G and C are bar chords. To fret a bar chord, press your index finger down firmly across *all* the strings on fret indicated.

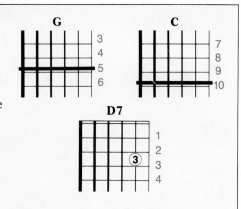

"Worried Man Blues"

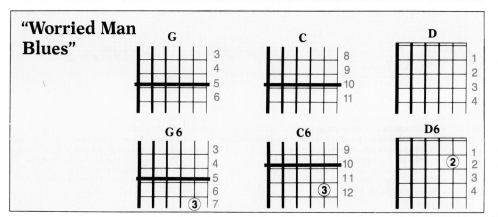

276

ALTERNATE TUNING: D MINOR

You can use this tuning to play "Drunken Sailor" and "The Wreck of the Edmund Fitzgerald."

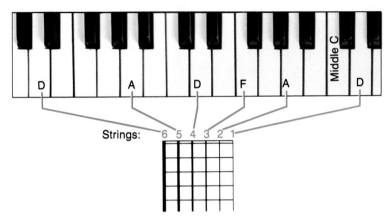

Strings: 6 5 4 3 2 1

"Drunken Sailor"

E minor is a bar chord (as are A minor and G major below). To fret a bar chord, press your index finger down firmly across all the strings on the fret indicated.

Em

D

"The Wreck of the Edmund Fitzgerald"

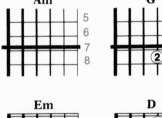

Am   G

Em   D

CHORAL SINGING

Detail from *Cantoria*, Luca della Robbia. MUSEO DEL OPERA DEL DUOMO, Florence

CHORAL SINGING

Focus: Checking Voice Range

Objectives
To identify and classify students' singing ranges in a group setting
To utilize a warm-up designed to develop resonance in the lower part of the tenor and baritone ranges

Materials
Recordings: "America": key of G
"America": key of B-flat
"America": key of C
Warm-Up 1

Vocabulary
Soprano, alto, tenor, baritone

279

CHORAL SINGING

TEACHING THE LESSON

1. Introduce identifying voice range.
Have the students:
• Discuss the information on singing ranges for young adults.
• Discuss why some voices sound higher and some sound lower. (Sounds are produced by the vocal cords vibrating together; vocal cords are of different lengths, thus affecting the range of individual voices.)
You may wish to use the following items as a basis for extended discussion.
1. Make certain the students understand the reasons for organizing the chorus according to voice range. (so that they are assigned voice parts that are within their range and to accommodate the physical changes that affect voice range and production)
2. Discuss the changes that are taking place in the students' voices. (As students become teenagers, many changes occur in their physical development. As boys develop physically their voices become lower in pitch. In the eighth grade, the degree of physical change among the boys will vary. Some of the boys become tenors or even baritones. Others will continue to sing in the high or middle ranges.)
3. Girls also experience physical change but the range of girls' voices does not reflect such a dramatic change in pitch. Their quality and range tend to stabilize and they are more easily classified as sopranos or altos.
4. Group or class testing is very quick and less intimidating than individual voice testing at this age level.
5. Since adolescent voices are unstable it is advisable to check voice ranges periodically.

CHECKING YOUR VOICE RANGE

Every person's voice has its own unique sound. However, the pitch range in which you sing falls into a group or category. These categories are: **soprano, alto, tenor,** and **baritone.**

This chart shows the approximate singing ranges for young adult singers.

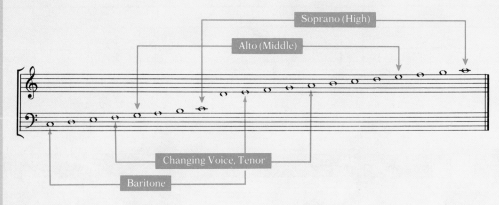

• Sing "America" in this key.

America

Words by Samuel F. Smith
Music by Henry Carey

My coun - try 'tis of thee, Sweet land of lib - er - ty,

Of thee I sing; Land where my fa - thers died, Land of the

pil - grim's pride, From ev - 'ry___ moun - tain-side Let__ free - dom ring.

If you can sing the upper octave more comfortably you probably are either a **soprano** or an **alto.**
If you can sing the lower octave more comfortably you are probably either a **changing voice,** a **tenor,** or a **baritone.**

280   Scale Tones: *ti₁ do re mi fa so la ti do¹ re¹ mi¹ fa¹ so¹ la¹*

E X T E N S I O N

- Sing "America" in this key.

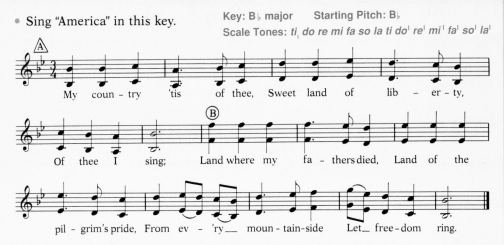

My coun - try 'tis of thee, Sweet land of lib – er - ty,

Of thee I sing; Land where my fa – thers died, Land of the

pil - grim's pride, From ev - 'ry__ moun - tain-side Let__ free - dom ring.

If you can sing the B section in the upper octave more comfortably you are probably a **soprano.**

If you can sing the B section in the lower octave more comfortably you are probably an **alto.**

- Sing "America" in this key.

Key: C major   **Starting Pitch:** C

Scale Tones: *ti, do re mi fa so la ti do¹ re¹ mi¹ fa¹ so¹ la¹*

My coun - try 'tis of thee, Sweet land of lib – er - ty,

Of thee I sing; Land where my fa – thers died, Land of the

pil - grim's pride, From ev - 'ry__ moun - tain-side Let__ free - dom ring.

If you can sing the A section in the upper octave more comfortably you are probably a **changing voice** or a **tenor.**

If you can sing the A section in the lower octave more comfortably you are probably a **baritone.**

281

CHORAL SINGING

6. Encourage the students (especially the boys) to request a voice range check when their assigned parts feel out of their range and cause strain.

7. Be aware of signs of strain: jaw forward and wrinkled brow, neck muscles and veins protruding, complaints about sore throats after singing, breaking or cracking voices while singing.

2. Identify voice range. Have the students:

- Sing "America" in the key of G. (Identify those who are singing the lower octave to determine later if they are changing voices, tenors, or baritones.)
- Sing "America" in the key of B flat. (Those who are singing the upper octave can be assigned to the soprano part. Those who are singing the lower octave can be assigned to the alto part.)
- Sing "America" in the key of C. (Those who are comfortable singing in the upper octave may be assigned to the changing voice/tenor part. Those who are comfortable singing in the lower octave may be assigned to the baritone part.)

3. Introduce vocal Warm-Up 1. Have the students:

- Focus on Warm-Up 1 as a technique to extend the range and resonance of the lower part of their voices. (This exercise is especially designed for those boys who are beginning to experience a change in their lower range. Have them sing an octave below the written notes.)

APPRAISAL

The students should be able to:

1. Define range and identify the basic voice categories—soprano, alto, tenor, baritone—for young adult singers.

2. Identify their own voice ranges and the ranges of the music they sing.

WARM-UP 1   Continue up to

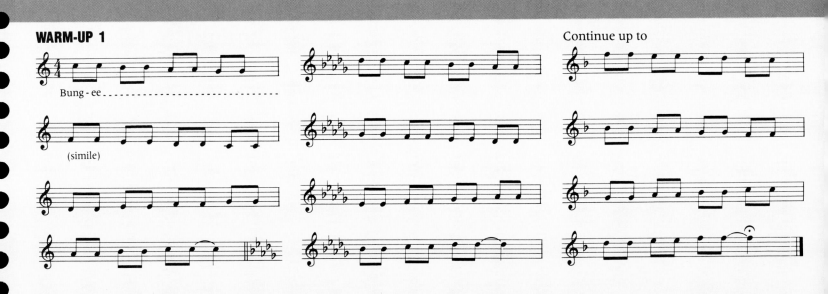

Bung - ee

(simile)

CHORAL SINGING

Focus: Producing a Good Choral Sound and Introduction to Targeting Vowels

Objectives
To develop correct singing posture and breathing techniques
To understand tone placement
To identify target vowels
To begin to develop independence of voice parts

Materials
Recording: "I'm Goin' Home on a Cloud"

Vocabulary
Breathing, posture, placement, vowel, target vowel

TEACHING THE LESSON

1. Introduce producing a good choral sound. Have the students:
• Discuss the information on how to produce a good choral sound.
• Demonstrate standing and sitting correctly. (Emphasize standing or sitting up straight with feet flat on the floor, and holding the chest high to help maintain proper air support.)
• Discuss the information on proper placement of tone.

HOW TO PRODUCE A GOOD CHORAL SOUND

11A CD 7

To **breathe** properly for singing, you must maintain good posture. Good **posture** means sitting or standing up straight, placing the feet flat on the floor, and holding the chest high so you have enough airflow to support the phrase you're singing. It's easy—try it.

Proper **placement** of tone means maintaining a sameness in the quality of sound throughout your vocal range. Proper placement is not achieved quickly. Practice it every time you sing a song.

Above, the Choir School of the Cathedral Church of St. John the Divine, New York. Right, the Chicago Children's Choir.

282

Vowels

Vowel sounds are important in singing because they are the sounds that are sustained, or held. Examine this diagram of **target vowels** and practice shaping each one with your lips to produce the correct sound. Every word in the text of a song will have at least one target vowel on which you can focus.

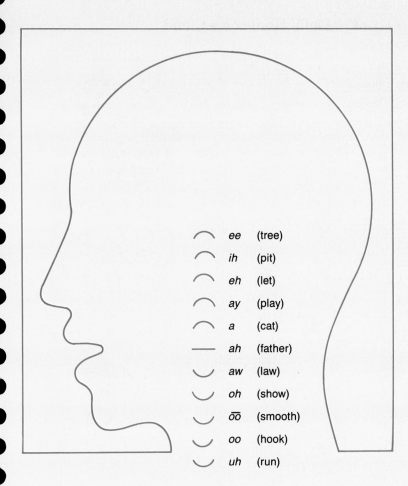

⌢	ee	(tree)
⌢	ih	(pit)
⌢	eh	(let)
⌢	ay	(play)
⌢	a	(cat)
—	ah	(father)
⌣	aw	(law)
⌣	oh	(show)
⌣	o͞o	(smooth)
⌣	oo	(hook)
⌣	uh	(run)

• Focus on producing clear vowels when you are learning to sing "I'm Goin' Home on a Cloud" on page 284.

283

2. Introduce targeting vowels. Have the students:
• Discuss the information on vowels.
• Experience the eleven target vowels by saying each word in the vowel spectrum slowly; identify other words that use each of these vowels.
• Identify the shape of the mouth and the position of the back of the tongue for each of the eleven vowel sounds. (For *ee, ih, eh,* and *ay,* the back of the tongue is high against the roof of the mouth. For *aw, oh, o͞o, oo,* and *uh,* the back of the tongue is low. The tongue is level for *a* and *ah.*)
• Notice the normal use of two vowel sounds (diphthong) in a word like play (*ay-ee*) and strive for pure vowel sounds.

CHORAL SINGING

3. Introduce "I'm Goin' Home on a Cloud." Have the students:
- Learn each of the four melodies by rote.
- Sing through each of the four melodies of "I'm Goin' Home on a Cloud," targeting the vowel sounds. (Encourage the students to focus on the shape of the mouth and the position of the tongue for each target vowel sound.)
- Form four groups and sing "I'm Goin' Home on a Cloud" in four parts.

APPRAISAL

The students should be able to:
1. Identify the characteristics of producing a good choral sound—good posture, proper breathing, proper placement of tone—and work towards achieving them.
2. Identify target vowels at the ends of phrases and produce them as pure vowel sounds.
3. Maintain independence of four equal voice parts while singing a partner song.

This spiritual is a partner song. It presents four different melodies that can be sung at the same time.

- Learn to sing each of the four melodies before performing them together.

Key: D major Starting Pitch: Part I: A Part II: D Part III: A Part IV: D
Scale Tones: *so, la, ta, ti, do ra re ma mi fa sa so la ta ti do'*

I'm Goin' Home on a Cloud

Piano Accompaniment on page PA 26

Spiritual
Arranged by Sean Deibler

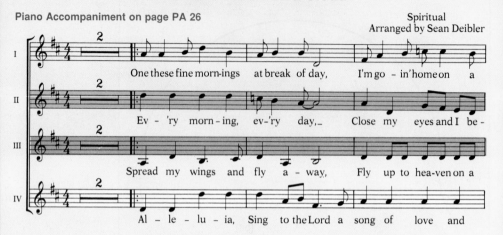

284

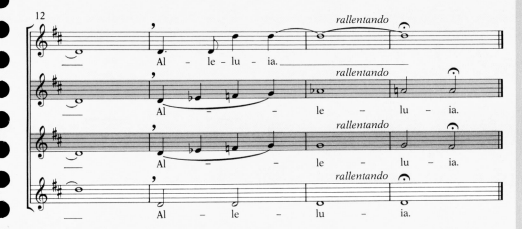

285

CHORAL SINGING

Focus: Introducing Consonants and Diction

Objectives

To identify consonant sounds
To understand diction and its importance
To develop crisp and precise diction in singing
To apply these skills to the performance of a two-part song

Materials

Recording: "Over the Sea to Skye"

Vocabulary

Consonant, diction

TEACHING THE LESSON

1. Introduce consonants. Have the students:
• Discuss the information on consonants.
• Experience the consonant sounds listed by thinking of and saying words that begin or end with each of those consonant sounds.
• Identify those sounds shaped by the lips (B, V, M, P) and those shaped by the tongue (D, J, T, S, G, C).
2. Introduce diction. Have the students:
• Discuss the definition of diction. (Emphasize that crisp and precise diction is important in making the words of a song understandable to the listener.)
• Find consonants in "Over the Sea to Skye" and practice saying them precisely.
3. Introduce "Over the Sea to Skye." Have the students:
• Clap the steady dotted half note beat as they listen to "Over the Sea to Skye."
• Read the text of the song slowly, focusing on the shape of the mouth and the function of the lips and tongue as they form each word.

Consonants 🌐 11A 💿 7

Key: G♭ major and G major   Starting Pitch: D♭   Scale Tones: See below.

• Say each **consonant** sound shown. Identify those sounds shaped by the lips and those shaped by the tongue.

B   V   M   P   D   J   T   S   G   C

Diction is the combination of vowel and consonant sounds that make words. Crisp and precise diction makes the words of a song understandable.

• Look for consonants in "Over the Sea to Skye" and practice singing them correctly.

Over the Sea to Skye

Piano Accompaniment on page PA 38

Words by Robert Louis Stevenson
Old Highland rowing song arr. by M.J.

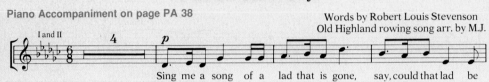

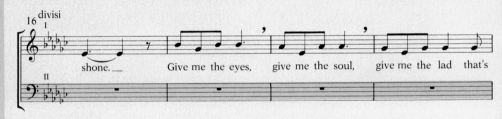

* Tacet (ta' set) means that Part II will not sing until indicated.

Scale Tones: G♭ major: *so͵ la͵ do re mi so la do' re' mi' so'*
               G major: *so͵ la͵ do re mi so la do' re' mi' so'*

286

CHORAL SINGING

• Follow the music to "Over the Sea to Skye" and listen for crisp and precise diction.
• Form two groups and learn their respective treble and bass clef voice parts by rote.
• Sing their parts softly on *oo* with the vocal accompaniment, and then with the instrumental accompaniment.
• Sing the song with the words, over-emphasizing the vowel and consonant sounds. Then sing the song again, under-emphasizing these sounds.
• Identify which performance contained greater rhythmic precision and clarity. (the first)

4. Perform "Over the Sea to Skye."
Have the students:
• Follow conducting gestures and sing "Over the Sea to Skye" with and without accompaniment.
• Silently sing and follow conducting gestures, breathing at phrase markings to indicate their attention.
• Perform with the instrumental track or keyboard accompaniment.
• Listen as the class, sections, or small groups perform the song. Discuss the performances.

APPRAISAL

The students should be able to:
1. Identify consonant sounds and perform them crisply and precisely.
2. Identify good diction in singing, know why it is important, and work towards achieving it.
3. Sing a simple two-part song and hold their own parts successfully.

288

289

CHORAL SINGING

Focus: Building a Choral Ensemble

Objectives
To reinforce an understanding of the characteristics of good choral singing including good posture, correct breathing, proper placement of tone, clear vowels, crisp consonants, and blend

To demonstrate an understanding of the characteristics of good choral singing through the use of specific warm-ups for correct breathing and support of the air flow, and proper placement of tone

To perform a choral composition with accompanying movement

Materials
Recordings: Warm-Up 2
"The Rhythm of Life"

Vocabulary
Blend

TEACHING THE LESSON

1. Introduce building a choral ensemble. Have the students:
• Discuss and review the information on the characteristics of good choral singing
• Sing Warm-Up 2 using these characteristics

2. Introduce "The Rhythm of Life." Have the students:
• Follow the music and listen to "The Rhythm of Life" while clapping the steady quarter note beat.
• Follow the music and, using good singing posture, softly sing the warm-ups as indicated.
• Learn and sing each part separately, focusing on pitch and rhythmic accuracy.
• Discuss the information on blend.

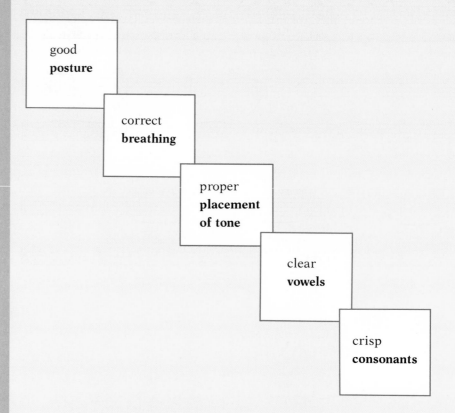

🔊 11A 💿 7 BUILDING A CHORAL ENSEMBLE

You have learned that characteristics of good choral singing include:

good **posture**

correct **breathing**

proper **placement of tone**

clear **vowels**

crisp **consonants**

To practice these characteristics of good singing, try these warm-ups with "The Rhythm of Life."

Maintain good posture so that you can breathe correctly to sustain and support the airflow. Sing each phrase of the song with the syllable *loo* in place of the words. For proper placement of tone, you should work for maintaining a sameness in the quality of sound throughout the song. Sing the syllable *vee* in place of the words. Then practice the words, working for clear vowels and crisp consonants.

One more characteristic of good choral singing is **blend**. You should blend your voice with those of the other singers to create a unified sound. This way the many individual voices sound like one. Keep this in mind as you sing "The Rhythm of Life" together.

290

E X T E N S I O N

WARM-UP 2

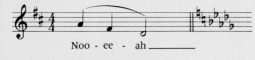

Noo - ee - ah

Continue down to

MOVEMENT DIRECTIONS FOR "THE RHYTHM OF LIFE"

All movements are performed in a standing, stationary position.

A mm. 9–12, right arm sweep from left to right—8 counts; mm. 13–16, repeat right arm sweep from left to right—8 counts.

B mm. 17–18, extend both arms above the head—4 counts; mm. 19–20, lower hands to top of head—4 counts; mm. 21–22, bring hands to shoulders—4 counts; mm. 23–24, lower hands to hips—4 counts.

C mm. 25–28, snap fingers (both hands) left to right on the beat—8 counts; mm. 29–32, repeat finger snaps, left to right—8 counts.

D mm. 33–40, Part I, repeat arm movements from rehearsal letter B; Parts II and III, repeat finger snaps from rehearsal letter C.

E mm. 41–48, Part I, repeat arm movements from rehearsal letter B; Part II, repeat finger snaps from rehearsal letter C; Part III, hitchhike motion with the right thumb, sweep to left every 4 counts—16 counts.

F mm. 49–56, repeat right arm sweep, left to right from rehearsal letter A—16 counts.

G mm. 57–64, repeat arm movements from rehearsal letter B (hands above head for 4 counts, hands on top of head for 4 counts, hands to shoulders for 4 counts, and hands on hips for 4 counts).

H mm. 65–72, Parts I and II, repeat arm movements from rehearsal letter G; Part III, extend both arms straight out and point with the index fingers for 16 counts.

Key: D minor, F minor, D minor **The Rhythm of Life**   Scale Tones: See below.
Starting Pitch: D

Piano Accompaniment on page PA 29

Words by Dorothy Fields (adapted)
Music by Cy Coleman
Arranged by Richard Barnes, adapted by V.L.

When I start-ed down the street last Sun-day,

Feel-in' might-y low and kind-a mean, Sud-den-ly a voice said,

"Go forth, neigh-bor! Spread the pic-ture on a wid-er screen!" And the

voice said, "Neigh-bor, there's a mil-lion rea-sons Why you should be glad in

all four sea-sons! Hit the road, neigh-bor, leave your wor-ries and strife!

Spread the re-li-gion of the rhy-thm of life." For the rhy-thm of life is a

pow-er-ful beat, Puts a tin-gle in your fin-gers and a tin-gle in your feet!

Rhy-thm on the in-side, rhy-thm on the street, And the rhy-thm of life is a

Sole Selling Agent for the Richard Barnes arrangement: Shawnee Press, Inc.; Delaware Water Gap, PA 18327.

Scale Tones: D minor: *si, la, ti, do re mi fa so la ti*
F minor: *re, mi, fa, fi, so, si, la, ti, do re mi fa*
D minor: *mi, fa, fi, so, si, la, li, ti, do di re ri mi fa fi so*

291

CHORAL SINGING

3. Perform "The Rhythm of Life."
Have the students:
• Use good singing posture and sing all parts with words, using the vocal and instrumental accompaniment. (Stress maintaining an even quality of sound throughout each vocal range, sustained vowel sounds, control of the airflow, and pitch and rhythmic accuracy.)
• Follow conducting gestures and sing the song without accompaniment.
• Silently sing and follow conducting gestures, breathing at phrase endings to indicate their attention.
• Follow conducting gestures and sing with the instrumental or keyboard accompaniment.
• Identify the characteristics of "The Rhythm of Life." (Emphasis should be on pitch and rhythmic accuracy, part singing, consonants at ends of phrases, targeted vowels, and blend.)
• Listen as the class, sections, or small groups perform. Discuss the performances.

APPRAISAL

The students should be able to:
1. Identify and demonstrate the characteristics of good choral singing—good posture, correct breathing, proper placement of tone, clear vowels, crisp consonants, and blend.
2. Perform simple choreographed movements to accompany a song.

I mm. 73–74, clap on the eighth rest, right arm sweep from left to right, 4 counts; mm. 75–76, clap on the eighth rest, hitchhike motion using left thumb, emphasizing beats, 4 counts; mm. 77–78, clap on eighth rest, finger snaps (both hands) left to right on the beat, 4 counts; mm. 79–80, clap on eighth rest, extend left arm straight forward and point with index finger, 4 counts; mm. 81–84, clap on quarter rest, slowly extend both arms (palms up) to ceiling, 8 counts.

292

293

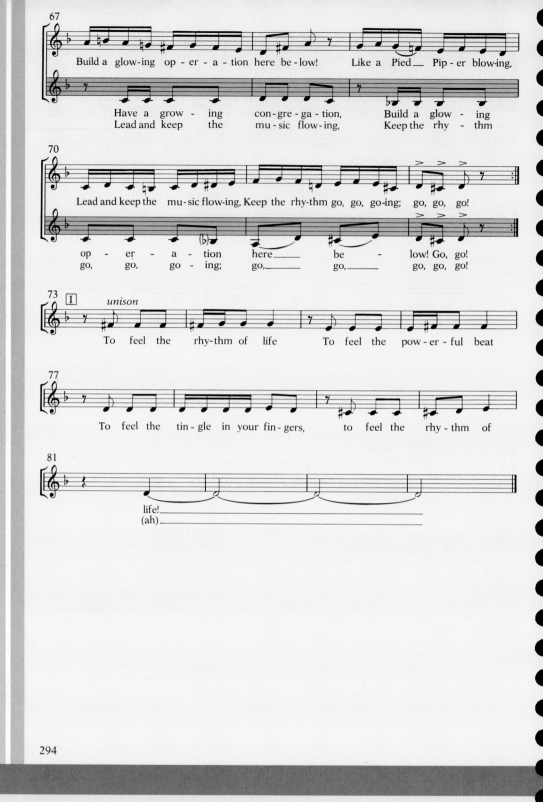

BUILDING MUSIC READING SKILLS

🔊 11B
💿 7

When someone can read music, he or she can look at a line or page of music and mentally hear how it sounds. The following preparations will help you develop your music reading skills.

Use the **tone ladder** to review the pitches of the major scale. Use syllables or numbers.

- See, hear, and sense the intervals between the pitches as you sing up and down the tone ladder.

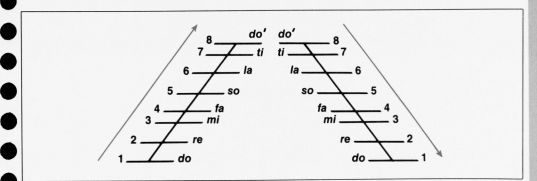

Preparation 1

- Clap this rhythm pattern.

- Add these pitches from the tone ladder to the same rhythm pattern. Sing the pitches with syllables or numbers.

When you sing pitches that are next to each other, for example, 1 to 2 or 3 to 2, the melody is said to move **stepwise**.

- Use the tone ladder to create your own stepwise melody to the same rhythm pattern.

295

CHORAL SINGING

Focus: Reading Steps and Skips

Objectives
To identify and read melodic patterns that move by steps and skips
To apply these music reading skills to the learning and performance of a two-part composition
To continue the development of skills and concepts of choral singing

Materials
Recording: "April Weather"
Copying Master C-1 (optional)

Vocabulary
Tone ladder, stepwise, skips

TEACHING THE LESSON

1. Introduce building music reading skills. Have the students:
- Discuss the information on building music reading skills.
- Review singing up and down the tone ladder in D major on syllables or numbers. (Emphasize seeing, hearing, and sensing the intervals between pitches as they sing.)
- Identify the pitches of the tone ladder as a major scale when placed on the staff.

2. Introduce Preparation 1. Have the students:
- Clap the rhythm pattern.
- Add the indicated pitches from the tone ladder to the same rhythm pattern and sing it with syllables or numbers. (Emphasize the concept of stepwise motion.)
- Create their own stepwise melodies using the tone ladder and the same rhythm pattern.

(You may wish to use Copying Master C-1 at this time.)

CHORAL SINGING

3. Introduce Preparation 2. Have the students:
• Use the tone ladder to help find the pitches in the beginning of "April Weather."
• Find the steps between pitches, skips, and repeated notes.
• Sing the melody with syllables or numbers.

4. Introduce Preparation 3. Have the students:
• Notice the square note at the beginning of each part that identifies the space or line that is *do* or 1.
• Identify which pitches are the same between the two parts.
• Sing the second part with syllables or numbers.
• Sing the two parts together.
• Find the melody and harmony parts in "April Weather." (mm. 6–9)
• Sing the third melody with syllables or numbers.
• Find where this melody is in "April Weather."

5. Introduce "April Weather." Have the students:
• Form two equal groups.
• Follow the music and listen to "April Weather."
• Follow the music and, using correct singing posture, softly sing first Part I and then Part II on short *doo* vowels for each note value with the accompaniment, focusing on pitch and rhythmic accuracy.

Preparation 2

• Use the tone ladder to help you find the pitches in the beginning of the melody of "April Weather."

Where are the steps between pitches? Where are the **skips,** or spaces, between pitches? Find the repeated pitches.

mm. 1–2, 2–3, 3–4 and with mm. 3–4; beginning–m.1, m.3; mm. 2, 3

Preparation 3

Here is the same melody with a second part as it appears in "April Weather."

• Practice each part separately. Then sing both parts together. Find this section in the music. mm. 6–9

• Use syllables or numbers to sing this pattern.

In which voice part do you find this pattern? I

Key: F major   Starting Pitch: C   Scale Tones: *so, la, ti, do re mi fa so la*

April Weather

Piano Accompaniment on page PA 44

Words by Lizette Woodworth Reese
Music by C. M. Shearer

𝅘𝅥 = c. 128

1. & 3. Oh, hush, my heart and take thine ease, For here is A-pril
2. The li-lac bush is sweet a-gain; Down ev-'ry wind that

(3rd time to 3rd ending)

wea - ther! The daf - fo - dils be - neath the trees Are all a - row to -
pass - es, Fly flakes from hedge-rows and from lane; The bees are in the

molto rit. on 2nd verse

- geth - er. The thrush is_ back with his_ old_ note; The scar - let_ tu - lips
grass - es. And Grief goes out, and Joy comes in, And care is_but a

- geth - er. Thrush is_ back with his_ old_ note; The scar - let_
grass - es. Grief goes out, and Joy comes in, And care is_

a tempo on 2nd verse

blow - ing; And white, ah, white as my love's throat The dog - wood boughs are
feath - er; And ev - 'ry lad his love can win, For here is A - pril

tu - lips blow-ing; And white, ah, white as my love's throat The dog-wood boughs are
but a feath-er; And ev - 'ry lad his love can win, For here is A - pril

1 & 2

grow - ing.
weath - er.

3

geth - er.

grow - ing.
weath - er.

geth - er.

297

6. Perform "April Weather." Have the students:

• Use correct singing posture and sing Parts I and II with words, with the vocal and instrumental accompaniment. (Stress maintaining an even quality of sound throughout each vocal range, sustained vowel sounds, control of the air flow, and pitch and rhythmic accuracy.)

• Sing the song with and without the instrumental accompaniment while following conducting gestures. (Emphasize eye contact, with attention to attacks and releases at the ends of phrases.)

• Silently sing and follow conducting gestures, breathing at phrase markings to indicate their attention.

• Follow conducting gestures and sing with the instrumental or keyboard accompaniment.

• Identify the characteristics of "April Weather." (Emphasis should be on pitch and rhythmic accuracy, evenness of vocal production, part singing, consonants at ends of phrases, and targeted vowels.)

• Listen as the class, sections, or small groups perform. Discuss the performances.

APPRAISAL

The students should be able to:

1. Identify the repeated, stepwise, and skipwise patterns in musical notation and sight sing them with some degree of success.

2. Recognize and perform simple rhythmic patterns using quarter and half notes.

3. Sing a simple two-part song and hold their own parts successfully.

CHORAL SINGING

Focus: Developing Skill in Reading Steps and Skips

Objectives
To reinforce the reading of melodic patterns that move by step in treble and bass clef

To apply these music reading skills to the learning and performance of a three-part composition

To continue the development of skills and concepts of choral singing

Materials
Recordings: Warm-Up 3
             "The Rose"

Vocabulary
Pickup

TEACHING THE LESSON

1. Introduce Preparation 4. Have the students:
- Discuss the information on the pickup.
- Clap or tap each of the three rhythm patterns in order.
- Listen for and identify the differences among the patterns.
- Find the third rhythm pattern in the musical excerpt.
- Sing the treble clef part on syllables or numbers.
- Sing the bass clef part on syllables or numbers.
- Sing both parts together using the words.

2. Perform Warm-Up 3. Have the students:
- Perform Warm-Up 3 before singing "The Rose."
- Focus on maintaining an even quality of sound (resonance) and experience the airflow (breathing) necessary to sustain a phrase.

Phrases in "The Rose" begin with an incomplete measure, called a **pickup.**

11B CD 7

Preparation 4

- Clap or tap these three patterns in order. Listen for the differences among the patterns.

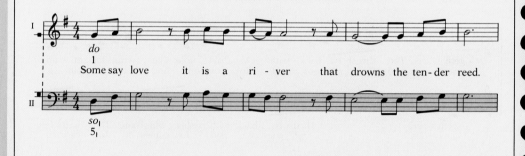

- Find the third pattern in the phrase below. pickup–m.2
- Form two groups. Sing this phrase in two parts. Notice that the lower part is notated in the bass clef.

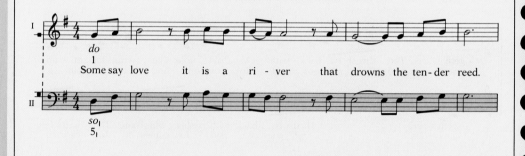

do
1
Some say love   it   is a   ri - ver   that   drowns the ten-der reed.

so
5

298

WARM-UP 3

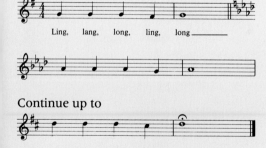

Ling,   lang,   long,   ling,   long ————

Continue up to

Key: G major   **Starting Pitch: G**   **The Rose**   Scale Tones: See below.

Piano Accompaniment on page PA 47   Words and music by Amanda McBroom
Arr. by V.L.

♩ = m.m. 60

I Some say love   it is a ri - ver   that
(ah)   (eh)

II Tacet until m. 19

5

drowns_ the ten - der reed   Some say love   it is a ra - zor   that
(ah)   (ee)   (ah)   (eh)

9

leaves_ your soul to bleed   Some say love___ it is a hun - ger   an
(ee)   (ah)   (eh)

13

end - less ach - ing need___   I say love___ it is a flow - er   and
(eh)   (ee)   (ah)   (eh)

17

you___   its on - ly seed.___   It's the heart   a - fraid of
(oo)   (ee)   (ah)

II   It's the heart   a - fraid of
(ah)

21

break - ing   that ne - ver___ learns to dance.   It's the dream   a - fraid of
(ih)   (a)   (ee)

break - ing   that ne - ver___ learns to dance.   It's the dream   a - fraid of
(ih)   (a)   (ee)

Scale Tones: *so₁ la₁ ti₁ do re mi fa so la do¹ re¹ mi¹ fa¹ so¹ la¹*   299

CHORAL SINGING

3. Introduce "The Rose." Have the students:
• Form two groups. Each group should be further divided for divisi sections.
• Follow the music and listen to "The Rose."
• Follow the music, using correct singing posture as they softly sing the unison section (mm. 1–18) with the accompaniment on short *doo* vowels for each note value, focusing on pitch and rhythmic accuracy.
• Learn Parts I and II separately, focusing particularly on the divisi sections in each part (mm. 19–52), while emphasizing pitch and rhythmic accuracy.

4. Perform "The Rose." Have the students:
• Use correct singing posture and sing Parts I and II with words and the vocal and instrumental accompaniment. (Stress maintaining an even quality of sound throughout each voice range, sustained vowel sounds, and control of the airflow.)
• Sing the song with and without the instrumental accompaniment while following conducting gestures. (Emphasize eye contact, with attention to attacks and releases at ends of phrases.)
• Silently sing and follow conducting gestures, breathing at phrase endings to indicate their attention.
• Follow conducting gestures and sing with the instrumental or keyboard accompaniment.
• Identify the characteristics of "The Rose." (Emphasis should be on pitch and rhythmic accuracy, evenness of vocal production, part singing, consonants at ends of phrases, and targeted vowels.)
• Listen as the class, sections, or small groups perform. Discuss the performances.

CHORAL SINGING

APPRAISAL

The students should be able to:

1. Identify stepwise and skipwise patterns in musical notation in treble and bass clefs, and sight sing them with some degree of success.
2. Recognize and perform simple rhythmic patterns using eighth notes, eighth rests, and half notes.
3. Sing a simple three-part song in treble and bass clefs and hold their own parts successfully.

*Optional divisi

300

think___ that love is on - ly for the luck - y and the strong, *Just re-*
(ah)

think___ that love is on - ly for the luck - y and the strong,
(ah)

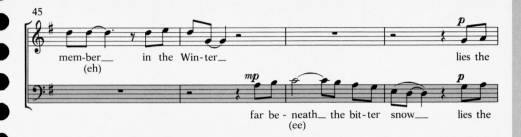

mem-ber___ in the Win-ter___ lies the
(eh)

far be - neath___ the bit-ter snow___ lies the
(ee)

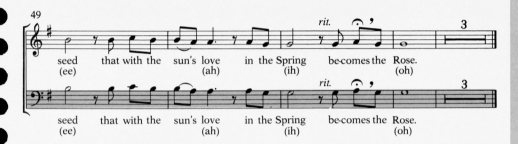

seed that with the sun's love in the Spring be-comes the Rose.
(ee) (ah) (ih) (oh)

seed that with the sun's love in the Spring be-comes the Rose.
(ee) (ah) (ih) (oh)

CHORAL SINGING

301

CHORAL SINGING **301**

CHORAL SINGING

Focus: Developing Music Reading Skills

Objectives

To develop skill in reading $^6_8$ meter

To reinforce the reading of melodic patterns that move by steps, skips, and repeated pitches

To apply these music reading skills to learning and performing a four-part composition

To continue the development of skills and concepts of choral singing

Materials

Recording: "Winter Carol"

Copying Master C-2 (optional)

TEACHING THE LESSON

1. Introduce $^6_8$ meter. Have the students:

• Discuss the information on $^6_8$ meter.

• Identify that in $^6_8$ meter the eighth note gets one count, the quarter note gets two counts, the dotted quarter note gets three counts, and the dotted half note gets six counts.

(You may wish to use Copying Master C-2 at this time.)

2. Introduce Preparation 5. Have the students:

• Form two groups. One group claps the steady eighth-note beat while the other group claps rhythm pattern A.

• Identify the pickup note at the beginning of the next melodic pattern.

• Clap the rhythm of this melody.

• Sing the melody with syllables or numbers.

• Locate the melody in "Winter Carol."

3. Introduce Preparation 6. Have the students:

• Sing up and down the tone ladder in F major to establish the key.

Many different meter signatures are used in music. So far, you have read music in $^2_4$, $^3_4$, and $^4_4$. The song "Winter Carol" is written in $^6_8$ meter. In $^6_8$, the eighth note (♪) is the beat note, and gets one count.

Preparation 5

• Form two groups to clap the eighth-note beat and the rhythm pattern.

• Clap the rhythm of the melody below. Look for the pickup note at the beginning of the melody.

• Sing the melody on syllables or numbers.

so do' fa so la so do' re' mi'
5 1' 4 5 6 5 1' 2' 3'

• Find this melody in "Winter Carol."

Preparation 6

• Sing this melody with syllables or numbers. Notice that this melody is notated in bass clef.

do re mi so fa mi
1 2 3 5 4 3

• Find this melody in "Winter Carol." Which vocal part sings it?

302

Key: B♭ major and D minor
Starting Pitch: F
Piano Accompaniment on page PA 52

Winter Carol

Scale Tones: See below.

Words by Jane Foster Knox
Music by Mark Wilson

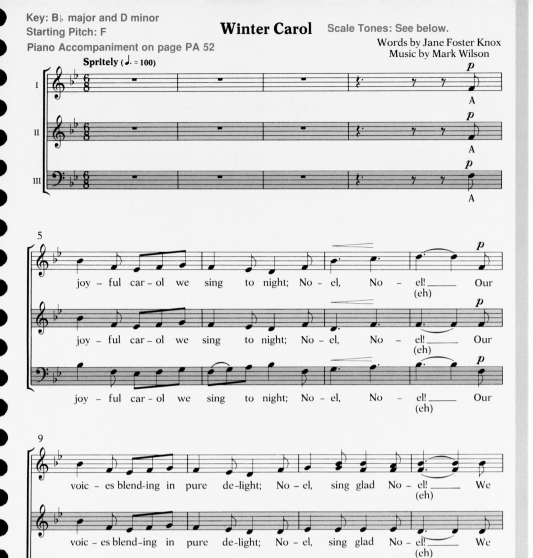

Spritely (♩. = 100)

joy – ful car – ol we sing to night; No – el, No – el! _____ Our
(eh)

voic – es blend-ing in pure de–light; No – el, sing glad No – el! _____ We
(eh)

Scale Tones: B♭ major: *fa, so, la, ti, do re mi fa so la ti do¹ re¹ mi¹*
D minor: *do, re, mi, fa, so, si, la, ti, do re mi fa so la*

303

CHORAL SINGING

• Identify the melody as being written in bass clef.
• Sing the melody with syllables or numbers.
• Locate the melody and which vocal part sings it in "Winter Carol."

4. Introduce "Winter Carol." Have the students:

• Sing up and down the tone ladder in B-flat major to establish the key. Form three groups.
• Follow the music and listen to "Winter Carol."
• Follow the music using correct singing posture, and softly sing the melody with the accompaniment on short *doo* vowels for each note value, focusing on pitch and rhythmic accuracy.
• Learn Parts I, II, and III separately for the first section (mm. 1–32), emphasizing pitch and rhythmic accuracy. Note when Parts I and II are in unison.
• Learn Parts I, II, and III separately for the second section (mm. 33–52), focusing on the changes from major to minor mode, and from ⁶⁄₈ to ²⁄₄ meter. Note when Parts I and II are in unison.
• Learn Parts I, II and III separately for the closing section (mm. 53–85), making certain to observe the ritardando and fermata in m. 81. Note when Parts I and II are in unison.

5. Perform "Winter Carol." Have the students:

• Use correct singing posture and sing all the parts with words and the vocal and instrumental accompaniment. (Stress maintaining an even quality of sound throughout each voice range, sustained vowel sounds, and crisp diction.)
• Follow conducting gestures and sing in three parts with and without the accompaniment. (Emphasize eye contact, with attention to attacks and releases at ends of phrases.)

CHORAL SINGING

- Silently sing and follow conducting gestures, breathing at phrase endings to indicate their attention.
- Follow conducting gestures and sing with the instrumental or keyboard accompaniment.
- Identify the characteristics of "Winter Carol." (Emphasis should be on pitch accuracy, evenness of vocal production, part singing, consonants at the ends of phrases, and targeted vowels.)
- Listen as the class, sections, or small groups perform. Discuss the performances.

APPRAISAL

The students should be able to:

1. Recognize the steps, skips, and repeated notes in a melodic pattern.
2. Perform simple rhythm patterns in $\frac{6}{8}$ meter.
3. Feel more confident about holding their own part in four-part choral singing.

304

fa – ces glow in the can – dle light. No – el, sing glad No – el! _____
(eh)

fa – ces glow in the can – dle light. No – el, sing glad No – el! _____
(eh)

fa – ces glow in the can – dle light. No – el, sing glad No – el! _____
(eh)

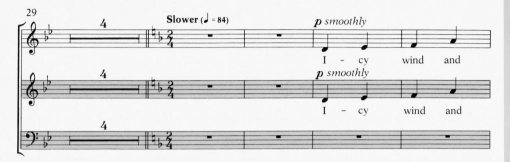

Slower (♩ = 84)   *p smoothly*

I – cy   wind   and

p smoothly

I – cy   wind   and

branch – es   bare;
(eh)

branch – es   bare;
(eh)

p smoothly

Shad – ows   danc – ing

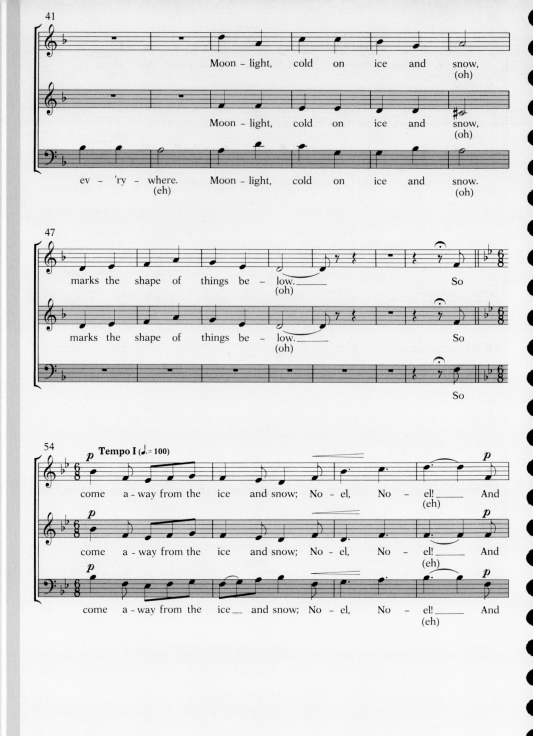

58

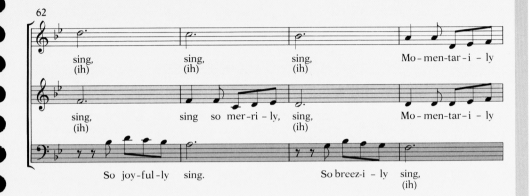

warm your-self by the fire's __ glow. No – el, sing glad No – el! __ We
(eh)

warm your-self by the fire's __ glow. No – el, sing glad No – el! __ We
(eh)

warm your-self by the fire's __ glow. No – el, sing glad No – el! __
(eh)

62

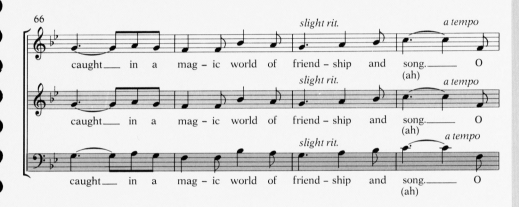

sing,   sing,   sing,   Mo – men-tar-i – ly
(ih)   (ih)   (ih)

sing,   sing so mer-ri – ly, sing,   Mo – men-tar-i – ly
(ih)   (ih)

So joy-ful-ly sing.   So breez-i – ly sing,
(ih)

66
                                        slight rit.   *a tempo*

caught __ in a mag – ic world of friend – ship and song. __ O
(ah)
                                        slight rit.   *a tempo*

caught __ in a mag – ic world of friend – ship and song. __ O
(ah)
                                        slight rit.   *a tempo*

caught __ in a mag – ic world of friend – ship and song. __ O
(ah)

CHORAL SINGING

CHORAL SINGING

Preparation 7

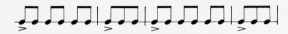 11B
CD 8

- Count aloud as you clap each beat. Emphasize the accented beats.

The same pattern can be shown in this notation.

You have just clapped alternating groups of six beats and three beats.

The rhythm structure of "Praise to the Lord" is based on the same grouping.

- Perform this rhythm pattern. Use a pat-slide motion for the half notes and dotted half notes, and clap for the eighth notes.

- Sing this melody on syllables or numbers. Then form groups and sing it as a two-part round.

309

E X T E N S I O N

CHORAL SINGING

Focus: Reading Changes in Meter

Objectives
To identify and read changes of meter
To apply these music reading skills to the learning and performance of a three-part composition with multiple meter changes
To continue the development of skills and concepts of choral singing

Materials
Recordings: Warm-Up 4
"Praise to the Lord"

TEACHING THE LESSON

1. Introduce Preparation 7. Have the students:
- Count aloud as they clap each beat of the first pattern, emphasizing the accented numbers.
- Discuss and perform the actual notation of the first pattern.
- Form two groups and perform the next pattern, using a pat-slide motion on the half and dotted half notes and clapping on the eighth notes.
- Sing the melodic pattern using syllables or numbers.
- Form two groups and sing the melodic pattern as a two-part round.

2. Introduce Warm-Up 4. Have the students:
- Read Warm-Up 4 using the rhythm in Preparation 7.
- Perform Warm-Up 4 at increasingly faster tempos.

WARM-UP 4

Vee Vee   Vee Vee   Vee Vee   Vee   Vee

Vee Vee   Vee Vee   Vee Vee   Vee   Vee

CHORAL SINGING

3. Introduce "Praise to the Lord."
Have the students:

• Find the last melodic pattern in Preparation 7 in "Praise to the Lord." (mm. 2–8)

• Form three groups.

• Follow the music and listen to "Praise to the Lord," lightly tapping the rhythm of the vocal part.

• Follow the music and, using correct singing posture, softly sing the melody with the accompaniment on short *doo* vowels for each note value, focusing on pitch accuracy and staccato movement.

• Sing the opening unison section (mm. 1–27) of "Praise to the Lord" slowly, without the accompaniment.

• Learn Parts I, II, and III separately for mm. 31–53. Note the canonic imitation and repetition among the three parts. Sing the parts together slowly.

• Learn Parts I and II separately for mm. 54–73. Again, note the canonic imitation between the two voices. Sing the parts together slowly.

4. Perform "Praise to the Lord." Have the students:

• Use correct singing posture and sing Parts I, II, and III with the words and with the accompaniment. (Stress maintaining an even quality of sound throughout each voice range, sustained vowel sounds, crisp diction, and pitch and rhythmic accuracy.)

• Sing the song with and without accompaniment while following conducting gestures. (Emphasize eye contact, with attention to attacks and releases at ends of phrases.)

• Silently sing and follow conducting gestures. (Have the students breathe at phrase endings to indicate their attention.)

• Follow conducting gestures and sing with the accompaniment.

Key: F major   Starting Pitch: F   **Praise to the Lord**

Scale Tones:
ta, do ra re ma mi fa sa
so lo la ta

M.J.

Piano Accompaniment on page PA 62

♪ = ♪ = 288 **throughout**

310

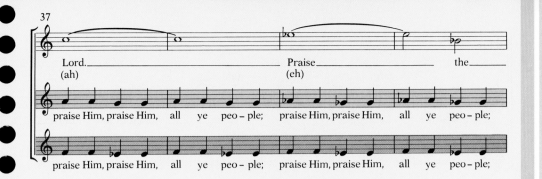

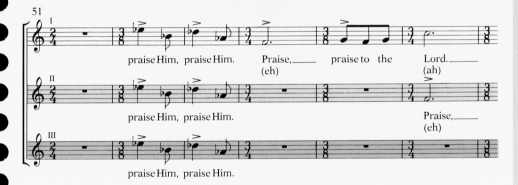

• Identify characteristics of "Praise to the Lord." (Emphasis should be on pitch and rhythmic accuracy, evenness of vocal production, part singing, consonants at ends of phrases, and targeted vowels.)
• Listen as the class, sections, or small groups perform. Discuss the performances.

APPRAISAL

The students should be able to:
1. Identify and read changes of meter with some degree of success.
2. Identify and read canonic and imitative writing between voice parts.

311

57

Praise,_____ praise to the Lord._____
(ah)

praise to the Lord._____ Praise,_____ praise to the Lord._____
(ah)   (eh)   (ah)

dim.

63

dim. *molto dim.* **pp**

Praise to the Lord._____ Praise to the Lord._____ Praise to the
(ah)   (ah)

molto dim. **pp**

(Lord)_____ Praise to the Lord._____ Praise to the Lord._____
                (ah)   (ah)

69

unison **ff** *rit.* *a tempo*

Lord. Oh, praise the Lord._____
(ah)   (eh)   (uh)   (ah)

unison **ff** *rit.*

(Lord) Oh, praise the Lord._____
          (eh)   (uh)   (ah)

unison **ff** *rit.*

Oh, praise the Lord._____
     (eh)   (uh)   (ah)

312

11B
CD 8

The song "Hanerot Halalu" is in minor.

Preparation 8

A **minor scale** uses the same scale tones as its **relative major scale**, but the tonal center is the sixth note of the major scale, la_1 (6), instead of on the first note, *do* (1).

- Use the tone ladder to sing the F major scale beginning on *do* (1) and the D minor scale beginning on la_1 (6).

Major and minor scales can be notated this way:

la₁ ti₁ do re mi fa so la ti do'

Preparation 9

- Sing this pattern to establish the tonal center for D minor.

- Sing this phrase from "Hanerot Halalu," which is in D minor.

la₁ do mi
6₁ 1 3

CHORAL SINGING

Focus: Reading Music in Minor Keys

Objectives

To introduce the minor mode in a two-part composition

To develop singing skills for the changing voice range

To continue the development of skills and concepts of choral singing

To continue developing skills in targeting vowels and combining diction and sustained vowels

To perform a two-part composition in Hebrew

Materials

Recordings: Warm-Up 5
            "Hanerot Halalu"
Copying Master C-3 (optional)

Vocabulary

Minor scale, relative major scale

TEACHING THE LESSON

1. Introduce Preparation 8. Have the students:

- Use the tone ladder and sing the F major scale beginning on *do* (1) and the relative D minor scale beginning on la_1 (6₁).
- Discuss the difference in sound between major and minor tonality.

(You may wish to use Copying Master C-3 at this time.)

2. Introduce Preparation 9. Have the students:

- Sing the first pattern to establish the tonal center for D minor.
- Sing the second pattern from "Hanerot Halalu," which is in D minor, on syllables or numbers.

CHORAL SINGING

3. Introduce "Hanerot Halalu." Have the students:
- Perform Warm-Up 5 to develop skill in changing between a bright vowel and a dark vowel.
- Locate the pattern from Preparation 9 in "Hanerot Halalu." (The pattern appears in measures 2–22 and 34–46.)
- Follow the music and listen to "Hanerot Halalu" to determine which part sings the melody. (Part I)
- Follow the music using correct singing posture, and softly sing the melody with the accompaniment on short *doo* vowels, focusing on an even quality throughout the voice range.
- Sing Part II softly on *doo* with the accompaniment.

4. Introduce the Hebrew words. Have the students:
- Listen to the recording with the Hebrew words and identify the sustained target vowel sounds.
- Perform with the vocal track of the recording.
- Perform with the instrumental track of the recording or piano accompaniment.

5. Perform "Hanerot Halalu." Have the students:
- Use correct singing posture and sing the song with and without the accompaniment while following conducting gestures. (Emphasize eye contact with attention to attacks and releases at ends of phrases.)
- Silently sing and follow conducting gestures. (Have the students breathe at phrase endings to indicate their attention.)
- Follow conducting gestures and sing with the instrumental or keyboard accompaniment.

Key: D minor   Starting Pitch: D **Hanerot Halalu**   Scale Tones: See below.
Piano Accompaniment on page PA 69

Words and music by Baruch J. Cohon
Arranged by Blanche Chass

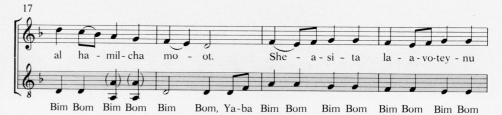

314   Scale Tones: *mi, fa, so, si, la, ti, do re mi fa so si la ti do' re' mi' fa' so' si' la'*

EXTENSION

WARM-UP 5

Continue up to

Ostinato (move up by half steps)

- Identify the characteristics of "Hanerot Halalu." (Emphasis should be on tonal accuracy, part singing, crisp diction, consonants at the ends of phrases, targeted vowels, and Hebrew pronunciation.)
- Listen as the class, sections, or small groups perform. Discuss the performances.

APPRAISAL

The students should be able to:
1. Identify the minor mode by sound.
2. Feel some degree of ease singing "Hanerot Halalu" in Hebrew.

315

PRONUNCIATION

Hanerot halalu anachnu
hä-ne-rôt' hä-lä-lōō' ä-näкн' nōō

madlikin
mäd-li-kin'

al hanisim v'al hat'shuot v'al
ä hä-nē' sim v'äl hä-chōō' ôt v'äl

hamilcha moot.
hä-mil' кнä môt.

Sheasita laavoteynu
she-ä-sē'tä lä-ä-vō-tä' nōō

bayamim hahem baz'man haze
bä-yä-mēm' hä-hem' bäz'-män' hä-zā'

al y'de kohanecha kohanecha
äl y'-dä kō-hä-nä' кнä kō-hä-nä' кнä

hak'doshem.
hä-k' dō' shem

V'hol sh'monas y'me Hanukah *(2 times)*
v'-hôl sh'-mō'näs y'-mä' hä' nōō-kä

Hanerot halalu Hanerot
hä-ne-rôt' hä-lä-lōō' hä-ne-rôt'

halalu kodeshhem.
hä-lä-lōō' kō-desh'-hem'

TRANSLATION

We kindle these lights for the wonders and the redemptions Thou didst perform for our fathers through Thy holy priests. These Hanukah lights are holy and through them we sanctify Thy name.

Preparation 10

- Perform rhythm pattern A from "This Is Christmas" by pat-sliding the half notes, patting the quarter notes, and clapping the eighth notes.

- Perform rhythm pattern B with the same body percussion. Make no sound on the rests.

- Form two groups and perform both patterns at the same time.

Preparation 11

- Sing these parts on syllables or numbers.

- Find these parts in "This Is Christmas." mm. 13–16

317

E X T E N S I O N

CHORAL SINGING

Focus: Reinforcement of Reading Stepwise Melodies

Objectives
To reinforce reading melodic patterns that move by step in treble and bass clefs
To apply these reading skills to the learning and performance of a three-part composition with a part for changing voice
To continue the development of skills and concepts of choral singing

Materials
Recordings: Warm-Up 6
              "This Is Christmas"
              Warm-Up 7

TEACHING THE LESSON

1. Introduce Preparation 10. Have the students:
- Perform rhythm pattern A from "This Is Christmas" by pat-sliding the half notes, patting the quarter notes, and clapping the eighth notes.
- Perform rhythm pattern B using the same body percussion, making no sound for the rests.
- Form two groups and perform both patterns at the same time.
- Locate patterns A and B in "This Is Christmas." (A, mm. 33–34; B, mm. 5–11)

2. Introduce Preparation 11. Have the students:
- Sing the melody with syllables or numbers. Carefully observe the quarter rests.
- Find the melody in "This Is Christmas." (You may wish to use Warm-Up 6 at this time.)

WARM-UP 6

Noo Noo Noo   Noo Noo Noo

Noo Noo Noo   Noo   Noo   Noo
      Noo Noo

CHORAL SINGING

3. Introduce "This Is Christmas." Have the students:
- Divide into three voice parts.
- Follow their respective parts in the music as they listen to "This Is Christmas."
- Read and sing the opening section (mm. 5–29) with the accompaniment. Note that parts are in unison.
- Learn Parts I, II, and III separately for mm. 31–55. Note that Parts I and III are in octaves, and all parts are in unison in mm. 47–55. Sing parts together slowly.
- Learn Part I separately for mm. 57–71. Note that Parts II and III are the same as in mm. 39–45. Sing the parts together slowly.
- Learn Parts I, II, and III separately for mm. 71–82. Note that parts are in unison in mm. 76–82. Sing parts together slowly.

4. Perform "This Is Christmas." Have the students:
- Sing Warm-Up 7 before performing "This Is Christmas" to learn to sing in contrasting styles. (Remind the students to keep their jaws relaxed.)
- Use correct singing posture and sing Parts I, II, and III with the words and with the accompaniment. (Stress maintaining an even quality of sound throughout each voice range, sustained vowel sounds, and crisp diction.)
- Sing with and without the accompaniment while following conducting gestures. (Emphasize eye contact with attention to attacks and releases at ends of phrases.)
- Silently sing and follow conducting gestures. (Have the students breathe at phrase markings to indicate their attention.)
- Follow conducting gestures and sing with instrumental or keyboard accompaniment.

Key: F major Starting Pitch: A **This Is Christmas**

Piano Accompaniment on page PA 74

Scale Tones: See below.

Words by Keith W. Derrickson and Jane Foster Knox
Music by Keith W. Derrickson

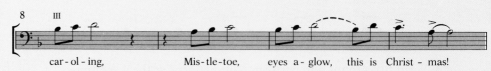

318   Scale Tones: *so, la, ti, do re mi fa so la ti do¹ di¹ re¹ mi¹ fa¹ so¹ la¹ ti¹*

E X T E N S I O N

WARM-UP 7

Nah noh nah noh ----------

Continue up to

CHORAL SINGING

• Identify the characteristics of "This Is Christmas." (Emphasis should be on pitch accuracy and evenness of vocal production. Others may include part singing, consonants at the ends of phrases, and targeted vowels.)
• Listen as the class, sections, or small groups perform. Discuss the performances.

APPRAISAL

The students should be able to:
1. Read and perform stepwise melodic patterns and simple rhythms using whole, dotted half, half, quarter, dotted quarter, and eighth notes fairly successfully.
2. Sing in three parts with confidence.

CHORAL SINGING

68
for shar - ing. Christ-mas is the sea-son, the sea - son for love. It's
Eve will soon be here. Child - ren, eyes a - glow,___ it's Christ - mas! It's
fill the air, Can-dle-light shin-ing bright, this is Christ - mas! It's

72
Christ - mas!___ Re - mem - ber tid-ings of love___ and good cheer,
Christ - mas! Re - mem - ber tid-ings of love___ and good cheer,
Christ - mas! Re - mem - ber tid-ings of love___ and good cheer,

76 I and II
(cheer) And spread the spi - rit of Christ - mas through all
III
(cheer) And spread the spi - rit of Christ - mas through all

80 I and II
the year.
III
the year.

CHORAL SINGING

Focus: Reading Traditional and Nontraditional Notation

Objectives

To develop skills in reading nontraditional music notation

To apply these music reading skills to the learning and performance of a two-part, nontraditional composition

To continue the development of skills and concepts of choral singing

Materials

Recordings: "Radiator Lions"
Warm-Up 1

TEACHING THE LESSON

1. Introduce Preparation 12. Have the students:

• Discuss some of the unusual ways the voice is used, and the visual differences in notation in Preparation 12.

• Follow the directions for each example and practice performing the various techniques required. (See additional performance instructions below.)

• Find these passages in "Radiator Lions." (m. 1; mm. 11–12; mm. 35–41)

SOME UNUSUAL VOCAL STYLES

Some twentieth-century choral music requires singers to use their voices in unusual ways. In "Radiator Lions" you will sing, say, and whisper the words.

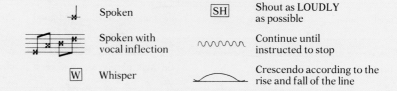 11A, 12A 7, 8

Preparation 12

"Radiator Lions" contains many short spoken and sung passages.

Symbol Explanations

Spoken		SH	Shout as LOUDLY as possible
Spoken with vocal inflection		∿∿∿	Continue until instructed to stop
W	Whisper	‿	Crescendo according to the rise and fall of the line

• Follow the directions for each to know when to sing, speak, or whisper.

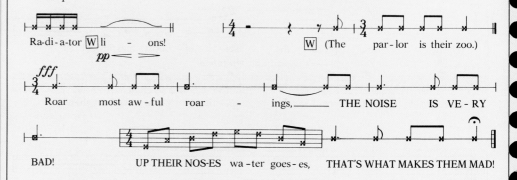

Ra-di-a-tor [W] li – ons! *pp*

[W] (The par-lor is their zoo.)

fff Roar most aw-ful roar-ings,——— THE NOISE IS VE-RY

BAD! UP THEIR NOS-ES wa-ter goes-es, THAT'S WHAT MAKES THEM MAD!

322

Key: G minor/modal (where applicable)   Starting Pitch: G
Scale Tones: See below.
Radiator Lions

I and II   Piano Accompaniment on page PA 82

Words by Dorothy Aldiss
Music by M.J.

Freely

Ra - di - a - tor li - (hi ········) ons ········

George lives in an a-part-ment and his moth-er will not let him keep a

dog   or poll-i-wog   or rab-bit   for a pet.   So

Very broadly, much vibrato   rit.

he   has   ra - di - a - tor   li -   ons.   W (The

a tempo

par-lor is their zoo.)   They   love to fight but ne-ver bite un-

-less   W George tells them to.   George lives in an a-part-ment   and his

moth - er   will   not   let   him   keep a   dog   or   pol - li - wog   or

Very broadly, much vibrato

rab-bit   for a pet.   So   he   has   ra - di - a - tor

Scale Tones: *mi̖ fa̖ so̖ la̖ ta̖ ti̖ do di ra re ri ma mi so*

323

CHORAL SINGING

2. Introduce "Radiator Lions." Have the students:

• Form two groups. (Group II should be twice as large as Group I. Group II should perform the sounds as many times and as loud as possible.)

• Follow the music and listen to "Radiator Lions," focusing on the performance of the various nontraditional techniques required.

• Read and sing the opening section of "Radiator Lions" (mm. 4–28) with the accompaniment on short *doo* vowels, focusing on pitch accuracy and staccato articulation.

• Sing Warm-Up 1, page 281, before performing measures 30–34 of "Radiator Lions" to develop an even tone quality throughout the range.

• Learn parts for mm. 30–41, carefully observing tempo changes and dynamic and expression markings. Note that at the fermata at the end of measure 41 Part II continues as Part I is cut off. Part II stops when the final sound runs out of breath.

• Read and sing the closing section (mm. 43–50). Note that this is a repetition of material from the opening section, and should be sung in a staccato style.

3. Perform "Radiator Lions." Have the students:

• Use correct singing posture and sing the piece with the words and with the accompaniment. (Stress maintaining an even quality of sound throughout each voice range, sustained vowel sounds, crisp diction, and exaggeration of spoken and whispered tone qualities.)

• Sing the song with and without the accompaniment while following conducting gestures. (Emphasize eye contact with attention to attacks and releases at the ends of phrases.)

CHORAL SINGING

- Silently sing and follow conducting gestures. (Have the students breathe at phrase endings to indicate their attention.)
- Follow conducting gestures and sing with the instrumental or keyboard accompaniment.
- Identify the characteristics of "Radiator Lions." (Emphasis should be on pitch accuracy and evenness of vocal production, part singing, consonants at the ends of phrases, targeted vowels, staccato style, nontraditional techniques, and so on.)
- Listen as the class, sections, or small groups perform. Discuss the performances.

APPRAISAL

The students should be able to:

1. Identify, read, and perform the different types of nontraditional choral techniques in "Radiator Lions" with some degree of success.

2. Identify, read, and perform changes of meter with confidence.

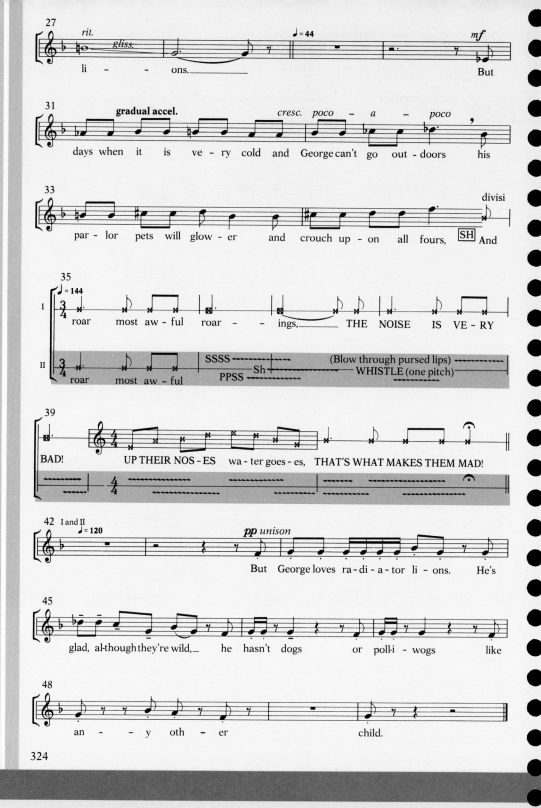

324

CHORAL BLEND

Remember that one characteristic of good choral singing is blend. Blending your voice with those of the other singers creates a unified sound. Focus on making a smooth sound as you sing *Sanctus*.

Preparation 13

Sanctus requires you to sing in a very sustained style, with smooth changes between chords.

- Listen to *Sanctus* for the chord sounds most often used.
- Sing the three main chords used in *Sanctus* on pitch numbers.

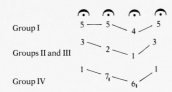

In *Sanctus* these chords are notated like this.

325

CHORAL SINGING

Focus: Reinforcing Choral Blend

Objectives
To reinforce techniques of choral blend
To apply choral blend to learning and performing a four-part composition in German
To continue the development of skills and concepts of choral singing

Materials
Recordings: *Sanctus*
Warm-Up 8

TEACHING THE LESSON

1. Introduce choral blend and Preparation 13. Have the students:
- Discuss the information on choral blend.
- Listen to *Sanctus* for the chord sounds used most often. (I, IV, V)
- Form four groups and sing the three main chords used in *Sanctus,* using the numbers given.

CHORAL SINGING

2. Introduce *Sanctus*. Have the students:
• Perform Warm-Up 8 to help emphasize legato singing.
• Form four groups.
• Read and sing the opening section of *Sanctus* (mm. 1–16) with the accompaniment. Work on individual parts separately, if needed. Focus on pitch accuracy, legato style, and a balance and blend of all voice parts.
• Read and sing measures 17–32 with the accompaniment. Work on individual parts separately, if needed. Focus on pitch accuracy, legato style, and a balance and blend of all voice parts.

3. Perform *Sanctus*. Have the students:
• Use correct singing posture and sing all parts with the words and the accompaniment. (Stress maintaining an even quality of sound throughout each vocal range, sustained vowel sounds and blend.)

Key: F major   Starting Pitch: Part I: A   Part II: F   Part III: C   Part IV: F

Piano Accompaniment on page PA 86

Scale Tones: See below.

Sanctus

Franz Schubert (1797–1828)

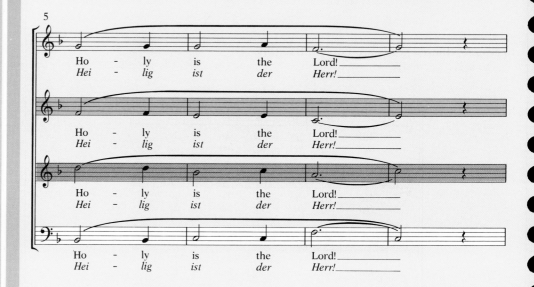

326

Scale Tones: *mi, fa, so, la, ta, ti, do re mi fa so la ta ti do' re' mi' fa' so' la'*

E X T E N S I O N

WARM-UP 8

CHORAL SINGING

• Listen to the recording of the German words and identify the sustained target vowel sounds.
• Perform *Sanctus* with the German words and accompaniment.
• Sing the piece with and then without instrumental accompaniment while following conducting gestures. (Emphasize eye contact with attention to attacks and releases at ends of phrases, and in particular, blend.)
• Silently sing and follow conducting gestures. (Have the students breathe at phrase markings to indicate their attention.)
• Follow conducting gestures and sing with instrumental or keyboard accompaniment.
• Identify the characteristics of *Sanctus*. (Emphasis should be on pitch accuracy, evenness of vocal production, part singing, consonants at ends of phrases, targeted vowels, legato style, blend, and so on.)
• Listen as the class, sections, or small groups perform. Discuss the performances. (Encourage the students to try performing *Sanctus* a cappella, that is, without accompaniment.)

APPRAISAL

The students should be able to:
1. Define and achieve a good choral blend with moderate success.
2. Sustain the air flow to the ends of phrases.
3. Hold their own parts successfully in four-part singing.
4. Perform a song in German.

PRONUNCIATION

Heilig, heilig, heilig,
hī′lig hī′lig hī′lig

heilig ist der Herr!
hī′lig ist dār hār

Heilig ist nur Er!
hī′lig ist nō͞or ār

Er, der nie begonnen,
ār dār nē be-gôn′ nen

er, der immer war,
ār dār im′ mer vär

Ewig ist und waltet,
ā′vig ist ōo͞nd val′tet

Sein wird immer dar!
sīn vērd im′mer där

CHORAL SINGING

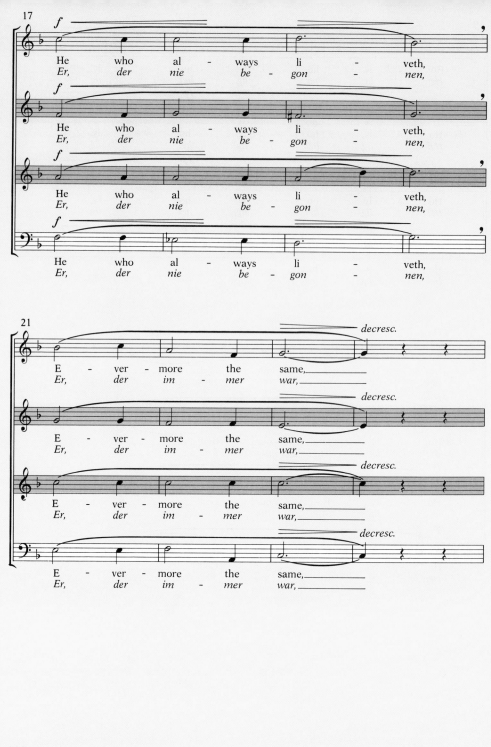

328

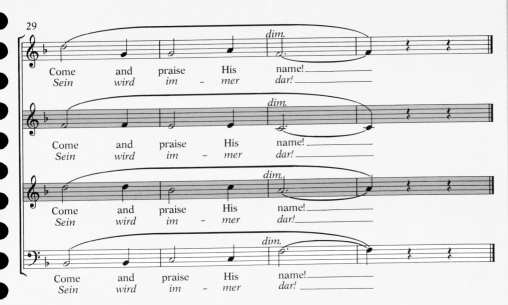

CHORAL SINGING

Focus: Developing Boys' Voices

Objectives
To perform a two-part accompanied choral composition for boys' voices
To continue developing singing skills and concepts

Materials
Recording: "The Promised Land"

TEACHING THE LESSON

1. Introduce Preparation 14. Have the students:
• Discuss and review the meaning of syncopation and syncopated rhythm.
• Perform the syncopated rhythm pattern from "The Promised Land" as indicated, patting the quarter notes and clapping the eighth notes.
• Locate the pickup notes in the melody pattern.
• Sing the melody pattern with the words.
• Locate the melody pattern in "The Promised Land."

2. Introduce "The Promised Land." Have the students:
• Form two groups. (If you choose not to perform this selection with only boys' voices, use the following voice arrangements: sopranos and tenors on Part I, altos and baritones on Part II; or, tenors and baritones on Part I, sopranos and altos on Part II.)
• Follow the music and listen to "The Promised Land," focusing on their respective parts.
• Read and sing the opening section of "The Promised Land" (mm. 5–38) with the accompaniment. Note where the melody changes from one part to the other.

Preparation 14

• Perform this syncopated rhythm pattern from "The Promised Land" by patting the quarter notes and clapping the eighth notes.

• Sing this melody. Look for the pickup note. "On"

On Jor-dan's storm - y banks I stand_ and cast a wist - ful eye

The *8* below the treble clef in Part I means you should sing one octave lower than the music is written.

The Promised Land
Piano Accompaniment on page PA 91

Pioneer hymn
Arr. by Carl J. Nygard, Jr.

On Jor-dan's storm - y banks I stand__ and

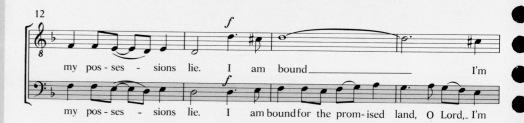

cast a wist - ful eye   Ca - naan's fair and_ hap - py land_ where
cast a wist - ful eye To__ Ca - naan's fair and_ hap - py land_ where

my pos - ses - sions lie. I am bound_____ I'm
my pos - ses - sions lie. I am bound for the prom-ised land, O Lord,_ I'm

Scale Tones: D minor: *la₁ ti₁ do re mi fa fi si la ti do¹*
E♭ minor: *mi₁ fi₁ si₁ la₁ ti₁ do re ri mi fa fi so si la*

330

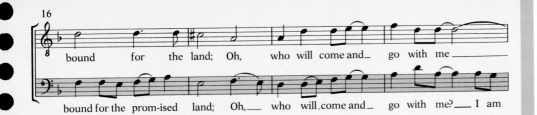

bound   for   the land; Oh,   who will come and_   go with me _____
bound for the prom-ised land; Oh,_ who will .come and_ go with me? _ I am

(me)_ to the prom - ised   land? _____   *mp*   There gen -'rous fruits   that
bound for the prom - ised   land. _____   *mp*   There gen -'rous fruits_   that

nev - er   fail on trees im - mor - tal   grow; There   rocks   and   hills   and
nev - er   fail on trees im - mor - tal   grow; There_   rocks   and_   hills   and

brooks and vales with_ milk and hon - ey flow.   *f*   I'm   bound _____
brooks and vales with_ milk and hon - ey flow.   *sub. f*   I   am bound for the prom - ised

(bound) O   Lord,   I'm   bound _____ for the land, Oh,
land,   O   Lord, I'm   bound for the prom - ised   land,   Oh, _____

CHORAL SINGING

• Follow the music using correct singing posture, and softly sing both parts with the accompaniment on a *vee* vowel, focusing on pitch accuracy and voice placement.

3. Perform "The Promised Land." Have the students:

• Use correct singing posture and sing the song with the words and with the accompaniment. (Stress maintaining an even quality of sound throughout the voice range, targeted vowel sounds, and blend and balance between parts.)

• Sing the song with and without the instrumental accompaniment while following conducting gestures. (Emphasize eye contact with attention to attacks and releases at ends of phrases.)

• Silently sing and follow conducting gestures. (Have the students breathe at phrase endings to indicate their attention.)

• Follow conducting gestures and sing with the instrumental or keyboard accompaniment.

• Identify the characteristics of "The Promised Land." (Emphasis should be on pitch accuracy and evenness of vocal production, part singing, consonants at ends of phrases, targeted vowels, and blend and balance between the parts.)

• Listen as the class, sections, or small groups perform. Discuss the performances.

APPRAISAL

The students should be able to:

1. Identify and perform simple syncopated rhythms found in "The Promised Land."
2. Perform a two-part composition for boys' voices successfully.

331

CHORAL SINGING

35
who will __ come and go with me? I am bound for the prom - ised
who will __ come and go with me? I am bound for the prom - ised

38
land.
land.

p much slower
Soon will the Lord __ pre -

p much slower
Soon will the Lord pre -

42
f *a tempo*
pare my soul for joys be - yond __ the skies, Where __ nev - er - end - ing

f *a tempo*
pare my soul for joys be - yond __ the skies, Where nev - er - end - ing

46
pleas - ures roll __ and __ prais - es __ nev - er die. I am
pleas - ures roll __ and prais - es nev - er die. I am

49
bound for the prom - ised land, O Lord, I'm bound for the prom - ised
bound, O Lord, I'm bound _____

332

land; Oh,___ who will__come and go with me? I am bound
(bound) for the land, Oh, who will__come and go with me? I am bound, O

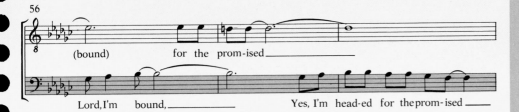

(bound) for the prom-ised___
Lord, I'm bound,___ Yes, I'm head-ed for the prom-ised___

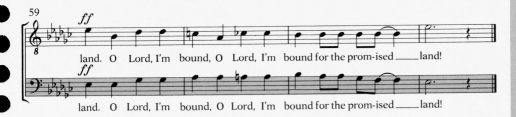

ff
land. O Lord, I'm bound, O Lord, I'm bound for the prom-ised ___land!
ff
land. O Lord, I'm bound, O Lord, I'm bound for the prom-ised ___land!

333

CHORAL SINGING

Focus: Reading Eighth- and Sixteenth-Note Rhythms

Objectives
To develop skill in reading eighth- and sixteenth-note rhythms

To continue to apply these reading skills to learning and performing a three-part accompanied composition

To continue developing singing skills and concepts

Materials
Recordings: Warm-Up 9
"To the Morning"

TEACHING THE LESSON

1. Introduce Preparation 15. Have the students:
• Clap the first two rhythm patterns, carefully observing the ties.
• Clap the third rhythm pattern as they say the words.
• Find the third rhythm pattern in "To the Morning."

2. Introduce "To the Morning." Have the students:
• Perform Warm-Up 9 to establish an even tone throughout the range.
• Form three groups.
• Follow the music using correct singing posture, and softly sing the three parts with the accompaniment on short *doo* vowels, focusing on rhythmic accuracy.
• Work on individual parts if necessary.

3. Perform "To the Morning." Have the students:
• Use correct singing posture and sing with words, with the vocal and instrumental accompaniment. (Stress maintaining an even quality of sound throughout the vocal range, target vowel sounds, and blend and balance between the parts.)

🌐 12A 💿 8   Key: C major   Starting Pitch: D   Scale Tones: See below.

Preparation 15

"To the Morning" has various combinations of quarter notes, eighth notes, and sixteenth notes.

• Clap the following rhythms in preparation for reading "To the Morning." Be careful to observe the ties.

• Clap the following rhythm as you say the words.

Watch-ing the sun,___ watch-ing it come

• Find this pattern in "To the Morning." beginning

To the Morning

Piano Accompaniment on page PA 96

Words and music by Dan Fogelberg
Arr. by D. H. Arthur

Watch-ing the sun, watch-ing it come, watch-ing it come up o-ver the

roof – – tops   Cloud-y and warm,   may-be a

storm,   you can   nev – er quite tell from the   morn – – ing, And it's

storm,   you can   nev – er quite tell from the   morn – – ing, And it's

334

Scale Tones: *so₁ la₁ do di re mi fa so la ta ti do' re' mi'*

EXTENSION

WARM-UP 9

Yah - - - - - - - - - - - - - - - - - - -

Continue down to

go-ing to be a day,__ there is real - ly no way to say__ "no"__ to the

go-ing to be a day,__ there is real - ly no way to say__ "no"__ to the

18

morn - ing.___ Yes, it's

morn - ing.___ Yes, it's

20

go-ing to be__ a day,__ there is real - ly no-thing left to say__ but come on__

go-ing to be__ a day,__ there is real - ly no-thing left to say__ but come on__

22

morn - ing.___ Wait-ing for__ mail, may-be a tale

morn - ing.___ Wait-ing for__ mail, may-be a tale

27

(tale) from an old friend or e - ven a lov - er.

(tale) from an old friend or e - ven a lov - er.

335

CHORAL SINGING

• Sing the song with and without the accompaniment while following conducting gestures. (Emphasize eye contact with attention to attacks and releases at ends of phrases.)
• Silently sing and follow conducting gestures. (Have the students breathe at phrase endings to indicate their attention.)
• Follow conducting gestures and sing with the instrumental or keyboard accompaniment.
• Identify the characteristics of "To the Morning." (Emphasis should be on pitch and rhythmic evenness of vocal production, part singing, consonants at ends of phrases, and targeted vowels.
• Listen as the class, sections, or small groups perform. Discuss the performances.

APPRAISAL

The students should be able to:
1. Perform eighth- and sixteenth-note rhythms in "To the Morning."
2. Sing a three-part song with confidence.

336

sea - sons,   and may - be   they   change,   and

sea - sons,   and may - be   they   change,   and

47 I *rit.*   *mp*   *freely*

may - be   true   love   is not   so   strange.

II *rit.*   *mp*   *freely*

may - be   true   love   is not   so   strange.

III *rit.*   *mp*   *freely*

may - be   true   love   is not   so   strange.

51   2   F   *a tempo*   *legato*

Ooh

2   *a tempo*   *legato*

Ooh

2   *a tempo*   *legato*

Ooh

57 I   G

The suns of the day,__ now they hur-ry a - way,   now they are gone   un - til   to-

II and III

The suns of the day,__ now they hu-rry a - way,   now they are gone   un - til   to-

337

Preparation 16

Like "Praise to the Lord" and "Radiator Lions," "Chartless" has changing meters.

- Form two groups to tap the steady beat and the rhythm pattern.

- Sing these melodies separately, then form two groups and sing them together.

Preparation 17

The middle section of "Chartless" requires the singers to perform the same melody, but to begin at different times.

- Learn to sing this melody. It has no meter signature. Follow the rhythm of the words as you sing.

I   nev - er   spoke with   God,_____   Nor   vis - it - ed   in   heav'n_____

- Perform this melody. Each person should begin at a different time.

339

CHORAL SINGING

Focus: Developing More Skills in Reading Traditional and Nontraditional Notation

Objectives

To continue to develop skills in reading nontraditional notation

To reinforce reading and performing meter changes

To apply these reading skills to learning and performing a three-part, unaccompanied composition

To continue the development of skills and concepts of choral singing

Materials

Recording: "Chartless"

TEACHING THE LESSON

1. Introduce Preparation 16. Have the students:
- Discuss and review the concept of changing meter.
- Form two groups. Group 1 taps the steady beat while Group 2 taps the rhythm pattern. Then reverse the groups.
- Read and sing the two melodies separately, then together, focusing on the balance and blend of the two parts.

2. Introduce Preparation 17. Have the students:
- Read and perform the melody
- Form three groups and have each perform the melody beginning at different times. (You may wish to begin at five-second intervals.)

CHORAL SINGING

3. Introduce "Chartless." Have the students:

• Read and sing the opening section of "Chartless" (through the second ending, mm. 1–15) with the recording. Work on parts separately, if needed.

• Do the free rhythm section (following the second ending) as practiced in Preparation 17.

• Read and sing the closing section (mm. 20–28) with the recording. Work on parts separately, if needed.

4. Perform "Chartless." Have the students:

• Use correct singing posture and sing the composition with the words. (Stress maintaining an even quality of sound throughout the voice range, sustained vowel sounds, crisp diction, and precision of the improvised section.)

• Sing the composition while following conducting gestures. (Emphasize eye contact with attention to attacks and releases at ends of phrases.)

• Silently sing and follow conducting gestures. (Have the students breathe at phrase endings to indicate their attention.)

• Identify the characteristics of "Chartless." (Emphasis should be on pitch accuracy and evenness of vocal production, unaccompanied part singing, consonants at ends of phrases, targeted vowels, and so on.)

• Listen as the class, sections, or small groups perform. Discuss the performances.

APPRAISAL

The students should be able to:

1. Read and perform meter changes and nontraditional notation with some success.

2. Apply these skills in a three-part song.

Chartless

Key: G (nondiatonic) Scale Tones: See below.

Words by Emily Dickinson
Music by C. M. Shearer

Starting Pitch: Part I: G Part II: C Part III: F

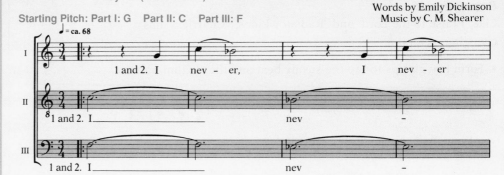

340 Scale Tones: *fa₁ sa₁ lo₁ ta₁ do ra re ma fa sa lo ta do¹ ra¹ ma¹ mi¹ fa¹*

♩ = ca. 128

know I how a heath-er looks, And be____ I nev - er spoke with God,
what a wave____ must

yet know I how a heath-er looks, ____must be.____ I nev - er
and what a wave____

about 5 seconds

(I)____ how heath - er looks,
(a)____ wave____ must be.

about 10 seconds

Nor vis - it - ed in heav'n;____

spoke with God,____ Nor vis - it - ed in heav'n;____

I nev - er spoke with God,____ Nor vis - it - ed in heav'n;____

Tempo I

Yet cer - tain____ am I of the

Yet cer - tain____ am I of the

Yet cer - tain am I of the

solo or soli I know.____

choir

spot As if the chart were giv - en.

spot As if the chart____ were giv - en.

spot As if the chart____ were giv - en.

*Each singer begins independently, singing each syllable at about ♩=128. After singing both lines of poetry twice, singers should hold the gathering note (⬜) until the last voice finishes singing "heav'n."

341

CHORAL SINGING

Focus: Developing Independence of Voice Parts

Objectives

To develop independence of voice parts

To apply music reading skills to learning and performing a three-part composition

To continue developing singing skills and concepts

Materials

Recording: "Sing Me Home"

TEACHING THE LESSON

1. Introduce Preparation 18. Have the students:

• Divide into three groups.

• Practice saying the words in rhythm and then singing each of the four examples.

• Locate each example in "Sing Me Home." (1: mm. 18–20; 2: mm. 32–36; 3: mm. 44–48; 4: mm. 58–60)

• Discuss which examples are the most similar, and which are the most contrasting.

2. Introduce "Sing Me Home." Have the students:

• Form three groups.

• Read and sing the opening section of "Sing Me Home" (to m. 36) with the accompaniment.

• Follow the music, using correct singing posture, and softly sing all parts with the accompaniment on an *oo* vowel, focusing on pitch accuracy and placement of tone.

• Work on parts separately, and then in various combinations (Parts I and II, I and III, and II and III) to develop independence of each voice line.

Preparation 18

The words *sing me home* are repeated throughout this song, but with different melodies and in different voice parts.

• Practice saying the words in rhythm, then singing the different sounds of the same phrase below.

Which examples are similar? Which are contrasting? 1 and 4, 2 and 3 are similar

342

Key: B♭ major   Starting Pitch: D

Scale Tones: See below.

Like a folk song, ♩ = 40-48

Sing Me Home

Words and music by Carl J. Nygard, Jr.

Piano Accompaniment on page PA 104

expressively

Sing me home, _____ sing me

When I'm tired of the road, sing __ me

When I'm tired of the road, sing __ me

home. _____ When I'm tired of the road, sing me

home. _____ Where the sun meets the sky's blue _____

home. _____ Where the sun meets the sky's blue

home. _____ Where the sun meets the sky's blue

dome _____ comes a song, let the song _____ sing me

dome (blue dome) comes a song, let the song sing me

dome (blue dome) comes a song, let the song sing me

Scale Tones: *do͵ re͵ mi͵ fa͵ so͵ si͵ lo͵ la͵ ta͵ ti͵ do re mi fa so si lo la ti do¹ re¹ mi¹ fa¹*

343

CHORAL SINGING

3. Perform "Sing Me Home." Have the students:

• Use correct singing posture and sing with the words and the vocal and instrumental accompaniments. (Stress maintaining an even quality of sound throughout each voice range, targeted vowel sounds, and blend and balance between the parts.)

• Sing the song with and without the instrumental accompaniment while following conducting gestures. (Emphasize eye contact with attention to attacks and releases at ends of phrases.)

• Silently sing and follow conducting gestures. (Have the students breathe at the end of phrases to indicate their attention.)

• Follow conducting gestures and sing with the instrumental or keyboard accompaniment.

• Identify the characteristics of "Sing Me Home." (Emphasis should be on pitch and rhythmic accuracy and evenness of vocal production, consonants at ends of phrases, targeted vowels, and blend and balance between the parts.)

• Listen as the class, sections, or small groups perform. Discuss the performances.

APPRAISAL

The students should be able to handle their voice parts successfully in a three-part song while continuing to develop reading and singing skills.

344

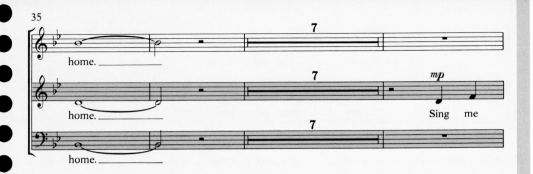

345

346

73

Sing me home sing __ me home. ____

Sing me home, sing me home. ____

home, ____ sing me home. ____

77

p dim. e rit. *pp*

Oo ____ sing me home. ____

p dim. e rit. *pp*

Oo ____ sing me home. ____

p dim. e rit. *pp*

Oo ____ sing me home. ____

CHORAL SINGING

Focus: Reading Quarter-Note Triplet Rhythms

Objectives
To develop skill in reading quarter-note triplet rhythms
To continue developing singing skills and concepts in a four-part song

Materials
Recording: "Dream a Dream"

Vocabulary
Quarter-note triplet

TEACHING THE LESSON

1. Introduce Preparation 19. Have the students:
• Clap the first rhythm pattern.
• Substitute a quarter-note triplet for the half notes. (You may wish to clap or pat on the first and third beats of each measure.)
• Find the new pattern in "Dream a Dream."
• Clap the pattern from the song, then say the words in rhythm.

2. Introduce Preparation 20. Have the students:
• Clap the rhythm, then say the words in rhythm.
• Sing Part I, then sing both parts, concentrating on smooth phrasing.

Preparation 19   🌐 12B   💿 8

• Clap this pattern.

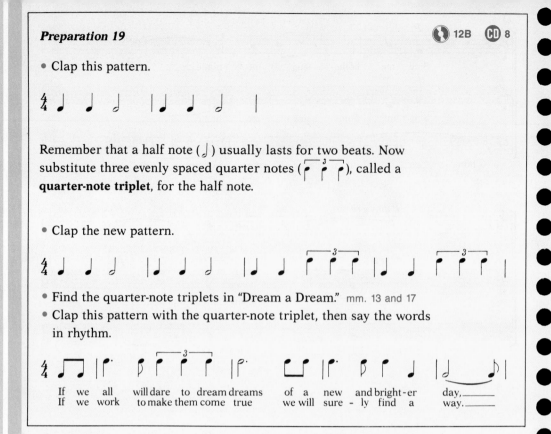

Remember that a half note (𝅗𝅥) usually lasts for two beats. Now substitute three evenly spaced quarter notes (𝅘𝅥 𝅘𝅥 𝅘𝅥), called a **quarter-note triplet**, for the half note.

• Clap the new pattern.

• Find the quarter-note triplets in "Dream a Dream." mm. 13 and 17
• Clap this pattern with the quarter-note triplet, then say the words in rhythm.

If we all will dare to dream dreams of a new and bright-er day,_____
If we work to make them come true we will sure-ly find a way._____

Preparation 20

Long, flowing phrases give this song a beautiful effect. The pattern in Preparation 19 should be sung on one sustained breath. Here is the same pattern with pitches added.

• Sing Part I in unison. Then form groups and sing both parts as you work for in-tune singing and smooth phrases.

(so) 5
If we all will dare to dream dreams of a new and bright-er day,_____

(mi) 3
If we all will dare to dream dreams of a new and bright-er day,_____

348

Dream a Dream Scale Tones: See below.

Key: B♭ major   Starting Pitch: D
Piano Accompaniment on page PA 114

Words and music by Ed Robertson

1. Dream a dream of a new to-mor-row when the
2. Dream a dream of a world u-ni-ted when the

peo-ple learn to love their fel-low man.___ Dare to hope for a
na-tions choose to lay their wea-pons down.___ Dare to hope for a

Dare to hope for a
Dare to hope for a

Dare to hope for a
Dare to hope for a

peace - ful morn-ing when we've learned to walk to-geth-er hand in
day of glad-ness when the world can let a smile re-place a

Scale Tones: *do, re, mi, fa, so, lo, la, ta, do re mi fa so lo la ta ti do¹ re¹ mi¹ fa¹*   349

CHORAL SINGING

3. Introduce "Dream a Dream." Have the students:
• Divide into four voice parts.
• Read and sing the opening section of "Dream a Dream" (mm. 4–12) with the accompaniment.
• Use correct singing posture and softly sing all parts with the accompaniment on an *oo* vowel, focusing on pitch and rhythmic accuracy and legato style.
• Work on the parts separately, then in various combinations to develop independence in each voice line.

4. Perform "Dream a Dream." Have the students:
• Use correct singing posture and sing with the words and the vocal and instrumental accompaniments. (Stress maintaining an even quality of sound throughout voice range, targeted vowel sounds, and blend and balance between the parts.)
• Sing the song with and without the accompaniment while following conducting gestures. (Emphasize eye contact with attention to attacks and releases at end of phrases.)
• Silently sing and follow conducting gestures. (Have the students breathe at phrase endings to indicate their attention.)
• Identify the characteristics of "Dream a Dream." (Emphasis should be on pitch accuracy, evenness of vocal production, blend, part singing, consonants at the ends of phrases, and targeted vowels.)
• Listen as the class, sections, or small groups perform. Discuss the performances.

APPRAISAL

The students should be able to:
1. Read and perform quarter-note triplets in a vocal score.
2. Sing a four-part song with increasing confidence.

12

hand.
frown.____ If we all will dare to dream dreams of a

hand.
frown. If we all will dare to dream dreams of a

hand.
frown. If we all will dare to . dream dreams of a

hand.
frown.____ If we all will dare to dream dreams of a

15

new and bright - er day,____ if we work to make them come

new and bright - er day,____ if we work to make them come

new and bright - er day,____ if we work to make them come

new and bright - er____ day,____ if we work to make them come

18

true, we will sure - ly find a way.____

true, we will sure - ly find ____ a ____ way.____

true, we will sure - ly find a way.____

true, we will sure - ly find____ a____ way.____

350

Dream a dream,_____ dare to hope,_____
of the world we long to see for the day when men are
Dream a dream, dare to hope,
Dream a dream, dare to hope,

may-be we_____ can make it hap - pen soon.
free and dreams come true._____ Dream a dream of a
some - times dreams come true._____ Dream a dream of a
some - times dreams come true._____ Dream a dream of a

may-be some-day we can see our dreams come true.
new to-mor-row may-be some-day we can see our dreams come true.
new to-mor-row may-be some-day we can see our dreams come true.
new to-mor-row may-be some-day we can see our dreams come true.

351

CHORAL SINGING

Focus: Imitative Style

Objectives
To perform a song in imitative style
To continue developing singing skills and concepts

Materials
Recordings: Warm-Up 10
               ''Chichester Prayer''

TEACHING THE LESSON

1. Introduce Preparation 21. Have the students:
• Count and clap the rhythms from ''Chichester Prayer.''
• Combine the two patterns, being aware that Part II follows Part I.
• Clap measures 16–19 in rhythm, say the words in rhythm, and then add the pitches.
• Find and work on other similar places in the song.

2. Introduce Preparation 22. Have the students:
• Clap the two parts shown, first separately and then together, being aware that Part I follows Part II.
• Read the words in rhythm, then add the pitches.
• Compare the two parts.

Preparation 21

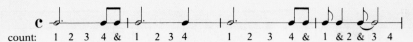

• Count and clap this rhythm pattern from "Chichester Prayer."

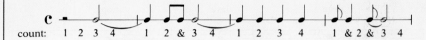

count: 1   2   3   4   &   1   2   3   4   1   2   3   4   &   1 & 2 & 3   4

• Now count and tap this pattern.

count: 1   2   3   4   1   2 & 3   4   1   2   3   4   1 & 2 & 3   4

The two patterns look like this when they are combined. Try them together.

In "Chichester Prayer," this combination of one voice following the other first occurs in measures 16 through 19.

• Clap measures 16–19 in rhythm, say the words in rhythm, and then add the pitches.
• Find other places in the music where similar patterns follow one another in the voices. mm. 24–29, 42–end

---

Preparation 22

• Clap these parts. Then form groups and clap them together.
• Read the words in rhythm, then add the pitches.

I
(pray)___   *mp dim.*   To love   more dear – ly___   *rit.*   Each day
          do   *fa*
          1   4

II
(pray)___   *mf*   *dim.*   To see   more clear – ly___   To fol-low more near – ly___   *rit.*
          do   *fa*
          1   4

How are the two vocal parts similar and different? They are identical except where they start.

352

E X T E N S I O N

Key: E♭ major   Starting Pitch: G **Chichester Prayer**

Scale Tones: See below.

Piano Accompaniment on page PA 121

Words attributed to Richard of Chichester
Music by Carl J. Nygard, Jr.

I — Day by day, O Lord, three—

II — Day by day, O Lord, three

8 — things I pray;— Day by day, O Lord, three— things I pray:

— things I pray;— Day by day, O Lord, three things I pray:

12 — (pray) Day by— day, O

— (pray) Day— by— day,

18 — Lord, three things I pray. Day by— day, O

— (day) O Lord, three things I pray. Day— by— day,

22 — Lord, three things I pray: To see Thee more clear - ly.—

— (day) three things I pray: See more clear - ly—

Scale Tones: *so, la, ti, do re mi fa so la ti do¹ re¹*

353

CHORAL SINGING

3. Introduce "Chichester Prayer." Have the students:

• Perform Warm-Up 10 to continue to develop support for the four-measure phrases.

• Divide into the two voice parts.

• Read and sing the opening section of "Chichester Prayer" (mm. 5–23) with the accompaniment.

• Use correct singing posture and softly sing both parts with the accompaniment on a *loo* vowel, focusing on pitch accuracy and legato style.

• Work on the parts separately, then in different combinations, to develop independence in each voice line.

4. Perform "Chichester Prayer." Have the students:

• Use correct singing posture and sing the song with and without the accompaniment. (Stress maintaining an even quality of sound throughout the vocal range, targeted vowel sounds, blend, and balance between the parts.)

• Sing the song with and without the accompaniment while following conducting gestures. (Emphasize eye contact with attention to attacks and releases at ends of phrases.)

• Silently sing and follow conducting gestures. (Have the students breathe at phrase endings to indicate their attention.)

• Follow conducting gestures and sing with the accompaniment.

• Identify the characteristics of "Chichester Prayer." (Emphasis should be on pitch accuracy and evenness of vocal production, part singing, consonants at the ends of phrases, and targeted vowels.)

• Listen as the class, sections, or small groups perform. Discuss the performances.

WARM-UP 10

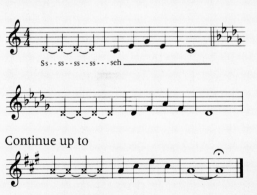

Ss - - ss - - ss - - ss - - seh ——

Continue up to

CHORAL SINGING

APPRAISAL

The students should be able to read and perform a song in which one part follows the other, while maintaining their own part successfully.

354

Key: D major   Starting Pitch: D   Scale Tones: *do re mi fa so la ti do¹*   12B   8

Preparation 23

- Listen to "Alleluia I." How many phrases do you hear? How are they different? Two; one moves in skips, the other in steps.
- Sing this pattern. Which phrase does it sound most like? I

do¹
l¹

- Compare this pattern with the first phrase of "Alleluia I." How are they different? The last two measures change.
- Sing the entire round on pitch syllables or numbers.

Alleluia I

Anonymous

Al – le – lu – ia,   al – le – lu – ia.

A – – – men,   a – – – men.

355

E X T E N S I O N

PRONUNCIATION
Alleluia.
ä-lä-lōō′ yä
Praise the Lord.

CHORAL SINGING

Focus: Additional Rounds for Sight Reading

Materials
Recordings: "Alleluia I"
    "Alleluia II"
    "Jubilate"
    "O Music, Sweet Music"
    "Mystery Tune" ("Joyfully Sing")

TEACHING THE LESSON

General directions for introducing a round. Have the students:
- Study and perform each Preparation.
- Divide into the number of parts indicated to perform the round.
- Follow the music while listening to the round.
- Review text pronunciation as necessary.
- Follow the music using correct singing posture, and sing the round in unison.
- Perform the round with the words, using vocal and instrumental accompaniments.

CHORAL SINGING

Preparation 24

- Sing this triad pattern. This pattern contains C, E, G, C', the pitches in the C major chord.

Both "Alleluia II" and "Jubilate" are based on this C major triad. Warming up with these sounds will help you sense the tonal center of both rounds.

- Find these pitches in "Alleluia II" and "Jubilate."
- Sing "Alleluia II" on pitch syllables or numbers.

Preparation 25

- Form two groups to perform the steady beat and the uneven rhythm pattern.

- Find this pattern in "Jubilate." Part III
- Tap all the rhythms in "Jubilate," then sing the round on pitch syllables.
- When you have learned both rounds, try writing new words to each.

Alleluia II

Key: C major   Starting Pitch: C   Scale Tones: *do re mi fa so la ti do'*

Anonymous

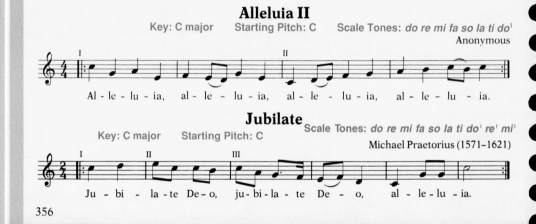

Al - le - lu – ia, al - le - lu – ia, al - le - lu – ia, al - le - lu – ia.

Jubilate

Key: C major   Starting Pitch: C   Scale Tones: *do re mi fa so la ti do' re' mi'*

Michael Praetorius (1571–1621)

Ju – bi – la - te De - o, ju - bi - la - te De – o, al - le - lu – ia.

356

PRONUNCIATION

Jubilate   Deo, alleluia.
yōō-bē-lä'tā dā'ō ä-lā-lōō' yä
Rejoice in God, alleluia.

Preparation 26

The meter of this round is $\frac{2}{2}$, which means that the half note (♩) has the steady beat.

- Lightly tap this rhythm.

- Add words as you tap it again.

Mu - sic,   mu - sic,   let the cho-rus ring!

- Find this pattern in the round, then sing it on pitch syllables or numbers. Part III

Notice that the last measure has only one and a half beats. Where is the other half-beat? in the first pickup notes at the beginning of the round

O Music, Sweet Music

Words and music by Lowell Mason

O — mu - sic, sweet mu - sic, thy— prais - es we will sing, We—

will— tell of the— plea - sure and— hap - pi -ness you— bring.

Mu - sic,   mu - sic,   let the cho - rus ring!

357

CHORAL SINGING

Preparation 27

- Play or tap this pattern.

- Say the pattern in rhythm using "la."

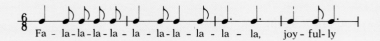

Fa - la-la-la-la - la - la-la - la - la - la,   joy - ful- ly

- Find all the places in the "Mystery Tune" where this pattern appears. Practice singing it with pitch syllables or numbers. Work for a smooth choral blend in all voices. mm. 1–4, 7–10, 22–25, 28–31

Preparation 28

In measure 34 of this round, the meter changes from $\frac{6}{8}$ to $\frac{2}{4}$. Since both $\frac{6}{8}$ and $\frac{2}{4}$ have two beats to a measure, the beat stays constant when you change to the new meter.

- Tap the steady beat as you say the rhythm using "la." Keep the feeling of 2 when you come to the $\frac{2}{4}$ section. This will help you make a smooth change.

358

Mystery Tune

Key: E♭ major   Starting Pitch: B♭

Traditional German round
Arr. M.J.

Scale Tones: *so, la, ti, do re mi fa so do¹*

TIME LINE

Michael Praetorius 1571–1621

1600

1620 Mayflower lands at Plymouth Rock

Jean Baptiste Lully 1632–1687

1643 Louis XIV becomes king of France at age 5

1650

Johann Pachelbel 1653–1706
Henry Purcell 1659–1695

1666 Newton discovers Law of Gravity

Antonio Vivaldi 1678–1741
Johann Sebastian Bach 1685–1750
George Frederick Handel 1685–1759

1700

Franz Joseph Haydn 1732–1809
John Stafford Smith 1750–1836

1750

Wolfgang Amadeus Mozart 1756–1791

1769 James Watt patents his steam engine

Ludwig van Beethoven 1770–1827

1775

1775 American Revolution (ended 1783)
1776 American Declaration of Independence

Francis Scott Key 1779–1843

1787 American Constitutional Convention
1788 John Fitch invents steamboat
1789 French Revolution; George Washington first
     president of United States
1791 Bill of Rights
1793 Eli Whitney invents the cotton gin

Franz Schubert 1797–1828

1800

1803 Louisiana Purchase
1804 Napoleon crowned emperor; Lewis and Clark
     expedition

Fanny Mendelssohn Hensel 1805–1847

1807 Robert Fulton builds first commercial
     steamboat; London streets lighted by gas

Felix Mendelssohn 1809–1847
Frédéric Chopin 1810–1849
Robert Schumann 1810–1856

1812 War of 1812

Richard Wagner 1813–1883

1815 Napoleon defeated in Battle of Waterloo

1819 First steamship crosses Atlantic

1825 Opening of the Erie Canal
1825 First public railroad opened in England

1825

Johannes Brahms 1833–1897

1838 Daguerre takes first photographs

Georges Bizet 1838–1875
Modest Mussorgsky 1839–1881
Peter Ilyich Tchaikovsky 1840–1893

Edvard Grieg 1843–1907
Nicolai Rimsky-Korsakov 1844–1908

1844 First telegraph message transmitted

1846 First use of ether as an anesthetic

1848 California Gold Rush; first Women's Rights
     Convention

361

TIME LINE

TIME LINE

1850

John Philip Sousa 1854–1932

Cécile Chaminade 1857–1944
Giacomo Puccini 1858–1924

Claude Debussy 1862–1918

1860 Civil War (ended 1865)
1863 Gettysburg Address; Emancipation Proclamation
1865 Abraham Lincoln assassinated

Scott Joplin 1868–1917

1869 First American transcontinental railroad

James Weldon Johnson 1871–1938
Ralph Vaughan Williams 1872–1958
W.C. (William Christopher) Handy 1873–1958
Arnold Schoenberg 1874–1951
Charles Ives 1874–1954
Robert Frost 1874–1963

1875

1876 Alexander Graham Bell invents telephone
1877 Thomas Edison invents the phonograph

1879 Edison invents improved incandescent electric light bulb

Igor Stravinsky 1882–1971

Ferdinand ("Jelly Roll") Morton 1885–1941
Gertrude ("Ma") Rainey 1886–1939
Ernst Toch 1887–1964
T.S. (Thomas Stearns) Eliot 1888–1965

Sergei Prokofiev 1891–1953

1885 Louis Pasteur develops milk "pasteurization"
1886 Statue of Liberty unveiled in New York Harbor

Bessie Smith 1894–1937
William Grant Still 1895–1978

1895 Wilhelm Roentgen discovers X-rays

George Gershwin 1898–1937

1898 Spanish-American War

1900

Louis Armstrong 1900–1971
Harry Partch 1901–1974
Langston Hughes 1902–1967
Ogden Nash 1902–1971

1901 Guglielmo Marconi transmits wireless telegraph signals across Atlantic
1902 Pierre and Marie Curie discover radium
1903 Wilbur and Orville Wright make first successful airplane flight
1904 First sound moving picture
1905 Albert Einstein offers Theory of Relativity
1906 San Francisco earthquake and fire

1908 Model T Ford produced
1909 Robert Peary and Matthew Henson reach North Pole

Milt Hinton 1910–

1910 Discovery of the South Pole; discovery of protons and electrons

John Cage 1912–
Morton Gould 1913–
Benjamin Britten 1913–1976

1912 *Titanic* disaster

Milton Babbitt 1916–
Eve Merriam 1916–
Lou Harrison 1917–
Leonard Bernstein 1918–

1914 Opening of the Panama Canal; World War (ended 1918)

1917 Russian Revolution

362

Dave Brubeck 1920–	1920 First commercial radio broadcast; suffrage (19th Amendment)
Katsutoshi Nagasawa 1923– **Paul Desmond** 1924–1977 **Pierre Boulez** 1925–	**1925**
	1927 Charles Lindbergh's flight across the Atlantic; first television transmission
Burt Bacharach 1928–	1928 Sir Alexander Fleming discovers penicillin 1929 New York stock market crash; beginning of worldwide depression
Claude Bolling 1930– **Stephen Sondheim** 1930–	
Shel Silverstein 1932– **Isao Tomita** 1932– **John Williams** 1932– **Krzysztof Penderecki** 1933–	1933 Nazi Revolution in Germany
Terry Riley 1935–	
Philip Glass 1937– **Gordon Lightfoot** 1938–	1939 World War II (ended 1945)
Trevor Nunn 1940–	
David Fanshawe 1942– **George Harrison** 1943– **Vangelis** 1943–	
Andrew Lloyd Webber 1948– **Stephen Schwartz** 1948– **Rick Springfield** 1949–	

1950

1950 Vietnam War (ended 1975)

1957 Launching of *Sputnik,* first earth satellite

1961 First successful manned orbital space flight
1962 Cuban missile crisis
1963 President John F. Kennedy assassinated
1965 First "walk" outside spaceship by an
astronaut
1968 Martin Luther King, Jr., and Robert F. Kennedy
assassinated
1969 First men land on the moon
1971 Voting age lowered to 18 years

1975

1976 U.S. celebrates its bicentennial on July 4;
Viking I and II landers set down on Mars

1981 Sandra Day O'Connor becomes first woman
appointed to the Supreme Court; first
reusable spacecraft, space shuttle *Columbia,*
travels into space and returns to earth
1983 Sally Ride becomes the first American woman
to travel in space
1984 First mechanical heart implanted in a human
1985 Worldwide Live Aid concert to benefit famine
victims in Ethiopia
1986 Statue of Liberty centennial celebration;
Hands Across America, nationwide joining of
hands to benefit the homeless in America
1987 *Voyager* makes first nonstop flight around the
world without refueling

363

TIME LINE

GLOSSARY AND INDEXES

ABA form a three-part form in which there is repetition after contrast, 21

AB form the organization of a composition into two different sections, 3

accent (>) placement of emphasis or stress on certain beats, 3

art song music written for solo voice and instrumental accompaniment, usually keyboard, 111

atonal music music characterized by the absence of a tonal center and equal emphasis on all twelve tones of the chromatic scale, 92

ballad a song that tells a story, 130

bar lines lines separating measures, 18

baroque style the common musical characteristics reflected by the music composed between 1600 and 1750, 17

bitonality harmony created by playing two different tonalities at the same time, 108

blues a melancholy style of American music characterized by flatted notes and a syncopated, often slow jazz rhythm, 104

calypso style folk-style music from the Caribbean Islands, 10

canon a form of music in which different vocal or instrumental parts take up the melody, successively creating harmony, 82

changing meter a combination of various meters, 48

chord three or more pitches sounding together, 4

classical style the common musical characteristics reflected by the music composed between 1750 and 1830, 17

coda concluding section, 20

compound meter meter whose beat can be subdivided into threes and/or sixes, 61

consonance the sounding of a combination of tones that produces little tension, 80

crescendo getting louder, 13

decrescendo getting softer, 13

development the expanded treatment of a musical idea, 147

dissonance the sounding of a combination of pitches that create harmonic tension and sound incomplete, 108

dominant chord a chord built on the fifth tone of a scale, 11

dotted quarter note the basic beat in compound meter, 60

duple beats grouped into sets of two, 18

dynamics levels of loudness and softness, 13

eighth note (♪) a symbol for a sound in music that is one-eighth as long as the sound of a whole note, 8

eighth rest (𝄾) a symbol for an interval of silence between tones lasting as long as an eighth note, 8

expressionism a movement in the arts characterized by the artist's concern with the expression of feelings about an object or event rather than realistically depicting the object itself, 93

forte (*f*) loud, 13

found objects sources of tone color that are ordinary items that wouldn't usually be thought of as musical instruments, 181

free form a composition that changes from one performance to the next, 158

half note (♩) a symbol for a sound in music that is one half as long as the sound of a whole note, 4

harmony a musical combination of tones or chords, 80

home tone the focus or tonal center of a scale, or system of tones, 80

homophonic music having one melodic line with the other parts providing harmony, 83

irregular meter a mixture of duple and triple meters in a repeating pattern, 48

jazz a style of American music originated in the South by black Americans. It is characterized by strong, prominent meter, improvisation, and dotted or syncopated rhythms, 52

key scale or system of tones in which all the notes have a definite relationship to, and are based on, the tonal center or keynote, 100

key tone the focus or tonal center of a scale or system of tones, 11

legato music that sounds smooth, 141

major chord a chord that consists of the first, third, and fifth notes of a major scale, 25

measures groups of beats, 18

meter the organization of beats into recurring sets, 18

minor chord a chord that consists of the first, lowered third, and fifth notes of a major scale, 25

modulation transition from a section of music based on one key to a section based on a different key, 100

monophonic music having a single melodic line with no accompaniment, 83

motive a short musical unit that keeps its basic identity through many repetitions, 127

natural (♮) symbol indicating that a sharp or a flat should be cancelled, 25

Ondes Martenot a precursor to the present-day synthesizer, 178

oratorio a dramatic musical composition usually set to a religious text and performed by solo voices, chorus, and orchestra, without action, special costumes, or scenery, 83

ostinato continuous repeating of a passage, 54

phrases the building blocks of form, 120

piano (*p*) soft, 13

pipe organ keyboard instrument whose sound is produced by wind moving through pipes, 172

pizzicato music played by plucking the strings of a stringed instrument with the finger instead of bowing the strings, 106

polyphonic music having two or more independent melodic parts sounding together, 83

polyrhythm a combination of two or more different rhythm patterns played at the same time, 70

polytonality a combination of two or more tonalities (keys) played at the same time, 108

GLOSSARY AND INDEXES

365

GLOSSARY AND INDEXES

prepared piano piano that has been altered by items of wood, metal, rubber, etc., placed between the strings of the piano, 175

program music a composition whose title or accompanying remarks link it with a story, idea, or emotion, 50

quadruple meter beats that are grouped into sets of four, 40

quarter note (♩) a symbol for a sound in music that is one fourth as long as the sound of a whole note, 3

quarter rest (𝄽) a symbol for an interval of silence between tones lasting as long as a quarter note, 3

reggae style popular music from the Caribbean Islands, 5

register the range of a voice or instrument, 102

Renaissance style the common musical characteristics reflected by the music composed between 1450 and 1600, 17

retrograde a melody that is performed backwards, 88

rhythm pattern a combination of long and short sounds which is repeated, 3

ritardando gradual slowing of the tempo, 20

romantic style the common musical characteristics reflected by the music composed between 1830 and 1900, 17

root the lowest pitch of each chord, 11

salsa a style of Latin dance music originating in Cuba. It is characterized by exciting rhythm and jazz and blues styles and harmonies, 70

serial music atonal music written using a technique based on the successive repetition of all twelve tones of the chromatic scale in a fixed order, 90

simple meter meter whose beat can be divided into twos and/or fours, 40

sonata allegro a musical form that uses the overall design of exposition, development, and recapitulation, 149

staccato music that sounds crisp and detached, 141

steady beat the underlying beat or pulse, 3

steel drums "homemade" percussion instruments found in the West Indies, 182

strophic form form in which the music is repeated with each new verse or stanza of text, 130

style quality that is characteristic of a culture, individual, or historical period, 2

subdominant chord chord based on the fourth tone of the scale, 104

symphony long orchestral work organized into three to five movements, 149

syncopation rhythm pattern that has unexpected sounds and silences, 10

synthesizer an instrument for producing electronic music that combines sound generators and modifiers in a single control system, 179

synth-pop popular music that uses synthesized tone color, 30

tempo the speed of the beat, 8

366

ternary form (ABA) a three-part form in which there is repetition after contrast, 21

texture the character of the different layers of sound in music, 83

Theremin first electronic musical instrument, invented by and named for Leon Theremin, 178

tonality the relation of melodic and harmonic elements between the tones of any major or minor scale to the home tone, 80

tone color the unique sound of each instrument or voice, 13

tone row a type of pitch organization made up of all twelve tones of the chromatic scale that has no tonal center and in which all pitches are equal, 90

tonic chord a chord built on the first tone or key tone of a scale, 11

triple meter beats grouped into sets of three, 18

twelve-bar blues chord pattern often used in blues music based on the I, IV, and V chords, 104

twentieth-century style the common musical characteristics reflected by the music composed since 1900, 17

whole note (𝅝) a symbol that represents a sound that lasts for four beats in meter, 4

GLOSSARY AND INDEXES

GLOSSARY AND INDEXES

LISTENING SELECTIONS

GLOSSARY AND INDEXES

GLOSSARY AND INDEXES

ALPHABETICAL SONG INDEX

CLASSIFIED INDEX

371

GLOSSARY AND INDEXES

PHILOSOPHY OF THE SERIES

The distinctive character of *Music and You*, Grades 7 and 8, has been achieved by integrating varied approaches and modes of learning into an experientially based, carefully sequenced curriculum that provides for the unique learning and motivational needs of adolescent students. The approach used in Grades 7 and 8 of the *Music and You* series is a synthesis of the Kodály, Orff Schulwerk, and Dalcroze approaches, as well as other proven practices and current research about adolescent learning styles. All concepts and skills are presented in an easy-to-use, *sequential* format. Lessons in Grades 7 and 8 were field-tested to ensure their appropriateness for adolescent students.

The articles in the pages that follow describe the varied approaches and special areas emphasized in *Music and You*.

CONTENTS

ORGANIZATION AND SEQUENCING OF THE SERIES

The *Music and You* program is carefully structured to ensure continuous growth in musical skills and understanding. A survey of the content from the early to the later units reveals a logical, step-by-step development of understandings and skills. For example, in the study of form, the basic principles of unity and variety are developed before progressing to additive forms, such as binary, ternary, and rondo.

Music and You offers a flexible curriculum to meet the diverse needs of Grades 7 and 8 school music courses. Each book provides a flexible organization of general music units, choral singing, instrumental skill development, and special study sections of high interest. Each of these four parts can be taught independently or integrated with one another for courses from six weeks to a full year in length.

The first eight units of each book may be used for a six-week, nine-week, or semester course in general music. Concepts and music reading skills are taught through listening lessons, songs, instrumental accompaniments, and various topics of study. The material in Unit 1 forms the foundation for all the units that follow and should be taught first as the "core" unit.

The choral, instrumental, and special study sections that follow the general music units provide additional repertoire, and offer opportunities to develop vocal and instrumental skills and to help students continue to grow in their understanding of different styles of music.

The **Scope and Sequence** chart on pages xiv–xv of each Teacher's Edition shows the overall plan for the grade level. This chart shows the objectives according to eight specific elements of music and summarizes what is taught and measured in each unit.

The Learning Process in *Music and You*

The sequence of learning that is built into each level of *Music and You* may be shown in this way:

> 1. EXPERIENCE/PREPARE
> 2. IDENTIFY/LABEL
> 3. PRACTICE
> 4. CREATE
> 5. EVALUATE
> 6. MAINTAIN

This process incorporates the key stages outlined in both the Kodály and Orff approaches to music education, as well as in general taxonomies of learning. Creativity is an integral part of each stage of learning. At the experiential level, creativity is exploratory. After a concept is labeled and practiced, the creative tasks are more directed and specific in nature.

Successful learning takes place when there is continual emphasis on *lesson-by-lesson* development of skills and understanding. The **Unit Overview** chart, which precedes each unit, outlines this progress. The chart shows the unit's overall objectives, including the measurable objectives, which are evaluated at the end of the unit, as well as the specific skills and concepts taught in each lesson.

The **lesson plans** in *Music and You* are carefully structured to support the learning sequence. Each lesson plan includes the following:

- *Focus* (generally one musical element)
- *Objectives* (clearly stated in behavioral terms)
- *Setting the Stage* (a motivating activity and often a review of previously learned material)
- *Teaching the Lesson* (a step-by-step, logical presentation from the known to the unknown)
- *Reinforcing the Lesson* (a review and/or preview that relates the lesson focus to other material)
- *Appraisal* (observable behaviors for measuring student achievement)

Additional material provided in the **Extension** section at the bottom of most pages may include More Music Teaching Ideas, as well as background information, supporting materials, curriculum connections, higher-level thinking activities, and suggestions for students with special needs and talents.

Review and Evaluation pages at the end of each unit summarize the unit's content and offer both an informal check for understanding and a formal assessment of conceptual learning. The formal written Evaluations are provided in the Teacher's Copying Masters and are also recorded.

Choral, instrumental, and special study sections follow the eight general music units in Grades 7 and 8 of *Music and You.* These sections can either be integrated into lessons from the general music units or taught separately.

The first special study section in Grade 7, **American Popular Music,** explores the development of different types of American popular music from 1900 to the present. Background information on famous composers and performers is provided, as well as opportunities for students to accompany some of the songs in the section. The **Musical** in Grade 7, "Those Who Have Gone Before" by Hank Beebe, serves as a review of the American Popular Music unit. It includes songs, a complete script, and suggestions for staging and costumes.

Two special study sections in Grade 8 lead students to develop familiarity with and knowledge about different musical styles. **Western Musical Styles** presents a survey of Renaissance, Baroque, Classical, Romantic, and twentieth century music. **Music of the World's Cultures** introduces students to music from around the world, including types of instruments and key characteristics.

ADOLESCENT LEARNING STYLES

Marked by the beginning of the transition from childhood to adulthood, adolescence is a time of growth and change. Students at this age exhibit widely varying individual characteristics intellectually, emotionally, socially, and physically. Lessons in *Music and You* are designed to address the special needs and learning styles of adolescent students as they learn music skills and concepts sequentially.

Intellectually, adolescence is a time of transition from the use of concrete thinking to more abstract thought processes. At this age some students may be highly dependent on concrete learning experiences, while others are functioning in more abstract modes. Due to varying rates of student development, when facts and ideas are presented to students, lessons in Grades 7 and 8 relate them to tangible examples.

Activities in the lessons in *Music and You* serve to develop the emotional needs and self-esteem of each student. The social needs of students are met by providing experiences ranging from individual to cooperative learning group activity. Teachers can assist students by using activities that require appropriate levels of involvement for their students and by encouraging the development of independence as well as a sense of group responsibility.

Recent research in adolescent learning theory suggests that the instructional environment for adolescents should include physical activity, meaningful participation, and opportunities to demonstrate competence and achievement. *Music and You* encourages the creation of a learning environment based on these principles by including meaningful "hands-on" activities, such as instrumental performance, singing, moving, and/or composing, as an integral part of each lesson.

Play-Along Accompaniments, a special feature of *Music and You,* provide a strategy for meaningful, physical activity. Play-Alongs are simple rhythmic, melodic, or harmonic scores for students to perform on Orff and percussion instruments, recorder, guitar, and keyboard as they listen to recorded music. These activities advance sight-reading and performance skills while helping students to focus on the music and become active participants and performers.

The content of each *Music and You* lesson is geared to reflect the interests of adolescents. Lessons start with a musical activity designed to challenge the student, as well as to provide a sense of competence and achievement. These activities motivate the students from the start, encouraging them to focus on the material as a means of engaging their interest.

Music and You provides a wealth of opportunities for adolescents to experience success as they learn and perform. Such experiences are among the most powerful tools for promoting student learning, development, and involvement.

THE KODÁLY APPROACH

The Kodály approach emphasizes the teaching of music literacy skills through the use of folk and composed music of the highest quality. It is based on the philosophy of the Hungarian composer, musicologist, and educator Zoltán Kodály (1882–1967), who believed that music belongs to everyone—that the ability to read and write music is the right of every person. Kodály stressed that music education should begin with the very young, that it must be centered on singing, and that children should first learn their "musical mother tongue," the folk songs of their cultural heritage, before exploring music of other cultures. This strong awareness of cultural identity, he believed, provides the best means for understanding music.

The Kodály approach develops musicianship through the sequential teaching of all concepts. It employs a logical teaching sequence that progresses from the known to the unknown, one step at a time. The learning sequence starts with basic rhythm concepts, simple melodic patterns (beginning with *so-mi*), and basic coordination skills, and progresses gradually to conscious knowledge of pentatonic and other commonly used scales. To build solid learning, the teacher guides the students to experience concepts in many different ways, leading them to conscious awareness of the names and symbols for the concepts, and then to discover and come to deeper understanding on their own as they practice and create, using the concepts they have learned.

Ear training is achieved through the use of relative solmization, a movable *do* system in which pitch syllable names indicate relationships among pitches in a key, rather than absolute pitch. This system, often supported by the use of hand signs, provides excellent training for in-tune singing and sight reading.

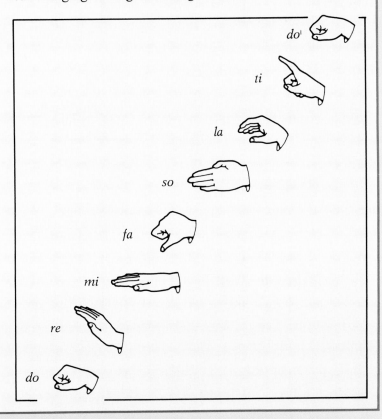

The Kodály approach requires constant attention to expressivity in all musical activities. Teachers learn to monitor the moods and feelings of their students and to vary activities to keep the sound vital and in tune. Some of the strategies used by Kodály educators to help students achieve good vocal development and musicianship include choosing songs with appropriate vocal ranges, modulating to different keys, and using expressive movement and inner-hearing games.

Lessons in Grades 7 and 8 of *Music and You* review basic rhythmic and melodic concepts learned in elementary school while gradually expanding students' knowledge, conceptual understanding, and music-making skills. Individual vocal and instrumental examples are taken directly from the music to be performed. This helps maintain the focus on the musical result rather than on mere technical drill. Emphasis on proper vocal development throughout the *Music and You* series is compatible with the Kodály approach. Both share the goal of developing the ability of all students to sing well and to enjoy singing. They also share the philosophy that music is not just for the educated elite but for everyone, and that everyone is entitled to reach the highest possible level of musicianship.

THE ORFF APPROACH

The Orff approach is a philosophy of musical development that builds understanding of concepts and skills through active involvement in speech, movement, singing, playing instruments, and drama. Developed by German composer Carl Orff (1895–1982), the approach emphasizes creativity and is based on the instinctive learning behavior of students.

The primary materials used are folk and composed music of high quality. Much of the music comes from the students' own culture and is an extension of familiar musical repertoire and experiences. From this music, students isolate basic melodic and rhythmic "building blocks." Once identified and internalized, these building blocks provide students with a musical vocabulary with which they can build their own creations.

Each musical concept is developed sequentially. Students first experience the concept aurally and physically, in imitation of the teacher. Next, the concept is labeled and, through extensive exploration, reinforced. Finally, students develop their own creations, using the concept. Improvisation and movement are encouraged throughout the learning process.

Speech exercises that use familiar rhymes, sayings, and other patterns, often accompanied by body percussion sounds, provide the basis for rhythmic study. These sounds are sometimes transferred to unpitched and pitched instruments. Melodic study, as with the Kodály approach, begins in the primary grades with the interval of a descending third, *so-mi* (5–3), and in the intermediate grades with *do-re-mi* (1–2–3). It gradually develops into the complete pentatonic and, finally, to the diatonic scales.

Rhythmic and melodic awareness and independence are developed by adding borduns (accompaniments using the first and fifth steps of the scale), ostinatos (simple repeated patterns), and other accompaniment techniques to melodies. Later, borduns with melodic ornamentation of the first kand/or fifth steps of the scale (moving borduns) are used. Harmonic development then proceeds to pedal point and various shifting chord patterns, expanding the tones used in improvisation as the complete major and minor scales and other modes are gradually introduced.

While not required, Orff instruments provide a variety of timbres and an excellent source of motivation for student aesthetic response. Designed originally by Orff, the instruments are distinctive for their unique suitability for students without compromising musical quality.

Orff instruments include xylophones, metallophones, and glockenspiels, all in various ranges (bass, alto, soprano). The instruments are usually diatonic, with additional F-sharp and B-flat bars that replace the F and B bars when keys other than C major or A minor are used. Timpani, recorders, guitars, other low-pitched stringed instruments, and a wide variety of unpitched percussion instruments are often used. The *Orff instrumentarium*, as this collection is called, is ideal for creative accompaniments for songs, stories, and poems, and for creating opportunities to develop improvisational, compositional, and ensemble playing skills.

Students in Grades 7 and 8 may need additional motivation to play Orff instruments, since they may associate them with their elementary school experiences. Consequently, *Music and You* varies the traditional approach for teaching an orchestration. The process of learning first by rote, then speaking, singing, playing, and creating, is expanded to include score reading. The teacher may assist students in clapping the rhythms in each part as they follow the score located either in their texts or on Copying Masters. The class is then divided into small groups, with each group responsible for accurately preparing one part of the accompaniment to be played with the full ensemble.

Lessons in *Music and You* suggest the use of Orff instruments, along with keyboards, resonator bells, recorders, and guitars, for the performance of melodic patterns and chordal accompaniments. Improvisation, always at the core of the Orff approach, extends at Grades 7 and 8 to include improvised instrumental riffs in jazz style, playing tone clusters with a contemporary sound, and using instruments as sources for new combinations of sounds.

THE DALCROZE APPROACH AND MOVEMENT

Movement is a natural means of expression. Children move instinctively to sound, expressing themselves in movement, gestures, speech, and song. These instinctive responses are the basis of the Dalcroze approach to the teaching of music.

Émile Jaques-Dalcroze, a Swiss music educator (1865–1950), incorporated the natural responses of the body into the study of music through movement, which he called *eurhythmics* from the Greek roots *eu* and *rhythmos*, meaning good flow or good movement. He believed that students must experience musical sounds through movement before translating them into musical notation.

Dalcroze noticed that sudden changes in rhythm or tonal patterns, tempo, or articulation could seriously affect his students' level of performance and their interpretation of music. Since students instinctively feel rhythmic vibrations in the muscles, Dalcroze felt that they should be encouraged to use the entire body to awaken "rhythmic consciousness" and respond to "expressive nuances." Dalcroze's eurhythmic exercises promote sharper communication between all the body senses to help students feel and physically respond to musical concepts through movement. Eurhythmic exercises also help students develop listening, concentration, memory sequencing, quick-reaction, coordination, ear training, and ensemble skills.

The movement activities in Grades 7 and 8 of *Music and You* are carefully sequenced and serve to reinforce the musical concepts introduced in the lessons. Students are prepared for all spatial movement activities before they leave their seats. For example, students are asked to clap or pat a beat or pattern at their seats before stepping it. The activities progress from simple to more complex in a logical, sequenced manner. For example, the students are asked to clap or pat the beat, then step the beat, then step the beat while clapping shorter durations such as eighth notes. The students may be further challenged when asked to perform three rhythmic lines simultaneously, such as stepping the beat while clapping an ostinato and singing the melodic rhythm.

Patterned dances in *Music and You* are presented in a logical order of skill development. Since most patterned dances are based on locomotor movements, related locomotor skills are isolated and practiced before being integrated into more complex dance patterns.

Although eurythmics is often considered to be all there is to the Dalcroze approach, the development of internal aural and rhythmic/muscular skills, as well as of improvisational skills, is of equal importance. Internal aural skills ("inner hearing" of pitch and harmonic relationships) are developed in *Music and You* through activities such as omitting (thinking) specific pitches in a song. Dalcroze believed that development of the inner rhythmic/muscular sense would help students perform music more accurately and expressively. This is achieved in *Music and You* through movement activities that involve such things as bouncing, rolling, and catching a tennis ball and using large and small movement gestures.

Dalcroze believed that the skill of improvisation is the ultimate goal for students. According to Dalcroze, for a student to improvise successfully in a musical and expressive manner, he or she must have experienced and developed an inner sense of rhythm, phrase, meter, pitch relationships, harmonic tension and resolution, musical unity and contrast, imitation and variation, and the expressive elements of dynamics, tempo, and articulation. In this way improvisation is the manifestation of musical understanding.

In Grades 7 and 8 of *Music and You*, students are given many opportunities to create and improvise with varying combinations of instruments, speech, singing, and movement. Activities include creating rhythm patterns, rhythmic accompaniments, body percussion patterns, speech chants, question/answer phrases, ostinatos, rondos, movement sequences, and compositions utilizing the musical elements being studied. Students are continually challenged to find another way of performing their music or to change or create a new version or accompaniment.

Through the Dalcroze approach, students are encouraged to integrate the use of visual, aural, and kinesthetic senses to develop their musical skills and understanding and their abilities to create and perform their own music. Dalcroze activities are characteristically challenging and fun. Students engaged in Dalcroze activities usually listen more attentively, respond more quickly and accurately, and become totally involved with the musical experience. The integration of numerous Dalcroze activities throughout Grades 7 and 8 of *Music and You* helps make the difference between the students' perception of music as an intellectual discipline and of music as an expressive, aesthetic experience involving body, mind, and spirit.

THE ADOLESCENT SINGER

Music and You is based on the philosophy that experiencing music through singing should be an integral part of the music program. Songs have been carefully chosen with respect to the interests and unique singing abilities of adolescents.

Particular attention has been given to the boy's changing voice. Songs selected for the series employ ranges that foster the development of mid-range, *bel canto* singing. This style of singing helps the students build confidence in their changing voices and promotes good intonation.

Suggested vocal ranges for students in Grades 7 and 8 are given below:

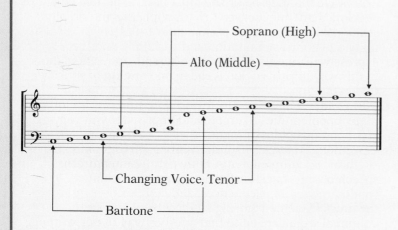

Lessons in Grades 7 and 8 of *Music and You* address the specific needs and problems of adolescent singers as they explore and develop their singing voices. The following summarizes key issues and suggestions for adolescent singers:

1. Help students to determine range and describe vocal tone color. By experimenting with singing in different keys, each student should be able to determine his or her current singing range. Following strategies in *Music and You*, students will become aware of tone color and develop a vocabulary to describe the basic properties of vocal sound.

2. Accommodate the adolescent singer. If the young adolescent has difficulty singing in tune while learning new songs, it may be because of the limited vocal range of the changing voice. Suggestions as to how to accommodate the limited ranges of the changing and changed voice are detailed in the lessons in *Music and You.*

3. Provide experiences singing in harmony. *Music and You* introduces harmony through simple ostinatos, rounds, canons, and descants. Optional instrumental parts are provided to support students singing the harmony part. The tinting of the vocal parts in the pupil books helps students locate and learn to follow the harmony part.

4. Develop vocal technique. Suggestions for helping students improve their tone quality through the development of basic singing and vocal production skills are found in the lesson plans of *Music and You.* Vocalises are included to help students expand vocal range, improve tone quality, develop resonance, and improve diction.

CHORAL SINGING

The material in the Choral Singing sections in Grades 7 and 8 of *Music and You* is designed to be used as additional repertoire for choirs, ensembles, and glee clubs, or to be integrated into general music classes. These choral selections have been carefully chosen and sequenced to accommodate the development of vocal technique, part singing, music reading, and repertoire.

Basic vocal techniques, including proper diction, vowel unification, breath support, tone placement, and range and register expansion are fostered through warm-ups that are applied directly to the choral literature. These warm-ups are notated in the Teacher's Editions and are on the recordings as well. The repertoire is carefully sequenced so that early choral selections have limited ranges, simple rhythmic and melodic patterns, and a short, repeated phrase structure. As the sequence advances, the students progress in their use of the changing voice from cambiata to baritone (for boys), from polyphonic to homophonic harmonic content, and from simple to more complex and sophisticated rhythmic and melodic patterns. Text settings at the beginning are syllabic, while melismatic passages are introduced later in the developmental sequence. The demands of longer, more sustained phrase patterns further into the sequence continually reinforce the development of breath support.

Independence in part singing is developed through simple ostinatos, rounds, canons, and descants. These experiences prepare students for performing repertoire that is set in a homophonic chordal texture. To help students follow their parts, difficult melodic, rhythmic, and harmonic patterns are isolated in a special Preparation box that precedes the selection.

The development of music reading skills is directly tied to the musical repertoire. Sight-reading hints in the Preparation boxes allow the students to focus visually on selected patterns before reading them in the choral selection. These previews help students to sing with greater accuracy and to learn the music more quickly.

Of equal importance in the development of music reading skills is the singer's acquisition of a tonal vocabulary of intervallic relationships that will promote accurate intonation. Familiar tonal patterns are reinforced through sight-reading activities. Experiences with "inner hearing" through the use of the tone ladder (scale) are included to help expand the tonal vocabulary.

In addition to its value in sequentially teaching students how to sing, the musical repertoire in *Music and You* has been carefully selected for its musical quality and appeal to adolescent singers. Selections reflect a variety of musical and historical styles, seasonal repertoire, and songs in foreign languages.

KEYBOARD, GUITAR, AND RECORDER

Instrumental activities in *Music and You* are designed to promote student understanding of and familiarity with the keyboard, guitar, electric bass, and recorder. In addition to teaching performance techniques, instrumental activities in *Music and You* also reinforce the concepts and music reading skills that are integral to the program. For example, by playing chord roots and full chords on guitar and keyboard, students may demonstrate their understanding of the concepts of rhythm, harmony, and form developed in the lessons.

The *special keyboard and guitar sections* in Grades 7 and 8 contain additional instrumental instruction that develop playing and note-reading skills through Play-Along accompaniments. These sections include instructional material at varied levels to accommodate students who may have had previous experience with the instruments.

In Grade 7, the Play-Alongs accompany the musical selections found in the "American Popular Music" section. The keyboard sequence in Grade 8 offers Play-Along accompaniments to folk and popular music and emphasizes improvisational and music reading skills.

Keyboard and guitar experiences begin with two-chord accompaniments and extend to five-chord accompaniments. In Grade 8, specific guitar performance techniques, such as the shuffle, hammer-on, and arpeggio, are also included. Recorder experiences begin with three-pitch melodic accompaniments and extend to six- and seven-pitch accompaniments.

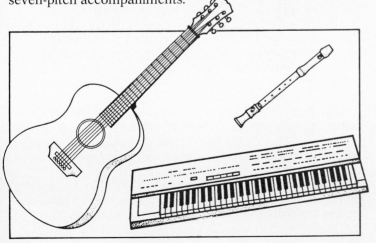

THE LISTENING PROGRAM

The development of listening skills is an important objective in the *Music and You* instructional program. Music is an *aural* art, and listening is the avenue through which most students will continue to participate in music after the middle/junior high school experience.

Lessons in *Music and You* provide a structure for actively involving students in the analysis of the music. Students show their understanding of musical concepts such as phrase structure, dynamic change, sectional contrast, and melodic contour in an observable and appraisable manner as they respond to music by making a tangible signal or creative movement response. Creative movement responses can also reflect higher-level thinking processes, for example, when students are asked to decide how to respond to show the contrast between two themes or sections. In addition, by following listening maps that are visual or verbal representations of the sounds, students maintain interest in and involvement with the selections.

The listening experiences in *Music and You* are carefully structured to help students understand and absorb what they are hearing. In Grade 7, the listening program begins with short selections. Longer selections are gradually introduced as the students' listening and analytical skills become more advanced.

Repeated listening is a necessary part of the development of discerning listeners. The resulting familiarity may expand the repertoire of music that students enjoy hearing. Repetition of listening selections in *Music and You* is encouraged by cross-referencing related materials across units.

The varied Listening Maps and analysis charts in *Music and You* provide diverse formats for structuring and focusing the students' listening. The maps may include geometric shapes that represent form, notation with patterns to be read or played, and musical symbols for such things as dynamics and tempo. Some include pictures of featured instruments and may combine several types of graphics. Many of these maps are on the reproducible Teacher's Copying Masters located in the Teacher's Resource Package for each grade and on the Transparencies provided with the Teacher's Edition.

COOPERATIVE LEARNING

Research shows that cooperative learning is one of the most powerful strategies for instruction available. Cooperative learning activities encourage students to spend more time on task and to rehearse information orally, resulting in *increased achievement*. Emphasis on group work requires students both to explain their point of view and to listen to others, stimulating *cognitive development at advanced levels*. During cooperative learning activities, students *grow in self-esteem* as a result of supporting one another and helping one another to learn for mutual gain. In addition, as students enjoy the process of learning and achieve more, cooperative learning activities *promote liking for school*.

What Is Cooperative Learning?

Five elements must be present for small-group learning to be cooperative:

1. *Positive Interdependence*. Lesson structure ensures that groups sink or swim together. This may be done by division of labor, limiting resources, assigning roles, and giving joint rewards.
2. *Face-to-face Interaction*. Socially acceptable interaction is required to achieve the lesson goal.
3. *Individual Accountability*. The group is responsible for the learning of each individual. Every student's mastery of material is assessed in some way.
4. *Interpersonal and Small-group Skills*. One social skill-building goal is assigned for the period.
5. *Group Processing*. The teacher and/or group members determine the effectiveness of the group in accomplishing the assigned task.

Other characteristics usually found in cooperative settings are heterogeneous groupings, shared responsibility for group leadership, and observation, analysis, and feedback on group functioning by the teacher.

Music and You provides many opportunities for cooperative learning, both in the lessons and in the Extension sections at the bottom of lesson pages.

Cooperative learning may be used for an entire lesson or for only part of the class period. The following are general guidelines to keep in mind when planning cooperative learning lessons:

1. Identify the subject matter and social goals.
2. Identify the appropriate group size, from two to six.
3. Set a time limit for the activity, including your explanation of the task and evaluation time.
4. Determine how to assign students to groups. (This is usually done in random order.)
5. Determine classroom arrangement to permit group members to see and hear each other.
6. Explain the learning task, the social skills expected, time limitations, and criteria for evaluation. Identify a stop signal. Check that students understand instructions.
7. Have the students form groups and work on the task. Observe group interactions, taking notes.
8. At the end of the assigned period, have the students share and evaluate their products and group functioning.

The cooperative learning activities in *Music and You* are organized to introduce sequentially the social skills required for effective group work. The activities guide students as they acquire the skills of basic communication, listening, eye contact, sound-level control, taking turns, sharing limited resources, and defending ideas when they differ from those of others. These skills, developed throughout *Music and You*, will bring added excitement and higher-level learning to the music class, while building lifelong social skills.

SPECIAL LEARNERS

Just as no music class is composed of students who all look alike, neither does any class consist of students who all learn alike. The challenge to teachers is to provide music instruction for integrated groups of learners while simultaneously avoiding lower musical expectations for students with different learning rates and styles. This challenge can be met by observing and trying to understand the unique learning abilities of each student.

The focus in *Music and You* is on success for all students. **Special Learners** suggestions appear in the Extension section of many *Music and You* lessons. Often, the same strategy will work for students with a wide variety of special needs. For this reason, most of the Special Learners suggestions are not restricted by labels that identify one particular exceptionality. Many of the suggestions recommend adapting materials or activities to help all students participate successfully in music class.

Students who are mainstreamed into music class are usually categorized as Educable Mentally Handicapped, Learning-disabled, Physically Handicapped, Visually Impaired, or Auditorily Impaired. Each of these categories covers a vast spectrum of abilities and needs; two or more students with the same exceptionality might participate quite differently in musical learning. The variety of musical activities provided in every *Music and You* lesson, combined with the many suggestions for special learners, makes it possible to plan successful music lessons for integrated groups of students.

Suggestions for Special Learners

Listed below are the kinds of learners given special consideration in *Music and You* and some of the recommendations provided for their specific exceptionalities.

Educable Mentally Handicapped. Students described by this label are identified by an intelligence test score below the norm combined with inappropriate adaptive behavior.

Practices such as using a slower rate of presentation, increasing repetition, the inclusion of concrete experiences, and teaching smaller amounts of material at a time are most often suggested for helping mentally handicapped students. Many of these recommendations have been incorporated into the Special Learners suggestions in *Music and You*. These suggestions are intended to serve as guidelines that can be adapted to fit the learning needs of individual students. In addition, the lesson plans are structured to provide repetition of songs and listening selections for all students.

Learning-disabled. The label of learning disability is an "umbrella" term. Students in this category might be poor readers, poor in arithmetic, or poor in writing. The causes of these academic deficits can be a combination of various perceptual problems.

Some learning-disabled students may become confused by text pages that are colorful and highly illustrated. These learners may succeed when notation or graphics are extracted from the page and enlarged.

Physical Handicaps. The suggestions for physically handicapped students in *Music and You* are offered to assist the teacher in designing appropriate alternative activities. Many physically handicapped students may require alternative musical responses when their peers are engaged in creative or structured movement activities.

Auditory Disabilities. Students with auditory disabilities may demonstrate hearing losses ranging from deafness to far lesser degrees of hearing impairment. Special Learners suggestions in *Music and You* that suggest a slower rate of presentation and clarification of materials will assist these students.

Visual Disabilities. The creation of tactile learning aids and manipulatives may be necessary for use with some visually impaired students, while for others the enlargement of notation, graphs, or song texts may be adequate. Many of the Copying Masters at each grade level of *Music and You* will provide a useful source of such materials.

SONGS IN SIGN LANGUAGE

Signing a song adds an expressive dimension to singing that is aesthetically appealing to the eye. Sign language can enhance the performance of a song and, as in choral choreography, can add meaning for the participant as well as for the observer.

Students should understand that the use of sign language in songs is conceptual rather than literal. The objective is to paint a picture of the song by visual means, and therefore it is not necessary to sign every word. The overall meaning of the song is signed.

In conversation, words that do not have specific signs are finger-spelled using the manual alphabet. Finger-spelling, however, is usually avoided in signing songs. If a particular phrase or idea does not lend itself clearly to sign, a combination of sign, gesture, and/or mime may be used.

Signing instructions, including illustrations, may be found in the *Music and You* Teacher's Editions. Students learn that sign language does not rely solely on the use of the hands. They discover that facial expressions and body movements are also important in conveying the mood of a song. Positive emotions are expressed with an upward motion. For an upturned "smile," the hands, body, and face move up with a lift. For unhappy emotions, the gestures of the face, body, and hands move downward. When teaching signs to a song, remind students that only part of the meaning is transmitted through the hands; the face and body must tell the rest.

Encourage students to make signs flow from one to the next, and to keep in mind the rhythm of the song and the flow of each phrase. The signing of songs should include very large movements, so that the audience can see them easily.

When signing a song, the students should always *sing* all of the words, even though they may not sign all of them. For best visual results in performance, the students should wear solid colors contrasting to skin color, so that the hands are highlighted against their clothing.

The signing suggestions in *Music and You* are one approach to learning forms of sign. As students gain familiarity and confidence with signing, they will enjoy creating their own schemes for signing favorite songs.

African American Music (See also Ethnomusicology)

Bebey, Francis. *African Music: A People's Art*. Chicago: Chicago Review Press, 1975.

Burgie, Irving. *The Caribbean Song Book: Songs of Puerto Rico, Jamaica, Cuba, Barbados, Dominican Republic, Haiti, Trinidad, Bahamas: Plus Nine Island National Anthems: For Voices in Harmony*. Compiled and arranged. Hollis, N.Y.: Caribe Music Corp., 1977.

Edet, Edna S. *The Griot Sings: Songs from the Black World*. Collected and adapted. New York: Medgar Evers College Press, 1978.

Glass, Paul. *Songs and Stories of Afro-Americans*. New York: Grosset & Dunlap, 1971.

Johnson, James Weldon, and J. R. Johnson, eds. *The Books of American Negro Spirituals*. 2 vols. in 1. Jersey City, N.J.: Da Capo Press, 1977.

Jones, Bessie, and Bess L. Hawes. *Step It Down: Games, Plays, Songs, and Stories from the Afro-American Heritage*. Athens, Ga.: Univ. of Georgia Press, 1987.

Nketia, Joseph H. *The Music of Africa*. New York: W.W. Norton & Co., 1974.

Roberts, John S. *Black Music of Two Worlds*. New York: Riverrun Press, 1985.

Southern, Eileen. *The Music of Black Americans*. 2d ed. New York: W.W. Norton & Co., 1983.

Cooperative Learning

Dishon, Dee, and Pat W. O'Leary. *A Guidebook for Cooperative Learning: A Technique for Creating More Effective Schools*. Holmes Beach, Fla.: Learning Publications, 1984.

Johnson, David W., Roger T. Johnson, and Edythe Johnson Holubec. *Circles of Learning: Cooperation in the Classroom*. Alexandria, Va.: Association for Supervision & Curriculum Development, 1984.

Slavin, Robert E. *Cooperative Learning: Student Teams*. 2d ed. Washington, D.C.: National Education Association, 1987.

Slavin, Robert E., Shlomo Sharan, Spencer Kagan, Rachel H. Lazarowitz, Clark Webb, and Richard Schmuck, eds. *Learning to Cooperate, Cooperating to Learn*. New York: Plenum Publishing Corp., 1984.

Dalcroze (See also Movement)

Abramson, Robert M. *Rhythm Games*. New York: Music & Movement Press, 1973.

Aronoff, Frances W. *Move with the Music: Songs and Activities for Young Children, A Teacher-Parent Preparation Workbook Including Keyboard*. New York: Turning Wheel Press, 1982.

———. *Music and Young Children: Expanded Edition*. New York: Turning Wheel Press, 1979.

Findlay, Elsa. *Rhythm and Movement: Applications of Dalcroze Eurhythmics*. Princeton, N.J.: Birch Tree Group, 1971.

Jaques-Dalcroze, Émile. *Rhythm, Music, and Education*. rev. ed. Translated by Harold F. Rubenstein. London: The Dalcroze Society, 1980.

Early Childhood Music

Andress, Barbara. *Music Experiences in Early Childhood*. New York: Holt, Rinehart & Winston, 1980.

Aronoff, Frances W. *Music and Young Children: Expanded Edition*. New York: Turning Wheel Press, 1979.

Bayless, Kathleen M., and Marjorie E. Ramsey. *Music: A Way of Life for the Young Child*. 3d ed. Columbus, Ohio: Merrill Publishing Co., 1987.

Birkenshaw, Lois. *Music for Fun, Music for Learning: For Regular and Special Classrooms*. 3d ed. Toronto: Holt, Rinehart & Winston of Canada, 1982.

Lawrence, Marjorie. *What? Me Teach Music?* Sherman Oaks, Calif.: Alfred Publishing Co., 1982.

McDonald, Dorothy C., and Gene M. Simons. *Musical Growth and Development: Birth Through Six*. New York: Schirmer Books, 1989.

Nye, Vernice T. *Music for Young Children*. 3d ed. Dubuque, Iowa: William C. Brown Publisher, 1983.

Wood, Donna. *Move, Sing, Listen, Play*. Toronto: Gordon V. Thompson Music, 1982.

Ethnomusicology (See also African American Music)

Anderson, William M. *Teaching Asian Musics in Elementary and Secondary Schools*. rev. ed. Danbury, Conn.: World Music Press, 1986.

Anderson, William M., and Patricia Shehan Campbell. *Multicultural Perspectives in Music Education*. Reston, Va.: Music Educators National Conference, 1989.

George, Luvenia A. *Teaching the Music of Six Different Cultures*. rev. ed. Danbury, Conn.: World Music Press, 1988.

May, Elizabeth, ed. *Musics of Many Cultures: An Introduction*. Berkeley and Los Angeles: Univ. of California Press, 1982.

Kodály

Choksy, Lois. *The Kodály Context*. Englewood Cliffs, N.J.: Prentice-Hall, 1981.

———. *The Kodály Method: Comprehensive Music Education from Infant to Adult*. 2d ed. Englewood Cliffs, N.J.: Prentice-Hall, 1988.

Daniel, Katinka S. *Kodály Approach, Method Book One*. 2d ed. Champaign, Ill.: Mark Foster Music Co., 1979.

———. *Kodály Approach, Method Book Two*. Champaign, Ill.: Mark Foster Music Co., 1986.

———. *Kodály Approach, Method Book Three*. Champaign, Ill.: Mark Foster Music Co., 1987.

———. *Kodály Approach: Method Book Two—Song Collection*. Champaign, Ill.: Mark Foster Music Co., 1982.

Szonyi, Erzsébet. *Musical Reading and Writing*. Translated by Lili Halápy. Revised translation by Geoffrey Russell-Smith. 8 vols. London and New York: Boosey & Hawkes Music Publishers, 1973–79.

———. *Solfège According to the Kodály-Concept*. Keckemet, Hungary: Zoltan Kodály Pedagogical Institute of Music, 1975.

Listening

Bernstein, Leonard. *The Joy of Music*. New York: Simon & Schuster, 1963.

Copland, Aaron. *What to Listen for in Music*. New York: McGraw-Hill Book Co., 1988.

Hoffer, Charles R. *The Understanding of Music*. 5th ed. Belmont, Calif.: Wadsworth Publishing Co., 1985.

Machlis, Joseph. *The Enjoyment of Music*. 4th ed. New York: W.W. Norton & Co., 1977.

Miller, Samuel D. "Listening Maps for Musical Tours." *Music Educators Journal* 73 (October 1986): 28–31.

Movement (See also Dalcroze)

Boorman, Joyce L. *Creative Dance in the First Three Grades*. Toronto: Harcourt Brace Jovanovich, Canada, 1969.

———. *Creative Dance in Grades Four to Six*. Toronto: Harcourt Brace Jovanovich, Canada, 1971.

———. *Dance and Language Experiences with Children*. Toronto: Harcourt Brace Jovanovich, Canada, 1973.

Joyce, Mary. *First Steps in Teaching Creative Dance to Children*. 2d ed. Mountain View, Calif.: Mayfield Publishing Co., 1980.

Staton, Barbara Rustin. *Move into Music*. 4 vols. Morristown, N.J.: Silver Burdett, 1981. (Available through Merrill Staton Enterprises, Alpine, N.J. 07620-1079.)

Weikart, Phyllis. *Teaching Movement and Dance: Intermediate Folk Dance*. Ypsilanti, Mich.: High/Scope Press, 1984.

Orff

Burnett, Millie M., and Patti S. Wiggins. *Today's Creative Children: Sing, Play and Move*. Dubuque, Iowa: Kendall/Hunt Publishing Co., 1983.

Frazee, Jane, and Kent Kreuter. *Discovering ORFF: A Curriculum for Music Teachers*. Valley Forge, Pa.: European American Music Distributors Corp., 1987.

Keetman, Gunild. *Elementaria, First Acquaintance with Orff-Schulwerk*. Valley Forge, Pa.: European American Music Distributors Corp., 1974.

Keller, Wilhelm. *Introduction to Music for Children*. Translated by Susan Kennedy. Valley Forge, Pa.: European American Music Distributors Corp., 1974.

Nash, Grace C., Geraldine W. Jones, Barbara A. Potter, and Patsy S. Smith. *Do It My Way: The Child's Way of Learning*. Sherman Oaks, Calif.: Alfred Publishing Co., 1977.

Orff, Carl, and Gunild Keetman. *Music for Children*. English version adapted from Orff-Schulwerk by Margaret Murray. 5 vols. London: Schott & Co., 1958–66.

———. *Music for Children*. Canadian (North American) version adapted from Orff-Schulwerk by Doreen Hall and Arnold Walter. 5 vols. London: Schott & Co., 1956.

Regner, Hermann, ed. *Music for Children*. Vol. 2, *Orff-Schulwerk*. Valley Forge, Pa.: European American Music Distributors Corp., 1977.

Shamrock, Mary. "Orff Schulwerk: An Integrated Foundation." *Music Educators Journal* 72 (February 1986): 51–55.

Signing

Gadling, Donna C., Pastor Daniel H. Pokorny, and Dr. Lottie L. Riekehof. *Lift Up Your Hands: Inspirational and Patriotic Songs in the Language of Signs*. Washington, D.C.: National Grange, 1975.

Humphries, Tom, Carol Padden, and Terrence J. O'Rourke. *A Basic Course in American Sign Language*. 18th ed. Silver Spring, Md.: T.J. Publishers, 1980.

Kannapell, Barbara M., and Lillian B. Hamilton. *Songs in Signed English*. Washington, D.C.: Gallaudet College Press, 1973.

Riekehof, Lottie L. *The Joy of Signing*. 2d ed. Springfield, Mo.: Gospel Publishing House, 1987.

Sternberg, Martin. *American Sign Language*. New York: Harper & Row Publishers, 1987.

Weaks, Donna Gadling. *Lift Up Your Hands*. Vol. 2, *Favorite Songs with Sign Language Interpretation*. Washington, D.C.: National Grange, 1980.

Special Learners

Alvin, Juliette. *Music for the Handicapped Child*. 2d ed. London and New York: Oxford University Press, 1976.

Atterbury, Betty W. *Mainstreaming Exceptional Learners in Music*. Englewood Cliffs, N.J.: Prentice-Hall, 1990.

———. "The Perplexing Issues of Mainstreaming." *Bulletin of the Council for Research in Music Education* 94 (1987): 17–27.

———. "Success in the Mainstream of General Music." *Music Educators Journal* 72 (March 1986): 34–36.

Beer, Alice S., Natalie L. Bellows, and Anna Mae D. Frederick. "Providing for Different Rates of Music Learning." *Music Educators Journal* 68 (April 1982): 40–43.

Bitcon, Carol Hampton. *Alike and Different: The Clinical and Educational Use of Orff-Schulwerk*. Santa Ana, Calif.: Rosha Press, 1976.

Darrow, Alice-Ann. "Music for the Deaf." *Music Educators Journal* 71 (February 1985): 33–35.

Graham, Richard M., and Alice S. Beer. *Teaching Music to the Exceptional Child: A Handbook for Mainstreaming*. Englewood Cliffs, N.J.: Prentice-Hall, 1980.

Herlein, Doris G. "Music Reading for the Sightless— Braille Notation." *Music Educators Journal* 62 (September 1975): 42–45.

Lam, Rita C., and Cecilia Wang. "Integrating Blind and Sighted Through Music." *Music Educators Journal* 68 (April 1982): 44–45.

Nocera, Sona D. *Reaching the Special Learner Through Music*. Morristown, N.J.: Silver Burdett, 1979.

Robbins, Carol, and Clive Robbins. *Music for the Hearing Impaired and Other Special Groups: A Resource Manual and Curriculum Guide*. St. Louis, Mo.: MMB Music, 1980.

Vocal Development/Choral Music

Bartle, Jean Ashworth. *Lifeline for Children's Choir Directors*. Toronto: Gordon V. Thompson Music, 1988.

Diercks, Louis H. "A Guide to Improving the Diction and Tone Quality of the Choir." *The Choral Journal* 15 (October 1974): 9–10.

Heffernan, Charles W. *Choral Music: Technique and Artistry*. Englewood Cliffs, N.J.: Prentice-Hall, 1982

Marshall, Madeleine. *The Singer's Manual of English Diction*. New York: G. Schirmer, 1953.

May, William V., and Craig Tolin. *Pronunciation Guide for Choral Literature*. Reston, Va.: Music Educators National Conference, 1987.

Rao, Doreen. *Choral Music Experience: Education Through Artistry*. Vol. 1, *Artistry in Music Education*; Vol. 2, *The Artist in Every Child*; Vol. 5, *The Young Singing Voice*. New York: Boosey & Hawkes, 1987–.

Swears, Linda. *Teaching the Elementary School Chorus*. Englewood Cliffs, N.J.: Prentice-Hall, 1984.

CLASSIFIED INDEX

Unsquare Dance, by Dave Brubeck, 54

Variations on "America," by Charles Ives, 109

"Wedding of Kijé, The," from *Lieutenant Kijé Suite* by Sergei Prokofiev, 205

Wellington's Victory, by Ludwig van Beethoven, 154

Wellington's Victory Theme Montage, 153

Mainstreaming. *See* Special Learners

Major/Minor, 11, 25, 27–28, 37, 80–81, 100, 103, 107, 109, 111, 114, 303, 313

Melodic Direction
listening for, 98, 100, 238–240
retrograde, 87–89, 92

Melodic Patterns, 88, 141, 242, 244–245, 248–249, 251, 296, 302, 309

Melodic Themes, 102, 153, 192, 200, 202, 204–205

Melody. *See also* Pitch
creating, 5, 11, 107, 228
variation on tune, 109

Meter
changing, 42, 44, 48, 50–51, 62–63, 69, 302, 309, 339, 358
compound, 60–61, 63, 66, 68–69, 302
duple, 18, 21, 23, 36, 40–41, 43, 45, 140, 253
irregular, 17, 48–50, 52-55
listening for, 63
quadruple, 40–41, 43, 45, 69
triple, 18, 21, 23, 30, 36, 40–41, 43, 45, 266

Minor. *See* Major/Minor

Minor Songs
Drunken Sailor, 261
Follow the Drinkin' Gourd, 271
Ghost Ship, The, 272
Hanerot Halalu, 313–316
Mi Caballo Blanco, 100
Michael and Ridgeley: "Careless Whisper" (listening), 121
Promised Land, The, 330–333
Wreck of the Edmund Fitzgerald, The, 130–131, 267

Modulation, 100, 102–103

Motives. *See* Duration/Rhythm, rhythmic; Pitch, melodic

Movement
conducting patterns, 41, 44–45, 66
patterned, 174
and phrases, showing, 120–121, 123
show choir, 290

Musicians. *See* Biographies

Music Reading. *See* Reading Notation

Ostinatos. *See also* Creative Activities
example of
Brubeck: *Unsquare Dance* (listening), 52
performing of, 54

Part/Unison Songs. *See also* Rounds/Canons
four-part
Dream a Dream, 349–351
Sanctus, 326–329
partner
I'm Goin' Home on a Cloud, 284–285
three-part
Chartless, 340–341
Praise to the Lord, 309–312
Rhythm of Life, The, 291–294
Sing Me Home, 343–347
This Is Christmas, 318–321
To the Morning, 334–337
Winter Carol, 303–308
two-part
April Weather, 297
Chichester Prayer, 353–354
Hanerot Halalu, 314–316
(Life Is a) Celebration, 123–125
Love Song, 46–47
Memory, 64–65
Mi Caballo Blanco, 100
Misty, Moisty Morning, 170–171
Our World, 28–29
Over the Sea to Skye, 286–289
Promised Land, The, 330–333
Radiator Lions, 323–324
Rose, The, 299–301
Run Joe, 10–11
unison
African American spiritual: "Ev'ry Time I Feel the Spirit" (listening), 207
America, 147, 280–281
Climbing Up to Zion, 98
Drunken Sailor, 261
Follow the Drinkin' Gourd, 271
Ghost Ship, The, 272–273
Samiotissa, 55
Smith and Orzabal: "Head over Heels" (lyrics, listening), 34
Staines: "River" (listening), 78–79, 274–275

That's What Friends Are For, 42–43
Wabash Cannonball, The, 265
Web, The, 90–91
Worried Man Blues, 269
Wreck of the Edmund Fitzgerald, The, 130–131, 267

Patriotic Songs
America, 108–109, 147, 280–281
Dream a Dream, 349–351

Pentatonic Songs
African American spiritual: "Ev'ry Time I Feel the Spirit" (listening), 207
Ahrirang, 82
Climbing Up to Zion, 98

Percussion. *See* Instruments, Playing; Tone Color

Phrases
and form, 16, 120–123
melodic, 89, 120, 348, 355
movement showing, 120–121, 123
singing through, 123, 287, 297, 303, 314, 318, 348
teacher cues for following, 121

Pitch. *See also* Minor Songs; Pentatonic Songs; Reading Notation; Scales; Skip/Leap
atonal, 92, 200, 202, 205
bitonality, 108–110
chords
definition of, 235
dominant, 10–11, 103–104, 236–237, 325
pattern, twelve bar-blues, 104–105, 242–247, 249, 251
progression of, 235, 242, 248
seventh, 244
subdominant, 104, 236–237, 325
tonic, 8–11, 14, 36, 103–104, 236–237, 325
consonance, 108, 110
dissonance, 108, 110
drone, 213
harmony, 80–81, 99, 104, 108–109, 296
intervals, 244, 295, 313
keys/scales, 11, 80–81, 100–101, 103–104, 107–108, 220, 225
listening for, 109, 148
major/minor, 11, 25, 27–28, 37, 80–81, 100, 103, 107, 109, 111, 114, 303, 313
melodic direction
listening for, 98, 100, 239–240
retrograde, 87–90, 92
melodic motives, 141, 148
melodic patterns, 88, 242, 244–245, 248–249, 251, 296, 302, 309

Tone Ladder, 295–296, 302, 313

Unison Songs. *See* Part/Unison Songs

Vocal/Choral Development
boys' voices, 131, 280–281, 330
breathing, 64, 67, 82, 131, 170, 296–298
choral sound, 282, 290, 325-326, 330–331, 339
consonants, 42, 67, 123, 286, 297, 303, 309, 314, 326, 331, 334, 341
diction, 42, 170, 286, 303, 309, 314, 318

expression and style, 131, 170
girls' voices, 281
legato singing, 11, 64, 131, 326, 348, 352
marcato singing, 11
phrases, singing through, 64, 123, 287, 297, 303, 314, 318, 348
pitch accuracy, 28, 291, 297, 299, 303, 309, 318, 324, 341–342
pitch syllables or numbers, 295–296, 298, 302, 309, 313, 317, 325, 339, 353, 355–356
posture, 64, 170, 282, 296–297, 299, 303,

309, 314, 318, 323, 326, 331, 334, 339, 342, 348, 355
resonant quality, 298, 303, 309, 314, 318, 323, 330, 341
rhythmic precision, 42, 55, 64, 67, 123
staccato singing, 309, 323
voice range, 55, 82, 280–281
vowels, 42, 67, 82, 123, 170, 283–284, 291, 297–299, 303, 309, 314, 318, 323, 325–326, 330–331, 341–342, 348
warm-up exercises, 281, 290, 295, 309, 313–314, 317–318, 326, 334, 353

TEACHER'S NOTES

TEACHER'S NOTES

TEACHER'S NOTES

TEACHER'S NOTES

TEACHER'S NOTES

TEACHER'S NOTES

TEACHER'S NOTES

ACKNOWLEDGMENTS

Grateful acknowledgment is given to the following authors and publishers. In the case of songs and poems for which acknowledgment is not given, we have earnestly endeavored to find the original source and to procure permission for their use, but without success. Extensive research failed to locate the author and/or copyright holder.

Beckenhorst Press Inc. for the music to "Over the Sea to Skye" by Robert Louis Stevenson, arranged by Michael Jothen. Copyright © 1985 by Beckenhorst Press, Inc. All rights reserved. Used by permission; "Praise to the Lord" by Michael Jothen. Copyright © 1979 by Beckenhorst Press Inc. All rights reserved. Used by permission.

Boosey & Hawkes Inc. for *Lieutenant Kijé Suite* by Sergei Prokofiev. Used by permission of Boosey & Hawkes, Inc., publisher and copyright owner.

CPP/Belwin, Inc. for "Dream a Dream" by Ed Robertson. Copyright © 1977 Studio 224. Assigned to Belwin-Mills Publishing Corp. c/o CPP/Belwin, Inc., Miami, FL 33014. International Copyright Secured. Made in USA. All Rights Reserved. Used by Permission; "Love Song" from *Pippin* by Stephen Schwartz. Copyright © 1972 by Stephen Schwartz. All rights for the world administered by Jobete Music Co., Inc. and Belwin-Mills Publishing Corp., c/o Filmtrax Copyright Holdings, Inc. International Copyright Secured. Made in USA. All Rights Reserved. Used by Permission; "To the Morning" by Dan Fogelberg. Copyright © 1975 by APRIL MUSIC INC. and HICKORY GROVE MUSIC. ADMINISTERED BY APRIL MUSIC INC. All rights of April Music Inc. assigned to SBK Catalogue Partnership. All rights controlled and administered by SBK APRIL Catalogue.

Dunvagen Music Publishing, Inc. for "Floe" from *Glassworks*, by Philip Glass. Copyright © 1982 Dunvagen Music Publishing, Inc. Reprinted by permission. All rights reserved.

Mark Foster Music Co. for "Hanerot Halalu" composed by Baruch J. Cohen, arranged by Blanche Chass, 1961. Used by permission of Mark Foster Music Company.

Harper & Row Publishers, Inc. for "Backward Bill" and illustration from A LIGHT IN THE ATTIC, by Shel Silverstein. Copyright © 1981 by Snake Eye Music, Inc.

Henry Holt and Co. for "Bravado," by Robert Frost. Copyright © 1947, © 1969 by Holt, Rinehart and Winston, Inc. Copyright © 1975 by Lesley Frost Ballantine, Reprinted from THE POETRY OF ROBERT FROST edited by Edward Connery Lathem, by permission of Henry Holt and Co., Inc.

Jenson Publications Inc. for "Our World" music by Lana Walter, words by Jane Foster Knox. Copyright © 1985 Jenson Publications, Inc. International Copyright Secured. Made in U.S.A. All rights reserved; "Winter Carol" by Mark Wilson and Jane Foster Knox. Copyright © 1980 by Jenson Publications, Inc. International Copyright Secured. Made in U.S.A. All rights reserved. Used by permission.

Julie Music Corp. for "Mi Caballo Blanco," by Francisco Flores del Campo. Copyright © 1971 by Julie Music Corp. All rights reserved. Used by permission.

Kodaly Center of America for "I'm Goin' Home on a Cloud" arranged by Sean Diebler, 1981. Copyright KCA Choral Series published by Kodaly Center of America.

Mineral River Music for "River," by Bill Staines from IF I WERE A WORD, THEN I'D BE A SONG. Copyright © 1977 Mineral River Music.

Moose Music Ltd. for "The Wreck of the Edmund Fitzgerald," by Gordon Lightfoot. Copyright © 1976 Moose Music Inc. Used by permission.

Music Sales Corp. for "Un bel dì vedremo" from MADAMA BUTTERFLY by Puccini, libretto by Giuseppe Giacosa and Lorenzo Illica. Used by arrangement with G. Schirmer, Inc., U.S. agent for G. Ricordi.

The New Music Company for "Radiator Lions" by Michael Jothen and Dorothy Aldis, reprinted and set to music by permission of G.P. Putnam's Sons from EVERYTHING AND ANYTHING by Dorothy Aldis. Copyright © 1925–1927, © renewed 1953–1955 by Dorothy Aldis. Music copyright © 1987 by The New Music Co. Used by permission. All rights reserved; "This Is Christmas" by Keith W. Derrickson and Jane Foster Knox. Copyright © 1987 by The New Music Co. Used by permission. All rights reserved.

Carl J. Nygard, Jr. for "The Promised Land," "Sing Me Home," and "Chichester Prayer." Copyright © 1986 by Carl J. Nygard, Jr. All rights reserved.

Random House, Inc. for "Dreams" and "April Rain Song" by Langston Hughes, from THE DREAM KEEPER AND OTHER POEMS by Langston Hughes. Copyright © 1932 by Alfred A. Knopf, Inc. and renewed 1960 by Langston Hughes. Reprinted by permission of Alfred A. Knopf, Inc.

Marian Reiner for "Rainbow Writing" by Eve Merriam, from RAINBOW WRITING by Eve Merriam. Copyright © 1976 by Eve Merriam. All rights reserved. Reprinted by permission of Marian Reiner for the author.

G. Schirmer, Inc. for "Tonight" quintet from WEST SIDE STORY by Leonard Bernstein and Stephen Sondheim. Copyright © 1957 by Leonard Bernstein and Stephen Sondheim. All rights reserved. Used by arrangement with G. Schirmer, Inc.

Shawnee Press, Inc. for "The Ghost Ship" from REFLECTIONS OF A LAD AT SEA by Don Besig and Nancy Price. Copyright © 1982 by Shawnee Press, Inc., Delaware Water Gap, PA 18327. All rights reserved. Used with permission; "The Rhythm of Life" by Cy Coleman, words by Dorothy Fields (adapted), arranged by Richard Barnes. Copyright © 1966, 1969 by Cy Coleman, Dorothy Fields, Notable Music Co., Inc. Sole Selling Agent for the Richard Barnes arrangement: Shawnee Press, Inc.; Delaware Water Gap, PA 18327.

C. M. Shearer for "April Weather" (words by Lizette Woodworth Reese) and "Chartless" (words by Emily Dickinson). Copyright © 1986 C. M. Shearer. All rights reserved.

Silver Burdett and Ginn for English words to *Samiotissa* by D. A. Vergoni and Stella Phredopolous, from SILVER BURDETT MUSIC LEVEL 5 PE (Centennial Edition) by Bennett Reimer, Mary Hoffman and Albert McNeil. English words copyright © 1985 Silver Burdett Company. Reprinted by permission. Music reprinted courtesy of Michael Gaetanos.

Songs of Freedom for "Climbing Up to Zion," words and music by Wintley Phipps. Published by Songs of Freedom, ASCAP. Copyright © 1983. Used by permission.

Sheldon Vidibor for the poem "Backward Bill," from A LIGHT IN THE ATTIC by Shel Silverstein, Harper & Row, 1981. Copyright © 1981 Snake Eye Music, Inc.

Virgin-Nymph Music Inc. for the words to "Head over Heels," by Curt Smith and Roland Orzabal. Copyright © 1985 Virgin Music (Publishers) Ltd. Published in the U.S.A. and Canada by Virgin-Nymph Music Inc. All rights reserved. Used by permission.

J. Weston Walch for "Eraser Piano Tees" from ZOUNDS, by Dorothy Gail Elliot. Copyright © 1976 J. Weston Walch, publisher. Used by permission.

David Ward-Steinman for "The Web" by David Ward-Steinman. Poem by Susan Lucas. Copyright © 1976 by David Ward-Steinman.

Warner Brothers for "That's What Friends Are For," words and music by Carole Bayer Sager and Burt Bacharach. Copyright © 1982, 1985 WB MUSIC CORP., WARNER-TAMERLANE PUBLISHING CORP., NEW HIDDEN VALLEY MUSIC & CAROLE BAYER SAGER MUSIC. All Rights Administered JOINTLY by WB MUSIC CORP. & WARNER-TAMERLANE PUBLISHING CORP. All rights reserved. Used by permission; "The Rose," words and music by Amanda McBroom, arranged by Vincent Lawrence. Copyright © 1977 by WARNER-TAMERLANE PUBLISHING CORP. All rights reserved. Used by permission.

Welk Music Group for "(Life Is A) Celebration," by Rick Springfield. Copyright © 1976 Vogue Music. (c/o The Welk Music Group, Santa Monica, CA 90401). International Copyright Secured. All rights reserved. Used by permission.

Some line drawings of musical instruments reprinted by permission of Harvard University Press from NEW HARVARD DICTIONARY OF MUSIC by Don M. Randel. Copyright 1987 by the President and Fellows of Harvard College.

PHOTO CREDITS:
© BOB ADELMAN: 76T. © CLARA AICH: 31, 90, 164TL, 176–7 all, 234–40 all, 256–8 all, 276, 277. PETER ARNOLD INC.: © Klaus D. Francke, 54–5; © Jacques Jangoux, 219; © Stephen J. Kraseman, 80B. ART RESOURCE, NY: 88; Giraudon, 22–3T, 27, 92, 144–5, 165, 195, 199R, 226T; Kavaler, 118T; Scala, 22–3B, 26–7, 93L, 139T, 144, 145, 163T, 192, 255L, 278R. © CLIVE BARDA/London: 69T,B. © VICTORIA BELLER-SMITH: 164TR,BR.

© BETH BERGMAN: 77T. THE BETTMANN ARCHIVE, INC.: 1T, 50, 93R, 110B, 188R, 197, 226B. BLACK STAR: © Herman Kokojan, 162–3; © Bob Krist, 58–9. BMG MUSIC: RCA Red Seal Label, 179B. LEE BOLTIN PICTURE LIBRARY: 1R, 6R. © SAM BROWN: 99. CAMERA 5: © Ken Regan, 133T. CARAMOOR CENTER FOR MUSIC AND THE ARTS, Katonah, NY: 178T. © MICHELE CLEMENT: 97L. THE CLEVELAND MUSEUM OF ART: Gift of the Hanna Fund (CMA 51.355), 19T. BRUCE COLEMAN, INC.: © Jane Burton, xT. CORDIER & EKSTROM GALLERY, NY: 48. CORDON ART, Baarn, Holland: 39TL. CULVER PICTURES, INC.: 24. MARISA DEL RE GALLERY, NY: 59BL, 119B. LEO DE WYS, INC.: © Roy Gumpel, x–1. DPI: © Pictor, 211B. © MARJORY DRESSLER: 83 all, 95 all, 128B, 148. © FRANK DRIGGS COLLECTION: 52–3, 53R, 104, 105. ENVISION: © Tim Gibson, 55, 214T. FPG INTERNATIONAL: © B. Staley, 208, 223T. © AL FRANCEKEVICH: 18L,R, 41, 45, 66T,B, 168, 174 all. FRUMKIN/ADAMS GALLERY, NY: 156L. LYNN GOLDSMITH, INC.: © Dave Hogan, 32–3T, 122R; © Steve Jennings, 30B; © Bliss Morris, 4–5; © Fabio Nosotti, 30T; © Duncan Raban/Stills, 77R. © JAMES HEFFERNAN: 196–7, 198. HISTORICAL PICTURES SERVICE, CHICAGO: 103, 134. THE IMAGE BANK: © Murray Alcosser, 96R; © Nancy Brown, 12L; © James H. Carmichael, Jr., 162T; Foto Franco Villani, 9B; © M. Friedel, 227; © Mitchell Funk, 139B; © Garry Gay, 39B, 76B, 97R; © D. Hiser, 80T; © Janeart Ltd., 152BR; © Lou Jones, 42; © Robert Kristofik, 59BR; © Elyse Lewin, 279R; © H. Loebel, 221; © S. Maeda, 38–9; © Marcel ISY-SCHWART, 229T; © David Muench, 76–7; © A.M. Rosario, 118–9; © A. Upitis, 152BL; © Eric L. Wheater, 211T; © Art Wolfe, 152TL. © ROBERTA INTRATER: 12R. © LEANDRE

JACKSON: 206 all. THE JOFFREY BALLET CO.: © Herbert Migdoll, 72–3T. KURZWEIL MUSIC SYSTEMS: 173, 233R. MAGNUM PHOTOS, INC.: © Marilyn Silverstone, 209, 214B. MEMORY SHOP: 188L, 202–3, 203T. THE METROPOLITAN MUSEUM OF ART: The Alfred Stieglitz Collection, 1949 (49.70.40), 146. © DANLEE MITCHELL: 183. THE MUSEUM OF FINE ARTS: M. and M. Karolik Collection (47.1202), 139C. THE MUSEUM OF MODERN ART, NY: Oil on canvas, 50 x 50", given anonymously, 128T; sheet metal and wire, 30-1/2 x 13-1/8 x 7-5/8", gift of the artist, 162B. NATIONAL FILM ARCHIVE LONDON: 205. By courtesy of the NATIONAL PORTRAIT GALLERY, London: 86B. NAWROCKI STOCK PHOTO: © Robert Lightfoot III, 77B, 138T, 282B. THE NELSON-ATKINS MUSEUM OF ART, Kansas City, MO: gift of the Friends of Art (F77-34), 157B. THE NEW YORK PUBLIC LIBRARY PICTURE COLLECTION: 194–5. THE NEW YORK TIMES: © Leonard Kamjler, 58. PHILADELPHIA MUSEUM OF ART: The A.E. Gallatin Collection (52-61-96), 157T. PHOTO RESEARCHERS, INC.: Archiv, 19B, 23, 86T, 114, 115T,B, 189, 190–1, 191T, 199L, 233C; © Marcello Bertinetti, 223BR; © Brian Brake, 228–9T, 229B; © Bruce Frisch, 180; © Dr. Georg Gerster, 223BL; Farrell Grehan, 278–9, 282T; © George Holton, 222, 224; © Richard Hutchings, 254L; © George E. Jones III, 152TR; © Y. Machatschek, 101; © Lawrence Migdale, 172B; © Peter Miller, 84; © Bruce Roberts, 278L; © Leonard Wolfe, 213. PHOTOTEQUE: 203B. THE PICTURE CUBE: © Karen Buchanan, 164C; © Milton Feinberg, 141. RAINBOW: © Christiana Dittmann, 9T,C. RETNA, LTD.: © John Bellissimo, 39TR; © Andy Freeberg, 72–3B, 182; © Gary Gershoff, 32–3B, 70; © Ian Hooton, 32L; © Daryl Pitt, 133B; © Michael Putland, 4L, 122L; © David Redfern, 52BL,

53B; © Paul Slattery, 5L. H. ARMSTRONG ROBERTS, INC.: © K. Scholz, 26; © Zefa, 254R. KEVIN ROCHE JOHN DINKELOO AND ASSOCIATES: 210B. SHOOTING STAR: © Judi Lesta, xB, 5R. Courtesy of STEINWAY & SONS: 138B. STOCK BOSTON: © Bill Gallery, 232, 255R. THE STOCK MARKET: © David Barnes, 126TR; © Ed Bohon, 126TL; © Robert Frerck, 210T; © Alan Goldsmith, 232–3; © Doug Handell, 38T; © Ted Horowitz, 118B; © David Hundley, 25; © Harvey Lloyd, 1B; © Ted Mahieu, 172T; © J. Messerschmidt, 68; © Proctor, 96–7; © John Ries, 126B; © Jim Rudnick, 138–9; © Ken Straiton, 13. © HARRY SUMMERFIELD: 181. MARTHA SWOPE PHOTOGRAPHY, INC.: 44, 59TR, 62L,R, 63, 72T. SYGMA: © Tony Frank, 167; © Ted Thai, 129. THE TATE GALLERY, London: 6L, 156R. © MICHAEL LE POER TRENCH: 96L. UPI/BETTMANN NEWSPHOTOS: 52BR. © JACK VARTOOGIAN: 217R, 222–3. © LINDA VARTOOGIAN: 72B. VASARELY CENTER, NY: 58T. WHEELER PICTURES: © Michael Melford, 163C; © Peter Tenzer, 140–1. WHITNEY MUSEUM OF AMERICAN ART: 50th Anniversary Gift of the Gilman Foundation Inc., the Lauder Foundation, A. Alfred Taubman, an Anonymous Donor (and purchase) (80.32), photo by Geoffrey Clements, 119T. WOODFIN CAMP & ASSOCIATES: © Marc & Evelyne Bernheim, 208–9, 215, 217L, 218; © David Burnett, 110T; © Tim Eagan, 38B; © Thomas Hopker, 228–9B; © Richard Nechamkin, 175T.

ILLUSTRATIONS:
Cover Design and Illustration:
Heather Cooper

Illustration Credits:
Istvan Banyai, Cynthia Watts Clark, Carolyn Croll, Fred Marvin, Michael McNelly, Deborah Pinkney

MUSIC AND YOU

USER'S SURVEY

We would like to hear about your experiences using *Music and You* and your suggestions for future revisions. Once you are familiar with *Music and You*, please take a few minutes to respond to this survey. Then remove the page from the book, fold, staple or tape, and return it to us, using the pre-paid postage stamp on the other side.

A. YOUR BACKGROUND

1. Which of the following best describes you? *(Circle one.)*

   a. classroom teacher

   b. music specialist/teach in a music room

   c. music specialist/travel from room to room

   d. music specialist/travel from school to school

   e. Other *(Explain.)* _____

2. What grades do you teach?

3. How frequently do you teach music (per class, per week)?

   a. less than once   **b.** once   **c.** twice   **d.** more than twice

4. How long is each music class period? _____

5. Which of the following music teaching approaches do you currently use? *(Circle one or more.)*

   a. Kodály   **b.** Dalcroze

   c. Orff   **d.** Other *(Explain.)* _____

B. SONG MATERIAL

1. What percentage of each type of song material would you like in a music text? *(Indicate percentages to total 100%.)*

   Folk _____   Composed _____

2-1 In Column 2–1 below, indicate the ideal percentage of each category of song that you would like in a music text? *(Indicate percentages to total 100%.)*

2-2 In Column 2–2 below, circle your rate of satisfaction with the amount of song material from each category in *Music and You:* too few (–), just right (ok), too many (+).

	Column 2-1 (Ideal)	Column 2-2 (*Music and You*)
Folk/Traditional	_____	– ok +
Foreign Language	_____	– ok +
Holiday and Seasonal	_____	– ok +
Patriotic	_____	– ok +
Popular/Contemporary	_____	– ok +
Show Music	_____	– ok +
Other	_____	– ok +

C. MUSIC AND YOU

1. Circle the description that best describes your opinion about the length of lessons in *Music and You*.

   a. too short   **b.** just right   **c.** too long

2. Use the chart below to indicate your answers *for each area listed.* Circle your answers for each grade that you teach. (– = *not adequate,* ok = *adequate,* + = *more than adequate*)

   a. appropriateness of the skills and concepts presented
   b. quality of folk song material
   c. quality of composed song material
   d. diversity of song styles
   e. number of rounds, descants, and harmony parts
   f. number of opportunities for students to play instruments
   g. number of opportunities for students to move to music
   h. frequency of evaluation

	K	1	2	3	4	5	6	7	8
a.	– ok +	– ok +	– ok +	– ok +	– ok +	– ok +	– ok +	– ok +	– ok +
b.	– ok +	– ok +	– ok +	– ok +	– ok +	– ok +	– ok +	– ok +	– ok +
c.	– ok +	– ok +	– ok +	– ok +	– ok +	– ok +	– ok +	– ok +	– ok +
d.	– ok +	– ok +	– ok +	– ok +	– ok +	– ok +	– ok +	– ok +	– ok +
e.			– ok +	– ok +	– ok +	– ok +	– ok +	– ok +	– ok +
f.	– ok +	– ok +	– ok +	– ok +	– ok +	– ok +	– ok +	– ok +	– ok +
g.	– ok +	– ok +	– ok +	– ok +	– ok +	– ok +	– ok +	– ok +	– ok +
h.	– ok +	– ok +	– ok +	– ok +	– ok +	– ok +	– ok +	– ok +	– ok +

D. RECORDINGS

1. Do you use CDs or plan to use them in the next five years? *(Circle one.)*   yes   no

2. Use the chart below to indicate your answers for *each aspect* of the *Music and You* recordings listed. Circle your answers for each grade that you teach. (– = *not adequate,* ok = *adequate,* + = *more than adequate*)

   a. overall quality of arrangements
   b. use of student voices as compared to adult voices
   c. use of acoustic instrumentation as compared to electronic

	K	1	2	3	4	5	6	7	8
a.	– ok +	– ok +	– ok +	– ok +	– ok +	– ok +	– ok +	– ok +	– ok +
b.	– ok +	– ok +	– ok +	– ok +	– ok +	– ok +	– ok +	– ok +	– ok +
c.	– ok +	– ok +	– ok +	– ok +	– ok +	– ok +	– ok +	– ok +	– ok +

3. Please explain what you like and/or dislike about the recorded lessons.

2. Please list any specific songs and/or listening selections you would like in your next music series. Include grade levels for each.

E. GENERAL

1. Are there additional ancillary materials that you would like included in *Music and You?* If so, please describe.

3. Any other comments?

① *Fold down along dashed line*

② *Fold down along dashed line so mailing and return addresses are visible*

FROM

_____
Name (Optional)

_____
Address (City/State/Zip)

_____
School

_____
Home Telephone (Optional)

Would you like to be contacted regarding reviewing for future music-related materials from Macmillan?

            yes   no

Thank you for taking the time to complete this questionnaire. Please fill in your name and complete mailing address above, and we'll be happy to send you a *free gift.* If you have further thoughts about what you would like in a music text, your favorite songs, or other comments about *Music and You,* we would enjoy hearing from you. You can write us at the address listed on this mailer.

STAPLE OR TAPE TO CLOSE